PRAGMATISM AND LAW

Pragmatism and Law
From philosophy to dispute resolution

MICHAL ALBERSTEIN
Bar Ilan University, Israel

DARTMOUTH

© Michal Alberstein 2002

All rights reserved. No part of this publication may be reproduced, stored in a retrieval system or transmitted in any form or by any means, electronic, mechanical, photocopying, recording or otherwise without the prior permission of the publisher.

Published by
Dartmouth Publishing Company
Ashgate Publishing Limited
Gower House
Croft Road
Aldershot
Hampshire GU11 3HR
England

Ashgate Publishing Company
131 Main Street
Burlington, VT 05401-5600 USA

Ashgate website: http://www.ashgate.com

British Library Cataloguing in Publication Data
Alberstein, Michal
   Pragmatism and law : from philosophy to dispute resolution.
   - (Law, justice and power)
   1.Dispute resolution (Law) 2.Law - Philosophy
   I.Title
   347'.09

Library of Congress Control Number: 2001095456

ISBN 0 7546 2208 8

Printed and bound in Great Britain by MPG Books Ltd, Bodmin, Cornwal

Contents

Preface   *vi*
Introduction   *ix*

1 The Maturing of the Pragmatic Idea in Law and Society
 (Or: The Fall, and the Rise of 'Philawsophy')   1

2 Settled Law and the Law-That-Is-Not-But-Ought-To-Be:
 The Pragmatic Philosophy of Dispute Resolution
 (Or: Why Couldn't Henry Hart Speak?)   100

3 Taking Sides: Margins and Phases of Pragmatics of Legal
 Process Disciples (Or: The Pragmatists That We Are)   185

4 In Search of the Dispute: On Lawyers and Legal Philawsophers
 at Harvard Law School (Or: Some Private Hope and Public Irony)   251

5 From Philawsophy to Dispute-Resolution (Or: Layers of
 Mediation, and Models of Engagements in Reality)   321

Concluding Notes   341

Bibliography   346
Index   355

Preface

The personal narrative behind the writing of this book might itself seem fictional, though the following 'story' has solid positivistic 'materials' to count on: An Israeli woman departs for America, and her husband stays behind, in the army where he must fulfill his military obligation in south Lebanon, in the field and away from home. Choosing not to be frustrated by this situation and pursuing my academic career, I arrived at Harvard Law School with my little son in 1996, and went through the LLM year mostly alone, visiting Israel once, then becoming pregnant. I was exposed to chicken pox due to my son having contracted the disease, then caught the disease myself, going through the ordeal of genetic counseling and high risk pregnancy. Finally, I gave birth to a healthy baby girl, graduated from the LLM program, and was accepted to the SJD doctoral program. After staying in Israel for a year following the birth of my daughter, I came back to Cambridge in the United States. Since then, thankfully, my life has grown much more calm and normal, with my whole family back together. Now we are back in Israel, our home country.

I live within the timetable of a mother. No 'reading' of my 'thesis' can neutralize the fact that 'the maturing of my writing', if such a thing occurred, was accompanied by nurturing my first child as I lived alone in Boston, a *de facto* single mother; by being pregnant, giving birth, and nursing my second child; by caring for them both throughout my writing and my journeys back and forth between Israel and the US. My children's existence as a world balancing the demands of academic life is inseparable from the scope of my claims that, on the one hand, might seem as pretentious as the grand project they try to attack, but on the other hand, stay loyal only to some private idea of the dispute, of family life, of life that is always in a hurry, not because 'time is money' but just because it is precious and short, because of the children, because of the work to be done.

In another (public) version of this personal narrative, my experience at Harvard Law School was, throughout, an effort to mediate my interest in two diverse fields of studies: dispute-resolution, and jurisprudence or philosophy. Upon my arrival in the new place, I thought of introducing Jean-François Lyotard's notion of 'differend', to acknowledge the potential hidden in mediation, and I soon understood there is no intellectual space for such an effort. Now, five years later, I can go back to this neglected book and understand how I was persisting in my own differend, or that of my thesis writing, all along.

> As distinguished from a litigation, a differend [*differend*] would be a case of conflict, between (at least) two parties, that cannot be equitably resolved for lack of a rule of judgment applicable to both arguments. One side's legitimacy does not imply the other's lack of legitimacy. However, applying a single rule of judgment to both in order to settle their differend as though it were merely a litigation would wrong (at least) one of them (and both of them if neither side admits this rule). Damages result from an injury which is inflicted upon the rules of a genre of discourse but which is reparable according to those rules. A wrong results from the fact that the rules of the genre of discourse by which one judges are not those of the judged genre or genres of discourse.[1]

In many ways, my thesis tries to expose and reveal the differend between the two genres of discourse I would like to dwell in. It crafts an intellectual history of these discourses and shows their family resemblance, as well as the difference between them. It tries to endure the inherent repetitive abyss between the different kind of pathos, which these fields demand, to expose the wrong in their detachment. Still, it has a hope for a healing, for a mediation, since the concluding historical event of this thesis writing is my moving back to another promised land (Israel), where the American history I tell has no direct bearing. The discourse of dispute-resolution can be built in a new land as originally having a humanist and intellectual significance and depth, and in that sense I conclude and open my writing with my first child of interest, that of dispute-resolution A mediation theoretical design constructed in Israel is thus the last chapter of this book, and is inspired from this hope of transformation. The latest 'Middle East crisis', and the following catastrophes which shake our global village, only reinforces my belief (though it is a day-to-day struggle) that a new language of resolving conflict should emerge here, and that it must, if hope is still allowed.

I owe many thanks for the general hospitable treatment of Harvard Law School and the academic environment, where the writing of the thesis, which is the basis for this book, took place. I wish to express my appreciation and thankfulness to the academic as well as the administrative staff of the graduate program for their support and help. My nomination as a Byse Fellow for the academic year of 1999–2000 was a great honor for me, and the chapters of this book were constructed along the lines of a seminar I gave at Harvard at the fall of 1999 as part of this nomination.

---

1 Jean-François Lyotard, *The Differend: Phrases in Dispute* (1988) 1983, xi.

I am grateful to a few special people that I would like to name here. First of all, I am indebted to my doctoral thesis supervisor, Duncan Kennedy, from whom I have learned a great deal about teaching, who gave me a sense of the place, and who balanced my fantasies with his patience, in a way that helped me to work with them. The permission to resist and respect him at once, and his readiness to lend himself for help and good advice time and time again, together with his warmth and kindness, were the ongoing gift of my staying here and I thank him deeply for that.

Second, I owe many thanks to my thesis' oral committee members, Professors Frank Sander and Stanley Cavell, who from their very different disciplinary locations helped me to mediate my diverse academic interests. I also extend my great appreciation to my second reader, Professor Terry Fisher, who agreed to come on board towards the latter stages of the work. Thanks are due also to my editor, Robbie Frandsen, who helped me to fight my second language problems, as well as to preserve its first hand singularities. Then, to my family: my mother Sara Alberstein, who is my shelter and support source, my flying rescue team for each childhood disease or family catastrophe; to my son Dor, the elder of my children, who came to America when only three years old with his mother, alone, and helped me to learn a lot about proportions and care; to my husband and friend Nadav Davidovitch, who stayed back in Israel, traveling back and forth and back again to rebuild our little family. Handling and sharing our cooperate dynamic communal life together is a precious present I treasure each day, thanks to him; and to my little one, Shir, who was born as part of this whole project, in between the continents, and has graduated from my womb to the encounter with the new land.

Gratitude goes out to another friend who became almost a family member, Roei Amit, who sits in Paris all these years, but his support and (electronic) presence throughout the last four years have been for me a source of peace and learning.

Finally, I would like to dedicate this thesis, not in the front page or in the usual framework, but in this bottom line of the preface, to my late father, Dov Alberstein, son of Rivka and Yakov-Shimon. My arrival in the US and at Harvard is very much a part of the work of mourning his unexpected death, of the terrible loss of his presence as a guide and as my authoritative figure. If I would describe myself as speaking from a place, I would certainly like it to be as his inheritor: of his Jewish orthodox narratives and texts, of his humanism, of his humor and love, and most of all, if I am very lucky, of his style of writing.

Miki Alberstein, Tel-Aviv, Israel

Introduction

Formalities

The book is a textual analysis of the American legal discourse, and of its unfolding through time and place in terms of the pragmatic idea. At the locus of my writing stands the jurisprudence of the 1950s as a constitutive moment, from which any narration is done in terms of 'before' and 'after'. By following the various appearances of pragmatism in time and place, I try to trace the singularity, the American stamp in historical narratives that emphasize both the general and the universal. The iconic role of Harvard as representing this singularity, and as providing the various 'discursive knots' of 'the legal American' in each era, is another recurrent theme within this attempt.

The first chapter of the book, 'The Maturing of the Pragmatic Idea in Law and Society (Or: The Fall, and the Rise of 'Philawsophy')', begins with the emergence of pragmatism as a discursive search for an American origin. Pragmatism is presented as a narrative with a few tenets, and I examine its relation with Darwinian science, religious thinking, and resistance to European thinking in this context. Its anti-foundationalist mode is examined in relation to the scientific foundation it did assume, and as being equivalent, in a sense, to another prevailing 'theory' of the twentieth century – psychoanalysis. The pragmatism of law arising through two stages of an antecedent origin of Holmes, and 'the next step' of Legal Realism, are described as a genre of discourse complementary to that of general pragmatism: professional, ironic, obsessed, theoretically obscure. This genre recurs in contemporary discourse, and I also describe it through reference to 'three legal prophets', one of which is Duncan Kennedy.

The second chapter, entitled 'Settled Law and the Law-That-Is-Not-But-Ought-To-Be: Hart and Sacks and The Pragmatic Philosophy of Dispute-resolution (Or: Why Couldn't Henry Hart Speak?)', describes the core of my thesis, which is the discursive moment of the 1950s as a constitutive stage. In the realm of the theory of law, I describe the coming together of the ironic and the general pragmatic discourses to produce a post-war, common-sense understanding of the world and of the legal apparatus functioning within it. An equivalent counter-path of the post-war era is the operation of the activist Warren Court with its famous *Brown* decision. The various narrations of this era by intellectuals within law, as well as by scholars outside the legal discourse, are presented as being divided along the lines of externals and internals, progressive-interpretives and professionals. The progressive-humanist drive is presented as organizing the internals' reading of the post-war era, and is incomprehensible to external viewers.

'Taking Sides: Margins and Phases of Pragmatics of Legal Process Disciples (Or: The Pragmatists That We Are)', the third chapter, describes trajectories and resistances to the Legal Process scholarship in contemporary jurisprudence. By focusing on Roberto Unger from the left, Richard Posner from the right, and Owen Fiss at the center, I try to expose different 'taking' of the original narrative of pragmatism and some various reformulations of its principles. In Fiss's writing, I diagnose 'settlement aversion' and examine his Yale-like relations with the dispute-resolution discourse at Harvard; in Posner's writing, I discern 'an original text' pragmatism, adopting this formula of modernity as the truth to apply; in Unger's texts, I follow an internal, anti-formalist Marxist legal mode to transform the world through the deviationist work of the body, which loses its intellectual hope to work from within law through the years and is becoming straightforward and external as its counterpart, the work of Roger Fisher.

The fourth chapter, 'In Search of the Dispute: On Lawyers and Legal Philawsophers at Harvard Law School (Or: Some Private Hope and Public Irony)', returns to the Harvard of today as an iconic example of the current pragmatic knot in the American legal discourse. I examine the discourse of dispute-resolution and negotiation against the intellectual one, and discern the original complementary genres of pragmatism I have delineated thus far. The 'return' of ideas as 'problem solving' or 'private ordering' and 'neutral principles' into the heat of the academic debate through the realm of the practice is described as revitalizing ideas long ago abandoned in the theoretical public sphere. What characterizes today the intellectual map is that through the split between the theoretical and the practical, the intellectuals are denied access to reality due to their irony and diversity, while the practical scholars are indeed activists, eager to improve and induce progress, while holding, at least to some extent, an optimistic 1950s style of discourse in their actions. At this point, I describe Ronald Dworkin's writing as responding to the Legal Process jurisprudence as well, while enacting the Holmsian myth of the detached intellectual who lives within law.

Finally, the last chapter, 'From Philawsophy to Dispute-resolution (Or: Layers of Mediation and Models of Engagement In Reality)' escapes the whole previous effort to provide an analysis of the legal discourse, and turns to the land of dispute-resolution and mediation where utopia still has a space, in my view. I try briefly to draw a map of developing models of mediation, and to suggest a contemporary model, which might address our turbulent reality of conflicts nowadays. The chapter begins with models of war inspired by the 1950s and describes a 'scientific' approach, which dominates the discourse to this day. This approach assumes antagonistic and hyper subjective encounters between rational individuals. I continue to explore models of peace making which incorporate ideas of subjectivity that emerge in the following decades. The most updated model I describe – the interpretive one – borrows the interpretive prevailing mode of the current discourse of adjudication, and returns to it to suggest a mediation notion based on identity conversations between diverse dispute-resolution professionals and between academic scholars.

The division between and within the chapters does not follow the above linear demarcations. I open each chapter with a line of arguments but then allow the narrative to flow, to tell the story behind the ideas without staying committed to their order or logic. In each chapter, I interfere with events and similarities from other chapters, from other times, which means to imply that there is one big story behind the diverse presentations of it. The recurrent pattern throughout my writing is the interaction between incommensurable discourses, which produce a certain American performance near one another. The crucial moment of the post-war era is a crisis and a transition point in my thesis, precisely because the incommensurables seem to unite in that hegemonic moment within the Legal Process text, a unification that has unique political and theoretical characteristics that affect coming generations. The intellectual conditions I describe in Harvard Law School today seem in a way to repeat the 1950s mediation of the incommensurable; but my 'map' tries to explain how, in a year-2000 contemporary climate, the harmony is achieved, paradoxically, through a discursive split. From another angle, my effort is to describe an intellectual theoretical pathos that enables a professional investment which becomes a discursive world to inhabit. The 'philawsophical' pathos that I follow from Holmes' writing through that of Duncan Kennedy, which is balanced in the post-war era, has a political quality and a theoretical fascination inaccessible to the outsiders of the legal discourse (and process). The concluding chapter which draws the dispute-resolution map, reveals a more dispersed and fresher discourse for mediators to inhabit. My purpose is to offer it a narrative that might advance new mystique for this developing discipline and professional identity.

For the formal history of pragmatism and for an effort to define this notion, I recommend a close reading of Part 3.4, which discusses Richard Posner, bringing forward some of his texts that deal with these issues. If there is one, bottom-line first wisdom that I want to emerge from my writing, it is the impossibility of providing such a definition.

Discourse

To say that I try to go beyond some dichotomies is to repeat the clichés. Still, I must declare that I indeed try to do so and more – not to merely go beyond, but to go right through, to endure them with passion: the internal and the external; the fantastic and the real; the progressive and the conservative; the theoretical and the practical; the philosophical and the common sense-like; the literary and the scientific. My writing is as much about fiction as about reality – reality as a fiction, as a story, a text, which unfolds through time-and-place matrices, and where the various dichotomies find their play each time in different ways.

In some sense, and in accordance with the pragmatic specter and with my focus on the jurisprudence of the 1950s at Harvard, my writing is itself a 'reasoned elaboration'. Reason, as I analyze it in my writing, operates in the 1950s as the navigating force between the public and private. In my writing, I would like it to navigate between my 'private' and the public I was encountering through a focus on negotiation and dispute settlement, and not through the authoritative mechanism (or metaphor) of adjudication. The writing strives for an interaction and an exchange: for the uniqueness of an event and not for the one big answer (or question).

My style of writing repeats the resistances I have described above. Refusing to accept the dichotomy between literary and academic writing, I try to maintain this narrative structure, both within the chapters and throughout the thesis. A story is told about the American legal theoretical discourse, one which unfolds through the succession of time and place, and surrounds the Legal Process Materials on all sides, 'before' and 'after', below and above. This is on the diachronic scale. On the synchronic scale, there again is a recurring structure: that of pragmatism in various appearances; that which juxtaposes the grand, hysterical story against the rigorous little work of the details and their complex diverse interaction. It begins with the emergence of the pragmatic idea, which is already contaminated with another (legal) view while in full bloom, and continues through the internal splits within law between Harvard and Yale, between progressives and conservatives, between theoreticians and practical people. Among these couples, one is always committed to some obscure work, denying the other's prerogative in describing reality and intervening in it.

Their relation, nevertheless, is complementary, and reflects an American picture of a legal-political-academic moment. The narrative quality is balanced by an argumentative opening in most chapters (the structure again neither neat nor formal). The last chapter is the supplement and the exception to the complex map drawn in the previous ones, since it aspires to enter a younger discourse, that of dispute-resolution. In this realm, as far as my current contextual perspective enables me to see, the internal-external interactions described before still has not materialized. The sequence of it is thus more linear and constructed as a theoretical manifesto of the proper meta-discourse to describe the business of mediation.

Being faithful to the pragmatic specter that haunts my paper, my writing tries to avoid the claim to apply *any* theory. Many theories operate within my texts, but in a process equivalent with what my writing describes, they have become a body, a sensitivity of reading that cannot be ascribed directly to the 'origin' anymore. Whatever texts are at stake – deconstruction, psychoanalysis, literary themes, or some philosophical wisdom – I cannot claim to master them in any way, or to have the ability to restate their 'origin' without operating my own incorporation, my own interpretive violence. This is why I avoid positing any grand theory as my ultimate guiding methodology. I try to read with what I am: with my legal and philosophical education and passions, with my location as a stranger, with my intellectual sensors of resistance. Overall, the most prevalent passion I find in the writing is that of resistance: for the American, the intellectual, the practical, and the theoretical, a resistance that functions as an energy source; I believe it to be a search for the human that can never be articulated. It is resistance, also in a way a kind of love, of craving that tries to preserve and work on the friend-enemy tension that exists in any relationship, which is part of living (and letting live).

Histories

History, in my text, is a story we tell from a certain point in time and place. I give up completely the idea of writing what 'really happens'. There is no real access to that idea, because it is always a matter of retrospective reflection and recapturing. Things we see from one point in time we do not see from another. This explains why most of my descriptions of 'what happened' are formulated in the text in a quote, functioning somehow like ornaments, through someone else who spoke them. It is always important when, exactly, he or she is telling them, and in what position in relation to the legal discourse. In this way, the grand story becomes a network of stories and projections, anxieties and counter-projections, where interactions are repeated but never in the same way, and where an amorphic singularity of pragmatism functions repeatedly as an object of desire and identification.

The above 'second-hand'-textual quality of the historic narratives explains why the names of the books are important: *The Revival of Pragmatism*, *The Emergence of American Philosophy*, *The American Evasion of Philosophy*. They all present the interest, the bias, the inevitable lens for a certain reading, and I am interested in exposing this interest and not the 'real' events. In a way, my choice of Harvard as an iconic place from which to examine the 'intellectual climate' of an era emphasizes the way that the imagined center continually reproduces the relevant narrative typical of a time, just because of its fantastic or 'second-hand' quality of being believed to be The American Place. For the singular dispute, or the so-called 'everyday life', none of the big stories matters. But they do. Exposing the arbitrariness in a signifying chain might help to demystify it, although there is always another one to come. To expose the proper names of some stories might shake up a bit our grid of understanding them, but there is always another grid to come, having its own proper name.

Between the quotations, I have a story myself, and in a way I am trying to work with my bias, my pragmatic specter (of using a theory) throughout the thesis. I have an interest in describing the textual medium of the history at stake, to show, through what I think are contemporary eyes, some 'underlying' structure for the unfolding of the diverse histories. I put aside any claim of the texts to possess a truth (and in a way, they all tell the truth) and try to characterize their aesthetic and discursive characteristics through their development. In that sense, the texts are examined in my writing as aesthetic works of art, as symbols and scripts signaling to one another, developing dependent upon one another, and having their own language of interaction. To say that there is much more happening there than just love or hate is actually also to describe the strength and uniqueness of family ties, of discursive relations as family ties and of genres of discourses that hold together in their uniqueness by holding the same name (or at least having some relation to it). Indeed, the thesis which is the basis of this book was originally named: *Pragmatism and American (Il)Legal Family Ties: Obsession, Hysteria, and Problem Solving*. Through the transformation into a book format, the title became much more simple: from philosophy to dispute-resolution, from philawsophy and an archeological quest into genres of discourses, to the art of the real, of reality of dispute-resolution in its becoming, and through the aspiration for an interpretive healing. The last chapter, which deals with models of mediation as reflecting intellectual phases, begins to address this hope.

Informalities

In some way I trace the singular within the claiming to be general and abstract. I trace the American (as pragmatist), its relations with the political (which is a kind of singularity in each time and place), and especially, the various representations of it in relation to the canonical view. The canonical view or the 'American legal theory' that I seek to capture is itself a singularity, a sickness, an obsession, an occupation that neglects other, more burning problems – the disputes. In one sense, I can claim that what characterizes my work is an anti-formalist mode – one that refutes being formally characterized as such, which tries to bring itself to its end/new beginning.

My writing is, at bottom, about fantasies: It starts with the fantasy of the foreigner (coming from another Promised Land, in some readings the original one), reaching a new land, trying to understand its grammar. It develops with reflections on the contradictions myself as this foreigner finds between the 'grammars' I can read, the genres of discourse I inhabit, which are dispute-resolution and jurisprudence. It moves on to trace this contradiction in the fantastic origin of this other land, in history, in histories, and in storytelling. The return to Israel, in this sense, and to its 2000 spectacle of dispute escalation, reinforced for me the uniqueness of the 'stranger' position and brought forward the problematic of providing a grand theory which is external to a location in time and place. My last 'Israeli' chapter tries to capture my current fantasy of a mediation model in our multicultural society, and the ongoing events in our world confirm for me that such a model has not yet been tried. Between the fantasies or the stories or the texts, within the delicate intercourse between them, arises reality, my reality – but actually, some reality that I hope can reveal something to another, at least to one. But this in itself is not sure. The multifarious reading possibilities that exist for any text suggest that it is always a matter of addressing one reader, expecting the violence and gift of their interpretation, of their re-reading. This one modest hope for the singular is again coming back to the dispute as the only place we can reach at last, the dispute that we can only hope to settle.

Chapter 1

The Maturing of the Pragmatic Idea in Law and Society (Or: The Fall, and the Rise of 'Philawsophy')[1]

1.1 Introduction

This chapter deals with the maturing of the pragmatic idea in law. My aim is to follow the specific way in which the pragmatic sensitivities have been applied to adjudication and to locate this phenomenon in the broader cultural level. Within this framework, I will trace the American within the pragmatic, examine both the Emersonian legacy and the Darwinian enchantment, and describe the relationship between legal and general pragmatism. I trace the legacy of Oliver Wendell Holmes Jr through its discursive characteristics, and show some examples for its manifestation in his followers' texts. The progressive canonical legal narrative will be examined through this sequence as well.

There are a few sub-arguments for this endeavor. First, there is a central role for the notion of pragmatism in defining the American and accounting for intellectual developments within law and society in the promised land. By using pragmatism as a text, which functions as a proper name, a singular identity that wears different costumes in time and place, I try to trace its operation within the theoretical legal discourse.

Second, pragmatism is described in this chapter as having a central role in the constitution of the American subject. In other words, for the sake of explicating my interest in a current focus on dispute resolution in law, I will begin with religious and naturalistic motives in the nineteenth century, pursue them with Darwinian science, and try to show their connection to the emergence of the pragmatic text and to the ostensibly simple idea of 'problem solving'.

---

[1] 'Philawsophy' is a concept near 'philosophy' and substituting for it, based on my claim that through pragmatism, philosophy in America has become the science of 'the legal elephant', an expression I discuss later, referring to Thomas Grey's article.

Third, there is proximity between the philosophical and legal discourse at the time of their emergence that accounts for the centrality and dominance of the academic legal discourse within the US intellectual realm of today. I describe, through a contemporary lens, the mythological foundation of the legal discourse as a substitute for philosophy, which preserves its pathos, and reorganize it around the particular elements that constitute the legal discourse. I try to capture the complementary relation between the two realms by offering a line of discursive correlative characteristics.

Fourth, a basic argument will be that the pragmatic idea in law has emerged beside what is considered classical, or general, pragmatism as its masculine discursive correlate. I will describe a philosophical discourse that is general, hysteric, external, practical, and progressive, and beside it a legal antecedent discourse (that of Holmes) that is professional, obsessive, internal, theoretical, and conservative. The next jurisprudential step of the Legal Realists' school will be read as a progressive re-inscription of the Holmsian legacy through the operation of an intellectual movement, and again as a resistance to a 'general' discourse of pragmatism, this time within law.

Fifth, along the lines of my arguments above, there is a continuity that can be articulated between Oliver Wendell Holmes, the originator of the pragmatism of law, his follower Llewellyn in his portrayal of the 'next step', and the contemporary Duncan Kennedy and his commitment to internal critique and to 'living within law'. By putting these three individuals under the same rubric of 'legal prophets', I emphasize the pragmatic unique characteristics of their 'legacy'. At the current turn of the century, it seems that Kennedy portrays a decline of the internal philawsophical pathos and defines it as the 'viral strain'. This portrayal can account for a decline of a mode of legal professional-identity mystique, which is examined in other chapters of this book.

1.2   Origins

In his book *The American Evasion of Philosophy: A Genealogy of Pragmatism*,[2] Cornell West posits Ralph Waldo Emerson in the mid-19th century as prefiguring 'the dominant themes of American pragmatism',[3] claiming that he 'enacts an intellectual style of cultural criticism that permits

---

2   Cornell West, *The American Evasion of Philosophy* (1989).
3   Id., at 9.

and encourages American pragmatists to swerve from mainstream European philosophy'.[4] West depicts Emerson as a proto-pragmatist and a prophet,[5] and whether or not this is true, equivalent accounts depict Emerson as the originator of the American voice. Examples can also be found in contemporary books, like *The Revival of Pragmatism* (1998)[6] or a 1999 book, *Classical American Pragmatism: Its Contemporary Vitality.*[7]

> With the exception of Jonathan Edwards, whose originality sets him apart, philosophers in America from the time of the Puritans to that of Emerson were mainly engaged in transmitting the schools of European philosophy to the New World ... The point to be stressed in this development is that, although these ideas from abroad affected American patterns of thought, they did not spring from the experience of America as a new country facing the problems posed by the need to civilize a continent, build cities, establish representative government, provide for public education, and cope with the inevitable conflicts of interests arising for a growing nation made up of many different nationalities. *In short, although America was open to all these intellectual currents from abroad, it had not yet found its own philosophical voice. That was to happen in time, first through the writing of Emerson and later through those of the pragmatists – Pierce, James, Dewey, and Mead* ...[8] (my emphasis, M.A.).

---

4   Id.
5   The epitaph to the Emerson chapter of West is a quote from Henry James, Sr: 'Mr. Emerson was never the least of a pedagogue, addressing your scientific intelligence, but an everyday unconscious prophet, appealing exclusively to the regenerate heart of mankind, and announcing the speedy fulfillment of the hope with which it had always been pregnant. He was an American John the Baptist, proclaiming tidings of great joy to the American Israel'. Id.
6   *The Revival of Pragmatism* (Morris Dickstein, ed., 1998), 3, 5, 72–5, 351–7.
7   See also Stanley Cavell, *What's the Use of Calling Emerson a Pragmatist?* Id., at 72.
8   See John E. Smith, 'Introduction', in *Classical American Pragmatism: Its Contemporary Vitality* (1999), 1–2: 'With the exception of Jonathan Edwards, whose originality sets him apart, philosophers in America from the time of the Puritans to that of Emerson were mainly engaged in transmitting the schools of European philosophy to the New World ... The point to be stressed in this development is that, although these ideas from abroad affected American patterns of thought, they did not spring from the experience of America as a new country facing the problems posed by the need to civilize a continent, build cities, establish representative government, provide for public education, and cope with the inevitable conflicts of interests arising for a growing nation made up of many different nationalities. In short, although America was open to all these intellectual currents from abroad, it had not yet found its own philosophical voice. That was to happen in time first through the writing of Emerson and later through those of the pragmatists – Pierce, James, Dewey, and Mead ....'

There is a 'revival of pragmatism', and of the 'vitality' of it, in contemporary terms or in more classical ones,[9] and within that revival is an effort to come back to the origin, to re-read it. I will try to capture a few basic Emersonian ideas that, in my view, recur later in pragmatic thought, and constitute some basic characteristic of the American subject as it appears in the legal texts I examine.

A primary message of the Emersonian individualism, which has its roots in Transcendentalist perception and in religious thought, is the evasion of the past, scorn for the authority of the old traditions, and the call to invent oneself anew. Emerson begs us not to count on generalities or past convictions.[10] We must be courageous enough to face the 'outside world' as it is reflected within ourselves, and to dare to be radically individualistic.

> The scholar is that man who must take up into himself all the ability of the time, all the contributions of the past, all the hopes of the future. He must be a university of knowledge. If there is one message more than another which should pierce his ear, it is: the world is nothing, the man is all; in yourself is the law of all nature, and you know not yet how a globule of sap ascends; in yourself slumbers the whole of Reason; it is for you to know all, it is for you to dare all.[11]

'I had better never see a book than to be wrapped by its attraction clean out of my own orbit ... Books are for the scholar's idle times. When he can read God directly, the hour is too precious to be wasted in other men's transcript of their readings.'[12] Emerson brings this romantic and also religious speech named 'The American Scholar' to the Harvard scholar of 1837,[13] and Holmes

---

9   The two above mentioned books indeed capture the flexible texture of pragmatism, which, having a central role in defining the American, is revived and revitalized through different genres of discourse in different ways. The 'classical American pragmatism' book includes discussions of James, Pierce, Dewey and Mead as having immediate baring for the academic discussions of today. The 'revival' book is reading the 'classical' texts through an interpretive mode and a contemporary 'wave' of pragmatism.

10 'Emerson's alternative to modern philosophy was neither to replace it with a new philosophical problematic nor to deny it by means of a strict and severe skepticism. Rather he *evades* modern philosophy, that is, he ingeniously and skillfully refuses: (1) Its quest for certainty and its hope for professional. i.e., scientific, respectability; (2) its search for foundations. This distinctly American refusal is the crucible from which emerge the sensibilities and sentiments of future American pragmatists': Smith *supra* note 8, at 36.

11 Ralph Waldo Emerson, Selected Essays (Larzer Ziff, ed., 1982), 103–4.

12 Id., at 88–9.

13 'The isolation is enacted in "The American Scholar," whose occasion is enviably if not frighteningly distinctive. Whoever Emerson invokes as belonging to the class of scholars

dubs it later as a 'national intellectual declaration of independence'.[14] As at any foundational moment, the declaration can be grasped only retrospectively, and as I will try to show, only in its inherent impossibility, in its mythical core. 'We have listened too long to the courtly muses of Europe ... The mind of this country, taught to aim at low objects, eats upon itself ... we will work with our own hands; we will speak our own mind.'[15] And also: 'Perhaps the time is already come when it ought to be, and it will be something else; when the sluggard intellect of this continent will look from under its iron lids and fill the postponed expectation of the world with something better than the exertions of mechanical skill.'[16] Here, perhaps, lies the paradox, or the mythical flavor, of this whole idea, resting in the fact that we can never simply speak 'ourselves', nor work with 'our own hands' using raw and basic materials.[17] We can never begin from scratch, just as we cannot step out of language, out of culture.[18] We are ever within a tradition, using certain idioms, commenting or transforming but always heavily situated within history.[19] There is, as Stanley Cavell offers, a 'hitch' and a 'catch' here:

> that commencement day at Harvard in the summer of 1837 – himself, his audience (whether as poets, preachers or philosophers) – the principal fact about the class is that it is empty, the American scholar does not exist. Then who is Emerson? Suppose we say that what motivates Emerson's thinking, or what causes his call for the American scholar, is Emerson's vision of our not thinking. Is this plain fact of American history – that we are, we still find ourselves, looking for the commencement of our own culture'. Stanley Cavell, *Conditions Handsome and Unhandsome: the Constitution of Emersonian Perfectionism* (1988), 35.

14   West, *supra* note 2, at 12.
15   Emerson, *supra* note 11, at 104.
16   Id., at 83.
17   'Why should not we also enjoy an original relation to the universe? Why should not we have a poetry and philosophy of insight and not of tradition, and a religion by revelation to us, and not the history of theirs? ...why should we grope among the dry bones of the past, or put the living generation into masquerade out of its faded wardrobe? The sun shines to-day also. There is more wool and flax in the fields. There are new lands, new men, new thoughts. Let us demand our own works and laws of worship': Id., *Nature*, 35.
18   For the problematics of locating the conceptual 'origin' without finding it already 'contaminated' with the supplement of its retelling, in history and in text, see Jacques Derrida, *Of Grammatology* (Gayatri Chakravotry Spivak, trans., 1976), 1967.
19   'Emerson's theodicy essentially asserts three things: that the only sin is limitation, i.e., constraints on power; that sin is overcomable; and that it is beautiful and good that sin should exist to be overcome. Emerson's articulation of this theodicy led Sydney Ahlstorm to suggest that Emerson is in fact the theologian of something we may almost term "the American religion" and Harold Bloom to conclude that Emerson's "truest achievement was to invent the American religion"': West, *supra* note 2, at 17.

Can Emerson be understood as wishing to replace philosophy? But isn't that wish really what accounts for the poignancy, or dialectic, of Emerson's call, the year Thoreau graduated college, not for a thinker but for Man Thinking? The American Scholar is to think no longer partially, as a man following a task delegated by a society of which he is a victim, but as leading a life in which thinking is of the essence, as a man whose wholeness, say whose autonomy, is in command of the autonomy of thinking. *The hitch, of course, is that there is no such human being. 'Man in history, men in the world today are bugs, spawn' (The American Scholar). But the catch is that we aspire to this man, to the metamorphosis, to the human – hence that we can be guided and raised by the cheer of thinking*[20] (my emphasis, M.A.).

Another basic characteristic of the Emersonian theodicy is its *naturalistic* character. 'The basic nature of things, the fundamental way the world is, is itself incomplete and in flux, always the result of and a beckon to the experimental makings, workings, and doings of human beings. Language, tradition, society, nature, and the self are shot through with contingency, change, and challenge.'[21] The naturalistic foundation of this construction of culture is prevalent in Emerson's texts, and continues to operate later in pragmatism in its various manifestations through time and place.

> The eye is the first circle; the horizon which it forms is the second; and throughout nature this primary figure is repeated without end. It is the highest emblem in the cipher of the world. St. Augustine describes the nature of God as a circle whose centre was everywhere and its circumference nowhere.[22]

This description of nature assumes its existence as given and unquestionable. Although the metaphysics and epistemology are here embedded in religious thought and in that way are still pre-modern, the basic structure of nature as given, and the subject as re-constituting itself within it, recurs in the pragmatic American thought that follows Emerson, accompanying us still today. The later insertion of evolutionary theories to modernize this conception will remain embedded in this structure.

> There are no fixtures in nature. The universe is fluid and volatile. Permanence is but a word of degree. Our globe seen by God is a transparent law, not a mass

---

20 Stanley Cavell, *The Senses of Walden* (2nd edn, 1981), 130.
21 West, *supra* note 2, at 15.
22 Emerson, *Circles*, *supra* note 11, at 225.

of facts. The law dissolves the facts and holds it fluid.[23]

'The natural world may be conceived of as a system of concentric circles, and we now and then detect in nature slight dislocations which apprise us that this surface on which we now stand is not fixed, but sliding.'[24] The encounter with nature is a complex, reflexive process where 'nothing is secure but life, transition, the energizing spirit', and where there is 'no truth so sublime but it may be trivial tomorrow in light of new thoughts'.[25] 'Life is a series of surprises'[26] within this thought, but what is not questioned and thereby stays philosophically unexamined is the obvious existence of nature and of experience within it. There is no critical effort to examine the whole notion of 'the common' or 'the natural', and within corresponding religious circles above, philosophy assumes this foundation. The 'transcendentalist' posture of Emerson apparently deals with the controversy between 'materialists and idealists; the first class founding on experience, the second on consciousness'.[27]

> The first class beginning to think from the data of the senses, the second class perceives that the senses are not final, and say, the senses give us representation of things, but what are the things themselves they cannot tell. The materialists insist on facts, on history, on the force of circumstances and the animal wants of man; the idealists on the power of Thought and of Will, on inspiration, on miracle, on individual culture.[28]

But despite the association with the rational against the empiricist debate in philosophy, despite the familiar ring of the expression 'things themselves' with Kantian philosophy, despite the manifest interest in critical examination of these attitudes, there is the assumption that these modes of thinking are 'both natural', and that there is a universe separate from 'me'. In Stanley Cavell's terms, 'We are in a state of "romance" with the universe; we do not possess it but our life is to return to it, in ever-widening circles.'[29] He continues, 'Emerson's most explicit reversal of Kant lies in his picturing the intellectual hemisphere of knowledge as passive or receptive and the intuitive or instinctual hemisphere as active or spontaneous. Whereas for Kant the basis of the *Critique*

---

23 Id., at 226.
24 Id., at 233.
25 Id., at 237.
26 Id.
27 Id., *The Transcendentalist*, 239.
28 Id.
29 Cavell, *Senses of Walden*, supra note 20, 128.

of Pure Reason is that "concepts are based on the spontaneity of thought, sensible intuitions on the receptivity of impressions." Briefly, there is no intellectual intuition.'[30] Whether Kant undervalued intuition in his German-European mode of thinking, Cavell's perception of Emerson's American intuition is loaded with metaphysics of its own.[31]

> Nature hastens to render account of herself to the mind. Classification begins. To the young man every thing is individual, stands by itself. By and by, it finds how to join two things and see in them one nature; then three, then three thousands ... But what is classification but the perceiving that these objects are not chaotic, and are not foreign, but have a law which is also a law of the human mind ... The ambitious soul sits down before each refractory fact; one after another reduces all strange constitutions, all new powers, to their class and their law, and goes on forever to animate the last fibre of organization, the outskirts of nature, by insight.[32]

The animation of organization, the obsession with classification, the counting ('three, three thousands'), the scientific image of the scholar and the operation of the human intellect and genius – none of these images has ceased to function with the decline of the religious pathos. They seemed still to haunt and influence the constitution of a nation whose largeness and complexity, combined with a potent economic impulse, corresponded with the Emersonian inscription of the American spirit.[33] We can find this same idea of experience and reality in flux some fifty years later in Dewey's writing.

> It goes without saying that man begins as a part of physical and animal nature. In as far as he reacts to physical things on a strictly physical level, he is pulled and pushed about, overwhelmed, broken to pieces, lifted on the crest of the wave of things, like anything else ... Thus to be conscious of meaning or to have an idea, marks a fruition, an enjoyed or suffered arrest of the flux of events.[34]

---

30 Id., at 129.
31 See the discussion of Cavell's 'pragmatism', *infra* text to 42n–46n.
32 Id., *The American Scholar*, 86.
33 'For Emerson, the modern world needs self sustaining and self overcoming individuals who would flex their intellectual, social political and economic muscles in order to gain wisdom, i.e., to see the miraculous in the common, and to build the Kingdom of man over nature': West, *supra* note 2, at 16.
34 John Dewey, 'Experience, Nature and Art', in John Dewey, *Experience and Nature* (1925), 233.

And also in William James's praise of what Richard Rorty calls 'romantic polytheism':[35]

> Old-fashioned theism was bad enough, with its notion of God as an exalted monarch, made up of a lot of unintelligible of preposterous 'attributes;' but, so long as it held strongly by the argument from design, it kept some touch with concrete realities. Since, however, Darwinism has once for all displaced design from the mind of the 'scientific', theism has lost that foothold; and some kind of an immanent or pantheistic deity working *in* things rather than above them is, if any, the kind recommended to our contemporary imagination.[36]

Darwinism is assumed here to legitimately condition the religious and philosophical ideas. The evolutionary picture it provides switches the 'pragmatic need' of external entities like God or the transcendental or the human notions of Kant. Instead there is an organic notion of working from within, of a romantic existence within nature and pantheism or polytheism which in James' texts mediate between empiricism and rationalism.[37] Hilary Putnam calls this mode 'direct realism'.[38]

The philosophical impulse at Emerson's time already assumes the prevalence of the scientific epistemology, meaning that man questions his limits and begins philosophizing within a positive picture of natural reality and nature given to scientific inquiry.[39] This prevalence is built later into the modern (non-religious) account of the American, in pragmatism, by the incorporation of Darwin's evolutionary theory to establish a philosophical account of the human animal.[40]

---

35 Richard Rorty, 'Pragmatism as Romantic Polytheism', in *The Revival of Pragmatism*, *supra* note 6, at 21.
36 Wlliam James, 'What Pragmatism Means', in William James, *Pragmatism: A New Name for Some Old Ways of Thinking* (1907), 56.
37 Id., at 110–11.
38 See Hilary Putnam, 'Pragmatism and Realism', in *The Revival of Pragmatism*, *supra* note 6, at 37: 'What I understand by the term direct realism here is not a particular metaphysical theory, but rather our implicit and everyday conviction that in experience we are immediately aware of such common objects of trees and buildings, not to mention other people.' Putnam claims that James was the first to successfully put forward a direct realist picture.
39 Referring to language, which is today considered the most fundamental dimension on which both the discourse on science and religion appears, Emerson holds a very representational image: 'Language is a third use which Nature subserves to man. Nature is the vehicle of thought, and in a simple, double, and three-fold degree. 1. Words are signs of natural facts. 2. Particular natural facts are symbols of particular spiritual facts. 3. Nature is the symbol of spirit': Emerson, *Nature*, *supra* note 11, at 48.
40 See infra text to 55n–59n.

> All science has one aim, namely to find a theory of nature ... Philosophically considered, the universe is composed of Nature and the Soul. Strictly speaking, therefore, all that is separate from us, all which philosophy distinguishes as the *not me*, that is, both nature and art, all other men and my own body, must be ranked under this name, *Nature*. In enumerating the values of nature and casting up their sum, I shall use the word in both senses; – in its common and its philosophical import. In inquiries so general as our present one, the inaccuracy is not material; no confusion of thought will occur. *Nature*, in the common sense, refers to essences unchanged by man; space, the air, the river, the leaf.[41]

But one thing we know today is that even the most natural 'essences' like 'space, air, the river' are changed by man (and woman). Not only are they changed; their 'naturality' is also assumed in our gaze – our perspective changes the essence of the quantum particles; our industry shapes the depiction of the natural resources or the reservoir; our technology affects the remoteness and neutrality of space. There is no 'common sense-natural' level beyond reflection, which is not constructed in language.

The later characteristic brings me to another impulse of Emerson's, which is *the embrace of the ordinary*. This is the third claim whose development I would like to examine.

> The literature of the poor, the feeling of the child, the philosophy of the street, the meaning of household life are the topics of the time ... I ask not for the great, the remote, the romantic; what is doing in Italy or Arabia; what is Greek art, or provincial minstrelsy; I embrace the common, I explore and sit at the feet of the familiar, the low.[42]

This is a very strong humanist call, a basic democratic idea in defining the American. Emerson's considered romantic attraction to the ordinary is related to his 'mythic conception of the exceptional individual as America',[43] and to the evasion of the past described above.[44] Stanley Cavell calls this impulse 'meta-snobbery: snobbery over not being a snob'.[45] He himself

---

41 Emerson, *Nature*, *supra* note 11, at 36.
42 Id., *The American Scholar*, 102.
43 West, *supra* note 2, at 19.
44 See *supra* text to 10n–19n.
45 'The moral vulnerability of Emerson's and Thoreau's impatience may be described as a temptation to meta-snobbery, snobbery over not being a snob (like pride in transcending pride), an apparent effort to exempt oneself from the condition of morality (the divided human condition) by surpassing it': Cavell, *Conditions Handsome and Unhandsome*, *supra* note 13, xxi.

searches for the ordinary (*In Quest of the Ordinary* as one of his books is titled) in opera,[46] in Hollywood movies,[47] in the discussion and elaboration of 'moral perfectionism',[48] and perceives this quest as a search for the American voice in philosophy. Cavell is occupied with describing the abyss between American and European philosophy by contrasting the European's de-construction with the Emersonian and Austinian embrace of the ordinary. While European thought chooses to go against metaphysics through metaphysics, Americans do so through the ordinary. Cavell's quest for the ordinary is interesting, and offers, in my view, a more psychoanalytic mode of 'return'. Still, the ordinary 'itself' in his texts – 'natural everyday language', marriage life, 'the woman's voice' in opera or in 'the melodrama of the unknown woman' – are undoubtedly discursively constructed, and have no simple, non-ideological essence. They all come back to the old Emersonian myth in the name of looking for the American.[49]

If access to the ordinary – nature, the poor, or the woman's voice – is inherently barred, as my above claim implies, that is also why Emerson's

---

46 See 'Opera and the Lease of Voice', in Stanley Cavell, *A Pitch of Philosophy: Autobiographical Exercises* (1994), 130.
47 Stanley Cavell, *Pursuits of Happiness* (1981). Stanley Cavell, *Contesting Tears: the Hollywood Melodrama of the Unknown Woman* (1996).
48 See Cavell, *Conditions Handsome and Unhandsome*, supra note 13.
49 See, for example, the descriptions on the cover of some of Cavell's books: 'This book is an invitation to the life of philosophy in the United States, as Emerson once lived it and as Stanley Cavell now lives it – in all its topographical ambiguity ... The result of Cavell's struggle to defend the Austinian heritage, in its "democratic" defense of the ordinary, by restoring the distinctive voice and tone that he takes Derrida to neglect is to my knowledge the most suggestive discussion of the distinctive status of tone and voice in response to the two philosophical traditions epitomized, however ironically, by Derrida and Austin (*A Pitch of Philosophy*). These lectures by one of the most influential and original philosophers of the twentieth century constitute a sustained argument for the philosophical basis of romanticism, particularly in its American rendering. Through his examination of such authors as Emerson, Thoreau, Poe, Wordsworth, and Coleridge, Stanley Cavell shows that romanticism and American transcendentalism represent a serious philosophical response to the challenge of skepticism and underlie the writings of Wittgenstein and Austin on ordinary language ... In *Quest of the Ordinary* is all about the kinship of philosophy and literature and the misfortune for the Anglo-American world of their too strict separation ...' (*In Quest of the Ordinary*) 'In these lectures, Stanley Cavell situates Emerson at an intersection of three crossroads: a place where both philosophy and literature pass; where the low traditions of English and German philosophy shun one another; where the cultures of American and Europe unsettle one another' (*Conditions Handsome and Unhandsome*). All the covers end with the same line: 'Stanley Cavell teaches philosophy at Harvard University.'

'snobbery over non-snobbery' may be the worst vanity. Conscious humility is inherently arrogant: how can he 'embrace' the common without mastering the discourse that decides what is common, what is gentile, and who is not covered by this discourse at all (who and what is the Other)? We can find some indication to that in Emerson's actual racism,[50] in his inaction and impotence in the political realm,[51] in his attitude towards woman, the Native, in his scorn for the masses. So long as the common and low are constructed in language, their discursive operation can manipulate and reinforce exiting structures of injustice.

Another cultural offspring of this call can be found later in Dewey's 'democratic faith in common people',[52] in the lower cultural level, in the scorn for high theory and for intellectuals, in the praise of practice and of 'little projects', and in the contemporary Roger Fisher's activist tone (which I describe elsewhere).[53]

Trying to summarize the Emersonian legacy described above, the initial pathos of evasion, of inventing everything anew, of finding a grand theory and of rebelling against all past convictions is accompanied by a low, case-sensitive practice, by a 'little-things' private existence. They combine into a market economy of the individual.

> Needless to say, the centrality of provocation and stimulation in a discourse is the product of and helps reproduce a market culture – that is, a market culture in which the past is effaced, the social concealed, and the future projected by the arbitrary clashing wills of individuals ... When freed of ritual, religious, or juridical restraints, a money medium can imbue life itself with a pervasive and ongoing sense of risk, a recurrent anticipation of gain and loss that lends to all social intercourse a pointed transactional quality.[54]

---

50 West, *supra* note 2, at 28–35. 'I saw ten, twenty, a hundred large lipped, low-browed black men in the streets who, except in the mere matter of language, did not exceed the sagacity of the elephant. Now is it true that these were created superior to this wise animal, and designed to control it? And in comparison with the highest orders of men, the Africans will stand too low as to make the difference which subsists between them and the sagacious beasts inconsiderable. It follows from this, that this is a distinction which cannot be much insisted on.' From Emerson's journals, quoted by West, 29.
51 Id., at 21.
52 Id., at 24.
53 See the chapter 'In Search of The Dispute: On Lawyers and Legal Philawsophers at Harvard Law School (Or, Some Private Hope and Public Irony)'.
54 West, *supra* note 2, at 26.

The combination of the *ex ante* grand theory, made of analytical tools and scientifically based (or the product of 'the genius', as described in Emerson) combined with an ex-post sensitivity to the case and the deference of criteria, is repeated later in pragmatism and in the Legal Process writing,[55] at times (post-World War II) when American legal thought is assumed to speak in a 'collective voice'.

Coming back to the incorporation and transformation of the three Emersonian ideas described above into the 'story' of pragmatism, which emerged at the turn of the century, the first significant fact to notice is the geographical and intellectual proximity between Emerson and the 'Metaphysical Club', assumed to be the originator of the pragmatic idea. New England – Cambridge – Harvard are again a focal point for the emergence of the new account of the American. This time, there is an effort to sort religion out from theory, and to the forefront (and background) of theoretical thought arrives the Darwinian Science. The epistemology and metaphysics of this scientific discourse become the foundation of the first purely 'modern' American philosophizing.

If we locate pragmatism within the broader picture of intellectual life around 1900, we can see it as a kind of knot in the tapestry, a pulling together of threads that reach into other areas of thought, with many other consequences – threads that, running back into the nineteenth century, include the emergence of theories of cultural pluralism and political progressivism; the fascination with pure science and the logic of scientific inquiry; the development of probability theory as a means for coping with randomness and uncertainty; the spread of historicist approaches to the study of culture; the rapid assimilation of the Darwinian theory of evolution; and the Emersonian suspicion of institutional authority.[56]

This complex account of pragmatism's 'pulling together' of diverse intellectual threads – cultural pluralism, political progressivism, the fascination with pure science, the spread of historicist approaches to the study of culture – is offered by Louis Menand in 1997 in an introduction to a new reader of pragmatic texts. One of William James' book implies this 'sameness' logic too: *Pragmatism: A New Name for Some Old Ways of Thinking*. Although this reading is possible, I would suggest that pragmatism's value and influence

---

55   See the chapter 'Settled Law and the Law-That-Is-Not-But-Ought-To-Be: Hart and Sacks and the Pragmatic Philosophy of Dispute Resolution (Or: Why Couldn't Henry Hart Speak?)'.

56   *Pragmatism: A Reader* (Louis Menand, ed., 1997), xxvi. The opening phrase of Menand's introduction is 'Pragmatism is an account of the way people think.'

are due precisely to its not being a 'knot in the tapestry', 'a new name for some old thinking' or 'a putting together of threads'. From one possible perspective, it is always such a knot, but its many different readers imply no fixed point of narration, revealing only a source for projections and cravings. Pragmatism should be read as a rupture, as a new beginning, a foundational moment, which, as in the discussion of the 'American Scholar', is always mythical, and ceaselessly acknowledged retrospectively. This focus does not claim to challenge the complex play of other ideas, including European thought and other discourses, in the creation moment and in later developments. My reading aims to organize the genealogical diversity while stressing my limited project of dispute resolution in law, through my inhabitance within contemporary texts of psychoanalysis and deconstruction. The centrality of Newtonian science for the emergence of pragmatism and the development of a certain style of American philosophizing is narrated by me, accordingly, through a post-structural psycho-analytic mode of inquiry.

> Kantian ethics appears at the same moment when the disorienting effect of Newtonian physics is left ... It was Newtonian physics that forced Kant to revise radically the function of reason in its pure form. And it is also in connection with the question raised by science that a form of morality has come to engage us; it is a morality whose precise structure could not have been perceived until then – one that detaches itself purposefully from all reference to any object of affection, from all reference to what Kant called the *pathologisches objekt*, a pathological object, which simply means the object of any passion whatsoever.[57]

What Jacques Lacan offers here, in his textual psychoanalysis, is that something disorienting in Newtonian physics brought Kant to establish the realm beyond the mechanistic and the 'utilitarian' on the one hand, and beyond the passionate and affectionate on the other. A Kantian morality that detaches itself purposefully from all reference to any object of affection is presented in Lacan's text as answering the need to leave science a space while keeping the philosophical pathos. It is a moment of foundation, with its mythological flavor, as before, and the product is a key inscription of modern Western subjectivity.[58]

---

57 Jacques Lacan, *The Seminar Of Jacques Lacan*, Book VII: *The Ethics Of Psychoanalysis* (Jacques Alain Miller, ed., Dennis Porter, trans., 1986), 1959–960, 76.
58 'In truth, I believe that the achievement of a form of subjectivity that deserves the name contemporary, that belongs to a man of our time, who is lucky enough to be born now, cannot ignore this text': Id., at 77.

Can it be the fact that, in America, things happened differently? That the epistemological base of the inscription of American subjectivity can be found in Darwinian and not Newtonian science? That the 'disorienting' role was ascribed in America to the Darwinian style of science? I think one can argue for that, and show how the previous religious hints can be re-read through the frame of Darwinian evolution and combined with Hegellian ideas to establish a metaphysics of the human animal.[59] The world of Darwin was not deterministic nor mechanistic. 'It was a processive and unfinished world',[60] shot through with chance and contingency, and there was probably no felt 'need' to produce a philosophy that transcended it. This concrete scientific foundation will continue haunting the intellectual evolution in America long after the Darwinian trend is over. Its truth is, in a way, assumed, and its existence is no longer a burning question. Still it is the local context of many philosophical inquiries, which assume a given natural medium of movement without questioning it. Philosophy in Europe will take Kant to a more radical idealism, and eventually through Heidigerr to a call against metaphysics, and to a consequent discursive post-structural analysis of this whole sequence. But the Americans will take their own route, one that does not assume Kant as a founding moment. Instead of a philosophy that differentiates itself from

---

59 An idea which seems to recall this argument appears in David Depew's introduction to *Pragmatism: From Progressivism to Postmodernism* (Robert Hollinger and David Depew, eds, 1995), 3–4. 'The sphere to which Kant assigns pragmatic ideas largely coincides with what was left of the old purposive or teleological Aristotelian worldview, from which Kant could not bear entirely to part after modern science had mechanized the world-picture. Pierce realized, however, that since James Clerk Maxwell, Ludwig Boltzman, Josian Willard Gibbs, and Charles Darwin, science itself had been changing. A second scientific revolution was revealing a much less deterministic and mechanistic world than the one portrayed by Newton, Laplace and Kant. It was a processive and unfinished world, shot through with chance, contingency, and seat-of-the-pants adaptations, yielding its contours, therefore, to statistical and probabilistic forms of reasoning. concluded that in such a world *all* our ideas must be pragmatic in something like Kant's sense. In an inherently changing world, the determinacy of which shapes up mostly behind us, ideas guide us from one point of inquiry to another. Because the world itself, however, and not just our ideas about it, is in process, our changing ideas can point toward objects, or be objective, rather than merely calling attention to the contrast between our mutable subjectivity and a reality that is assumed to be invariant, as Kant had it.' This account of Depew is problematic in a sense. It emphasizes the gap I describe by assuming a 'correct' one vision of 'the world', which Kant did not see, and Pierce, thanks to Darwin, does see. It also assumes the leaner line between Newton and Darwin and claims for a progress narrative (from Newton to Darwin), a claim that does not correspond even with existing theory of science studies, and especially not with any discursive perspective of science.

60 Id.

science, establishing a realm beyond the mechanic, an evolutionary science beyond the mechanic is establishing a philosophy of the body, of the ordinary, the romantic existence of an open-ended contextual inquiry. This epistemology assumes a given natural existence before contemplation (the ordinary, the common, 'natural language', natural selection, the 'world'), and within it a contemplative space for constructions of theories for development of the self.[61] When the evolution base declines, after the 1950s, other foundational texts arrive to revive pragmatism, such as the economic or the interpretive, but as I will try to reveal through my writing, some strong Emersonian American impulse operates constantly beneath and within the discourse. I call it the pragmatic idea; but it may also be called the American one.

> The recognition that the intellectuals who rallied to pragmatism were preoccupied with the place of science in modern life is the point at which to begin an assessment of pragmatism's role in the lives of Americans who cared about it. The writings on meaning, truth, goodness, and other basic philosophical issues on account of which Pierce, James, and Dewey became known as pragmatists were the apex of a larger intellectual edifice constructed by these three men and their followers in response not only to the great epistemological and metaphysical questions of post-Kantian thought, but also to the desire for a way of life consistent with what they and their contemporaries variously perceived as the implications of modern science. Pierce, James, and Dewey were conspicuous leaders, among Americans, in the effort of Western intellectuals to find and articulate such a way of life.[62]

This was, indeed, as David Hollinger suggests, an intellectual edifice in response to science, but in contrast to the universality he tries to depict, it was unique to American thought and fascinated with a particular kind of science – the Darwinian one. The singularity of pragmatism in its American emphasis is manifested also in the particular details of its told emergence: The people who 'established' this philosophy, its place of birth in New England.

---

61 For the relationship of this perception to feminist thought see John Patrick Diggins, 'Pragmatism and Its Limits', in *The Revival of Pragmatism, supra* note 6, at 225. He brings the opinion that 'Dewey's philosophy helped women liberate themselves by showing that truth was a fixation of the dominant class, that there would be no neutral take on reality, and that "experience is to be understood as an affair of the intercourse of a living being with its physical and social environment". The idea that feminism begins when traditional philosophy ends "is certainly a dictum of our times".'
62 David A. Hollinger, 'The Problem of Pragmatism in American History: A Look Back and a Look Ahead', in *Pragmatism: From Progressivism to Postmodernism, supra* note 59, at 20.

The term was introduced to the world by William James in a lecture called 'Philosophical Conceptions and Practical Results', which he delivered on a visit to the University of California at Berkeley in 1898. In it James presented what he called the principle of Pierce, the principle of pragmatism, which he defined as follows: 'To attain perfect clearness in our thought of an object ... we need only consider what effects of a conceivably practical kind the object may involve – what sensations we are to expect from it, and what reactions we must prepare. Our conception of these effects, then, is for us the whole of our conception of the object, so far as that conception has positive significance at all.'[63]

William James, the brother of the writer Henry James and the son of a well-known Bostonian family, was 'one among many others',[64] but also 'a type of the epoch',[65] 'a man who put his stamp on his community and on his society'.[66] He was a Harvard professor[67] who had fame and respect in his country and abroad. The term pragmatism being assumed to be 'introduced to the world' by him is not a coincidence.[68]

In his book *The Rise of American Philosophy: Cambridge, Massachusetts 1860–1930*,[69] Bruce Kuklick describes this emergence of pragmatism in relation to the 'challenge of Darwinism' that the 'Unitarian philosophy' at Harvard confronted.[70] 'As scientists accepted Darwin, the Unitarian philosophers foundered. Believing that natural selection entailed atheism and that man could justify his existence only with religion, they could not integrate the developmental hypotheses into their creed.'[71] This occurred just after the

---

63 Pragmatism, *supra* note 56, at xiii.
64 Kim Townsend, *Manhood at Harvard: William James and Others* (1996), 25. The name of the book 'recalls an autobiographical work by James' brother Henry': *A Small Boy and Others*.
65 Id., at 26.
66 Id.
67 Id., at 25–6. 'And inasmuch as Harvard strove to become the most influential educational institution in the country during the years that James taught there, all the while that higher education itself was becoming the means by which young men made their way in society, there is ample justification for imagining William James at the center of a much larger circle.'
68 See also William James, 'What Pragmatism Means', in *Pragmatism, supra* note 56, 95: 'This is the principle of Pierce, the principle of pragmatism. It lay entirely unnoticed by anyone for twenty years, until I ... brought it forward again and made a special application of it to religion. By that date (1898) the time seemed ripe for its reception. The word pragmatism spread, and at present it fairly spots the pages of the philosophic journals.'
69 Bruce Kuklick, *The Rise of American Philosophy: Cambridge Massachusetts 1860–1930* (1977).
70 Id., at xix.
71 Id.

'philosophical bulwark that Harvard philosophers provided against Emerson heresies'.[72] The settling response to this challenge came from 'a group of brilliant young men with legal and scientific training'.[73]

> A group of younger men who have studied at Harvard but were unaffiliated with its philosophic faculty and uncommitted to its doctrines were devising ways to meet the theological crisis without giving up essential religious claims. A mechanistic interpretation of Darwin might destroy religion and lead to a fatalistic atheism. Some thinkers feared that it might eventuate in passivity, suicide, or a mindless absorption with trivia as people tried to preserve their sanity in a meaningless universe. But individuals might understand evolution differently. As the Unitarian credo became moribund, Bowen's students and associates – Chauncey Wright, Charles Pierce, and William James among them – worked out the principle of pragmatism in an informal society called the metaphysical club and, individually, different pragmatic philosophies. The principle allowed for changes in beliefs over time, defining a belief as a habit of action and not as some abstruse mental entity. By arguing a la Darwin, that survival was somehow the test of intellectual as well as biological fitness, these men were able to reconcile the new science to a new religion.[74]

'The metaphysical club' was formed in the years 1871–72 in Cambridge and 'its core consisted of six men: William James, Oliver Wendell Holmes Jr, Charles Pierce, Chauncey Wright, Nicholas St. John Green, and Joseph Bangs Warner'.[75] Holmes taught Jurisprudence at Harvard Law School at that time. 'The men were Harvard educated exclusively.'[76] 'As James has written to Holmes, the society was "to be composed of none but the very topmost cream of Boston manhood".'[77]

These men discussed different ideas in their meetings, including 'the practical significance of every proposition',[78] but what is quite clear today is

---

72 Id.
73 Id., at 49.
74 Id., at xix.
75 Id., at 47.
76 Id., at 48. Also see 47: 'William James was abroad in 1867 and 1868. From Berlin, in January 1868, he wrote to his friend Oliver Wendell Holmes, Jr: 'When I get home, let's establish a philosophical society to have regular meetings and discuss none but the very tallest and broadest questions ... It will give each one a chance to air his own opinion in a grammatical form, and to sneer and chuckle when he goes home at what damned fools all the other members are – and may grow into something very important after a sufficient number of years.'
77 Id., at 48.
78 Id., at 49.

The Maturing of the Pragmatic Idea in Law and Society   19

that the depiction of them as the origin also had some 'metaphysical' impulse. Kuklick says, 'The club had no secretary and no record of debate. As Pierce later wrote, the proceeding had all been in winged words.'[79] Menand shows that none of the several accounts of Pierce in his papers match one another. He said that Pierce himself was in Washington most of the time. 'Holmes, by all accounts, including his own later recollection, was immersed in his first major scholarly project, a revision of Kent's *Commentaries on American Law*, which was published in 1873, and gave little time to anything else.' Chauncey Wright went to Europe in July and did not return until November.[80] He concludes, 'It is hard to know just how self-conscious and cohesive a group the metaphysical club Pierce described really was for anyone but, in retrospect, Pierce himself.'[81]

Whether or not there was this founding moment, there is definitely an interest in articulating it at Harvard,[82] and in the beginning of the century Pragmatism was a theme in intellectual life. West suggests, in this context, that 'the major role of William James *as a figure in the American pragmatist tradition* is that of Emersonian individualist, moralist, meliorist, popularizer, and intellectual hero to crucial factions of the refined and reformist middle class'.[83] The infiltration of pragmatism into more 'low culture'[84] has resulted also in some 'formalizations' of previous Emersonian ideas in a more modern scientific framework. 'James' favorite rhetorical strategy in support of his fervent individualism and comforting "middle-of-the-roadism" is the juxtapositions of exorbitant polar positions.' After putting forward a long list of oppositions (tender minded-tough minded, rationalistic-empiricist, idealistic-materialistic), he 'attempts primarily to dissolve the distinctions by combining the best of each, rejecting the rest, and affirming the protean pluralism that occupies middle space'.[85]

79　Id.
80　Pragmatism, *supra* note 56, at xvii.
81　Id., at xviii.
82　See also West, *supra* note 2, at 42: 'The first articulation of American Pragmatism – members of the Metaphysical Club in Cambridge, Massachusetts – were learned professionals principally interested in demystifying science and, a few, in modernizing religion.'
83　West, *supra* note 2, at 55.
84　'James took it upon himself to translate and transform his conversations with these traditions (the European philosophical traditions, M.A.) into a language intelligible to educated middle-class Americans. Hence, his lectures or essays sound not like books but rather like juicy intellectual gossip that beckons the audience and readers to eavesdrop on what is being said. James want us to taste the milk in the coconut and be nourished.' Id., at 56.
85　Id., at 57.

> The role of pragmatism is that of 'a happy harmonizer' and a mediator and reconciler ... that 'unstiffens' our theories. She has in fact no prejudices whatever, no obstructive dogmas, no rigid canons of what shall count as proof. She is completely genial. She will entertain any hypothesis, she will consider any evidence.[86]

We will find this rhetoric later in Dworkin's writing and in the negotiation people's chart,[87] where it is presented as common-sense wisdom (in negotiation), or as the true spirit of liberalism (in Dworkin). The idea is that of going beyond oppositions, of finding a mediating point. Pragmatism is a woman. (Later in Carol Gilligan's writing, I find the woman she depicts is actually the pragmatist, or a version of her.) She is 'a happy harmonizer'; she is America. 'Of course, these assumptions chime well with the Emersonian theodicy of optimism, moralism and voluntarism.'[88]

But it was John Dewey who brought pragmatism to its 'official' peak, by adding the 'public' dimension to the more psychological stories of James and Pierce.[89]

Dewey did not have an 'exclusive Harvard education'.[90] Born in Vermont

---

86 Id. See also William James, 'What Pragmatism Means', in *Pragmatism, supra* note 56, at 110.

87 See the chapter 'In Search of The Dispute: On Lawyers and Legal Philawsophers at Harvard Law School (Or, Some Private Hope and Public Irony)', PART 4.2.

88 Id.

89 'For his part, Dewey was even more committed than Pierce or James to deploying an adaptationist theory of meaning to arrive at redescriptions of experience. At the same time, Dewey did not believe that an adaptationist theory of mind allows each of us to count as true whatever helps us get up in the morning. Rather, what Dewey called the influence of Darwinism on philosophy should lead us to favor a range of redescriptions of experience in which individual life is characterized as social, and in which social life is described in interactive and cooperative terms that foster ongoing projects of social reconstruction through communal experimental inquiry and democratic decision making': in David Depew, *Introduction to Pragmatism: From Progressivism to Postmodernism, supra* note, 'Introduction' to 62, 6.

Regarding Pierce, see also West, *supra* note 2, 43: 'There are three fundamental claims in Pierce's pragmatism, first, that the most reasonable way of arriving at warranted and valid beliefs is by means of scientific method; second, that scientific method is a self-correcting social and communal process promoted by smoothly functioning habits, i.e., beliefs, upset by uncertain expectations, i.e., doubts, and whose sole end is "the settlement of opinion", and third, that this scientific quest is inextractibly linked, though in no way reducible, to the ultimate good of furthering "the development of concrete reasonableness", i.e., evolutionary love.'

90 Unlike the aristocracy that characterized the 'metaphysical club' members, Dewey was a WASP intellectual 'of humble social origins'. See David A. Hollinger, 'The "Tough-

and educated there, as well as at Johns Hopkins and Columbia, he began by embracing German idealism and in trying to 'demonstrate the compatibility of theology and evolution, religion and science'.[91] Referring to a paper Dewey wrote in 1887, Kuklick writes:

> Dewey implied that the early 1880s had revolutionized theology. The inherence of the psychical in the physical, spirit in nature, he wrote, would define future inquiry. Mind represented itself in the entire body in the fundamental mode of nervous adjusting or teleological activity. Darwinism established this principle in the universe. 'The structure of nature itself is such that it gives rise to ... purposive action.' The physical world for Dewey *wanted* to be spiritual. Intelligence was latent in matter. Evolution told how this happened. Physical causes had to be read as part of rational design. Through evolution the natural world was being transformed into the moral: 'This whole structure of the physical is only the garment with which the ethical has clothed itself ... The germ shall finally flower in the splendor of the moral life... The garment shall finally manifest the living from within ....' In evolution, Dewey said, God embodied himself in matter, just as the body incarnated the individual soul. All this, he concluded, was Saint Paul's message.[92]

What is interesting to see is that, in 1887, the religious pathos and foundation are very explicit, and the justification for theorizing is the need to reconcile the discourses of science and theology. At this time, pragmatism seems almost to derive from religion, but later it becomes the new religion, the foundation itself, the conditioning of a new kind of consciousness where religious excuses are not needed. From then on, anything not scientifically constructed, logical, argumentative, or structured will be considered outside the discourse, sometimes mystical and literary, later interpretive. Still, the hierarchy will dissolve and transform again afterward, in another rupture, through another version of pragmatism, in the post-post war era, though pragmatic ('deep moral') convictions and sentiments continue guiding until today. But we are still at the nineteenth century, where American modernity is taking off. 'In 1894, just as he was prying himself loose from the Social Gospel,

---

Minded" Justice Holmes, Jewish Intellectuals, and the Making of an American Icon', in *The Legacy of Oliver Wendell Holmes, Jr.* (Robert Gordon, ed., 1992). See also West, *supra* note 2, 76: 'As an organic intellectual of the urbanized, professional, and reformist elements of the middle class, Dewey had far more immediate impact on society than Emerson, Pierce, or James.'

91 Bruce Kuklick, *Churchmen and Philosophers: From Jonathan Edwards to John Dewey* (1985), 232.
92 Id., at 232.

Christianity and idealist philosophy ... Dewey left the University of Michigan to serve as chairman of the Philosophy Department of the new University of Chicago.'

For the Chicago philosophers, Hegellian naturalism and democratic communitaranism could triumph only if the primacy of practice over theory as the site at which intelligence is paradigmatically exercised could be philosophically defended. By 1903, Dewey and his students had turned out an impressive piece of cooperative philosophical work aimed at demonstrating precisely this. The idea of *Studies in Logical Theory* was to portray logic as a tool of discovery, mediating between problematic situation and problem solving response. The Chicago philosophers now asserted that a practical logic of discovery, in which matter and form are fused and refused through problem-solving innovation, would better account for the quality of necessity that had traditionally and rightly been ascribed to logic than any theory in which contingency enters through a theoretical gap between empirical content and logical framework.[93]

The idea that 'matter and form are fused and refused through problem solving innovation' might at first sight appear purely philosophical[94] but, as I will try to show, this concrete historical claim has become so 'commonsensical', so deep in the American culture, that we find it repeatedly on many cultural levels.[95] When Henry Hart tells the first-year students in 1948 that the lawyer is essentially a problem solver,[96] Roger Fisher tells 'the

---

[93] David Depew, 'Introduction', in *Pragmatism: From Progressivism to Postmodernism*, supra note 62, at 9.

[94] See also James T. Kloppenberg, 'Pragmatism: An Old Name for Some New Ways of Thinking?', in *The Revival of Pragmatism, supra* note 6, at 84: 'At the core of James' and Dewey's pragmatism was experience conceived, not as introspection, but as the intersection of the conscious self with the world. They conceived of knowing subjects as embodiments of reason, emotion, and values and they emphasized the inadequacy of philosophers' attempts to freeze, split apart, and compartmentalize the dynamic continuities and multiple dimensions of life as we live it ... They conceived of experience as intrinsically and irreducibly meaningful, and they insisted that its meanings were not predetermined or deducible from any all-encompassing pattern.'

[95] See, for example, Steven D. Smith, *The Pursuit of Pragmatism*, Yale L.J. 409 (1990). The author posits two common understandings of legal pragmatism: One as a forward-looking instrumentalism, and two as a hostility to abstract theory. The underlying theme of the article is itself pragmatic, what notion of pragmatism, if at all, will help 'to solve our problems'.

[96] Henry Hart, Harvard Special Collection, Box 22–9: Speech to first-year class of 1948, 'How to go about the job of studying law': 'My notion of a lawyer can be summed up in one word. To my mind he is essentially a problem-solver. A good lawyer, it follows, is one who is good at solving problems. A poorer lawyer is one who is not so good.'

world' in 1982 to engage in problem solving,[97] and in 1999, Robert Mnookin calls upon the lawyer to become a 'problem solver', they all rely on the same cultural source. 'By focusing on humans as social animals, Darwinian adaptationism, as Dewey understood it, provided a way of articulating a new Aristotelian naturalism in which, in an open, unfinished Piercean world, humans appear as problem-solving animals, and their linguistically mediated social environment seems as natural to them as water to fish.'[98]

The problem-solving innovation defuses matter and form; it is natural and given to the mind once you assume evolution as your founding theory. It is common sense. It is a variant on the Emersonian idea of 'experience' discussed above, which had its own construction of 'the world' against the soul.[99] In Dewey's *Experience and Nature*, this prevalence is emphasized again and again:

> The title of this volume, Experience and Nature, is intended to signify that the philosophy here presented may be termed either empirical naturalism or naturalistic empiricism, or, taking 'experience' in its usual signification, naturalistic humanism.[100]

> The objects of reflection in philosophy, being reached by methods that seem to those who employ them rationally mandatory are taken to be 'real' in and of themselves – and supremely real. Then it becomes an insoluble problem why the things of gross, primary experience should be what they are or indeed why they should be at all. The refined objects of reflection in the natural sciences, however, never end by rendering the subject matter from which they are derived a problem; rather, when used to describe a path by which some goal in primary experience is designated or denoted, they solve perplexities to which that crude material gives rise but which it cannot resolve of itself. They become means of control, of enlarged use and enjoyment of ordinary things.[101]

> When objects are isolated from the experience through which they are reached and in which they function, experience itself becomes reduced to the mere process of experiencing, and experiencing is therefore treated as if it were also complete in itself. We get the absurdity of experiencing which experiences only itself, states and processes of consciousness, instead of the things of nature.

---

97 See the discussion in the chapter 'In Search of the Dispute: On Lawyers and Legal Philawsophers at Harvard Law School (Or, Some Private Hope and Public Irony)'.
98 David Depew, 'Introduction', in *Pragmatism: From Progressivism to Postmodernism*, supra note 62, at 7.
99 See *supra* text to 19n-30n.
100 John Dewey, *Experience and Nature (The Paul Carus lectures 852–1919)* 1929 (2nd edn), 1.
101 Id., at 9.

> Since the seventeenth century this conception of experience as the equivalence of subjective private consciousness set over against nature, which consists wholly of physical objects, has wrought havoc in philosophy.[102]

There is havoc in philosophy, and in 1929 Dewey begins to reconstruct it in his book *Reconstruction in Philosophy*. His reference to experience, reduced 'to the mere process of experiencing', undoubtedly alludes to the 'cogito ergo sum' of Descartes. If thinking becomes an element of 'natural experience' that is not questioned (which does not have a metaphysic, an historical context, a discursive dimension), there are problems to solve (which can be theoretical) and goals to achieve (which can be redefined after they are reached), but there is no sense in reflecting on the reflection itself. We have to indulge ourselves in ideas through reflection but not question the 'naturality' of this very process.

Here arises a problem that, I think, haunts Dewey in his problem-solving 'preaching' – the problem of his own text. What problem does it try to answer, and how do we accept it and yet remain loyal to the nonessential pathos? If ideas are to serve us in an intense intellectual inquiry, what does the idea of 'inquiry' itself serve? How do we preserve it in an intellectual world that will question later the prevalence of science itself? This problematic will be the background to the 1960s rapture.

> Philosophy has abrogated to itself the office of demonstrating the existence of a transcendent, absolute or inner reality and of revealing to man the nature and feature of this ultimate and higher reality.[103]

But Dewey seems to fall to an equivalent arrogance when he argues for 'the scene of human clash of social purpose and aspirations' within 'a case of science'[104] as the ultimate foundation of his reconstructed philosophy.

> The organism acts in accordance with its own structure, simple or complex, upon its surroundings. As a consequence the changes produced in the environment react upon the organism and its activities. The living creature undergoes, suffers, the consequences of its own behavior. This close connection between doing and suffering or undergoing forms what we call experience.[105]

---

102 Id., at 13.
103 John Dewey, *Reconstruction in Philosophy* (1920), 23.
104 See Id., p. xviii, where he attacks the dichotomy between 'a case of science' and 'a case of philosophy'.
105 Id., at 86.

What sounds obsolete to us today, and even frightening in its inhuman scientific reduction, was central to Dewey's thought and to his time, operating in the background and even on the surface of the texts of that era's scholarship.

The intellectual impulse to exhaust ourselves with reason is ascribed to Descartes and other European philosophers, and the occupation with metaphysical questions is described as obsolete and compatible with previous conditions of life. 'Newfound wealth, the gold from the Americas and new articles of consumption and enjoyment, tended to wean men from preoccupation with the metaphysical and theological, and to turn their mind with newly awakened interest to the joys of nature and this life.'[106] This is a story of progress, and within it, philosophy has brought itself to its end.

> My growing feeling about Dewey's work, as I went through what seemed countless of his books, that Dewey was remembering something philosophy should be, but that the world he was responding to and responding from missed the worlds I seemed mostly to live in, missing the heights of modernism in the arts, the depth of psychoanalytic discovery, the ravages of the century politics, the wild intelligence of American popular culture. Above all, missing the question, and the irony of philosophy's questioning: whether philosophy, however reconstructed, was any longer possible, and necessary, in this world. Positivism's answer, the reigning answer in the professional philosophy of the America in which I was beginning to read philosophy, shared pragmatism's lack of irony in raising the question of philosophy – in the idea that philosophy is to be brought to an end by philosophy, which in a sense is all that can preserve philosophy.[107]

Cavell says that it was pragmatism's 'lack of irony' in attacking philosophy that he opposes. It is a common charge to blame Americans for having no sense of irony, but it seems irony is not lacking in the above discourse. ('Then it becomes an insoluble problem why the things of gross, primary experience should be what they are or indeed why they should be at all.') If irony is a discursive, metonymic operation of criticizing by putting a claim *near* another, without claiming to 'contradict' it directly, it is always also metaphoric in offering another meaning, that of the one who stands aside, but still within the same discourse. Is Cavell standing aside today in offering the literary, the opera, the art, and the music, or is he a part of reaffirming the cultural prevalence of the core, which is the scientific and committed 'rational' endeavor? It seems his 'non-ironic' embrace of the ordinary locates him as

---

106 Id., at 40–41.
107 Cavell, *Conditions Handsome and Unhandsome, supra* note 48, at 14.

offering a counter-ideology (that of the literary, the humanist intellectual, the art expert), but accepting the same 'American' mythologies as his opponents.

> Nothing could be more certain to Othello that Desdemona exists; is flesh and blood; is separate from him; other. This is precisely the possibility that tortures him. The content of his torture is the premonition of the existence of another, hence his own, his own as dependent, as partial. According to me further, his professions of skepticism over her faithfulness are a cover story for a deeper conviction; a terrible doubt covering a yet more terrible certainty, an unusual certainty. But then this what I have throughout kept arriving at as the cause of skepticism – the attempt to convert the human condition, the condition of humanity, into an intellectual difficulty, a riddle.[108]

This is a basic theme in Cavell. The Western philosophical effort to exhaust criteria and to be reasonable and 'impartial' leads to skepticism. It begins with Descartes, and in his effort to defeat the possibility of his isolation by introducing God.[109] It keeps on with the development of science,[110] with analytical philosophy and positivism that try to encompass the conditions of language. The conditions of humanity cannot be exhausted, and trying to do so may lead in movies to near-madness of the 'unknown woman',[111] or her sacrifice in the opera while she tries to raise her voice.[112] There is a need to come back to the ordinary and not stay entrenched in intellectual riddles.[113]

---

108 Stanley Cavell, *Disowning Knowledge* (1987), 138.
109 Id., at 126.
110 'For Dewey, representing the international view, knowledge is given in science and in the pre-scientific practices of the everyday, that is, the learning of problem solving. For Emerson, the success of science is as much a problem for thought as, say, the problem of religion is ... for Dewey the relation between science and technology is unproblematic, even definitive, whereas for Emerson the power manifested in technology and its attendant concepts of intelligence and power and change and improvement are in contest with the work, and the concept of the work, of realizing the world each human is empowered to think. For an Emersonian, the Deweyan is apt to seem an enlightened child, toying with the means of destruction, stinting the means of instruction, of provoking the self to work. For Dewey the texture of the philosophical text barely exists, except as superstition and resistance to social change ...': Cavell, *Conditions Handsome and Unhandsome, supra* note 107, at 16.
111 Cavell, *Contesting Tears, supra* note 47.
112 See Cavell, 'Opera and the Lease of Voice', in *A Pitch of Philosophy, supra* note 46, and also Catherine Clement, *Opera: Or the Undoing of Women* (Betsy Wing, trans., 1988), 1979.
113 I see it in Cavell as actually a *psychoanalytic* return to the ordinary – an ordinary which is no more simple or common, and which has the 'liberating function', and the human element only through its 'non-simple' dimension.

The problem with Othello, according to Cavell in the paragraph above, is that he tried to operate logic to control his jealousy.[114] He says that the terrible certainty Othello has is that Desdemona exists, 'is flesh and blood, separate from him'. The accusations of unfaithfulness are a cover story for the fact that 'he cannot forgive Desdemona for existing, for being separate from him, outside, beyond command, commanding, her captain's captain'.[115] But here is again the 'Cavellian' romantic embrace of the ordinary – of the mere existence in 'the world'. But is it not precisely the point where the ironic distance should be kept? Where an intellectual riddle should remain? It is not the obsession with logical criteria that is so tragic here. It is exactly the idea of 'pure existence'. Desdemona does not 'exist', as 'separate', in 'reality', and is 'flesh and blood'. Othello turns her into a fetish by letting his jealousy project her as such. Desdemona is in his fantasy, in his inner world. It does not help her not to be actually murdered, non-ironically. Thus, it can be said that Dewey's 'lack of irony' regarding philosophy and his call to overcome the metaphysical – skeptic dichotomy through a scientific inquiry are transformed in Cavell to such a call to do so through an aesthetic experience of art and literature.

But this is also a matter for further reflection. When Cavell says that 'in philosophy it is the sound which makes all the difference',[116] while comparing Dewey to Wittgenstein, he might mean that Dewey's cover story was too good, too economical, too wide to swallow other sentiments in philosophizing, in culture in general, sentiments like the literary one.[117] The combination of science, evasion of the past, a democratic idea of participation, embrace of the common and the natural, the huge place for reflection and imagination, all these elements under one philosophical roof of pragmatism have produced a deep cultural influence and resulted in following generations that do not even

---

114 'The torture of logic in his mind we might represent as follows: Either I shed her blood and scarred her or I did not. If I did not then she was not a virgin and this is a stain upon me. If I did then she is no longer a virgin and this is a stain upon me. Either way I am contaminated': Id., at 135.
115 Id., at 136.
116 Stanley Cavell, *Must We Mean What We Say?* (1969), 36.
117 See also Stanley Cavell, 'What's the Use of Calling Emerson a Pragmatist?', in *The Revival of Pragmatism*, supra note 6, at 72: 'To attest my good faith in this struggle over terms such as pragmatism, transcendentalism, and ordinary language philosophy, I acknowledge that if Emerson is the founder of the difference in American thinking, then later American thinkers such as Dewey and James are going to be indebted to Emerson. What I deny is that their thinking, so far as it is recognizable as something distinctly called pragmatism, captures or clarifies or retains all that is rational or moral in the Emersonian event.'

have the urge to ask the old questions. It is the feeling that Dewey's philosophy has 'solved' the problem, but now no place is left to breathe. In Cavell's term, a more open-ended thematic is needed to recover pragmatism, and Dewey, as Othello, through challenging the intellectual occupation with metaphysics, has exhausted the criteria too. There is no modesty in his theorizing.

> Principles and alleged truths are judged more and more by criteria of their origin in experience and their consequences of weal and woe in experience, and less by criteria of sublime origin from beyond everyday experience and independent of fruits in experience. It is no longer enough for a principle to be elevated, noble, universal and hallowed by time. It must present its birth certificate, it must show under just what conditions of human experience it was generated, and it must justify itself by its works, present and potential.[118]

And in a more current secondary presentation, by Hollinger:

> This faith is consistent with the pragmatic approach to truth as a form of utility, but is not entailed by it. Ideas, in this view, are instruments that not only can become true by doing their job in inquiry, but can also transform the environment to which they are applied. This effect takes place most obviously in the improvement of medical and industrial techniques, but the effect was held by Dewey and his followers to operate throughout experience even at the cognitive level, in the knowing relation itself. For Dewey, the entire knowing process is a manipulative one in which inquiries seek to rearrange, to their satisfaction whatever components of a given situation stimulated inquiry.[119]

The new epistemology, offered by Dewey, by recalling Emerson, and also by re-reading him (or misreading, as West suggests,[120] if such a thing exists), is the 'evasion of epistemology-centered philosophy', by positing philosophy as 'a mode of cultural critical actions that focuses on the ways and means by which human beings have, do, and can overcome obstacles, dispose of predicaments, and settle problematic situations'.[121]

---

118 Dewey, *Reconstructions in Philosophy*, supra note 103, at 48.
119 Hollinger, *The Problem of Pragmatism*, supra note 62, at 24.
120 West, *supra* note 2, at 76: 'For Dewey, Emerson signifies what Dewey himself actually tried to do. Dewey views Emerson as the founder and the inventor of the American religion – of the Emersonian evasion, theodicy, and refusal – yet he delineates his own project as the authentic content and substance of it. In this way, Dewey implicitly rejects Henry James, Sr.'s, view of Emerson as John the Baptist, with an American messiah yet to come. Instead, Dewey plays Joshua to Emerson's Moses, with Pierce a ground-breaking yet forgotten Aaron and James a brilliant and iconoclastic Eleazar.'
121 Id., at 86.

Dewey enables us to view clashing conceptions of philosophy as struggles over cultural ways of life, as attempts to define the role and function of intellectual authorities in culture and society. For Dewey, to take modern historical consciousness seriously in philosophy is first and foremost to engage in meta-philosophical reflection, to reform and reconstruct philosophy as a mode of intellectual activity. To reform and reconstruct philosophy is both to demystify and to defend the most reliable mode of inquiry in modern culture, namely, critical intelligence best manifest in the community of scientists. And to demystify and defend critical intelligence is to render it more and more serviceable for the enhancement of human individuality, that is, the promotion of human beings who better control their conditions and thereby more fully create themselves (i.e., advance creative democracy).[122]

This paragraph of West's has a powerful rhythm: After repeating the name Dewey four times in the introductory sentences,[123] he keeps repeating it, and then moves on in waves: 'to take modern historical consciousness seriously' is 'to reform and reconstruct philosophy'; to 'reform and reconstruct philosophy' is 'to demystify and to defend the most reliable mode of inquiry in modern culture'; 'to demystify and defend critical intelligence is to render it more and more serviceable for the enhancement of human individuality'. It is an inscription of individuality which has become so much like common sense for the modern mind that it might be hard today even to grasp how much it is mythological (the control of our conditions, the full creation of ourselves). There is no need to go afar or outside in order to see the limits of this claim. As in the 'problem-solving' discussion, the idea of a theory which 'solves the problem', a spirit that comes back to itself, individuality that is fully controlled, in an advanced creative democracy, contradict the basic assumptions of the pragmatic epistemology itself. It is not only that 'classical pragmatism' is more of a patchwork *bricolage* than Dewey makes it appear when he told a typically teleological Aristotelian Hegellian story about it in *The Development of American Pragmatism*,[124] as David Depew suggests. Claud Levi-Strauss has posited the notion of *bricolage* and examining it here can help to articulate the roots of pragmatic thinking:

> There still exists among ourselves an activity which on the technical plane give us quite a good understanding of what a science we prefer to call 'prior' rather than 'primitive', could have been on the plane on speculation. This what is

---

122 Id., at 71–2.
123 Id., at 71.
124 David Depew, *Pragmatism: From Progressivism to Postmodernism*, *supra* note 59, at 13.

commonly called 'bricolage' in French. In its old sense the verb 'bricoleur' applied to ball games and billiards, to hunting, shooting and riding. It was, however, always used with reference to some extraneous movement: a ball rebounding, a dog straying or a horse swerving from its direct course to avoid an obstacle. And in our own time the 'bricoleur' is still someone who works with his hands and uses devious means to those of a craftsman. *The characteristic feature of mythical thought is that it expresses itself by means of a heterogeneous repertoire which, even if extensive, is nevertheless limited. It has to use this repertoire, however, whatever the task in hand because it hand because he has nothing else at its disposal. Mythical thought is therefore a kind of intellectual 'bricolage' – which explains the relation which can be perceived between the two*[125] (The emphasis is mine – M.A.).

In contrast to the 'bricoleur', Strauss depicts the engineer or the physicist – the scientist, who submit their tasks to 'the availability of raw materials and tools conceived procured for the purpose of the project'.[126] In these terms, if pragmatism is a bricolage, it is based more upon its mythical Emersonian sources of origin and religious perceptions on the one hand and the Darwinian science and empiricist tradition on the other, than on a scientific method of inquiry[127] for which it calls. (What is the inquiry of the inquiry? Can any discourse depict a source without questioning it, while at the same time being conditioned on it?) But what is more crucial if we accept this claim (which is why acknowledging that pragmatism is a bricolage is not enough) is that this work is perceived as the engineering of a culture, and for years it was, and still is, 'used' for such a purpose. Even when the source is denied, whether it is the 'pre-modern' religious myths or the Darwinian scientific 'story', and after it is more or less intellectually dead (like today), the pragmatic (or is it the American?) keeps haunting, guiding; it is revived and announced, it turns into common sense, becomes implicit, hidden, and may wear an interpretive mode. It is the enormously appealing inscription of modern subjectivity that is conquering the world. Whether it is the spirit of capitalism or of the American, it has an economical and political role in each phase of each manifestation.

---

[125] Claude Levi-Strauss, *The Savage Mind* (George Weidenfeld, trans., 1966) 1962, 16–17.
[126] Id., at 17.
[127] 'We have already distinguished the scientist and the "bricoleur" by the inverse functions which they assign to events and structures as ends and means, the scientist creating events (changing the world) by means of structures and the "bricoleur" creating structures by means of events': Id., at 22.

Dewey's philosophy is seen as deeply embedded in a philosophical culture which is firmly precommitted to an array of core 'Lockeian' political values, an atomistic individualism of self-interested, if conformist, property owners, with little sense of the individual's social or institutional surroundings ... Once we recognize pragmatism's complacent acquiescence in this ethos, according to this interpretation, we can explain its concern with the application of 'scientific method' to social and political problems: assured of an unquestionable foundation of 'submerged convictions' about the ends towards which techniques are to be directed, Dewey and his followers are solely preoccupied with the means by which these ends might be achieved. This interpretation has been supported by the image of Dewey as the quintessential intellectual proponent of the culture and ideology of the United States. His pragmatism has been taken to be both expressive of, and a crucial influence on, twentieth-century American liberalism, and he has repeatedly been hailed as a 'national philosopher', 'the guide, the mentor and the conscience of the American people'.[128]

What made Dewey's ideas so enchanting in one stage, what made them disappear for a while after the 1950s, and how and why did they return? Is it a matter of death, of resurrection, of incorporation, of suppression? The answers this chapter and book will provide will be limited in scope by focusing on an adjacent professional discourse that has emerged and developed during the same time. A basic thread in my argument will trace the specific way in which the pragmatic operates through the economical and political conditions while trying to 'solve' different perceived 'problems' in different times and places. My focus on the legal discourse of Oliver Wendell Holmes Jr aims to capture through a contemporary lens the way in which an adjacent pragmatism, the one of law, develops and maintains a relationship with its original counterpart. It is only through this professional supplementary discourse that I will try to begin to address the questions above of the relation of a certain pragmatism to the political and economical conditions of its time. Through the lenses of this inquiry of the professional discourse, the characteristics of the original philosophical one will be examined. The contextualization of the pragmatic grand story above through its reflection in law in various times and places, combined with the articulation of the shift of the philosophical pathos into a professional theoretical discourse, will provide a complementary perspective to trace the pragmatic idea in its maturing process.

---

128 Matthew Festenstein, *Pragmatism and Political Theory: From Dewey to Rorty* (1997), 18.

1.3 Progressive History

In his book *The Transformation of American Law 1870–1960: The Crisis of Legal Orthodoxy*, Morton Horwitz tries to account for the role of Legal Realists within the American legal culture. Horwitz, a Harvard professor, portrays in his writing the canon of American Legal History:

> From the beginning of the twentieth century, Classical Legal Thought found itself confronted by an increasingly powerful critique of its basic premises. In one legal field after another, Progressive thinkers challenged both the political and moral assumptions of the old order and the structures of legal doctrine and legal reasoning that were designed to represent both assumptions as neutral, natural, and necessary.[129]

It is wrong, in Horwitz's view, to perceive Realism either as 'a coherent intellectual movement' or 'a consistent or systematic jurisprudence'.[130] It is more 'an intellectual mood than a clear body of tenets, more a set of sometimes contradictory tendencies than a rigorous set of methodologies or propositions about legal theory'.[131]

What is the 'intellectual mood' of the Realists? What makes their contradictory and dispersed claims so cohesive? What makes their appearance in legal history so dramatic and significant? Horwitz's answer is that 'above all, Realism continues the Progressive attack on the late nineteenth-century Classical Legal thought's attempt to distinguish sharply between law and politics, and to portray law as neutral, natural, and apolitical'.[132]

Horwitz writes his book in 1992, but the phenomenon he describes is narrated in different times by different people, and also have other significant historical dates to account for, other lines to delineate its context. One important point is what is considered the pre-emergence of the Realist movement: the work and influence of Oliver Wendell Holmes, the Realist's antecedent, who lived and wrote in the years 1841–1935, when the metaphysical club, mentioned above and pragmatism emerged in Cambridge, and an American philosophy began to take shape. Another period is the post-war era, where the kind of pragmatism announced by Holmes was transformed into collective consciousness, as manifested in the Legal Process course materials, which

---

[129] Morton J. Horwitz, *The Transformation of American Law 1870–1960: The Crisis of Legal Orthodoxy* (1992), 169.
[130] Id.
[131] Id.
[132] Id., at 170.

were delivered as an oral tradition without formally becoming a book until the mid-1990s. The 1990s themselves provide a context of their own to the reading of Horwitz and for the understanding of his reading of these different points in 'legal history' (which he produces).

What is the difference between Horwitz's account of the Realists and the post-war scholars' perspective of them? How is Holmes depicted differently at these different points in time, by other scholars as well? What is the relation to 'the political', and its diverse operations through time? What does it mean to be 'progressive' at each point in time? This section offers a few historical narratives of Holmes and the Realists that will expose the problematic that these questions put forward. The next discussion of two versions of pragmatism ('the pragmatism of law: the first two stages') will try to answer by offering a narration of its own. The remaining chapters of this book will deal with the same questions from different aspects and diverse points in time and place.

In 1947, in the influential book *Social Thought in America: The Revolt Against Formalism*, Morton White describes the Realists' phenomenon as part of an intellectual development which has reached its end.

> I have in mind the submersion of a certain style of thinking which dominated America for almost half a century – an intellectual pattern compounded of pragmatism, institutionalism, behaviorism, legal realism, economic determinism, the 'new history'.[133]

In 1947, a few years before pragmatism operates within law in the Legal Process Materials, and elsewhere as a kind of a 'collective consciousness',[134] White announces that the idea is dead:[135] 'It might be argued that these movements are not dead, but one cannot avoid feeling that they are past the peak of their influence.'[136] Holmes and Dewey are presented by him as sharing the same endeavor, which is 'a campaign to mop up the remnants of formal logic, classical economics and jurisprudence in America, and to emphasize that the life of science, economics, and law was not logic but experience in

---

133 Morton White, *Social Thought in America: The Revolt Against Formalism* (1947), 3.
134 See the discussion of the post-war scholarship and its endorsement of a 'common sense' pragmatism that was indeed theoretically dead at that time, in the chapter 'Settled Law and the Law-That-Is-Not-but-Ought-To-Be: Hart and Sacks and the Pragmatic Philosophy of Dispute Resolution (Or: Why Couldn't Henry Hart Speak?)'.
135 'Are we faced with a dead tradition – a chapter in American thought that is already behind us? Are we to perform an analysis or autopsy?': Id., 7. Referring to pragmatism in my writing, we always do both – analysis by autopsy and vice versa.
136 Id., at 3.

some streaming social sense'.[137] This is the revolt against formalism.

> The men we have studied share a number of intellectual traits. They all participated in an early revolt against formalism in social science, in a rejection of the patterns which dominated formed logic, classical political economy, formal jurisprudence, and barren political history ... It was not so much the logical coherence of their ideas that laid people to accept their works as though they were synoptic gospels; *it was rather the way in which they all seemed to contribute to the advent of a more rational society*[138] (my emphasis, M.A.).

There is a progress story of contribution to a more 'rational' society, and the more updated combination, according to White in 1947, is to take the 'rational' motive of the men he describes and combine it with a real progressive spirit. 'It made no difference that Holmes was a nineteenth-century liberal in his economics and that he made wisecracks about socialism and reformers,' says White, or that 'Weblen seemed to avoid political commitment.'[139] The important thing is that 'their followers overlooked such deviations'.

> The followers became pragmatists in epistemology; they tried to apply scientific method to moral and social problems; they sent their children to progressive schools; they defended social justice and civil liberties by citing Holmes' dissenting opinions; they voted socialist occasionally.[140]

In line with Horwitz's description above,[141] the followers are indeed the post-First World War generation, and the Legal Realists are part of their progressive offspring, dedicated participants in 'the revolt against formalism'. White depicts the 1880–1920 era as 'the golden age of liberalism in America, an age which closed intellectually just when its ideas became weapons again'.[142]

It seems interesting to examine what kind of death is at stake here. The children who went to progressive schools, the Holmesian inheritance and its authority and domination within the legal culture, the Realists' progressive attacks, the same book of White wherein he chooses Holmes' and Dewey's

---

137 Id., at 11–12.
138 Id., at 237.
139 Id.
140 Id., at 238–9.
141 See *supra* text to 129n.
142 Id.

way of a more 'natural law' perception[143] – all these phenomena indicate an enormous influence and 'work' of the 'revolt against formalism'. This revolt is actually the emergence of the pragmatic idea as the American philosophy, as a central and dominant theoretical account of the American spirit and culture. White's book is written right after the Second World War.

---

143 See id., 'Epilogue for 1957: Original Sin, Natural Law, and Politics', 247–80. White discusses the problematic of their theories and lines his reservations but still he takes their spirit to lead him (279). The equivalence between White's description of his bottom-line convictions and that of Dworkin in his 1999 article *Justice for Hedgehogs* is striking: 'It is hard to deny, of course, that we all have certain deep moral convictions, that we do firmly believe certain moral principles which we try to act on to the best of our ability. They make up, along with other beliefs, the foundation of our whole structure of belief ... They constitute our terminal beliefs. We want them to be consistent with each other and to fit in harmoniously and simply with other less confidently held beliefs; we want this structure to mesh with experience and feeling. We also, other things being equal, prefer to have other people adopt a similar system of beliefs ... What then, is the purpose of inventing a mysterious realm of essence *of which* our terminal beliefs are supposed to be true? Having gotten to the end of the line, why do we need to inch a bit further in the direction of darkness? Wouldn't it be saner to recognize that we all have our ultimate convictions at any moment, that they are not absolutely immune to change (though we can resolve, at our own peril, to make them permanently immune), that some people adopt the same beliefs as terminal and other don't? Who are the people we get along with? Very often the people with whom we have a great deal of agreement on these fundamental beliefs. Who are the people we quarrel with? Very often those with whom we don't share these beliefs. The point is that we and those whose lines, as it were, end up at the same terminal as ours shouldn't need the kind of mutual encouragement that comes from inventing a realm of essence beneath (or above) the terminal; and those who go in different directions are the last people in the world who are likely to use essence in the same way even if they agreed that there were such things' (276).

Except for the obvious antecedence to the negotiation people's slogan 'the bottom line is that there is no bottom line', which I discuss elsewhere in relation to Dworkin, there is an interesting politic of sameness in this pragmatic spirit, which continues to prevail in intellectual circles today. It is the idea that people who share my convictions and intellectual consciousness do not need to invent a realm beneath or above the terminal, and 'those who go in different directions' in any case are the last in the world who will use essence in the same way, 'if they agreed that there were such things'. This logic disenables genuine heterogeneous asymmetric interaction which does not assume assimilation. Among these Others who go 'in different directions' we can find today maybe the negotiation people; the lay-person who happen to have a dispute and do not know much on political theories; the indigent, who is the object of the reform of justice; and of course, the lay-lawyer, who is a skilled negotiator, but the 'essence talk' is not of his interest.

See also the discussion of Ronald Dworkin, *Justice for Hedgehogs* (Harvard colloquium draft 2/23/99), in the chapter 'In Search of The Dispute: On Lawyers and Legal Philawsophers at Harvard Law School (Or: Some Private Hope and Public Irony)', PART 4.3.

> Catastrophes are peculiarly suitable aids in tracing the history and development of ideas and intellectual currents. Wars and atomic bombs become devices for the dating of other events. They make so much seem absurd and so much seem old-fashioned that they serve as convenient reference points.[144]

White writes his post-war book while acknowledging the burden of the war, of atomic bombs, and of the need to be less dogmatic 'in an age that is crowded with dictators of principles who can read essences as easily as men used to read the stars'.[145] At the same time, his book is the naming of a new era, where 'the American' is becoming more dominant and influential, where there is a need to account for what *is* the American political philosophy. There is a need to narrate the American intellectual history and to identify a pattern of a 'revolt against formalism'. In an interesting way, the story is that of death, of ideas which have passed the peak of their influence. In the time when White writes his book, pragmatism is considered philosophically dead and the book seems to describe a historical phenomenon from a theoretical vacuum. At his era, pragmatism is no longer appealing in departments of philosophy, and has lost its enchanting stimulating force.[146]

> The decline of pragmatism belonged to a moment of deep pessimism in American thought, the moment of the Holocaust, of original sin. Of global cold war and nuclear stand-off. But the tragic realism and fashionable dark theology of the 1940s and 1950s proved as perishable as the progressive liberalism that preceded it. They were anchored in their cultural moment.[147]

This decline does not prevent pragmatism from functioning as a common-sense text in White's book, for example, and also in law. The emergence and dominance of the Legal Process school also can be explained by the pragmatic mode of the children who were brought up on these ideas, and upon the common-sense level that pragmatism has reached until then. In 1988, Garry Peller describes this phenomenon, as follows.

---

144 White, *supra* note 133., at 3.
145 Id., at 279.
146 See also Kloppenberg, *Pragmatism: An Old Name For Some New Ways Of Thinking?*, *supra* note 94, at 90: 'After Dewey died in 1952, his ideas faded quickly into the background. Even though one of the most prominent thinkers of the post-World War II period, Reinhold Niebuhr, shared many of Dewey's, and especially James', ideas, his critique of Dewey's optimism helped discredit pragmatism as too sunny minded for serious intellectuals.'
147 *The Revival of Pragmatism*, *supra* note 6, at 17.

The focus on institutional procedures rather than substantive results was a response to two overriding constraints that the fifties' legal scholars would have felt: first, the deep assumption of the relativity of knowledge and values within which it appeared that any substantive vision of justice would be controversial and therefore outside the boundaries of legitimate legal analysis; and second, the need to legitimate the realm of law generally, and the power of courts in particular, as something nobler than the 'raw' exercise of force. The first limitation flowed from the basic acceptance in American intellectual culture of the modernist critique of traditional nineteenth-century social thought in the first decade of the twentieth century; the second was rooted in the challenge to the legitimacy of relativism in modernist thought presented by the rise of fascism in Europe.[148]

The first constraint corresponds with the intellectual sequence White describes in his book as well.

> The split between legal realists and legal traditionalists was merely one facet of a broader rupture in American intellectual culture between two fundamentally opposed visions of the nature of knowledge, truth and society. Similar controversies had occurred in philosophy, economics, psychology, political theory, anthropology, and sociology since the twenties ... Within each field, there was one group of scholars identified as traditionalists who generally followed the nineteenth-century methodology, and who were confident about the ability of reason to provide objective and universal knowledge about the world. Posed against the traditionalists were modernists who criticized 'the metaphysics' of the traditionalists and offered instead a science 'relative to consequences rather than antecedence'.[149]

Peller describes the opposition between traditionalists and modernists as universal, and goes on to argue that 'within the American philosophy the modernist position was presented as pragmatism'.[150] The equivalent non-American modernism was manifested in his view by the creation of a new field of study, the sociology of knowledge. 'The very possibility of conducting a sociology of knowledge implied that epistemology could not be a foundational discipline for distinguishing true knowledge from falsity because what one took as knowledge was itself contingent and contextual, a derivative function of the social group in which one found oneself.'[151] This sociological

---

148　Gary Peller, 'Neutral Principles in the 1950s', 21 *Jour. L. Reform* (1988) 561, 572–3.
149　Id., at 573.
150　Id., at 575.
151　Id., at 574.

challenge characterizing modernism, where the Anglo-American foundationalist epistemology is assumed to be the source, seems like only one description among many of modernism. Still, what does look convincing to me is the idea that within American philosophy, the modern was the pragmatic.[152] In the American context, the revolt against formalism and the development of an anti-foundational mode of inquiry was a manifestation of the very mythological constitution of the American as having no foundation. It was perceived as non-problematic through the eyes of the children brought up on its texts. In the post-World War II 1950s, this modernism is incorporated into the legal sphere and is bounded by the substance-process dichotomy.

> The central jurisprudential project of the fifties thinkers was to incorporate legal-realist intellectual sophistication into the mainstream of American legal discourse while avoiding the most corrosive aspect of the realist message – that there was no analytically defensible way to distinguish law from politics. Their intellectual strategy had two basic dimensions: first, they acknowledged the realist point that there was no neutral, determinate basis for deciding the social issues arising in cases; second, the forties writers immediately domesticated this concession by limiting its application to the realm of 'substance'. At the level of 'process', however, neutral, apolitical, reasoned – that is, *legal* discourse was still possible (hence the name 'process theory').[153]

The second constraint that Peller describes is not the internal intellectual sequence in law and other academic disciplines. Like White, who refers to atomic bombs, it is external events that need consideration. The second limitation that the fifties legal scholars confronted 'was rooted in the challenge to the legitimacy of relativism in modernist thought presented by the rise of fascism in Europe'.[154]

> John Dewey's pragmatic compromise between the traditionalist conviction that moral authority depended on belief in the objectivity of truth and ethics, and the modernist assertion that such issues were necessarily contextual and relative became, by the fifties, the broad filter through which the first generation of post-War intellectuals in America would understand both their roles as intellectuals and the general legitimacy of American Society.[155]

---

152 See the discussion above, *supra* text to 53n–59n.
153 Id., at 567.
154 Id., at 573.
155 Id., at 580.

In contrast to the First World War, where the progressive post-war generation constituted opposition to the traditional regime,[156] the 1950s generation was occupied with regaining a unitary voice. The depiction of this era as 'the maturing of a collective thought'[157] is part of this phenomenon. Morton Horwitz acknowledge this difference too:

> American legal thought after World War II shared a strikingly similar agenda with many other areas of social thought. There was more similarity of approach between the different branches of thought during this period than at any time since the decade before the First World War. Then the issues generated by industrial capitalism had formed the central agenda for all categories of social thought. After World War II, much of the American intellectual outlook was shaped in reaction either to the trauma of Nazism or to continuing encounters with the savagery of Stalinism.[158]

The similar agenda in many areas of social thought, the need to sort out an American voice, the 'collective thought', are all part of a constitutive moment in American history. The equivalent reconciliation with the Civil War, and enforcement of equality standards toward blacks by the Warren court and the *Brown V. Board of Education* (1954) decision, are part of this phenomenon.[159] It is interesting to see how this 'self-definition' of a nation is done through the pragmatic ideal, and how it is part of the operation of an international war. At first it is the real war, where millions are murdered in unfathomable ways. Then there is the Cold War, where the 'happening' is much more on the level of war games, of ideologies and perceptions.

---

156 See the discussion of White, *supra* text to 38n–42n above.
157 Henry Hart, 'Foreword in The Time Chart of the Justices: The Supreme Court 1958 Term' 73 *Harv. L. Rev.* 84 (1959).
158 Horwitz, *supra* note 129, 250.
159 For this discussion see the chapter 'Settled Law and the Law-That-Is-Not-But-Ought-To-Be: Hart and Sacks and the Pragmatic Philosophy of Dispute Resolution (Or: Why Couldn't Henry Hart Speak?)'. Also Morton J. Horwitz, *The Warren Court and the Pursuit of Justice* (1998), 17: 'By the end of the nineteenth century, then, the Civil War Amendments had been interpreted to give almost no special constitutional protections to the former slaves, who were originally thought to be their principal beneficiaries. And despite the fifteenth amendment, which barred racial discrimination in voting, by the turn of the century virtually all southern blacks had been disenfranchised ... by the time *Plessy* was decided, the Supreme Court justices had themselves come to absorb and endorse the post-1877 political realities, which conceded to Southern whites a free hand in reestablishing and maintaining what would come to be romanticized as the "Southern way of life".'

The fifties was a decade in which the public culture was remarkably homogenous, free from the fundamental conflicts that had ripped through the country in earlier periods. America had just won a great war victory, and it dominated the world economically, politically, and culturally. The generation that governed America during the war (Hart's generation) and that fought the war (Sacks' generation) had tremendous confidence not only in the greatness of America, but also in the goodness of America – especially in contrast to 'godless communism', the new postwar totalitarian enemy. These intellectuals were open to the consensus politics and political theory that characterized America during the fifties.[160]

The challenge of fascism, according to this account, by Eskridge and Frickey, the new editors of the old Legal Process Materials,[161] was accompanied by 'the new postwar totalitarian enemy' – Communism. The unified voice of the American legal academy in the 1950s is part of setting its limits against 'the enemy' (the Communist, the Fascist) and through this transitional constitutive moment, legal realism, as well as Holmes' legacy, are perceived as dangerous, extreme, and not balanced enough. The diversity of the perceptions of Holmes through time is itself a lesson on the misleading idea of looking for one true history, as Robert Gordon shows:

The first significant appropriation was, famously, by the band of progressives including Felix Frankfurter, Harold Laski, Jerome Frank, and Max Lerner, who claimed Holmes on the basis of his dissents in free speech and social legislation cases as a 'liberal' reformer like themselves; and by rebellious legal theorists like Karl Llewellyn, who claimed him on the basis of his skepticism as a progenitor of the antiformalist movement known as Legal Realism ... In the 1940s, Roman Catholic natural lawyers and legal moralists like Lon Fuller found Holmes' skepticism toward ideas and absolutes and his apparent reduction of law to positive facts – to predictions of judicial decisions, synthesized from the dominant interests of society, ultimately grounded in brute force and brute biological instinct – dangerously akin to fascism. By the 1960s a growing crowd of critics, of whom the harshest and most penetrating was Yosal Rogat, had inspected Holmes' social views at close range and discovered in them the disdain for democracy, the contempt for liberal and socialist reformism and humanitarian sentiment, the Malthusian economics, the Darwinist sociology, the bleak yet

---

160 Henry M. Hart, Jr and Albert M. Sacks, *The Legal Process: Basic Problems in the Making and Application of Law* (William N. Eskridge, Jr and Philip P. Frickey, eds 1994), xii.
161 *The Legal Process Materials*, edited by Hart and Sacks, were ' ... the last great attempt at a grand synthesis of law in all its institutional manifestations' (Peller, *supra* note 148, 568). The book was not published until 1994, although the Materials were the text for a central perspective course at the Harvard Law School and other law schools for more than three decades.

The Maturing of the Pragmatic Idea in Law and Society 41

somehow enthusiastic acceptance of force as the basis of civilization, which have since become familiar elements of Holmes' historical persona ... By the end of the 1970s it appeared that the revision of Holmes' reputation had stripped him altogether of current usefulness ... Ironically, some of the same aspects from the revised Holmes that divided him from progressive liberals made him attractive to the conservative law and economic movement. There are probably few more devoted present-day Holmsians that Judge Richard A. Posner ...[162]

Holmes was perceived first as progressive, and later as anti-democratic. Jewish intellectuals and others in the post-World War I world depicted him as progressive,[163] while intellectuals of post World War II saw him as dangerous. Nowadays he is adopted by progressive legal thinkers, as well as by those more right-wing oriented, like Posner. They all perceive him as an oracle, and the multifarious lenses they hold, including the progressive one, I read as responses to the mythical script in Holmes' writing, that which constitutes the pragmatism of law.

The next section seeks to trace Holmesian legacy in its diversity, and through it to substitute the 'progressive history' with the discursive story, that of the pragmatism of law.

1.4 The Pragmatism of Law: The First Two Stages

Holmes, the Legal Realists' antecedent, was a Brahmin, born and bred in Boston, the son of a distinguished physician and poet. 'He was a "Yankee from Olympus",[164] a member of the "metaphysical club"',[165] as described above. In contemporary legal writing, there is the tendency to depict him as the oracle.[166]

---

162 See Robert W. Gordon, 'Introduction: Holmes' Shadow', in T*he Legacy of Oliver Wendell Holmes, Jr, supra* note 164, at 5–6.
163 See the discussion later, *supra* text at 166–9 regarding the article by David A. Hollinger, 'The "Tough-Minded" Justice Holmes, Jewish Intellectuals, and the Making of an American Icon', in *The Legacy of Oliver Wendell Holmes, Jr* (Robert Gordon, ed., 1992).
164 'Responsibility for effectively promoting Holmes as a cultural hero is often assigned above all to Frankfurter and Laski. These two largely "concocted", according to Grant Gilmore in 1977, "the picture of the tolerant aristocrat, the great liberal, the eloquent defender of our liberties, the Yankee from Olympus"': David A. Hollinger, 'The "Tough-Minded" Justice Holmes, Jewish Intellectuals, and the Making of an American Icon', in *The Legacy of Oliver Wendell Holmes, Jr* (Robert Gordon, ed., 1992), 223–4.
165 See *supra* text to 72n–81n.
166 See for example Horwitz, *supra* note 129, at 109–10: 'Almost everything that has been written about Holmes's legal theory has been written for the perspective of "winner's theory". Thus, much has been written about Holmes as the father of the later Legal Realist

Some indication of his relationship to 'Progressive' ideas can be found in David Hollinger's article 'The "Tough-Minded" Justice Holmes, Jewish Intellectuals, and the Making of an American Icon.'[167] Hollinger finds 'a perceived incongruity between the particular qualities attributed to him and the illiberal, if not reactionary, character of many of his actual social values and some of his judicial acts'.[168] In trying to discern how Holmes became such a cultural icon, Hollinger offers *Lochner* as one explanation.

The paradox is solved, we are sometimes told, by the fact that liberals were able to exploit the Lochner dissent, some free-speech opinions, a few of Holmes' other judicial acts, and certain themes in his theoretical writing. Since Holmes declined to defer to legislatures and since legislatures in the Progressive era tended to enact progressive legislation, Holmes looked liberal by disagreeing with court colleagues who wanted to invalidate that legislation on constitutional principles.[169]

Holmes was neither liberal nor progressive, according to Hollinger, but had an inclination to defer, which by default made him dissent in *Lochner*.[170]

---

movement, and his writing are studied for anticipations of pragmatism, anti-formalism, realism, functionalism, instrumentalism and modernism in law. Because he was noted for his brilliant, often revolutionary, but easily misunderstood aphorisms – "The life of the law has not been logic: it has been experience"; "general propositions do not decide concrete cases" – and because he was something of a cult figure for two generations of legal thinkers, there has been strong tendency to stereotype his contributions to American legal thought'.

And also Martin P. Golding, 'Jurisprudence and Legal Philosophy in Twentieth-Century America – Major Themes and Developments', 36 *J. Legal Educ.* (1986), 441: 'Jurisprudence and legal philosophy in twentieth century America may be said to have begun around 1880 with the publication of Oliver Wendell Holmes' book *The Common Law*. In this work, and in his widely read 1897 article "The Path of the Law", Holmes broaches, with varying degrees of emphasis, four themes that subsequently dominated American jurisprudence and legal philosophy: (1) the relation of law and morality, (2) the nature of legal rules and legal concepts, (3) the nature of judicial decision making and (4) the relation of law to the social sciences.'

167 Id., at 216.
168 Id., at 222: 'How could the author of "The Soldier's Faith" – a celebration of an unthinking and unquestioning obedience to orders and a vindication of violence for its role in "the breeding of a race for headship and command" – come to be a special darling of egalitarian, anti-imperialist intellectuals devoted to the life of the mind and to its political progressive uses?'
169 Id., at 223.
170 Compare also G. Edward White, *Justice Oliver Wendell Holmes: Law and The Inner Self* (1993), 327: '*Lochner* thus appeared to identify Holmes as a progressive judge, one sympathetic to legislative efforts to ameliorate the conditions of labor in industrializing America ... Holmes was suggesting in *Lochner* that the test for the constitutionality of

The Maturing of the Pragmatic Idea in Law and Society 43

In contrast to Dewey's pragmatism, which was supportive of the progressive project, the legal pragmatist Holmes had a more conservative approach. The following generation – the Legal Realists – have mistakenly depicted Holmes as their antecedent, while their agenda, as Horwitz and White suggested above, was progressive, and not merely theoretically pragmatic.

We can learn more on Holmes' figure from Thomas Grey in his article *Holmes and Legal Pragmatism*.[171] After describing Holmes as 'the great oracle of American legal thought',[172] he explains:

> In common with many American lawyers, I am fascinated by Holmes, a fascination compounded of repulsion and attraction. It is easy to list the man's repulsive aspect: his naïve attraction to pseudo-scientific eugenics, his fatalism, his indifference to human suffering, his egotism and vanity, his near-worship of force and obedience. But even when all that is taken into account, I am drawn on by Holmes' charms of person and of style, charms enhanced for the interpretive suitor by the complexities and paradoxes that shroud his character and thought. And the substance of his most famous teaching, the primacy of experience over logic, still seems to me the central, if obscure, truth of American legal thought: as Cardozo wrote, 'here is the text to be unfolded. All that is to come will be development and commentary.'[173]

When Grey says Holmes' teaching of 'the primacy of experience over logic' seems to him 'the central, if obscure, truth of American legal thought',[174] does he refer to the same 'central, if obscure' notion of 'experience' in Dewey's *Experience and Nature*,[175] or to pragmatism in general? What is the particular way in which the pragmatic sensitivity has developed in law, assuming pragmatism to be a cultural sensitivity rather than only some formal, fixed and external theory? Grey's discussion seems to adopt the latter idea.

First, he emphasizes Holmes' account of pragmatism, as if the question of his pragmatism depends on his evaluation of his pragmatist friends at that

---

> regulatory legislation – whether a given statute was "reasonable" or whether it infringed fundamental principles as they have been understood by our people and our law – was ultimately a test of majority opinion. If the public at large, through its legislative representatives, thought that the conditions of industrial labor should be regulated, the fact that judges thought the regulation "meddlesome interference with the rights of the individual" was irrelevant.'

171 Thomas C. Grey, 'Holmes and Legal Pragmatism', 41 *Stan. L. Rev.* (1989), 787.
172 Id.
173 Id., at 792.
174 Id.
175 Dewey, *supra* note 100.

time: James, Pierce, and Dewey. Holmes admired Dewey and never clarified why he condemned James' version of pragmatism, nor thought highly of Pierce's and James's ideas.[176]

Second, Grey's effort takes us through a kind of 'time tunnel' experience: we read Holmes' texts through neo-pragmatism, which Grey supports. He tries to solve the conflicts in Holmes' work by pointing to 'a characteristic paradox – the man was disabled by temperament, by experience, and by the historical context in which he found himself from adequately practicing the pragmatism he so eloquently preached'.[177] Holmes, in Grey's view, was actually aiming for the post-modern interpretive mode of pragmatism, but the context in which he found himself disabled him from acknowledging this. He suggests that 'we can understand the distinctively pragmatist cast to Holmes' legal thought if we take account of the recent revival and reinterpretation of pragmatism within Anglo-American philosophy'.[178] Grey admits that one of his motives is to have his own present say in the furtherance of a neo-pragmatic approach to legal theory.[179]

The problem with this attitude is that the pragmatic events were not linear, as I try to show throughout my work. There are only diverse lenses, perspectives in time through which we can read Holmes.[180] Re-announcing Holmes in contemporary terms is done today by Grey, but I will develop a different account locating Holmes in relation to James and Dewey by describing legal pragmatism as a special and separate mode within the pragmatist tradition, as the pragmatism of law. This argument will help illuminate the dominance and intensity of the intellectual academic legal discourse within the American academy. It will also help to sharpen my view as to what is the pragmatic specter.

Coming back to Grey, his basic notion of philosophy is already built into the pragmatic epistemology.

> On one side of this divide, English speakers (and some Austrian helpers) have tended to conceive of philosophy as an enterprise dedicated to exploring the foundations of knowledge through a rigorous account of natural scientific method, with the ultimate aim of extending that method to all areas of human inquiry. On the other side, European philosophy has long stood in an adversary

---

176 Grey, 'Holmes and Legal Pragmatism', *supra* note 171, at 788.
177 Id., at 788.
178 Id., at 789.
179 Id., at 792.
180 See *supra* text to 162.

relation to natural science and technology, pursuing the (often quasi-religious) search for meaning, sometimes culminating in a discovery of meaninglessness, through the exploration of culture and lived experience.[181]

In this condensed description of the philosophical tradition, logical positivism, a distinct phenomenon in the beginning of our century, has the primary role of establishing a tradition. Against it, in a footnote to the above paragraph is included a list of European philosophers from Descartes to Derrida (Kant, Hegel, Kirkegaard, Nietzsche, Ditthey, Heidegger, Sartre, Gadamer, Ricoeur). Nothing further is said of any of them. The complete submission of philosophy to science is presented as the standard, and the rich European tradition of philosophizing is reduced to 'a quasi-religious search for meaning'. The neo-pragmatists are said by Grey to resolve part of this tension by incorporating the 'European style of theorizing into American intellectual life'.[182] His depiction of core (positivism and pragmatism) and periphery (quasi-religious European search) still generates the question of American pragmatism. Does it have a 'religious' source, or a mythological one, a paradoxical? Is a search for meaning, embedded in a thick epistemology of science – naturalism and positivism, which are built into pragmatism – not biased? And if pragmatism is indeed admitted to be the 'American religion', what is the difference between it and any other religion, or a quest for it? Keeping these questions open and coming back to Grey, his depiction of philosophy 'as an enterprise dedicated to exploring the foundations of knowledge through a rigorous account of natural scientific method' enables him to delineate the pragmatic line in law as an elaboration of the positivist tradition, combined with a historicist lesson.

On the one hand is the utilitarian tradition:

> Bentham's instrumentalism applied the post-Enlightenment spirit of scientific positivism to law and politics. Central to this spirit was the conviction that, as Richard Rorty has put it, 'Natural science – facts about how spatio-temporal things worked – was all the Truth there was ... For positivists of the Benthamite persuasion, moral and political evaluation could proceed rationally only if evaluative discourse itself could be reduced to factual terms ... Thus utilitarianism became the prescriptive corollary of positivism. An action or a law was right to the extent it promoted pleasure or satisfaction, and prevented pain or frustration.'[183]

---

181 Id., at 790.
182 Id.
183 Id., at 795.

This state of mind is future-oriented, aiming towards social engineering: 'For all their differences, Kant, the philosopher behind German legal science, and Bentham, the founder of English analytical positivism, shared a commitment to liberate the human mind from its state of "tutelage" – the tutelage of the past, with its weight of customs, traditions, and inherited texts.'[184] Kant and Bentham share here the same endeavor, and against them 'there arose a romantic and conservative reaction based upon faith in the virtues of tradition, organic solidarity, and cultural particularity, and upon distrust of innovation and abstract reason'. This was the historicist tradition, which in Europe found its vehicle in the formation of the historical school of jurisprudence.

> The historicists argued that the basis of all law is custom, the set of evolved norms that gives a society its identity. According to their central metaphor, a community's law is like its language, a collective product, peculiar to its people and their history, gradually developed, a structure of contingent elements and rules, and yet one so deeply rooted in practice as to be almost entirely resistant to conscious modifications.[185]

As in the philosophy dichotomy, the two sides are not equal. The European school of history '... said nothing that was in substance new to English and American lawyers. Historical jurists only restated the conventional wisdom of "the common law tradition" as it had been articulated over the centuries by Coke, Hale, David Hume and Edmund Burke.'[186] In other words, the enlightened side (Kant, Bentham, utilitarians) was a liberating force from the historicist traditional side within the common law and, outside of it, in the European tradition.

> The enlightened argued that the only proper way to remove the law's haphazard excrescencies was to start from scratch (at least in imagination) and build up a new body of law by rational inference from first principles; the historical jurists responded that workable law must always be based in custom, and that no good could possibly come from conscious and instrumental law reform.[187]

This is an interesting mixture: repetitions of philosophical dichotomies (starting from scratch, rooted in custom) and philosophical figures (Kant,

---

184 Id., at 808.
185 Id.
186 Id., at 809.
187 Id.

Bentham, Mill) diffused into the legal tensions of past and future, common law, civil law, and America. It is as if the legal has become the only philosophical ("'the common law tradition" as it had been articulated over the centuries ... and translated into the language of political theory by David Hume ...'[188]), as if the legal intellectual discourse in America has received the role once ascribed to philosophy, before pragmatism evaded it. This impression will recur later in Grey's article as well as in other texts. Following his exposition of the dichotomy, he describes Holmes mediating between the poles through the concept of experience: 'Experience is tradition interpreted with one eye on coherence and another on policy.'[189] Holmes was skeptical of legal and political reform (the enlightened pole) and held 'an unconvinced conservatism'.[190] He was fascinated with the old ('Love the old', he wrote to Pollock. 'I feel ... to my finger tips ... a reverence for venerable traditions.'[191]) But he also 'had a capacity for self-critical distance from his antiquarianism'.[192] ('How delightful is the mixed emotion: half noble aesthetic – half fishy – that of the collector, with which one turns to ancient things.')[193] The pragmatic mediation was, according to Grey, 'like much pragmatist theory', essentially banal. 'At its most abstract level it concludes in truism.'[194]

> Pragmatism thus tends to be theoreticians armed with a presumptive suspicion of neat theories; this is not because they despise neatness, but because they know how obsessively those drawn to theorizing love it. Thus, typically, of pragmatist theory, Holmes' central point about judges' law was a critical one; law *isn't* logic in Langdell's exciting and geometrical precise sense. It was partly to avoid a discursive vacuum, and partly to nudge practice in the right direction, that he added the vague constructive alternative that 'law *is* experience', by which he meant an indefinite mixture of habit, instrumental reason, and the search for internal coherence. Dewey used the term 'experience', and his other

---

188 Id.
189 Id., at 814.
190 Id., at 812: '"I don't believe much in anything that is", he once wrote to John Henry Wigmore, "but I believe damned sight less in anything that isn't." Precisely because he "rarely could be sure" that one rule "tends more than its opposite to the survival and welfare of the society where it is practiced", he was slow to depart from precedent. "Precisely my skepticism, my doubt as to the absolute worth of a large part of the system we administer, or of any other system, makes me very unwilling to increase the doubt as to what the courts will do".'
191 Id., at 812.
192 Id., at 813.
193 Id.
194 Id., at 814.

favorite, 'situation', in very much the same way, as designedly vague terms meant to give a sense of partial closure and some approximate practical remapping of the conceptual space his critique has vacated.[195]

Grey and perhaps also Rorty, as he suggests,[196] have an interest in reading Dewey in this way. But as emphasized before, there was a concrete theory of science, one probably old-fashioned today, behind the concept of experience in Dewey.[197] This was the idea of 'thinking as an adaptive function of an organism, practical in the sense that it was *instrumental*',[198] and experience within this context was a consequence of the changes produced in the environment in reaction upon the organism and its activities.[199]

> In a transitive flip worthy of Nietzsche, Pierce reversed the Kantian hierarchy, and assimilated all human science, speculative philosophy, and moral inquiry into the category of the pragmatic. All judgments – scientific and moral as well as prudential and technical – were contingent, probabilistic, relative to a situation and to the interests of an agent or a community of agents. Thought was no longer to be conceived as something distinct from practice, but rather it simply *was* practice, or activity, in its deliberative or reflective aspect.[200]

But Grey is ambivalent toward 'classical' pragmatism. He praises the claim of thinking as contextual (this is the neo-pragmatists' position), but he tries to avoid the Darwinist origin.[201] According to him, Holmes shared this detest too:

> Excessive focus on the instrumental aspects of pragmatism, especially with emphasis on its evolutionary biological roots, readily makes it into the Philistine and readily reductive philosophy portrayed by its critics. Pragmatists treat human inquiry as a means, an instrument – but an instrument to what ends? As Holmes once said, the theory of evolution seems to decree constant attention to survival, so 'that man should produce food and raiment in order that he might produce yet other food and other raiment for the end of time.' And yet, as he added, 'Who does not rebel at that conclusion?' Well, not everyone does. Holmes himself associated the term 'pragmatism' with the world view of those who endorse the

---

195 Id., at 815.
196 Id.
197 See, for example, the *supra* text to 105n.
198 Grey, *supra* note 171, at 798.
199 Id.
200 Id., at 803.
201 Id., at 798–9.

same grimly Philistine 'food and raiment' creed, in which every activity is subordinated to some end external to itself, and nothing is done for its own sake.[202]

Grey keeps pointing to the reductive and primitive quality of the instrumental approach – by referring to this line in pragmatic thought and diminishing it, and by returning to the positivist tradition which he depicts as the core of philosophizing. This was, according to him, the Realist school's overemphasis upon claiming to follow Holmes,[203] and also the overemphasis of Roscoe Pound.[204] The true pragmatism, his own and that of Holmes and Dewey, is non-instrumental.

Actually, Grey's ambivalence parallels that of Holmes. Grey would prefer claiming that pragmatism's basic message is, as he said above,[205] 'Don't be obsessive with your theories.'[206] It is an appealing contemporary motto (which recalls 'The bottom line is that there is no bottom line', which I discuss elsewhere),[207] and depicting Holmes as supporting it makes him indeed 'disabled ... by the historical context in which he found himself from

---

202 Id., at 852.
203 'The Legal Realists in their critique of conceptual jurisprudence would later seek (without much success) to reorder the law around just "functional" and "real-world" topic headings. And ironically, the Realists claimed Holmes as their chief authority in the assault upon the classical doctrinal framework of legal thought – a framework that he had helped to build': id., 819.
204 '... it is instructive to compare Holmes' version of the ideal the lawyer should pursue with that stated by Roscoe Pound, who was probably the first significant American legal thinker to label himself "a pragmatist". Expounding his conception of "sociological jurisprudence", Pound wrote that legal scholarship should dedicate itself to a great task ... of social engineering, aimed at the creation of a system of law rationally designed with an eye to "precluding friction and eliminating waste ..." For one thing, the engineering metaphor creates false hopes for the technical solution of social problems by experts, wrongly suggesting that is justice is always better redescribed as "friction" and "waste". Further, it presupposes that so important an element in social life as law can remain simply a dependent variable, a means for achieving external ends': id., 860–61.
205 See the *supra* text to 195n.
206 Another illustration of Grey's 'time tunnel' reading of classical pragmatism in contemporaneous terms appears at another article of him: 'Pragmatists conceive of law as a cluster of activities too complex to be captured and subdued by any theory – the element of truth in anti-theoretical professionalism.' Or: 'Stated in general terms, pragmatist jurisprudence is a theoretical middle way between grand theorizing and anti-intellectual business-as-usual': Thomas C. Grey, 'Freestanding Legal Pragmatism', 18 *Cardozo L. Rev.* 21, 26, 38 (1996).
207 See the chapter 'In Search of the Dispute: On Lawyers and Legal Philawsophers at Harvard Law School (Or: Some Private Hope and Public Irony)', PART 4.2.

adequately practicing the pragmatism he so eloquently preached'.[208] The assertion that pragmatism was '... essentially banal ... concludes in truism',[209] and that 'it was partly to avoid a discursive vacuum, and partly to nudge practice in the right direction, that he [Holmes – M.A.] added the vague constructive alternative of *law is experience*'[210] blends with the need to eliminate the dominance of the evolutionary image both Holmes and Dewey maintained. Grey would rather Dewey used this concept in a vague way,[211] preempting the contemporary psychoanalytic call against obsession with theories. But except for the fact that this call has its hyperbolic character (how can one avoid being obsessive with one's theory of not being obsessive?), it is probably not what Holmes and Dewey had in mind when thinking of experience.

But there was, indeed, something central about experience, something obscure and at the same time attractive, producing much of the pragmatic legacy's power. Instead of describing it as an effort 'to avoid a discursive vacuum', it can be perceived, as Grey indeed suggests, as 'the central, if obscure, truth of American legal thought: as Cardozo wrote, "Here is the text to be unfolded. All that is to come will be development and commentary".'[212] If the truth/foundation are this text, and if this text is vague and only fills a discursive vacuum, what made it so influential? It begins to appear that the paradox lies somewhere in the 'central ... truth of American legal thought', and not only in Holmes' writing.

But there is something about experience, something as deep as the Protestant ethic or the capitalist spirit, and as transparent as 'nature' at the time and place of Dewey and Holmes. The 'Protestant ethic' that echoes in pragmatism was described before as having a role in modern development. Max Weber describes its infiltration into capitalist thought in his book, *The Protestant Ethic and the Spirit of Capitalism*. He says that 'The Puritan, ascetic lifestyle emerges as a response to the doctrine of predestination. This doctrine holds that God has already picked out who will be saved for heaven and who will be punished in hell.'[213] In the next stages, when the religious doctrine died, 'the spirit lived in a secularized form', manifest as an ascetic tendency of the Puritan (or the modern American): 'He gets nothing out of his wealth

---

208 Grey, *supra* note 171, at 788.
209 See *supra* text to 194n.
210 See *supra* text to 195n.
211 Id.
212 Id., 792, and above, *supra* text to 174n.
213 Randall Collins, 'Introduction', in Max Weber, *The Protestant Ethic and the Spirit of Capitalism* (Talcott Parson, trans., 2nd edn, 1998), xiii.

for himself, except the irrational sense of having done his job well.'[214] Weber probably had an interest or perspective of his own when narrating the paradigmatic capitalist as the Protestant, and describing the ultimate modernity and rationality as having developed in America. He describes a strong religious impulse of predestination which has become a principle of commodification, manifested also in the pragmatic idea of experience. Here, there is a convergence between the religious pathos and the Darwinian enchantment.

But the 'capitalist spirit' mentioned above is not only the sociological-historical dimension of it. A deeper characteristic might be perceived as its discursive structure. Jacques Derrida describes it when reading Marx: 'The whole movement of idealization that Marx describes, whether it is a question of money or of ideologems, is a production of ghosts, illusions, simulacra, appearances, or apparition. Later he will compare this spectral virtue of money with that which, in the desire to hoard, speculates on the use of money *after death*, in the other world.'[215] Money and commodities have a spectral dimension, and in the more theoretical market this quality can enhance a non-possessive discourse of generalities.

In the philosophical realm, this 'castrated' mode of the ideal, combined with a scientific 'direct' perception of 'the real' ('the world', or 'ordinary' as discussed before) are combined to justify the bringing of philosophy to its end, the call for creativity, and the democratic embrace of the common. In the legal sphere, it enabled aesthetic indulgence in legal criteria, from Holmes' time until the Legal Process decline and beyond. It is indeed the non-instrumental spin that is so appealing in pragmatism.

> ... reason is experimental intelligence, conceived after the pattern of science and used in the creation of social arts; it has something to do. It liberates man from the bondage of the past, due to ignorance and accident hardened into custom. It projects a better future and assists man in its realization. And its operation is always subject to test in experience. The plans which are formed, the principles which man projects as guides of reconstructive actions are not dogmas. They are hypotheses to be worked out in practice, and to be rejected, corrected and expanded as they fail or succeed in giving our present experience the guidance it requires.[216]

Plans and principles are only hypotheses to be worked out in practice. Nevertheless, it is not their actual outcome we are after.

---

214 Id., 72.
215 Jacques Derrida, *Specters of Marx* (Peggy Kamuf, trans., 1994), 1993, 45.
216 Dewey, *Reconstruction in Philosophy*, supra note 103, at 96.

Happiness is found only in success; but success means succeeding, getting forward, moving in advance. It is an active process, not a passive outcome. Accordingly it includes the overcoming of obstacles, the elimination of sources of defect and ill ... Upon the whole, utilitarianism has marked the best in the transition from the classic theory of ends and goods to that which is now possible ... But it was still profoundly affected in fundamental points by old ways of thinking. It never questioned the idea of a fixed, final and supreme end. It only questions the current notions as to the nature of this end; and then inserted pleasure and the greatest possible aggregate of pleasures in the position of the fixed end. Like every theory that sets up fixed and final aims, in making the end passive and possessive, it made all active operations *mere* tools.[217]

We can find the non-instrumental message already in Holmes's *Privilege, Malice and Intent* in 1894:[218] Decisions for and against the existence of privilege in tort can be decided only upon considerations of policy,[219] but 'when the question of policy is faced it will be seen to be one which cannot be answered by generalities, but must be determined by the particular character of the case, even if everybody agrees what the answer should be'.[220] The same pathos arises from Grey's description of Holmes' non-instrumental stress:

> He gave internal or practical legal writing the accolade 'philosophical' when it had, or aspired to, intrinsic intellectual interest along with its practical classificatory and decision guiding use. And he found ideas intrinsically interesting only when they were *general*. He 'hate(d) facts' and thought 'the chief end of man is to form general propositions', to which he always added the twist – meant to stress that he valued his generalities as ends in themselves, not for their utility – that 'no general proposition is worth a damn'.[221]

---

217 Id., at 183.
218 Oliver Wendell Holmes, 'Privilege, Malice and Intent', 8 *Harv. L. Rev.* (1894), 281.
219 'Distinguishing himself from the positions he had adopted earlier in *The Common Law*, Holmes contended that it is impossible to answer definitely the question whether a defendant who has injured someone but whose conduct was not blameworthy should be forced to pay damages to the victim. The choice between the negligence principle (defendant should be liable only if they were at fault) and the strict liability principle (defendant should be liable even if blameless), he now insisted, is a concealed, half conscious battle on the question of legislative policy, and if anyone thinks that it can be settled deductively, or once for all, I only can say that I think he is theoretically wrong, and that I am certain that his conclusions will not be accepted in practice': *American Legal Realism* (William W. Fisher, Morton J. Horwitz and Thomas A. Reed, eds, 1993), 5.
220 Id., at 283.
221 Grey, *supra* note 171, at 842.

But what is the exact relation between Dewey's and Holmes' perceptions? What can be inferred from the fact that 'while Holmes did express admiration for Dewey, he never made clear what it was that he admired'?[222] We find a few clues in Grey's account of their relations, one of which appears after he describes Dewey's psychology of action, which blurs the distinction 'between work and play on the one hand, and between play and art on the other'.[223] 'We must return our attention to Holmes, who of course was no radical, scarcely even liberal, and who had no faith at all in the advancement of human happiness by the economic reorganization of society.'[224]

In the same context, he described Holmes as 'a detached skeptic whose commitment to democracy was at best ambivalent'.[225] Holmes was neither a radical economic nor a bit of a feminist.[226] As already mentioned, his attitude toward legal and political reform remained, at bottom, 'an unconvinced conservatism'.[227]

> Because Holmes' conservatism in both its skeptical and its romantic mode was so pervasive, it is important to see that it has no necessary connection with the basic pragmatist tenets that he so well articulated. Dewey, for example, welcomed Holmes as a philosophical kindred spirit even while recognizing that the two of them disagreed on many of the political questions of the day. Dewey used pragmatist premises as a basis of an optimistic brand of activist liberal reformism.

Holmes was ironic, detached, devoted to a life of 'practical struggle' within the law, as a judge, and not as a spectator[228] (an 'actor' and not a 'witness', in Grey's terms regarding Holmes[229]). Yet throughout, he remained a philosopher, probably driven by the same initial motives he had when joining the metaphysical club.[230] His 'masculine' characteristics – insensitive, fascinated

---

222 Id., at 788.
223 Id., at 856.
224 Id.
225 Id., at 858.
226 Id., at 862.
227 Id., at 812.
228 Id., at 844: After the appointment to the Massachusetts Supreme Judicial Court, he wrote in a letter to James Bryce: 'To reject a share in the practical struggle of life which naturally offered itself' would be 'the less manly course ... I am glad on the whole that I stuck to actualities against philosophy (the interest of all actualities).'
229 Id., at 837–44.
230 Id., at 838–9: 'As a young Civil War veteran his passions were science, poetry, and philosophy; his companions at the time were the young writers and intellectuals of Boston and Cambridge, William and Henry James, Chauncey Wright, and Nicholas St. John

with logic in a counter-pragmatic fashion – are particularly emphasized when his work as a judge is described.

> In becoming a judge, Holmes entered a life to which, for all the scope it gave to his literary gifts, he was not wholly suited. Judging is an enterprise deeply concerned with 'practice and details', and neither Holmes' talents nor his inclinations lay in this direction. Generations of law students have marveled at the simple lack of informed common sense manifested by such judgments as his pronouncement that a motorist at a rail crossing must stop, look, and listen for a train, and get out of the car if necessary to do so, on pain of being found contributorily negligent.[231]

In the Supreme Court the same deficiency of not being 'a man of affairs' was repeated, according to Grey:

> Holmes in his judicial role adopted a kind of surrogate for Shaw's or White's sound instinctive sense of good public policy, his well known attitude of deference to legislative judgment. His reputation as a great judge rests largely on his many eloquent reiterations of his attitude in constitutional cases during a period of progressive legislative activity – and his reputation as a liberal statesman rests almost wholly on this basis.[232]

> As a judge, he was skilled at the conceptual aspect of the work ('untying knots', he called it), and he could follow the wishes that were given positive embodiment. But his very lack of connection to that community and lack of empathy with its central concerns disabled him from being the kind of 'great magistrate' that Lemuel Shaw had been.[233]

But this is not only the question of how Holmes operated as a judge, or how skeptical and conservative he was, and if he really had some 'common sense'. Instead of following Grey in his effort to examine how pragmatic

---

Green. He came to the law in 1865 not out of any sense of professional calling, but because he was, as he put it, "kicked", "thrown", and "shoved" into it. At first he doubted whether his "ragbag of details" was "worthy of the interest of an intelligent man". But he soon reconciled himself, not because of any attractions from the profession's practical side, but, on the ground that "law ... may be approached in the interests of science" and "opens a way to philosophy"': id., at 837–44.

'In 1876, writing as a young lawyer to the old philosopher Emerson, he said that what justified law to him was the path it opened to philosophy': id., at 847.

231 Id., at 845.
232 Id., at 849.
233 Id., at 850.

Holmes was, I would suggest that this was precisely Holmes' pragmatism: logical, ironic, not good at 'real affairs', professional, theoretically obscure, obsessive, internal. This *is* legal pragmatism.[234] It is related to what was once called, or still *is* called, classical pragmatism, that of James, Pierce, and Dewey; but in my view, considering the fact that they all emerged at once from the same cultural milieu, there are alchemic, metonymic discursive relations between legal and classical pragmatism, which at least from today's perspective can be seen as two complementary answers to the same call. I will describe the emergence of this distinct genre of pragmatism by using four of the above characteristics, as opposing their philosophical counterparts.

Professional (Against General)

While Pierce and James offer a distinct philosophical claim, claiming for the death of an old discourse and the emergence of a new one, Holmes does not give grand narratives. His formula of law as experience is obscured precisely because it is not the experience which Dewey speaks about. Holmes is a theorist of a professional discourse and as such, he does not have to say the grand theories. He assumes the existence of a body of law and upon this assumption establishes the idea of the life of the law.

His relation to the other members of the metaphysical club can validate that idea. For example, William James:

---

234 Examples of the incorporation of the philosophical pragmatism into law are pervasive all over the legal discourse and in different era. A very early one can be found in Benjamin N. Cardozo, *The Nature of the Judicial Process* (1921), 12–13: 'We are reminded by William James in a telling page of his lectures on pragmatism that everyone of us has indeed an underlying philosophy of life, even those of us to whom the names and the notions of philosophy are unknown or anathema. There is in each of us a stream of tendency, whether you choose to call it philosophy or not, which gives coherence and direction to thought and action. Judges cannot escape that current anymore than other mortals. All their lives, forces which they do not recognize and cannot name have been tugging at them – inherited instincts, traditional beliefs, acquired convictions; and the resultant is an outlook on life, a conception of social needs, a sense in James's phrase of the total push and pressure of the cosmos, which, when reasons are nicely balanced, must determine where choice shall fall. In this mental background every problem finds its setting. We may try to see things as objectively as we please. Nonetheless, we can never see them with any eyes except our own.' This psychological account of decision-making in terms of the pragmatic is part of the jurist who tries 'to philosophize'. When he operates in the legal world, he will take the more Holmsian mode of inquiry (but he will still read Cardozo).

In 1872 James was emerging from a nervous collapse that had lasted almost three years. After a wildly peripatetic education in Europe and America, he had finally graduated from the Harvard Medical School (the only course of study he ever completed) in 1869, at the age of twenty-seven, and immediately fallen into a state of lassitude, depression, and chronic ill health. Whatever the causes of his various symptoms, James seems to have explained them to himself in intellectual terms. He treated his depression as a kind of philosophical problem that might be relieved by coming up with a philosophical solution; and one day in 1870, in his diary, he announced a breakthrough.[235]

Holmes underwent his own crisis in a very different setting. In 1861, at the end of his senior year at Harvard, he enlisted in the Union Army (something James seems scarcely to have contemplated doing), and he served for three years, and in some of the bloodiest fighting of the Civil War. Although he later gave speeches in which he glorified the soldiers' blind allegiance to duty, Holmes hated war itself. He was seriously wounded three times ... Holmes did emerge from the war purged of illusions. He thought he had paid a high price for the privilege of losing them, and he was careful never to acquire any again.[236]

James experienced a depression, an internal collapse. His major effort became the existential act of surviving. He needed 'the will to believe'.[237] Holmes, on the other hand, encountered 'the real world', that of blood and cruelty.[238] He had no illusions. He 'developed an intimate friendship with William James', but eventually their personal relations 'became strained'.[239] 'Holmes was always unsympathetic to James' philosophical writings.[240] They

---

[235] Menand, *Introduction to Pragmatism*, supra note 56, at xviii.
[236] Id., at xix.
[237] William James, 'The Will to Believe', in *Pragmatism*, supra note 56, at 69–92.
[238] See also Robert W. Gordon, 'Introduction: Holmes' Shadow', in *The Legacy of Oliver Wendell Holmes, Jr*, supra note 164, I: 'The war experience may have laid the foundations of Holmes's aloof detachment, his disengagement from causes and distrust of enthusiasms, and the bleakly skeptical foundations of his general outlook, according to which law and rights were the only systems imposed by force by whatever social groups emerged as dominant in the struggle for existence. From his war service on, *he would repeatedly speak of personal and social life in military terms, as a fight carried on by soldiers blindly following incomprehensible orders*' (the emphasis is mine – M.A.).
[239] Menand, *supra* note 56., at xix.
[240] Grey describes the relation between Holmes and James in the appendix to his article starting from their youth: 'In their youth they were intense discussion partners and friends; Holmes could address James without any irony as "Oh! Bill, my beloved", while James called him in reply "my Wendly boy". But they were friends always conscious of serious differences. Thus in 1868 James wrote to Holmes that when they were together "I put myself involuntarily into a position of self-defense, as if you threatened to over-run my

seemed to him to promote, in their spiritual hopefulness, the very sentimental idealism he had rejected.'[241] He disrespected the religious sentiment in them.[242]

An equivalent relationship can be traced from descriptions of Holmes against Pierce. On the one hand:

> It is reasonable to expect that Holmes and Pierce shared much of their fundamental philosophical outlook. They each had Calvinist grandparents and Unitarian-leaning parents. They each went to Harvard and Europe for an education. Each had an intellectual father who was prominent in the mid-nineteenth century Cambridge community. They read many of the same books and cut their philosophical teeth on discussions with common contemporaries. Each was touched strongly by Emerson and Darwin; each was profoundly affected by the arguments of Bain and the resident Cambridge genius, Chauncey Wright.[243]

On the other hand, 'Holmes dismissed pragmatism as "an amusing humbug", and has rejected Pierce's ideas as well, saying that he was "overrated", observing that "his reasoning in the direction of religion ... reflects what he wants to believe".'[244] He also wrote critically on the collection of James' essays published after his death,[245] and all of these oppositions within pragmatism.

---

territory and injure my own proprietorship ..." As late as 1876 James was still close enough to Holmes to visit him and his wife on Cape Code, where, as he wrote to Henry, he saw Holmes' "virtues and faults" ... thrown into singular relief by the lonesomeness of the shore'; against that background Holmes appeared to James as 'a powerful battery, formed like a planing machine to gouge a deep self-beneficial groove through life': Grey, *supra* note 171 at 865.

Later, according to Grey, their temperamental differences put an end to their active friendship and in some letters to Pollock Holmes has used the following words: 'I think pragmatism an amusing humbug – like most of William James's speculations ....' 'James, he said, was not strong in "logic" or "abstract thinking", his talent was for "art and *belles lettres*" rather than "philosophy"; he had taken positions "fitted to please free thinking Unitarian parsons and the ladies"': id., at 866.

241 Menand, *supra* note 56., at xix.
242 The reference to religion suggests an important factor common to Holmes' rejection of the ideas of both James and Pierce: 'As to pragmatism ... I now see ... that the aim and end of the whole business is religious': Grey, *supra* note 171, at 866.
243 Catherine Wells Hantzis, *Legal Innovation Within the Wider Intellectual Tradition: The Pragmatism of Oliver Wendell Holmes, Jr*, 82 NW University School of Law (1988) 541, 546–7.
244 Grey, *supra* note 171, at 867.
245 Hantzis, *supra* note 243, at 547.

Although Pierce and Holmes shared common origins, their lives as adults could not have been more different. Holmes was wounded three times in the Civil War, while Pierce sat in the sidelines. Holmes led a phenomenally successful professional life, while Pierce wrote volume after volume in obscure poverty. While Pierce seems to ignore the political and legal issues of his day, Holmes was at the center of many of them.[246]

Holmes engaged himself in real life – in political and legal issues. He 'led a phenomenally successful professional life' and opposed the direct general contemplation of Pierce and James. The professional mode of his philosophical inquiries is a distinct characteristic of the discourse he bequeaths for coming generations.

Internal (Against External)

The legal theorist-style Holmes is busy with internal critique while assuming the body of law in which he dwells. Through this internal perspective, from within the body, he watches other spheres of law.

The suspicion that in philosophy was aimed at generalities and metaphysics, was pointed in law toward legal rules. It was the same pathos of questioning, but in law it was accompanied by a common-law tradition, and framed in a different context. Legal rules, in contrast to philosophical ideas, are prescriptions aimed at some action or inaction in the world. The English inheritance, with its tension between the common law as tradition and utilitarianism as modernism, as described above, in my view became for Holmes the equivalent to the natural world outside of law. He probably accepted and lived the evasion of the past, the American embrace of the ordinary, and the glorious advance of science, but actually needed not to 'hold' a philosophy in order to develop his professional discourse. Generalities in law were a distinct brand of generalities and jurisprudential thought could treat them uniquely. The experience idea he offered has given us a different version of pragmatism: more ironic, less intuitive, and internal to the legal sphere. The power of his philosophy, paradoxically, lies in its non-philosophical commitment to a given context, that of the law. In the legal domain, philosophy had still a chance, generalities were still embraced, principles still counted.

It is interesting to examine, in this context, Dewey's account of Holmes, in relation to *Logical Method and the Law*, an article Dewey wrote in 1925.

---

[246] Hantzis, *supra* note 243, at 548.

Justice Holmes has generalized the situation by saying that 'the whole outline of the law is the result of a conflict at every point between logic and good sense – the one striving to work fiction out to consistent results, the other restraining and at last overcoming that effort when the results become too manifestly unjust'.[247]

Dewey 'corrects' this conflict described by Holmes:

> What justice Holmes terms logic is formal consistency, consistency of concepts with one another, irrespective of the consequences of their application to concrete matter-of-fact. We might state the fact by saying that concepts once developed have a kind of intrinsic inertia on their own account; once developed, the law of habit applies to them. It is practically economical to use a concept ready at hand rather than to take trouble and effort to change it or to devise a new one. The use of prior ready-made and familiar concepts also gives rise to a sense of stability, of guarantee against sudden and arbitrary changes of the rules which determine the consequences which legally attend acts. It is the nature of any concept, as it is of any habit, to change more slowly than do the concrete circumstances with reference to which it is employed. Experience shows that the relative fixity of concepts affords men with a specious sense of protection, of assurance against the troublesome flux of events.[248]

In place of a picture of a conflict, we have one overarching, pragmatic explanation to the whole system of precedent and the emphasis upon tradition in law: The 'logic' of Holmes is consistency. This is the use of prior concepts. It is economical and enhances stability. The 'application' of the pragmatic science to law is done in a way equivalent to any other professional decision making – 'an intelligent farmer or business man or physician'.[249] The ideal is the 'scientific man', and 'it is natural and proper that we should ... treat ordinary "practical" reasonings leading up to decisions as to what is to be done as only approximations'.[250] Holmes could not accept this formula in relation to law. Even if it appealed to him, it was too empty, too 'philosophical', beginning from scratch. He believed in the life of the law.[251] In that sense, he

---

247 John Dewey, 'Logical Method and the Law', 10 *Cornell L. Quarterly* (1925) 17, 20.
248 Id.
249 Id., at 18.
250 Id.
251 'If we are to speak of the law as our mistress, we who are here know that she is a mistress only to be wooed with sustained and lonely passion – only to be won by straining all the faculties by which man is likes to a god. Those who, having begun the pursuit, turn away uncharmed, do so either because they have not been vouchsafed the sight of her divine figure, or because they have not the heart of so great a struggle': Julius J. Marke, *The Holmes Reader* (1955) 278.

promoted the life of the context beside the Deweyan pragmatic contextualization of any life.

> If your subject is the law, the roads are plain to anthropology, the science of man, to political economy, the theory of legislation, ethics, and thus by several paths to your final view of life. It would be equally true of any subject. The only difference is in the ease of seeing the way. To be master of any branch of knowledge, you must master those which lie next to it; and thus to know anything you must know all.[252]

Law is only a paradigm of academic learning in general, and such learning has become life. It is not only the commandment to dwell in law and be internal. It is also the demand to be internal and external at once, to 'know all'. Within the context of Holmes' legal discourse, law became nature, and within it, experience took the natural stance of a craft, within the great chain of life.

> The growth of the law is very apt to take place in this play: Two widely different cases suggest a general distinction, which is a clear one when stated broadly. But as new cases cluster around the opposite poles, and begin to approach one another, the distinction becomes more difficult to trace; the determinations are made one way or the other on a very slight preponderance of feeling, rather than articulate reason; and at last a mathematical line is arrived at by the contact of contrary decisions, which is so far arbitrary that it might equally well have been drawn a little further to the one side or to the other. The distinction between the groups, however, is philosophical, and it is better to have a line drawn somewhere in the penumbra between darkness and light than to remain in uncertainty.[253]

There is 'growth' in law, which takes place like an organic reaction: two cases suggest a general distinction and new cases 'cluster around the opposite pole and begin to approach one another'. At last, a mathematical line 'is arrived at by the contact of contrary decisions', but it seems that this whole process takes place in some natural medium where the metaphor of 'experience' serves as the organizing force.

In contrast to old-fashioned philosophical inquiries, the science of the law still has aesthetic appeal; 'a man may live greatly in the law' because it stimulates 'the large survey of causes' where thought may find its unity in an infinite perspective'.[254] 'Law, as "a part of man, and of one world with all the

---

252 Id.
253 From Holmes, 'The Theory of Torts', in Grey, *supra* note 171, at 821.
254 From Holmes, and Grey, id., at 846.

rest" teaches "the philosophical" lesson of the continuity of the universe.' And the law's true fascination, he said in the Emersonian peroration to *The Path of the Law*, lies in those 'remoter and more general aspects' wherein the lawyer can 'catch an echo of the infinite, a glimpse of its unfathomable process, a hint of the universal law'.[255]

Considering the circumstances in which these things are said and the overall consensus of that time and place regarding the death of philosophy, what is crucial about law is that it is still allowed to search for a universal law, to philosophize. Law is becoming philosophy, but the particular discourse of law at the time of Holmes (rules, principles, policies, positivism, instrumentalism, the common-law tradition and the nineteenth-century utilitarian discourse surrounding it) becomes the sole universe of philosophizing, becoming what nature once was to philosophy. 'The conflicting accounts of the legal elephant as experience, logic, and prediction',[256] in Grey's terms, can be recaptured here in their significance. Philosophy has become the science of the legal elephant (philawsophy or pil-osophy[257]) by combining the pragmatic scientific epistemology and infiltrating it into the concrete body – the corps – of the legal animal. When an enchanting real creature is assumed to exist, much of its development is often explained, like in the old story, through the blind search of its extremities. The law has a body, and within it we dwell.

The project behind *The Common Law* of Holmes, according to Grey, was thus avowedly doctrinal and conceptual.

To make known the content of the law; that is, to work upon it from within, or logically, arranging it from within, or logically, arranging and distributing it, in order, from its *summun genus* to its *infima species*, so far as practicable. Holmes sought to replace the old arrangement of Anglo-American private law, based on Blackstone and the writ system, with a new 'philosophical' structure organized around the categories of contract and tort.[258]

Working upon the content of law from within, and especially from within private law texts, which are considered the core of American law, has become a major intellectual engagement of the jurists of the coming century. Later on, when the Marxist spirit arrives into law through the neo-pragmatism of the Critical Legal Studies movement, this mode wears also the revolutionary aspiration to liberate society through the work from within the body.

---

255 Id.
256 Id., at 805.
257 'Pil' is the word for 'elephant' in Hebrew.
258 Grey, *supra* note 171, at 816.

Obsessive (Against Hysteric)

In contrast to the hysteric philosophical discourse of grand new narratives, Holmes establishes an ironic obsessive discourse which accepts the existence of the legal body as nature. There is no need to give big explanations of the world, of the human, of nature or the state, as in the pragmatism of Dewey. There is not a metaphoric lack to be covered by a theory of evasion. When the discourse or the body is assumed, the meaningful operation within it is the obsessive work with the particulars. The bad man's test and the prediction theory can be read, in my view, as a manifestation of this characteristic.

Coming back to Grey, 'Holmes developed the prediction theory during the early 1870s at the same time he was attending the meetings of the Metaphysical Club at which the pragmatic movement was founded.'[259] Grey writes in a period where dispute orientation is considered degrading for legal intellectuals. This is probably why he goes out of his way to explain the professional biases of Holmes' time.[260] The statement that 'the prophecies of what the courts will do in fact, and nothing more pretentious, are what I mean by the law', combined with 'the bad man's theory' ('for one who proposes to study "the law as a business with well understood limits", Holmes says it is heuristically useful to adopt the viewpoint of a "bad man" who cares only for 'material consequences'[261]), is the 'cynical acid' Grey describes.[262] Yet this pair is appealing, precisely *due* to their cynical dimension: The prediction of the moment after the decision-making in law, of this organic natural happening, is inherently impossible. If it is not the generalities and not social goals, what is left is a mathematical or an indexing device that will only re-conceptualize this impossibility. Still the need to capture this moment, to be the bad man, the persisting obsessive theoretician, is the business of the law in Holmes' pragmatism. It is the bad man, or more accurately the man (masculine) of pragmatism that insists on providing theories and predictions. Though there is no more foundation, there is still the life of the law.

In various ways, Grey shows how the logical impulse of Holmes was very strong, and much of his work 'was devoted to the abstract and conceptual ordering of doctrine into a structured and coherent system'.[263] He was a

---

259 Id., at 826.
260 See the discussion of Fiss's approach toward the Alternative Dispute Resolution movement in the chapter 'Taking Sides: Margins and Phases of Pragmatics of Legal Process Disciples (Or: The Pragmatists that We Are)', PART 3.2.
261 Id., at 833.
262 Id.
263 Id., at 816.

conceptualist and a formalist, like Langdell, according to Grey,[264] and not as the Realists have portrayed him.[265] 'He loved the logical manipulation of doctrine for its own sake nearly as much as Langdell did,'[266] but he re-channeled this attraction through the core idea of pragmatism. Logic, and accordingly, philosophy, became subordinate to the Deweyan-Holmsian-American idea of experience.

> For Langdell, the fundamental principles of the common law, once extracted by induction from the cases, had the status of axiomatic general truths; they *were the law*, and individual decisions shown to conflict with them were thereby shown to have been wrongly decided. Holmes, by contrast, considered the same general principles to be guidelines, rules of thumb, instruments of inquiry designed as practical aids to making sound decisions.[267]

The moment of decision-making in law is the crucial point from which to examine the validity of its generalities, but as Holmes' famous slogan in Lochner suggests, 'General propositions do not decide concrete cases.' It is also not a matter of choice among the principles or rules by the judge, because the whole pragmatic approach is to evade the old-fashioned, subject-object relation or moral questions which, years later, will bring Derrida to describe the role of the 'aporia' and justice in legal decision-making in his article, 'Force of Law: The "Mystical Foundation of Authority"'.[268]

> An aporia is a non-road. From this point of view, justice would be the experience that we are not able to experience ... Every time that something comes to pass or turns out well, every time that we placidly apply a good rule to a particular case, to a correctly subsumed example, according to a determinate judgment, we can be sure that law *(droit)* may find itself accounted for, but certainly not justice. Law *(droit)* is not justice. Law is the element of calculation, and it is just that there be law, but justice is incalculable, it requires us to calculate with the incalculable; and aporetic experiences are the experiences, as improbable

---

264 Id., at 822.
265 'The Legal Realists in their critique of conceptual jurisprudence would later seek (without much success) to reorder the law around just such "functional" and "real-world" topic headings. And ironically the Realists claimed Holmes as their chief authority in the assault upon the classical doctrinal framework of legal thought – a framework that he had helped to build': id., at 818.
266 Id., at 819.
267 Id., at 818.
268 Jacques Derrida, 'Force of Law: The "Mystical Foundation of Authority"', in *Deconstruction and the Possibility of Justice* (Drucilia Cornell et al., eds), 2.

as they are necessary, of justice, that is to say of moments in which the decision between just and unjust is never insured by a rule.[269]

In contrast to a 'universal' discursive picture of impossible interactions between law and justice, and to deconstruction, which questions them from within, the American Holmsian picture presents law that by definition, is 'never insured by a rule'. It is a separate universe, established on the debris of a 'metaphysical-philosophical' world that assumed justice. Its 'prediction-bad-man theory'[270] is the calculation of what cannot be calculated and thus leaves no room for the messianic spirit Derrida tries to read into law.[271] When he borrows Stanley Fish's 'fresh-judgment' expression to demonstrate the claim that 'for a decision to be just and responsible, it must be ... both regulated and without regulation',[272] he ignores the way in which a pragmatic epistemology has a built-in disbelief in the regulated side. Still, in law, due to the Holmsian legacy, the insistence on some regulation exists, and the Fiss-Fish encounter on this matter confirms this: For Fiss, there are still disciplining rules,[273] still metaphysics in philawsophy.[274]

The economy of this pragmatic legal discourse is obsessive, assuming a 'body' and working on its mastering, in contrast to the hysteric conditioning of the more 'philosophical' discourse that was produced by the emotional characters, like James, or the less aristocratic ones, like Dewey. Their discourse covers a lack, one all-encompassing in its theory.

---

269 Id., at 16.
270 See *supra* text to 257n–260n.
271 See also the comparison between Unger and Derrida in relation to empowered democracy against messianic democracy in the chapter 'Taking Sides: Margins and Phases of Pragmatics of 'Legal Process' Disciples (Or: The Pragmatists That We Are)'.
272 Derrida, *supra* note 268, at 23.
273 Owen Fiss, 'Objectivity and Interpretation', 34 *Stan. Law Rev.* 739 (1982); Stanley Fish, 'Fish v. Fiss', in Stanley Fish, *Doing What comes Naturally: Change, Rhetoric, and The Practice of Theory in Literary and Legal Studies* (1989), 120. Fiss promotes the notion of 'bounded objectivity', which is based on the idea that although adjudication is not the application of rules but the assignment of interpretation to public value, nihilism is avoided through the existence of disciplining rules which guide the judge. Against him Fish explains that no rule can ever bind or limit the judge's decision in a safe way, because as long as there are texts, even if they are called 'rules', there will always be a possibility to interpret them in various ways.
274 See the discussion of Fiss's disciplining rules in relation to the Holmsian legacy in the chapter 'Taking Sides: Margins and Phases of Pragmatism of Legal Process Disciples (Or: The Pragmatists that We Are)', PART 3.2.

Theoretically Obscure (Against Practical)

In an interesting way, the philosophical general discourse occupies the practical pole, because it is accessible, metaphoric, clear, easy to implement and deliver to next generations. The Dewyan theory has a dimension of engineering, as described above, as helping to promote the welfare state and capitalism, while the Holmsian discourse insists on obscurity, rigorousness and does not confer itself easily for understanding or for a common-sensical use.

Decision-making in law, according to Holmes, is a matter of organic happening,[275] of mathematics and scales. 'A fundamental legal concept, necessarily general and imprecise, applies with decreasing certainty to fact situations as they diverge from its paradigm instance.'[276]

> The only way to achieve certain and predictable law was to artificially fix 'a mathematical line' at some relatively arbitrary point within the penumbra where opposing concepts overlapped ... A principle was an indexing device that guided the lawyer to relevantly similar cases, while at the same time guiding the judge to the policy considerations relevant in deciding the hard cases that fell under it.[277]

The pragmatic legal spirit pervades here in its impossibility, in its castrated, open-ended mode, because if generalities do not decide cases, and neither do the social ends we would like to achieve, and if the decision itself is nothing but an organic occurrence, then some deep mystery lies in this icon who captures us in his pragmatic formula.[278] Grey's account of *Lochner* seems to illustrate this aversion-attraction attitude to the idea in its purity.

> Holmes' attitude toward the place of principles in legal reasoning is likewise illustrated when we put his slogan 'general propositions do not decide concrete cases' back into its context within his *Lochner* dissent. The general principle Holmes referred to was one he had just stated and relied on himself: 'A constitution is not intended to embody a particular economic theory'. He meant his famous slogan only to qualify, not to negate, the force of this general principle,

---

275 See *supra* text 253n.
276 Grey, *supra* note 171, at 821.
277 Id., at 822.
278 For a contemporary account of the same mysterious legal pragmatic happening, see Duncan Kennedy, in his discussion of the 'conflicting considerations consciousness' in Duncan Kennedy, 'From the Will Theory to the Principle of Private Autonomy: Lon Fuller's "Consideration and Form"', 100 *Colum. L. Rev.* 94 (2000).

a principle which would if accepted, 'carry us far toward the end'. The principle did not deductively decide *Lochner*; one might accept it and yet strike down the maximum-hours law, characterizing liberty of contract not as part of controversial and transient economic theory, but rather as a fundamental aspect of personal liberty. Yet Holmes believed that a judge who approached the case guided by this principle will be nudged in the direction of the correct decision.

The canonical power of the Holmsian view, and the background for his becoming the icon of so many schools of legal thought from diverse political ranges, [279] seems according to the discussion above to lie squarely in its promise to provide what it inherently cannot. It aims to preserve the secret inaccessible element of its theory by keeping it impractical. The need to continue using logic, to differentiate, conceptualize, count, and measure is enshrined for coming generations of legal scholars. In that way, there is still philosophy in law, because it can neither be brought to its end nor evaded. Nevertheless, this 'philosophical' occupation is only 'instrumental' for a coming moment of decision where no generality can decide the case deductively.

Coming back to the progressive history exposition,[280] and to the question of who were the Realists and what was Holmes in relation to them, it becomes clear that Holmes' political views were correctly questioned by Hollinger when discussing *Lochner*.[281] It turns out that the strength of Holmes lies exactly in providing an empty formula, constructed through pragmatic sentiments, which can later be filled by many camps according to their political interest. In contrast to Dewey's philosophy, this formula is not necessarily progressive. At the time of Holmes, when the American identity/modernity is just emerging, being political is being feminine, practical, is being Dewey: The hysteric discourse of philosophy as the emergence of American modernity is also accompanied by an account of the political in terms of the philosophical. The democratic legacy of Dewey includes a political philosophy, and is mobilizing the American modern perception of itself.[282]

---

279 See *supra* text to 161n–162n.
280 See part 1.3 above.
281 See *supra* text to 168n–169n.
282 And another quotation accounting for the political significance of Dewey's writing: 'If the inevitability of change was to be successfully faced by society as a whole, a philosophy of limited scope was surely needed by the class of managers and bureaucrats assigned to the task of supervising American public affairs. It can scarcely be a coincidence that the age in which pragmatism became popular was also the age in which American intellectuals were unprecedentedly engaged by the managerial ideal. Fully consistent with this ideal

His pragmatism has been taken to be both expressive of, and a crucial influence on, twentieth-century American liberalism, and he has repeatedly been hailed as a 'national philosopher', 'the guide, the mentor and the conscience of the American people'.[283]

Holmes, on the contrary, is responsive to a much more conservative call. As part of the theoretical posture, there are no practical immediate political consequences to his writing. In fact, it may be more probable that it has a conservative orientation.

The above characteristics of the Holmsian discourse offer the opposition between the obsessive, ironic, internal, obscure masculine discourse and the hysteric, metaphoric, external practical feminine one. Legal and philosophical pragmatism, under this description, represent two versions of resistance to the same need to define the American and to establish a new beginning. This opposition can be read also in light of the distinction between two versions of 'resistance to analysis', which Derrida describes in his book *Resistances of Psychoanalysis*. After offering two hypotheses regarding the limit of analysis in Freud's text one historical and the other structural, he continues:

> If one transposes these first two hypotheses into a history of reason, the distinction between them is like that between, on the one side, an Enlightenment progressivism, which hopes for an analysis that will continue to gain ground on initial obscurity to the degree that it removes resistances and liberates, unbinds, emancipates, as does every analysis, and, on the other side, a sort of fatalism or pessimism of desire that reckons with a portion of darkness and situates the unanalyzable as its very resource.[284]

The fatalism that represents the unanalyzable as its very core is that of Holmes, the progressivism which liberates and removes resistance is that of philosophical pragmatism. From another direction, these two modes can account for the couple of anti-foundational theories which dominated the

---

was the elevation of "bold, persistent experimentation" to the level of the principle in the rhetoric of the New Deal. Spare as pragmatism was, it was fleshy enough to support this much admired principle, to sustain an optimistic perspective on science, and to reinforce certain of the least contested, most familiar, and most security-providing ideals in American culture'; Hollinger, *supra* note 62, at 29.

283 Matthew Festenstein, *Pragmatism and Political Theory: From Dewey to Rorty* (1997), 18.
284 Jacques Derrida, *Resistances of Psychoanalysis* (Peggy Kamuf, Pascal Ann Brault ,1988) 1966, 16.

twentieth century – psychoanalysis and pragmatism.[285] This dichotomy also corresponds with the discursive hierarchy I describe, of the fatalist being the man, the dominant well-established social figure, and the enlightened progressive being the woman, the more remote marginal scholar, who is familiar with the body but does not own it. She will take care of the education of the children; the man will encounter the outside world. The Derridian European a-historical irony, in contrast to the American epistemology (mythology) of pragmatism presented by West of a movement within history, can be also played here against this text. Because if the deconstructor is indeed 'Bartleby the Scrivener',[286] who 'to every demand, question, pressure, request, order ... responds without responding, neither active no passive', then 'I would prefer not to',[287] as Derrida suggests.[288] And if 'at issue here is the movement of deconstruction that is not only counter-archeological but counter-genealogical',[289] then maybe 'the responsible man of the law', who is a 'tireless analyst'[290] in the Bartleby story, can be a philosophical tradition that is more 'historical' and concrete in its critique, tracing the specific conditions of humanity through the assumption of an ordinary existence, of 'the world' (the romantic Emersonian existence, as described elsewhere by Cavell[291]). It is

---

285 My argument which describes the proximity and difference between two complementary genres of discourse can be also structured and 'proved' in other ways. The reference to Freud, for example, in relation to Dewey, can for itself signify an equivalent play to that of the Holmes-Dewey relation I try to portray. Clarence Karier claims that Dewey and Freud represent two opposing figures of the turn of the century: the rebel and revolutionary. 'Freud was psychologically an authoritarian rebel, revolting against the Victorian ethic and the authoritarian social structure that frustrated his ambition ... The revolutionary ... is one "who overcomes his ambivalence toward authority because he frees himself from attachment to authority and from the wish to dominate others". If Freud was the rebel, John Dewey in this context was the revolutionary. Dewey was free from both the psychological and practical need to dominate others': Clarence J. Karier, 'The Rebel and The Revolutionary: Sigmund Freud and John Dewey', in *John Dewey: Critical Assessments* (J.E. Tiles, ed., 1992) 42, 44–5.

286 Derrida, *supra* note 284, at 24: 'Those who have read this immense little work by Melville know that Bartlesby is a figure of death, to be sure, but they also know how, without saying anything, he makes others speak, above all the narrator, who happens to be a responsible man of the law and a tireless analyst. In truth incurable.'

287 Id., at 24.

288 Id., at 30: '... and all this deconstruction is also a logic of the spectral and of hunting, of surviving, neither present nor absent, alive nor dead: "I would prefer not to", and so forth.'

289 Id., at 27.

290 Id., at 24.

291 See part 1.2 above.

true that Derrida himself, as a cultural oracle peering through some lenses, especially American ones, has a messianic progressive discourse as well. This happens when he speaks about justice and law (and cannot resist the Levinasic message), but the literary and philosophical contours of this call produce a 'double bar' for the legal academic. Thus it is not surprising that this 'feminine' style of treating law, and the general offering of a new vocabulary based on resistances to the European philosophical chain,[292] does not appeal to many American legal jurists. (This quest represents 'a quasi-religious search for meaning',[293] in Grey's terms above.) The hegemonies between these discourses are certainly not determined, and it is a matter of perspective, but through the American perception easily marginalized.

As the resistances analysis above implies, just as in a 'decent', traditional liberal family, there are role assignments in this relationship as well: the Dewey and James pragmatism became the 'happy harmonizer',[294] the one responsible for the education of the children, for cultural reforms and community projects. It enhances creativity, common sense, listening and pluralism (also within law today, at least in Harvard's negotiation studies, as I show elsewhere).[295] It became increasingly based explicitly on Darwinian science, and still dominates the social sciences of today. It is our 'common sense', our work, our organizational philosophy; it is in school, in family life. A world 'for itself', just as before the Cartesian critique emerged, or as the 'ordinary' in pragmatism, prevails in these realms, and in principle, this world can be observed and manipulated as in a laboratory experiment. On the other hand, legal pragmatism has remained the responsible, insensitive, rational and sophisticated actor. Overall, this discourse has no illusions, it is political, still

---

292 See id., at 28–30: 'Basically, what resists both the Kantian analytic and its dialectical critique is still an analysis, to be sure, but it is an analysis of the presence of the present that cannot give in to the necessity and the affirmation of a hetero-affection in the system of auto-affection and of the living presence of consciousness. This is what I tried to show *by setting out from* Husserl – which is also to say by leaving him behind and taking my distance from him – a certain Husserl... this hetero-affection of time, which is also its originary spacing, obviously led to a displacement, following a Heideggerrian movement, of the emphasis in Kantian Critique ...' and so forth. This parade of European philosophy is indeed central to the understanding of Derrida's thinking, and to the understanding of the use he makes with his foundating notions difference, double bind, aporia, iterability, supplement 'that are contradictory or incompatible between themselves, in their very *between,* in their interlacing, their chiasmatic invagination'.
293 See above, *supra* text to 180n.
294 See above, *supra* text to 85n.
295 See the chapter 'In Search of the Dispute: On Lawyers and Legal Philawsophers at Harvard Law School (Or: Some Private Hope and Public Irony)'.

believes in theory – that of the internal body of the law. Its detachment from 'the world' and its direct metaphysics are enacted later in the interpretive idea of the Herculean Judge of Hercules.[296] The only domain where metaphysics and principles do make sense is this one: the kingdom of law, projected by the oracle Holmes. This can also be inferred from Robert Gordon's claim that 'his influence, magnified into legend by the attention he has received, has helped to constitute the identity of the legal profession, the conception of the judicial function, and the role of the public intellectual in modern America culture'.[297]

But it is not that there is not love in the family of legal and 'general' pragmatism (hard and soft, masculine and feminine, metaphoric and ironic) or some complementary dialectical discursive relations that enable the interaction. The question is, of course, what do the children do, and what is the horizon of their choices in the promised land? The first generation of legal children of Holmes and Dewey are the Legal Realists. They represent the next step of the pragmatism of law. Their discourse will be described here as emerging in resistance to a general pragmatic discourse, this time within law.

Who were the Realists? Is their 'intellectual mood' that of progressivism, and in what way are they different from the generation that followed Holmes and preceded them? Grey clarifies in his Holmes article that 'all the leading Anglo-American legal thinkers of the period from about 1870 to 1920 were conceptualists in the same sense'[298] Holmes was. In that sense, they were different from the Realists 'breaking the general and abstract concepts of the law into narrow categories and type situations based in extra-legal experience'.[299] At the same time, they did not adhere to the Langdellian notion of legal science: 'They treated principles, categories, and taxonomies as instruments for use in the process of legal inquiry rather than its end result.'[300]

The term 'realism' itself needs clarification. There is an interesting opposition between what in philosophy was later termed 'the Realism-antirealism debate', and the way 'realistic jurisprudence' is perceived in the legal realm, which can demonstrate the specific role of legal thought in relation to the old style of philosophy.

Remember that in philosophy the word 'realism' often refers to the belief that

---

296 Id.
297 Gordon, *supra* note 238, at 5.
298 Grey, *supra* note 171, at 821.
299 Id., at 825.
300 Id.

abstract entities such as laws *really* exist, while in law 'realism' refers to the opposite, to the belief that abstract entities such as laws don't exist.[301]

When David Luban reminds us of this split, and when Michael S. Moore tries to revive a contemporary 'metaphysical realist' in the name of realism in philosophy,[302] they both have in mind a certain style of 'philosophy' that is scientific, logical, analytical, and positivistic. But more important is to see how their 'philosophical-professional' project is a refusal to take part in the philawsophy Holmes established and the Realist developed. Both refuse to acknowledge 'the life of the law'.

> General jurisprudence is not a possible enterprise for the skeptic, for it lacks a subject matter. Law (in general) and the legal system (in general) lack a context in which some sense could be made of them.[303]

Moore calls the Legal Realist an 'antirealist of the skeptical kind',[304] and grieves that 'the Legal Realists have so thoroughly applied their brand of philosophical antirealism to legal entities and qualities that it is difficult for us post-Realist generations even to understand what a Metaphysical Realist about law could believe'.[305] A Metaphysical Realist is an analytic-philosopher,

---

301 David Luban, 'What's Pragmatic about Legal Pragmatism', 18 *Cardozo L. Rev.* (1996), 43.
302 Michael S. Moore, 'The Interpretive Turn in Modern Theory: A Turn for the Worse?', 41 *Stan. L. Rev.* (1989) 871, 878: 'A metaphysical realist about some class of entities – say, real numbers in mathematics – is a person who holds certain particular versions of each of the metaphysical theories mentioned above. First, his ontology maintains both: (1) that the entities in question exists, and (2) that their existence is independent of any individual's mind or any community's conventions ... Second, a realist will hold a correspondence theory of truth, according to which the meaning of "is true" is given by the correspondence of some sentence to some mind and convention-independent state of affairs': id., at 878.
303 Id., at 888.
304 Id., at 877. And also at 888: 'Such a skeptic simply denies what both the legal realist and the legal conventionalist assert. Neither natural, moral, nor functional kinds exist for the skeptic; and the conventions relied upon by the conventionalist to define such kinds are completely indeterminate. Thinking this, the skeptic finds both legal texts (statutes, constitutions) and prior case decisions woefully indeterminate. His judge "interprets" legal texts by finding what he wants in them – for neither nature nor convention binds his interpretive efforts, the words of the legal texts becoming mere chameleons in his hands.'
  It is interesting to see how Moore imposes 'the interpretive turn', which happened after the Legal Realists' era, on their philosophical approach, which was probably based much more on the evolutionary idea of experience and not on interpretive incentives.
305 Id., at 972.

representing a distinct brand of a philosophical pathos that was evaded by pragmatism (later, this mode itself is evaded by the pragmatism of Rorty), and in a different way evaded by legal pragmatism. This mode of philosophizing seeks to analyze language and its relation to reality through yes and no questions and logical inquiry. It is interesting to see how, even under an analytical English lens, the legal pragmatist claims himself (him-the masculine type) as a distinct brand against the philosophical one. David Luban says it succinctly:

> Currently, pragmatism is often identified as a philosophical position that rejects the claim that practical activities require philosophical foundations. Grey goes further, arguing that legal pragmatism requires no philosophical foundations *including foundations in the philosophy that says the legal pragmatism requires no philosophical foundations*.[306]

Luban criticizes Grey's claim for *freestanding legal pragmatism*,[307] where Grey tries to show how pragmatism in law has emerged from the synthesis between the instrumentalist and contextualist strands in legal thought[308] (a mediation discussed above when referring to Grey's article on Holmes[309]). He also criticizes Holmes for his eclectic jurisprudence which can in no way be captured by an appeal to 'pragmatism'.[310] Philosophical pragmatism is, in his eyes, 'what used to be called "first philosophy", the subjects of metaphysics and epistemology, which nowadays include philosophical logic, meta-ethics, and the philosophies of the mind, of language, and of science'.[311] When he points above to the inconsistency in the claim that 'legal pragmatism requires no philosophical foundations, including foundations in the philosophy that says the legal pragmatism requires no philosophical foundation', I think he captures a deep truth of legal pragmatism: that indeed, mythological (impossible) self-foundation, autonomic life, kinship with the philosophic

---

306 Luban, *supra* note 301, at 46.
307 See Grey, *supra* note 206.
308 'The common lawyers and the utilitarian codifiers saw themselves and were seen by others as rival schools of legal theory presenting alternative and mutually inconsistent conceptions of law. The contribution of the American legal pragmatists, from Holmes through Roscoe Pound, Benjamin Cardozo, Karl Llewellyn, Lon Fuller, to Richard Posner, has been to argue instead that historical and instrumental jurisprudence present two compatible and equally necessary perspectives on the complex reality of law': id., at 24.
309 See *supra* text to notes 180–99.
310 Id., at 45.
311 Id., at 46.

strand, and, in a way, adoption of its basic ideas (no foundation; philosophy is no longer a hegemonic science), but a distinct character and a more 'tough-minded' approach. Legal pragmatism is an independent version of pragmatism, with a complex affinity to his philosophical sister.

But there is no universal 'first philosophy', as Luban would like to claim in favor of his criticism of Grey. There are only different philosophies, one near the other, and the legal one is indeed the tough-minded type. Luban examines the Realists using the philosophical analytic genre. Others use different lenses. As in this chapter's opening exchange, my effort to capture the Realist's pragmatic legacy will be trapped in the multifarious lenses that perceive them. The analytical philosophy is a later, marginal one within this spectacle (though it might dominate certain areas of law such as 'jurisprudence' at Harvard Law School[312]), and I will narrate the more hegemonic story as positing the 'realism' of the Realist (their 'reality principle'), the progress and the contribution of their writing, as the commitment to the pragmatic legal spirit.

This mainstream narration can be demonstrated by returning to Morton Horwitz:

> All Realists shared one basic premise – that the law had come to be out of touch with reality. Holmes' statement that 'the life of the law has not been logic, it has been experience' was its battle cry ... The perception that institutions were out of touch was not only a major theme of post-Lochner legal thought, but of American critical social thought generally ... The perception that law and life were out of sync produced many different forms of intellectual response. Many sought to show that while life had rapidly changed, law had lagged behind ... the distinction between law in books and law in action also led directly to an alliance between progressivism and reformist social science.[313]

The law was 'out of joint' with 'reality', according to the Realists, and there was then no analytical philosophic questioning of what reality is. Reality was the New Deal, was the World War just ended. 'The great depression and the early New Deal swept away the legitimating premises of the old order and

---

[312] For example, in a course of jurisprudence by Lewis Sargentich, offered in 1996–97, the rubric under which the Realists' ideas have been discussed was 'the predicament of Jurisprudence', differentiating between three types of liberal jurisprudence: 1. Formalism: Law as a formal doctrine (Langdell, Beal Weber); 2. Idealism: Law as Moral Reason: Idealism (Fiss, Fried); 3. Realism: Law as Political Choice (Frank, Llewellyn, Tushnet, Klare).

[313] Horwitz, *supra* note 129, at 188.

made things seem possible that just a short time before seemed impossible, if not illegitimate. Rebellion could be tolerated for a time.'[314] The prophet of the Legal Realist movement, Carl Llewellyn, is described as 'a rebel, a freak, a non-conformist'.[315] Another prominent figure in the movement, Jerome Frank, is described as suffering from a unique 'irreverence' and outright 'rebelliousness'.[316] N.E.H. Hull depicts them as the two 'enfants terribles'[317] who 'shook the legal heavens'.[318]

The figure of Llewellyn as a rebellious pragmatist-prophet becomes clearer when we compare him with another pragmatist who preceded him, Roscoe Pound. Actually, the whole emergence of the Realist movement is ascribed to the Pound-Llewellyn exchange regarding the existence and significance of 'a realist jurisprudence'.[319] ('The debate between Karl Llewellyn and Roscoe Pound over the future of American jurisprudence, in part a context of wills between the king and the would-be usurper, in part merely the public continuation of their private discourse, is perhaps the most famous controversy

---

[314] Id., at 187.
[315] Id., at 185.
[316] Id., at 177–8.
[317] N.E.H. Hull, *Roscoe Pound and Carl Llewellyn: Searching for an American Jurisprudence* (1997), 7.
[318] Id., at 8: 'Llewellyn's personal and professional ties to Frank were strong and fruitful. Between them, the two men carried the banner of legal realism. Llewellyn was skeptical of rules, and Frank worried that facts were little more than stories interested parties told, but between them they shook the legal heavens.'

See also Horwitz, *supra* note 129, at 175: '*Law and the Modern Mind* was published at a pivotal moment in the formation of the Legal Realist movement. If Llewellyn had coined the terms "Realism" only a few months before, Jerome Frank needs to be credited with first using the name "Legal Realism" in his book. It was through the collaboration between Llewellyn and Frank that a decision to proclaim the arrival of a new movement in legal thought crystallized, even as some of the named members of the movement refused to be drawn into any collective self-identification.'

[319] See Horwitz, *supra* note 129, at 170–71: 'Nothing has so shaped – and distorted – our picture of Legal Realism as the famous exchange over Realism between Karl Llewellyn and Roscoe Pound in 1930–1931. The list of twenty Realists complied by Llewellyn in response to Pound's criticism has completely dominated historians' subsequent understanding of the meaning and significance of Legal Realism ... Legal Realism received both its name and its designation as an intellectual movement when Llewellyn, a thirty-seven-year-old Columbia law professor, published an article in the *Columbia Law Review* of April 1930 entitled "A Realist Jurisprudence – The Next Step". Realism became famous when, a year later, the sixty-one-year-old dean of Harvard Law School, Roscoe Pound, at the height of his reputation as the only world class American legal thinker since Holmes, deigned to criticize realism.'

The Maturing of the Pragmatic Idea in Law and Society 75

in the history of American jurisprudence'.[320] I claim there is an equivalency between the relation of Dewey-James' general pragmatism to the Holmsian one, and the way Pound's sociological jurisprudence is related to the Realism of Llewellyn.[321] As in Dewey-Holmes' previous pragmatic play, the new jurisprudential constitutive act takes place in relation to another version of pragmatism, more pure in its theory (sociological), less political.

In the book, *Roscoe Pound and Karl Llewellyn: Searching for an American Jurisprudence*, Hull describes both Pound and Llewellyn as 'bricoleurs', who fix things 'by modifying whatever materials are at hand' to serve their purposes.[322]

> The bricoleur collects castoffs and odd items with the idea that they may be useful. So, too, did Pound and Llewellyn collect ideas from their vast reading of their predecessors in jurisprudence as well as of economists, social psychologists, sociologists and historians. They squirreled away ideas and then used them to construct their jurisprudential examinations of legal processes and the system of justice.[323]

Pound was borrowing from sociology,[324] while Llewellyn used 'new findings of economists'.[325] However, in Hull's text, the bricoleur is actually a pragmatist because, as in the Deweyan inscription above, he operates in a world where 'matter and form are fused and refused through problem-solving

---

320 Id., at 173.
321 For a discussion of this transition as related to the 'passage of American political, social, and intellectual history from a period dominated by the Progressive Movement to one dominated by the spirit of the New Deal', see G. Edward White, 'From Sociological Jurisprudence to Realism: Jurisprudence and Social Change in Early Twentieth-Century America', 58 *Va L. Rev.* 999 (1972).
322 Hull, *supra* note 317, at 10.
323 Id., at 10–11.
324 Id., at 12: 'Pound, voraciously curious, with his ability to speed-read, his command of nearly every European language, and his photographic memory, had access to an enormous range of ideas ... a great many of his writings themselves are summaries of others' scholarship on which he had implicitly drawn. In his three-part article in the *Harvard Law Review* on "sociological jurisprudence", for example, Pound reviewed the work of just about every important jurisprudent who preceded him in succinct and sharply etched summaries.'
    See also 44: 'Pound was formulating a new view of law and of science out of old materials, a *bricolage*, seeking an American jurisprudence by pruning away the errors of European thinkers and their American acolytes.'
325 Id., at 145. 'Llewellyn subscribed to the code of the *bricoleur*. And he tried to deploy the new findings of the economists in a way that Pound did not try to borrow from the sociologists.'

innovation'.[326] Llewellyn and Pound 'use' old and borrowed ideas to serve new purposes, but their myth-building is described by Hull through the pragmatic text, which has its own mythology ... It is still interesting to see how Pound's compact, all-encompassing sociological theory stands in contrast to Llewellyn's more complex legacy. Pound offers 'an orderly parade of schools and movements, each giving way to the next in an ever upward progress of jurisprudential acuity',[327] and is explicit in his organic perception of the law:[328]

> So if I were to write on jurisprudence, I should begin with the anatomy and histology of law as we know it now in civilized communities ... *It would not be necessary to define law.* Nothing organic can be defined ... It is like tying a string around a tree. The tree will grow and break the string. The law, too, will grow and break the strings tied about it by way of definition by past students, and learned writers have not availed to stop it ... The only thing to be insisted on is the futility of defining law or contending over a definition of it ...[329]

Llewellyn is more careful and ironic regarding a pervasive theory.[330] 'Pound, according to Llewellyn, had imposed a design of conscious causal process on what was undoubtedly an unconscious practical evolution followed by post hoc rationalizations. Pound was guilty of what Llewellyn later called, in his 1930 article, 'post-mortemizing'.[331] Again, we find the 'bad man's' insistent claim that, although the law (or philosophy) should not be defined, it still should, and it is this exact impossibility that should guide the jurist-intellectual.

---

326 See *supra* text to 93n.
327 Hull, *supra* note 317, at 2.
328 This has to do also with Pound's PhD in botany. See also id., at 44–5: 'He knew biology as well as he knew scholastic jurisprudence and hoped that concepts taken from the former could fill in the gaps left after he stripped the latter. He told Hershey, "Law like every super organic thing is essentially organic ..." Pound meant not an organism already evolved and now fixed in its morphology, but rather a living organism, changing and adapting ... The organic, evolutionary analogy thus refuted the positivist philosophy... The organic model was the "in" thing, and Pound's recourse to biology in an age when Darwinian models of human progress were all the rage could hardly be called original, but his gift was to catch the academic tide as it surged, not to anticipate it.'
329 Id., at 45–6.
330 Jerome Frank, *Law and The Modern Mind* (1970), 181: 'Pound was applauded for his views on the law as social engineering and his critique of mechanical jurisprudence, but blasted for his belief that somewhere beneath everything there was something definite and absolute. It was a remnant of the scholastic tendency to treat abstractions as independent entities.'
331 Id., at 146.

Perhaps the best course was to concentrate simply on what courts did (the conclusion of his 'New Trends'). At the very least, such an exploration would lead jurisprudents to examine all the tried and true categories of law. Researchers might test within the law to see if it is consistent and, from within, to see the effects of such classifications on actual outcomes.[332]

To live within law is better than to refute any definition altogether, or to provide a borrowed discipline to explain its essence. The scorn for 'pure theory' goes together with pragmatism, already common sense 'among our folk, as among the nations',[333] in Llewellyn's poetry. This new trend in legal thought has a progressive flavor, and a political and leftist antecedent and meta-discourse,[334] which were part of the 'post-World War I' reality (the Realist

---

332 Id., at 170.
333 Id., at 342: 'Among our folks, as among the nations/Justice is never a thing, but a quest./ The measure is always a little messed./But a man must manage without vacations/and, if he must, on shortened rations,/When questions press and press and are presses/For justice is never a thing but a quest/among our folk, as among the nations.'
334 A central contrast which is usually emphasized in the liberal contemporary narration of jurisprudential thought is the contrast of the conservatism of Pound and the activism leftist mode of Llewellyn. See *American Legal Realism, supra* note 219, at 50: By 1930, Pound had grown increasingly oracular and conservative. In the most shameful of his grand career, he was to accept an honorary degree from the University of Berlin in 1934. Llewellyn and Pound had by 1930 already divided over the Sacco and Vanzetti case, Pound keeping silent, Llewellyn offering a powerful radio address condemning the Massachusetts legal process on the eve of the execution. See also Horwitz, *supra* note 129, at 175: 'it is reasonable to suppose that Pound's silence affected Llewellyn's determination to characterize him as "a man partially caught in the traditional percept-thinking of an age that is passing" and one who showed "a tendency toward idealization of some portion of the status quo".'
  Hull describes in her book the correlation between Llewellyn's political involvement in the Sacco and Vanzetti case (two local activists in an anarchist workers' movement were accused and convicted of the South Braintree payroll robbery and murders. They were convicted and sentenced to death in a very controversial trial) and the later theoretical exchange with Pound. Hull depicts Pound as having a more 'cautious' approach (157–8: '... too open advocacy of the injustice of the case might jeopardize all that Pound had wanted to achieve ... Pound would certainly have jeopardized his deanship if he had gone public with his condemnation of the proceedings.') Llewellyn was more brave and 'did not weigh his vulnerability. He charged into the crusade from the condemned radicals, regardless of the consequences' (159–60). Hull claims that Llewellyn has used the responses he received for his petition against the execution as 'an index not of outrage of the fate of the two defendants, but of sympathy for his own views of law' (160). She tries to be apologetic for Pound and explains that although he found the petition 'too forthright on the merits of the case' (161), he wrote and promoted his own indirect protest. 'All in all, Pound's role in the Sacco-Vanzetti case and its aftermath helped to isolate him from his jurisprudential heirs because liberal view point was one index of the reformist jurisprudence' (166).

call) and the Great Depression. In fact, there is an 'external' aspect to this whole endeavor as part of an American effort for a scientification of law in a positivist direction, which depicts it as a social science. As Henry Schlegel (whom I discuss elsewhere[335]) suggests, the occupation with law as 'a scientific study, in the twentieth-century sense of science as an empirical inquiry into a world "out there",[336] was a central aspect of the Realists' work'. This emphasis of the Realists on facts (and also some aspects of the prediction theory of Holmes) is related to the American pragmatic sensitivity to the ordinary, to reality, and not to metaphysics, and can be read in Llewellyn's writing as well:

> Realism was first a way of looking at phenomena, letting that phenomena dictate their own arrangements and rules, rather than imposing general rules on the subject from the outside ... Realists, Karl Llewellyn knew, wanted to hold a realistic mirror to the law and then reformulate the law to match its realistic reflection.[337]

The appeal to social facts and the relation to social science were indeed a powerful call of the Realists. Still, its power, and the key to its becoming in a sense an orthodoxy are in its pragmatic repetition of the Holmsian call for a philosophy of the body. The earlier pragmatists such as Pound are now condemned for being too formal. The formalist, as in Duncan Kennedy's later description,[338] is the one who overestimates the power of any generality to establish a theory of law or to decide a concrete case. The powerful prophecy is the one that preserves the riddle, the pragmatic legal knot of the experience of the body, composed of rules, principles, and policies, and with less common-law elements. Another contrasting figure to bring forth in this context is that of Cardozo, with his 'philosophical' pragmatic style.

> Cardozo was one of the two greatest American common law judges of the twentieth century ... Cardozo's *The Nature of The Judicial Process* (1921), originally delivered as the Storrs Lectures at Yale Law School, remained perhaps

---

335 See the chapter 'Settled Law and the Law-That-Is-Not-but-Ought-To-Be: Hart and Sacks and The Pragmatic Philosophy of Dispute Resolution (Or: Why Couldn't Henry Hart Speak?)', parts 2.2.3, and 2.4.3.
336 John Henry Schlegel, *American Legal Realism and Empirical Social Sciences* (1995), 1.
337 N.E.H. Hull, 'Some Realism about the Llewellyn-Pound Exchange over Realism: The Newly Uncovered Private Correspondence 1927–1931', 1987 *Wisconsin L. Rev.* 921, 966 (1987).
338 See part 1.5 in this chapter.

the most widely read American work on legal thought for over half a century. No other book managed to capture the serene optimism of progressive jurisprudence or to convey its reformist conviction that 'the force which in our day and generation is becoming the greatest [influence] of them all, [is] the power of social justice ...'[339]

Horwitz, in the opening paragraph, narrates the progressive history, and his account of Cardozo, accordingly, posits him as managing 'to state the working premises of progressive jurisprudence'.[340]

> The confident ease with which Cardozo approached value questions captures one important tension within both pre-World War I Progressive jurisprudence and post-war Realism. In boldly disputing the legal positivism of Holmes ... and the analytical philosophers Austin, Holland, and Gray ... he asserted that it 'really matters' that 'the judge is under a duty to maintain a relation between law and morals, between the precepts of jurisprudence and those of reason and good conscience'.[341]

Cardozo 'portrayed judicial decision-making as more like a "strange compound which is brewed daily in the cauldron of the courts". The task was to let the different ingredients enter in varying proportions.'[342] It is more the hocus-pocus pragmatism of James that balances values than the rigorous study of Holmes, and this explains the popularity of Cardozo's writing. For Llewellyn and Frank, 'in the midst of the Great Depression' this analysis seemed 'to have been derived not from reason or analysis but from a generous but unrealistic faith in inevitable incremental progress'.[343]

> This contrast between Cardozo and Llewellyn does highlight the fact that there was a major shift toward value skepticism after the First World War. Legal Realists generally did not express the sort of self-assurance about values that Progressives were able regularly to muster.[344]

This is to say that it is not progressivism that is unique to Legal Realism in the internal jurisprudential narration, as was offered by Horwitz before.

---

339 Horwitz, *supra* note 129, at 189.
340 Id., at 190.
341 Id., at 191.
342 Id., at 192.
343 Id., at 190.
344 Id., at 191.

Progressives like Cardozo existed before, and they were pragmatic too. It is the inscription of a 'next step' of legal pragmatism, in the form of a rigorous re-enchantment with the body, through a rebellious gesture.

Dealing with 'real life' is considered being 'functional' at the time of the Realists and applies to social sciences in the Realists' era,[345] but it is not that this appeal has not been made before, as Grey said above.[346] It is that a new progressive spirit is built into an old Holmsian legacy, this rebellious act coming from Yale and Columbia against the canonical position of Harvard.[347] The tough-man-paradigm study of the law[348] is becoming the Wesley Newcomb Hohfeld's ('wonder boy from Yale') 'seminal' [349] article, 'Some Fundamental Legal Conceptions as Applied in Judicial Reasoning'.[350]

> The jurisprudential contribution of Hohfeld's *Some Fundamental Legal Conceptions* was, in its essence, a pragmatic exercise ... Hohfeld's analytical schema of jural relations was pragmatic to the extent that he tried to connect legal symbols to the human relationships they described. He did not believe in abstractions called 'rights' and 'duties'. He insisted that they be defined in relation

---

[345] See Laura Kalman, *Legal Realism at Yale 1927–1960* (1986), 96: 'The realists of the 1920s and 1930s are frequently remembered as revolutionaries who brought social sciences, social policy, and the functional approach into the classroom.'

[346] See *supra* text to note 217–note 220.

[347] Kalman, *supra* note 345, XI: 'Have there ever been two cities in such close proximity as New Haven and Cambridge so different in their atmosphere?' Harvard Law School professor Felix Frankfurter once asked Yale's Thurman Arnold. It is tempting to concur with this sharp contrast between Harvard and Yale. Certainly they have differed in the realms of legal theory and education. Indeed, so much of legal education at Yale has represented a rebellion against the Harvard approach that it would be impossible to understand Yale without studying Harvard.

And at 3: 'For well over a hundred years, the structure and content of legal training have followed the strictures of Harvard and Langdell. During the 1920s and the 1930s, however, a group of scholars known as legal realists developed a jurisprudence that challenged this education as having detrimental effects on unsuspecting students. Their attack grew out of their contempt for the conceptualistic legal theory upon which the Harvard training was based.'

[348] Hull, *supra* note 317, 105: 'He likened the application of his schema to find the "lowest common denominator of the law" through which "comparison becomes easy, and fundamental similarity may be discovered ... By such a process it becomes possible not only to discover essential similarities and illuminating analogies in the midst of what appears superficially to be infinite and hopeless variety, but also to *discern common principles of justice and policy underlying the various jural problems solved*".'

[349] Id., at 102.

[350] Wesley Newcomb Hohfeld, 'Some Fundamental Legal Conceptions as Applied in Judicial Reasoning', 23 *Yale L. J.* 16, (1913).

The Maturing of the Pragmatic Idea in Law and Society

to human beings ... He looked at the practical effect of legal relationships to distinguish many types of relationships and tried to apply more descriptive terms to label them.[351]

Hull continues to suggest that 'this singular piece of scholarship turned out to be a watershed for the Yale Law School, legal education, and American jurisprudence', and says that 'Pound's "sociological" approach differed considerably from Hohfeld's analytical one, but in the same fashion as David Hume's philosophical works stirred Immanuel Kant from his repose, so Hohfeld was stimulated by Pound's work.'[352] The analogy illustrates again the philawsophical pathos and pragmatic megalomania of the legal American legend, 'of law and life':[353] Pound is posited as David Hume. Hohfeld is awakened from his dogmatic slumber by him.

The marriage (following the Holmsian engagement) between social sciences and law is announced in the name of a call against the traditional legal education Harvard offered, considered 'blind, inept, factory-ridden, wasteful, defective, and empty'.[354]

> As the new century unfolded, it became clear that the vision of law held by Harvard conceptualists had not become reality. Litigation exploded ... Despite the best efforts of the conceptualist to identify the proper legal principles that would determine future judicial decisions ... legal certainty has disappeared ... Functionalism sought to aid the lawyer who confronted the welter of conflicting precedents and wondered which a judge would apply. The realists looked to the social sciences to help them reform jurisprudence. A determination to integrate law with the social sciences pervaded their functionalism... Their functionalism preached that law was one of the social sciences and that the social sciences should be examined to illuminate social policy. As Llewellyn said, 'The same acts of the same human beings are raw stuff for psychology, sociology, social psychology, economics, or law, or history, according to the chosen line of abstraction and of context'. Just as the same 'raw stuff' existed for all, so did the 'same inquiry: 'Whither do we want society to move?"[355]

---

351 Hull, *supra* note 317, at 104.
352 Id., at 102.
353 This is the name of a book written by Felix Frankfurter, later a Justice in the Supreme Court famous for his Harvard-like pragmatic approach. Felix Frankfurter, *Of Law and Life & Other Things that Matter* (1965).
354 Kalman, *supra* note 345, at 67.
355 Id., at 17–18.

This coupling with the social sciences disappears in one sense,[356] and reaches its peak (and end) in another, in the Legal Process jurisprudence, in what I will term the pragmatic philosophy of dispute resolution.[357] After the postwar, when the theoretical debate will wear an interpretive mode, there will be no more room for such 'realism'.[358]

'The polarities in Llewellyn's personality and intellect',[359] which Horwitz describes and Hull pictures, recall the old pragmatic couple James-Holmes, and suit a typical pragmatic descendent. The description of the complexity of his personality hints at his role as the new mythological prophet, the founder of a movement.[360]

> Though 'an emotional and intuitive ... person' – 'someone with poetic tendencies' – he loved 'technical complexity' in the law and chose commercial law, often regarded as 'one of the most prosaic and technical ... subjects ... '. Though he had an 'intensely religious nature', he was fanatically hostile to 'contemporaneous polysyllabic professionalized academic' philosophy. 'What the hell has Kant to do with *my* course on jurisprudence?' he thundered at a student who submitted a paper on the Kantian distinction between the 'is' and the 'ought'.[361]

---

356 Kalman describes in her book the decline of the unique style of Realism which developed at Yale until the 1940s and the incorporation of this tradition into the canon of Harvard formalism during the 1950s. The convergence of the Harvard–Yale legal education has resulted in much less emphasis on social sciences in the 1950s curriculum.

357 See the chapter 'Settled Law and the Law-That-Is-Not-But-Ought-To-Be: Hart and Sacks and the Pragmatic Philosophy of Dispute Resolution (Or: Why Couldn't Henry Hart Speak?)'.

358 For a discussion of the contemporary split in jurisprudential thinking of law and 'reality', and the discussion of Richard Posner's emphasis on the social sciences to promote a new professional identity in law, see the chapter 'Taking Side: Margins of Phases of Pragmatics of Legal Process Disciples (Or: the Pragmatists That We Are)'.

359 Id., at 186.

360 A quite equivalent fascination with the polarities in Llewellyn's personality can be found in William Twining, *Karl Llewellyn and the Realist Movement* (1973), ix: 'At first sight it may seem that few jurists can stake as strong a claim to singularity as Karl Llewellyn: the only American ever to have been awarded the Iron Cross; the most fertile and inventive legal scholar of his generation; legal theory's most colorful personality since Jeremy Bentham; the only common lawyer known to have collaborated successfully with an anthropologist on a major work; a rare example of a law-teacher poet; the chief architect of the most ambitious common law code of recent times; the most romantic of legal realists, the most down-to earth of legal theorists; the most ardently evangelical of legal skeptics; the most unmethodical of methodologists, and the least convertible of claims, the professor of one of the most exotic prose styles in all legal literature.'

361 Id.

The 'tough-minded' image characterizing Holmes before, against his 'philosophical' partners, plays here again, where the 'Realist' jurist is the one who commits himself (in Llewellyn's time it is probably only him-self) to 'work to depict the institution of law as it is, the law in action, and to do so vigorously and fairly'.[362] As in Holmes' diverse accounts of 'the legal elephant', which were a *bricolage* consisting of the existing ideas of his time, the Realist school has also many voices, different responses to the legal discourse of that era. Still, this jurisprudence is characterized as 'tough' and devoted to work, the man-like version of the legal discourse.

> As Cardozo put the matter, 'Realists', like Cardozo himself, are those who find that 'considerations of analogy, of convenience, of policy, and of justice' overwhelm the 'old jurisprudence of conceptions'. Llewellyn's was not a definition meant to foment debate; on the other hand, his fashioning of a 'movement' from it made it fairer game for attack. However bland Llewellyn's 'Realism', his was a critical concept – for what were judges and lawyers and academicians doing if they were not part of his 'Realist jurisprudence', if they were not tough-mindedly examining what law was actually about?[363]

But a tough-minded examination of 'what law was actually about' is an empty commitment. Like the prediction theory and the 'bad-man' insistence, there is no assured salvation in 'the work', because 'the work' is itself a metaphor, a discursive construct, a deep mythical organizing focus for the pragmatic jurist.

Coming back to some of Llewellyn's key terms used in support of his jurisprudential approach, we find the reinforcement of Holmes' pragmatic idea of the life of the law.

> His stylistic informality led him to coin phrases like 'situation sense' and 'law-stuff', which occasionally illuminate, but more often communicate a certain suffocating technocratic or scientific sensibility. Realism was 'a sound, horse sense technology'.[364]

The scorn for general propositions determining a case is repeated in this context; the appeal is to the 'concrete instance', where the crucial moment is the bottom line, and not the use of policy argument instead of legal rules. In

---

362 *American Legal Realism, supra* note 219, at 51.
363 Id., at 51–2.
364 Horwitz, *supra* note 129, at 186.

Joseph Singer's *Legal Realism Now*[365] this combination is described as an ambivalence between the making and finding functions of the judge. On the one hand, judges choose between conflicting lines of precedent, between broad and narrow interpretations of cases. On the other hand, 'the realists often made it seem as if judges could make these policy and precedential judgments without injecting personal political commitments into their decision making'.[366] This style of belief in rational thinking which works from the inside is unique to the pragmatism of law.[367]

> We have discovered in our teaching of the law that general propositions are empty. We have discovered that students who come eager to learn the rules and who do learn them, *and who learn nothing more,* will take away the shell and not the substance. We have discovered that rules *alone,* mere forms of words, are worthless. We have learned that the concrete instance, the heaping up of concrete instances, the present, vital memory of concrete instances, is necessary in order to make any general proposition, be it rule of law or any other, *mean* anything at all. Without the concrete instances the general proposition is baggage, impedimenta, stuff about the feet.

The Holmsian definition of law is repeated by Llewellyn in a more casual, 'common sense-like' terms:

> This doing of something about disputes, this doing of it reasonably, is the business of law. And the people who have the doing in charge, whether they be judges or sheriffs or clerks or jailers or lawyers, are officials of the law. *What these officials do about disputes is, to my mind, the law itself.*[368]

Law has a business, and to know it is a matter of professional investment and intensive work of the diverse actors around the dispute. Each has his own perspective, his working legitimate concept of the law. This formula, which is very appealing in its pragmatic structure (the doing, the experience, the work which cannot be reduced to generalities) focuses on the dispute as the organizing force for experience. After the post-war era, there is an effort to suppress and forget this orientation, and the pragmatic sensitivities are transformed to other

---

365 Joseph William Singer, 'Legal Realism Now', *Cal. L. Rev.* 467 (1988).
366 Id., at 502.
367 In John Dawson there is a parallel tension between what he defines as 'the overriding need for skepticism' and the need to supplement the law from other disciplines like economy, psychology and sociology. John Dawson, 'Legal Realism and Legal Scholarship', *J. Legal Educ.* 406, 407–8 (1983).
368 Karl N. Llewellyn, *The Bramble Bush: On Our Law and its Study* (1951) 12.

areas. But in Holmes' time, the practitioner's point of view is crucial for the theory of law. The metaphor for the legal worker is organic and the relation of the jurist to his materials in his world is that of a scientist to nature.

> The conception of law in flux, of moving law, and of judicial creation of law ... The conception of society in flux, and in flux typically faster than the law, so that the probability is always given that any portion of law needs reexamination to determine how far it fits the society it purports to serve.[369]

The Holmsian fascination with generalities, and the commitment to the rigorous study of the law as the core message of Realism for coming generations, becomes clearer when we consider the nearly forgotten 'marginal' Realism of Jerome Frank (the second 'enfant terrible' who carried the Realist banner with Llewellyn[370]). Frank took a more extreme critical position toward mainstream legal tradition, and had some constructive ideas of how to handle the study of law. He chose a different path to support a dispute resolution focus.[371]

> Whereas other Realists attributed the lawyer's inability to predict future decisions to the appellate judge's idiosyncratic manipulation of legal rules in the opinion, Frank placed most of the blame on the subjectivity of the facts. Once Frank himself became an appellate court judge in 1941, his faith in the appellate judge's consistency in using legal rules grew even stronger. By the late 1940s, he had abandoned his earlier interest in the appellate courts and had come to focus almost exclusively on the trial courts.[372]

This focus on the trial courts, and the idea that 'in contested cases, the trial judge's or the jury's findings of facts might bear no resemblance to the past events in dispute',[373] are accompanied by Frank's hope 'to induce thinking

---

369 Karl N. Llewellyn, 'Some Realism About Realism – Responding to Dean Pound', in *American Legal Realism, supra* note 219, at 72.
370 See *supra* note 318 and accompanying text.
371 For a discussion of Frank's idea of a clinical 'lawyers' school' see the chapter 'In Search of the Dispute: On Lawyers and Legal Philawsophers at Harvard Law School (Or: Some Private Hope and Public Irony)', part 4.4.
372 Kalman, *supra* note 345, at 165.
373 Id. 'First, testimony was fallible: witnesses sometimes lied, and honest witnesses frequently erred in observing events, in remembering their observations, and in communicating their memories to the courtroom. Second, trial judges and juries were imperfect: the personality and past of the judge or jury members might interfere with an accurate determination of who, if any, of the disagreeing witnesses, was telling the truth. It followed

about practicable new methods of bringing the judicial "findings" of fact closer to the "objective" facts as they actually occurred'.[374] The 'objective facts' exist within this discourse, like 'the ordinary' of Cavell above, and in fact, Frank uses 'ordinary language' philosophy to promote the transformation of law schools into clinical laboratories for the study of the ordinary,[375] for the search of the pragmatic experience.[376] His estimation that 'decisions of trial courts determined the fate of 98 percent of all litigated cases'[377] and the call 'to abandon an obsessively exclusive concentration on the rules'[378] took in Frank's time an academic theoretical mode. In Yale Law School, he tried to develop a clinical orientation.[379] He 'proposed that, just as medical students attended medical operations, so law students should attend "legal operations" in the trial and appellate courts'.[380] He spoke of developing a 'lawyers' school', and 'repeatedly stressed that the ideal law school "resemble a sort of sublimated law office". At its heart would be a legal clinic staffed by full-time professors who had considerable experience in practicing law and students who would serve as the professors' assistants.'[381]

But despite the fact that Frank's realism was 'formally' equivalent to, and perhaps even contained, Llewellyn's, as Frank himself suggested,[382] his voice does not reverberate like that of his counterpart. Putting aside his character as more extreme, and the problematic of his constructive ideas for a professionalization process of academic elite law schools as distinct from trade

---

that a trial court's decision in a case where oral testimony is conflicting, is usually the result of the combination of (1) a legal generalization – a particular law, i.e., a rule or principle – and (2) a unique subjective feature called the "facts". The "particular law", being a generalization, is not unique. But the particular decision is unique – since it is a product in part of something that cannot be generalized, i.e., the subjective reaction (of the trial court or jury) to the facts.'

374 Id., at 167.
375 See Jerome Frank, *Courts on Trial: Myth and Reality in American Justice* (1950).
376 See more discussion on this matter on the chapter 'In Search of the Dispute: On Peace Making and Law Teaching at Harvard Law School (Or: Some Private Hope and Public Irony)', part 4.4.
377 Id., at 166.
378 Id.
379 Id., at 171–2: 'Frank hoped that his reforms would be adopted at Yale, and Yale Law School became, as Felix Frankfurter observed, Frank's "spiritual home". Although he did not begin teaching fact-finding at the law school until 1946, he became a research associate there in 1932, thus beginning twenty five years of a loose affiliation with Yale.'
380 Id., at 170.
381 Id., at 171.
382 Id., at 166.

schools and as ideologically 'not practical',[383] something in his pragmatism could not preserve the Holmsian legacy. Maybe the aesthetic beauty of experiencing the generalities of legal rules could not be preserved in its obscurity when coming to facts. That is so if, as Frank suggested, the following is true:

> If legal certainty were to exist ... the lawyer had to be able to predict the court's decision in a future case. Such prediction called for 'an ability to foretell the facts'.[384]

> No one can predict the facts of a suit not yet commenced. Therefore no one can predict a court's decision in such a suit, even if all the rules are as fixed as the North Star.[385]

So maybe it is better to remain with the bad man's insistence regarding rules and leave the facts as not having academic interest. Through the intellectual legal perspective of today, which assumes a reality, which is barred in principle, this focus on the link to the actual disputes cannot be addressed. In Frank's writing, the skeptical position is posited as the natural mature development toward liberation from the father's authority.

> To the child the father is the infallible judge, the Maker of definite rules of conduct. He knows precisely what is right and what is wrong and, as head of the family sits in judgment and punishes misdeeds. The Law – a body of rules apparently devised for infallibly determining what is right and what is wrong and for deciding who should be punished for misdeeds – inevitably becomes a partial substitute for the Father-as-Infallible-Judge. That is, the desire persists in grown men to recapture, through a rediscovery of a father, a childish,

---

383 Id., at 186: 'The New Deal, as Jerold Auerbach has observed, had been a lawyer's deal. It had signaled the rise of the legal profession to a position of power within the national government. War had propelled lawyers even higher. When virtually every important official in the government – including the president – was a lawyer, it was not difficult to understand why law professors resisted proposals that would revolutionize legal education. Ultimately, perhaps, the most effective rejoinder to such complacency was Frank's: Harvard and Yale men controlled the country in spite of their legal education rather than because of it. Yet law professors were impervious to such observations. They placed too much faith in themselves and not enough in their students. *For Harvard and Yale professors alike, intellectual schizophrenia once again impeded change. As a lawyer and an academic, the law professor was bound to find lawyer-schools and policy science-schools repugnant*' (my italics, M.A.).
384 Id., at 165.
385 Id. This is the 'Frankian' message of the Holmsian prediction theory of law, but it is much more explicit in its impossibility.

completely controllable universe, and that desire seeks satisfaction in a partial, unconscious, anthropomorphizing of Law, in ascribing to the Law some of the characteristics of the child's Father-Judge. *That childish longing is an important element in the explanation of the absurdly unrealistic notion that law is, or can be made, entirely certain and definitely predictable*[386] (my italics, M.A.).

But this is not so simple. As Horwitz suggests, the 'dramatic and simple vision' of the book 'is proclaimed as if the writer is offering a blinding new truth to a humanity in darkness'.[387] In the legal realm, there is less appeal to 'new truths', offered by an 'irreverence' who acts 'in bad taste'.[388] The more balanced, ironic position is welcomed.

By adopting a libidinal perspective and trying to get rid 'of the need for father authority'[389] in law, Frank draws nigh to Grey's contemporary reading of Holmes' pragmatism, which says, 'Don't be obsessive with your theories.' It is interesting to examine in this context how he describes Holmes as 'the completely adult jurist'.[390]

> *The great value of Holmes as a leader is that his leadership implicates no effort to enslave his followers.* It would be grossly misusing his example to accept his judicial opinions or views on any question of law as infallible. It may well be assumed that he would be the readiest to urge a critical reconsideration of any doctrine he has announced. He has attained an adult emotional status, a self-reliance, a fearless approach to life, and, we repeat, he invites others to do likewise. We might say that, being rid of the need of a strict father, he can afford not to use his authority as if he, himself, were a strict father.[391]

---

386 Frank, *supra* note 330., at 259.
387 Horwitz, *supra* note 129, at 176.
388 Id., at 177.
389 Frank, *supra* note 330., at 259.
390 Id., at 270. His description of William James is interesting in its contrast to Holmes', who seems to have been born already mature. Id., at 18: 'William James' career is suggestive. As a young man "a sense of insecurity of life", a consciousness of a "pit of insecurity beneath the surface of life", so obsessed him that he was sized with that morbid melancholy "which takes the form of panic fear" and reached the point of suicidal mania. He might, he reports, have gone insane, if he had not clung to scripture-texts such as "The eternal God is my refuge". Suddenly he was "cured". And the cure consisted in a sudden shift to the positive delight in the hazardous, incalculable character of life. Life's very insecurity became its most inviting aspect.'
   The philosophical pragmatic discourse that aims to cover an insecurity, to recover a hysteria, to acknowledge and enjoy the incalculable character of life stands in contrast to the more obsessive pragmatic legal discourse which possesses a body and is occupied with knowing 'it'.
391 Id., at 276.

Holmes – the Brahmin, the Yankee from the Olympus of Beacon Hill in Boston – functions in Frank's work as 'the name of the father', as described in Jacques Lacan's text:[392] the symbolic origin of authority and law, deriving its power from its contradictory existence as substituting and at once constituting a metaphoric lack. In contrast to Lacan, this symbolic origin is functioning within the world of law (and not language), and in a concrete historical context, that of America and its pragmatic discursive coupling.

> If, like Holmes, we win free of the myth of fixed authoritarian law, having neither to accept law because from an authority resembling the father's, nor to reject it for like reason, we shall, for the first time, begin to face legal problems squarely. Without abating our insistence that the lawyers do the best they can, we can then manfully endure inevitable short-comings, errors and inconsistencies in the administration of justice because we can realize that perfection is not possible. The legal profession will then for the first time be in a position to do its work well.[393]

We have to learn neither to accept law because of its authority nor to reject it from that reason; instead, we should approach the 'problems squarely'. Then we can 'manfully endure' the inevitable 'shortcomings and inconsistencies'. The salvation is guaranteed in the balanced position of 'the work' on the concrete problems of dispute resolution, and under the metaphor of manful endeavor. This masculine pragmatic approach to pragmatic dispute resolution will find some articulation in the Legal Process Materials, and will be built into a much more harmonious and optimistic mediating picture, but later it will decline and be suppressed. A current revival of this idea, elaborated in its psychological-psychoanalytical emphasis, can be found in the negotiation literature at Harvard today.[394] Through pragmatism as 'common sense', and social sciences, which are embedded in a pragmatic epistemology, 'rule' skepticism and 'fact' skepticism are now celebrated again, but this time within a utopic approach to dispute resolution, and a feminine hysteric style of overcoming obstacles. What was considered radical and oppositional has become common sense nowadays, and the post-World War II era plays a crucial role in this process. The birth and growth of the pragmatic idea in law until the Realists' time is the foundation on which the next post-post-war rupture will occur.

---

392 Jacques Lacan is a French post-structural psychoanalyst scholar who offers a textual reading of Freud.
393 Id., at 277.
394 See the chapter 'In Search of The Dispute: On Lawyers and Legal Philawsophers at Harvard Law School: (Or: Some Private Hope and Public Irony)'.

The fascination with concepts, with logic and mathematical indexical lines, has remained since Holmes a primary characteristic of the legal intellectual. In law, this pathos is still allowed. In an ironic way, it is like Felix Cohen's 1935 description of the Von Ihering heaven (or hell?) of legal concepts.

> Some fifty years ago a great German jurist had a curious dream. He dreamed that he died and was taken to a special heaven reserved for the theoreticians of the law. In this heaven one met, face to face, the many concepts of jurisprudence in their absolute purity, freed from all entangling alliance with human life. Here were the disembodied spirits of good faith and bad faith, property, possession, *laches*, and rights *in rem*. Here were all the legal instruments needed to manipulate and transform these legal concepts and thus to create and to solve the most beautiful of legal problems. Here one found a dialectic-hydraulic-interpretation press, which could press an indefinite number of meanings out of any text or statute, an apparatus for constructing fictions, and a hair-splitting machine that could divide a single hair into 999,999 equal parts and, when operated by the most expert jurists, could split each of these parts again into 999,999 equal parts. The boundless opportunities of this heaven of legal concepts were open to all properly qualified jurists, provided only they drank the Lethean draught which induced forgetfulness of terrestrial human affairs. But for the most accomplished jurists the Lethean draught was entirely superfluous. They had nothing to forget.[395]

Is not the heaven of legal concepts still the sole home of the jurist-intellectual? Does 'the functional approach' directly encounter 'terrestrial human affairs', or is it still haunted by the idea that generalities do not decide concrete cases? If it is, but still insists on being innovative and critical, is it not suggesting the same formalist intellectual heaven-hell of aimless speculations, 'freed from all entangling alliance with human life?'. The difference is seemingly buried in the Holmsian idea of experience that the Realists have internalized (the children who went to progressive schools).[396]

Coming back to Horwitz' initial presentation of the significance of realism in law, and White's account of progressivism and the revolt against formalism in society, this section concludes by suggesting that the pragmatic mythological fall of philosophy in American society (which I somewhat characterize as feminine in my text) was accompanied by the revival of her (him) in law, and though what is left are only the various lenses through which to re-read this

---

[395] Felix Cohen, 'Transcendental Nonsense and the Functional Approach', 35 *Colum. L. Rev.* 809 (1935).
[396] See *supra* text to 312n.

The Maturing of the Pragmatic Idea in Law and Society 91

origin, it can still be narrated (from here and now) as the rise of philawsophy, of the belief in the life of the law, the life of the context. This process might have parallels in other professionalization processes, and in other disciplines and discourses. The next section suggests that at the turn of the current century it seems like this mode of professionalization and 'philawsophizing' is declining in favor of ideals that will be examined in other chapters.

1.5 Three Legal Prophets

Holmes and Llewellyn were the prophets of the first two stages of the pragmatism of law, but the mythology of living within law is not done, neither does the operation through different modes of pragmatism and in resistance to it. My next chapters try to map and describe the transformations of theoretical thought in terms of the argument presented above, but in this concluding part of the first chapter I would like to describe a contemporary progressive legal prophet, the assumed leader of the Critical legal studies movement in law.[397]

Duncan Kennedy, who on many occasions is described as the 'son of the Realists', in 1991 gives a contemporary manifestation of the Holmsian enchantment with the legal body:

> Although *A Semiotic of Legal Argument*, to which this is a European introduction, was written for an American audience, it is shamelessly European-theoretical in its approach. It is an attempt to summarize and extend one of the innovations of American legal studies – the appropriation for the analysis of legal argument of the structuralism of Saussure, Levi-Strauss and Piaget. The American introduction gives a post-modern, specifically Derridian, gloss to the enterprise.[398]

To be European is to be 'shamelessly theoretical', and even if this is true, what is it to be all American legal scholar? First of all, for Kennedy, it is taking the challenge of re-reading the American-Realist enterprise as already capturing the European contemporary 'post' theory. 'What we have appropriated these famous European for is the American project of radicalizing

---

397 The location of Kennedy in relation to other contemporary scholars from left and right is discussed in the chapter 'Taking Sides: Margins and Phases of Pragmatics of 'Legal Process' Disciples (Or: The Pragmatists That We Are)', part 3.1.
398 Duncan Kennedy, 'A Semiotics of Legal Argument', in *Essays on Adjudication 1973–1996*, 309, 317.

legal realism.'[399] One of the objections he depicts for his semiotic project in the European introduction is that his argument is 'just "no rule can determine the scope of its own application", well known since Wittgenstein, obvious to anyone who has read Derrida'.[400] When answering this claim, I understand him as returning to the old evasion in the idea of experience, the idea that decision-making is a natural 'happening'. It is no longer organic, but an event that is theoretically uninteresting, and lacks the painful medium of the choice Derrida circles.

> This article does not attempt to establish that policy analysis (broadly conceived) can or can't do anything. It describes how policy analysis works in practice – that is, what its textual content is and how practitioners manipulate it by operating on the elements of that given content. As a matter of fact, it appears that practitioners sometimes use policy argument to generate in their audience the experience of the necessity of a particular choice of rule definition. But this article does no more than describe the tools with which they sometimes succeed and sometimes fail at this task.[401]

The idea that there is a practice in which 'policy analysis works', and that 'the use' of policy argument is enabled to generate the experience of 'necessity of a particular choice of rule definition', which sometimes succeeds and sometimes fails, recurs in Kennedy's more recent book *A Critique of Adjudication*, when describing legal formality.[402] After distinguishing between two senses of formalism – denial of policy and overestimation of generalities in a particular case – he concludes by saying:

> Neither in the first nor the second sense is formalism a *method* distinct from deduction. It can be invalidated as a theory of law, but it can't be invalidated or disproved as a method, because it is a mistaken use of a method that is sometimes valid, rather than a method in itself.[403]

Formalism is a method that sometimes succeeds and sometimes not, like deduction. This implies that there is, in experience, some transparent possibility to 'apply' a norm, or to 'deduce' an outcome in a non-problematic way. An equivalent idea is repeated in his rich account of *Freedom and Constraint in*

---

399 Id.
400 Id.
401 Id., at 321.
402 Duncan Kennedy, *A Critique of Adjudication (Fin de Siecle)* (1997), 105–7.
403 Id., at 106–7.

Adjudication: A Critical Phenomenology,[404] when discussing 'the work'[405] of adjudicating. He suggests that 'one of the ways in which we experience law ... is as a medium in which one pursues a project, rather than as something that tells us what we have to do'.[406] In his words, 'Law constrains as a physical medium.'

> The metaphor of a physical medium does not help us solve the problem of just how constraining the law is. All it does is suggest that we should understand both freedom and constraint as aspects of the experience of work – chosen projects constrained by material properties of the medium – rather than thinking in the back of our mind of a transcendentally free subject who 'could do anything', contrasted with a robot programmed by the law.[407]

Freedom and constraint 'are aspects of the experience of work', and in the background there is the assumption of a sovereign, natural given subject who goes through the experience. I find the above descriptions embedded in the legacy of Holmes and his pragmatism.

> In the alternative post-modern version, it is wrong to interpret 'difference' as a logically necessary aspect of interpretation – it is merely an event that sometimes subverts the aspiration to presence through textuality. To elevate it to a logical necessity – to treat it as something inevitable, a 'truth' – would land us in the aporetically self-invalidating position of affirming the truth of the impossibility of truth, while the same time denying the actual experience of determinacy. Deconstruction is rather an event brought about by someone doing the work of deconstruction; whether it will 'happen' in any given case cannot be known in advance no matter how sure the deconstructer may feel that he or she will succeed.[408]

---

404 Duncan Kennedy, 'Freedom and Constraint in Adjudication: A Critical Phenomenology', in *Essays on Adjudication 1973–1996*, 45.
405 'The judge is neither free nor bound. I don't see it that way from inside the situation. From inside the situation, the question is, where am I going to deploy the resources I have available for this case? The issue is how should I direct my *work* to bring about an outcome that accords with my sense of justice. My situation as a judge (initial perceived conflict between "the law" and how-I-want-to-come-out) is thus quite like that of a lawyer who is brought a case by a client and on first run-through is afraid the client will lose. The question is, will this first impression hold up as I set to work to develop the best possible case on the other side?': id., at 49.
406 Id., at 53.
407 Id., at 54.
408 Kennedy, *supra* note 398, 322.

Difference is an 'event' that sometimes subverts the aspiration of presence; deconstruction sometimes 'happens' and sometimes does not. There is a given natural reality of 'someone doing the work of deconstruction', and above all, there is the experience of it, which may work or not, in correlation with what the interpreter feels. This is the experience of the pragmatist, who 'uses' theories and generalities while staying on a different level. This 'spectator' position is accompanied by a very sincere interest in mapping and playing with the 'body' of the law, with a legal universe composed of 'argument bytes', policy arguments 'in favor of or against a particular resolution of a gap, conflict or ambiguity in the system of legal rules'.[409] These bytes become language itself, and the structuralist message in Strauss[410] and Saussure[411] applies to them and inspire their emergence.

> As I see it, there are three basic elements to the proposed semiotic of legal argument. These are: (1) The idea of reducing the 'parole' of legal argument to a 'langue' composed of argument-bites (2) the idea of relating the bites to one another through 'operations', and (3) the idea of 'nesting', or the reproduction, in the application of a doctrinal formula, of the confrontation between argument-bytes that the formula purported to resolve.[412]

The application of the 'langue' and 'parole' distinction to the American vocabulary of legal argument are, in my view, part of the same Holmsian idea of 'the life of the law', of Grey's legal elephant that has become the sole world of the legal jurist. A certain discursive legal activity becomes a life, a body to examine, and within that life, philosophy is also allowed today.

To claim that words 'get their meaning' not from the things or ideas they signify

---

[409] Id., at 325.
[410] The source in structuralism of the idea of reducing legal argument to bites was Levi-Strauss's discussion of *bricolage* in the first chapter of *The Savage Mind*. Levi-Strauss relativizes the distinction between rationality or technical reasoning and the activity of myth making. In spite of its pretension to fit precisely whatever phenomenon it addresses, technical reasoning is inevitably the 'jerry-building' (*bricolage*) of an edifice out of elements borrowed from here and there, elements initially meant for other purposes (and themselves therefore jerry-built of yet other, earlier bits and pieces). Legal argument, understood as the deployment of stereotyped pro and con argument fragments, seems a particularly good example of *bricolage* masquerading as hyper-rationality: id., 352.
[411] 'This article attempts a further incorporation of structuralist ideas by recasting the "canons" analysis of argument-bites in the terms of F. Saussure, *Course in General Linguistics*. This represents a circuitous return to origin, since the idea of *bricolage* was itself an adaptation of the Saussurian theory of the sign': id., at 353.
[412] Id., at 351.

but from their relationship with other words is often presented in a way that is, to put it mildly, mystifying. I want here to make an analogous claim about argument bytes, but one that seems to me relatively straight-forward ...

To say that the 'meaning' of 'no liability without fault' depends on its existence in relationship to 'as between two innocents, he who caused damage should pay', is to say that if we imagine eliminating the latter phrase from the vocabulary of argument-bytes, then 'no liability without fault' would *ipso facto* become a different, and likely a more powerful and valuable argument than it is when it is counterable by 'as between two innocents ...'. Of course, there would still be other counters, such as 'but you were at fault'. And the situation might be one in which 'no liability without fault' seemed a weak or obtuse moral position, even though no stereotyped, familiar 'as between two innocents ...'. counterbyte was available.[413]

I think what Kennedy offers here, in a revision of the European mystical message of the arbitrariness of the sign, is again the mystery of experience – the 'straight-forward' claim about the operation of legal argument *in a context*, where the argument-byte is 'an indexing device', just as in the Holmsian picture above.[414] The question of whether one argument or the other applies is one of statistics, of an imaginary scale in which arguments become more or less powerful, but it is not a matter of overcoming the Saussrian bar or taking responsibility for the framing of the whole process, or for the choice it makes. There is no theoretical access to what happens in experience. Kennedy's contemporary writing on Fuller's *Consideration and Form* article repeats the same Holmsian message:

> When choosing a legal norm to cover a case, rational decision making selects from the continuum of normative possibilities the one that best accommodates (balances, maximizes, mini-maxes, or whatever) the conflicting considerations as they play out more or less strongly in the fact situation of which the case is an instance. The solution doesn't fully realize any consideration, nor does it ignore any that has force under the circumstances. The solution is responsive to the case, but only to the case seen as a specimen of a species of case, or situation-type.[415]

---

413 Id., at 342.
414 'The only way to achieve certain and predictable law was to artificially fix "a mathematical line" at some relatively arbitrary point within the penumbra where opposing concepts overlapped ... A principle was an indexing device that guided the lawyer to relevantly similar cases, while at the same time guiding the judge to the policy considerations relevant in deciding the hard cases that fell under it'. See text to fn 277, above.
415 Duncan Kennedy, 'Lon Fuller's Consideration and Form', *supra* note 278, 100 *Colum. L. Rev.* 94 (2000).

Rational decision-making is possible in law. It is not easy to capture its movement within the complexity of the normative possibilities that exist in any new case, but it happens, just like a natural event. The solution does not choose between 'consideration' and not. The solution is 'responsive to the case'.[416] Law, as in Holmes, is an indexing device for a reality in flux, which we can catch only through the conceptuality of the legal system.

His considered canonical article *Form and Substance in Private Law Litigation*,[417] a mandatory reading in many canonical collections of American legal thought, illustrates the way in which going beyond the policies and principles, and 'using' some philosophical theories of that time, like existentialism, is done through a deep commitment to the internal perspective of living within private law. Kennedy shows how 'the opposed rhetorical modes'[418] of policy argument – individualism and altruism – are transcended to reach 'a deeper level of contradiction'.

> At this deeper level, we are divided, among ourselves and also within ourselves, between irreconcilable visions of humanity and society, and between radically different aspirations of our common future.[419]

Going beyond the rhetoric is enlarging the discourse of law with more broad philosophical claims and showing the arbitrariness and indeterminacy of the application to policy alone. The deeper levels are themselves indeterminate and divide us 'within ourselves' and 'among ourselves', and this recalls, with Holmes' idea, that it is eventually not the policies which determine the case. It is experience, in Kennedy and in Holmes, and it is the hard, man-like work of the legal scholar who prefers not to give grand theories.

This endeavor is presented as radicalizing the Legal Realists' critique:

---

416 There is a very complex and interesting genealogical endeavor in Kennedy's article to capture the intellectual consequences and sources of Fuller's claim and its contribution to private law theory and legal theory in general. In this context, my effort is only to describe its discursive characteristics, and the choice of Fuller's writing as a paradigm of legal thought has to be read together with the chapter 'Settled Law and the-Law-That-Is-Not-But-Ought-To-Be: Hart and Sacks and the Pragmatic Philosophy of Dispute Resolution (Or: Why Couldn't Henry Hart Speak?)'.
417 Duncan Kennedy, 'Form and Substance in Private Law Adjudication', 86 *Harv. L. Rev.* 1685 1 (1976).
418 Id., at 1685.
419 Id.

The realists as a group were more preoccupied with the critique of what they saw as formalist argumentative techniques than they were with reflection on their own beloved alternative of policy analysis.

The extension of the 'bytes' analysis from statutory interpretation to policy discourse meant rejecting the 'reconstructive' impulse among the realists, which seemed (in 1970) to be an evasion of the more 'rationalist' or 'existential' implications of their own work. Policy discourse at the time seemed deeply implicated in, indeed the major vehicle for, the Cold War liberalism against which the anti-war movement, the civil rights movement and the women's movement were then aligning themselves.[420]

The Realists put emphasis on policy analysis against a political climate that was producing formalist argumentative techniques to prevent progressive acts of the state. Kennedy is one of the 1970s actors who extended the bytes analysis 'from statutory interpretation to policy discourse', while rejecting the 'reconstructive impulse' of the Realists in order to attack the use of policy discourse as 'the major vehicle of the Cold War Liberalism'.

It is again the question of theory as the experience of answering the political problem of the time. In 1991, when the article was written, there was no more Cold War or policy abuse in that sense to answer. Was it now time to attack the discourse of attacking or defending policy analysis altogether? In his recent book *A Critique of Adjudication (Fin de Siecle)*, it seems like this subversive political movement from within law is perceived already as a disease, as 'the viral strain', the strain 'whose relation to the body of thought is the theme'[421] of his whole book.

> This book is an attempt to develop and extend this American form of internal critique. To my mind, it is mainly through this project, rather than through philosophy or political theory, that American intellectuals have been participants in the larger, worldwide long-running project of left/mpm critique. American legal theory is one of the quasi-autonomous enclaves, like Western Marxist theory, phenomenology and hermeneutics, and now literary theory, where this project has developed like a Sartrean 'worm at the heart of being'.[422]

The 'dramatic historical moment when this critical strategy was first formulated' was, according to Kennedy, 'in 1894, when Oliver Wendell Holmes

---

420 Id., at 352.
421 Kennedy, *Critique of Adjudication, supra* note 402, at 73.
422 Id., at 82.

published his article, "Privilege, Malice and Intent".'[423] The Realists, who are the next step, have not asserted 'that adjudication was irredeemably ideological', as some of their 'pop academic'[424] views might assert. The critique was much more delicate through its pointing towards the reflection of the outside political world inside legal decision-making.

> I think it quite common to see the history of American thought about law in the twentieth century as a protracted debate about how to deal with the 'viral' tendency of internal critique, with the positions ranging from flat rejection to compromise to flat endorsement ... The course of the debate has been powerfully influenced by its situation as a distinct part of the general debate between left and right. The critique has been an evolving part of the general left-wing attack on particular rules and on the power of judges in general, and in itself logically unconnected to leftism.[425]

Considering the fact that this internal critique had all the variety of manifestations in legal thought, from rejection to compromise until endorsement, as my writing also tries to show, why does Kennedy call it 'viral?' 'The body fights the virus',[426] but isn't the virus the force of life of the body itself, the source of intellectual energy and political dominance? If the 'viral' tendency in his text is the pragmatism of law (i.e., a mode of discourse which is near the general pragmatic one, but through its professional investment is able to defy the general claims and speaks in terms of theoretical rigorousness and internal investments), then the uniquely intellectual American legal mode of analysis is constructed as a disease, perhaps as an obsession. In my writing, in order to understand its unfolding through time we must analyze the post-war incorporation of this virus. Beginning with Holmes, this mode does not have a strong political flavor, but continuing to the Realists it acquires an intellectual passion. In the post-war era there is 'a flat endorsement' of it into general pragmatism as constructing the external world into the conservativism of the 1950s. In our time it is endorsed by Kennedy, written by Dworkin, flatly rejected by Dworkin himself, Posner, and Owen Fiss. Roberto Unger seems to leave (left) it behind in his recent writing.[427]

---

423 Id., at 85.
424 Id., at 88. 'This was true even for some notorious "bad boys" as Jerome Frank, Thurman Arnold, Joseph Hutchenson, and Max Radin, all of whom were debunkers of the "myth of certainty".'
425 Id., at 89.
426 Id. at 91.
427 All these claims are examined in the rest of the chapters of this book.

What the three prophets Holmes, Llewellyn and Kennedy have offered law so far is life as a context that has its own inner wisdom. The next chapters are an effort to fill in the intellectual influence of the 1950s, as the transitional moment, in order to bridge the generation gap between these three men.

Chapter 2

Settled Law and the Law-That-Is-Not-But-Ought-To-Be: The Pragmatic Philosophy of Dispute Resolution (Or: Why Couldn't Henry Hart Speak?)

2.1 Introduction

The post-World War II era is a crucial transition point for understanding the play of the pragmatic idea in law, marking an intellectual moment that is both a rift and a shift, from which any narration is done in terms of 'before' and 'after'. It is also a significant moment for tracing the roots of the transformation and repression of the theoretical interest in dispute resolution in legal thought today.

As the previous chapter shows, until that time a distinct genre of pragmatism, a legal one, had developed alongside the more philosophical general version of the American, as offered by James and Dewey. Starting with Holmes, an internal obsessive ironic discourse developed, enduring the body of the law while putting aside the big philosophical questions. The next step in jurisprudence, operated by the Realist movement, reenacted this 'reality principle' of the legal jurists – a refutation of the big claims; a commitment to hard work; an insistence on playing with the generalities; and nevertheless, a command to predict their application (to be 'the bad man' who does so). Still, it was not until the post-war era that this account of American legal discourse was incorporated and received the official stamp of Harvard. Holmes and Llewellyn indeed mark the origin of the organizing myth of 'the life of the law' and the distinct notion of legal experience, but their writing is perceived to be in resistance to the 'old' classical discourse. They challenge the mainstream position and remain controversial and critical in relation to it. Holmes was an oracle, an originator of a unique style within his generation, while the Realists as the next phase constituted a group which expressed an 'intellectual mood' of progressive ness and rebel lion. It was not until the 1950s that their message could be incorporated as the official canon of

American legal thought. In this interesting moment, a mediation of the external (hysterical feminine) philosophical pragmatism and the internal (obsessive masculine) legal pragmatism could occur, and in that sense it can be said that a textual 'child' was born at Harvard, manifested in The Legal Process Materials of Henry Hart and Albert Sacks.[1] This child of Harvard, in its iconic role of representing the American, is a glorious and harmonious mediation of the pragmatic external view of 'the world' – legal institutions, the public and the private, politics and law – together with the pragmatic legal notion of experience as the indulgence in generalities and of law as a living body that should be inhabited. America of the post-war era produces '... the last great attempt at a grand synthesis of law in all its institutional manifestations'.[2] In order to understand what happened after this effort, as well as what had occurred before it, prominent texts of the era are examined in this chapter. The current inquiry can be divided, accordingly, into a few sub-arguments:

First, in the constitutive moment of the post-war period, there is a theoretical 'vacuum' in general philosophical pragmatism, and the Dewey-James ideas are no longer appealing as an object of academic inquiry. On the other hand, they become a type of common sense and operate as the transparent view of 'the world' and of political choices for the children who went to progressive schools and were raised upon Dewey's ideas. This common sense, combined with prevalent political theories of 'pluralism', conditions Legal Process jurisprudence.

Second, underlying the Legal Process notion of 'the legal' and 'the world', there are positivism, naturalism, an institutional perspective and an evolutionary image of human society. Within this image, the operation of law is captured through the pragmatic notions of reasoned elaboration, institutional settlement and the 'Grand Pyramid' of legal norms. The purposive quality of human interaction in general, and law in particular, as the fundamental condition is constructed throughout the Materials, helping to organize the above pragmatic notions as evading or overcoming the old dichotomies (is-ought, fact-value, reason-force, integrative-distributive).

Third, there was a difficulty in once again raising the common sense of the 'dead' theoretical pragmatism of that time to the level of a theory. It has to do also with the framework of the Legal Process Materials, which were the product of professional jurists (and not philosophers) in the 1950s who reflected

---

1   Henry M. Hart, Jr and Albert M. Sacks, *The Legal Process: Basic Problems in the Making and Application of Law* (William N. Eskridge, Jr and Philip P. Frickey, eds) 1994, at lxxxvii (hereinafter 'Hart and Sacks').
2   Gary Peller, 'Neutral Principles in the 1950s', 21 *U. Mich. J. L. Reform* (1988), 561, 568.

the local common sense of that time. This difficulty has a role in the portrayal of the Legal Process School as failing in terms of theory while having an enormous effect as a body of professional wisdom. The image of the late Henry Hart signifies this theoretical failure.

Fourth, the political climate of the post-war era produced an optimistic horizon of 'institutional settlement' for each value judgment by promoting the process approach as overcoming the grand public questions through the singularity of the dispute. This project, and the development of the 'reasoned elaboration' notion, actually emerged in resistance to the activism of the Warren Court, which was depicted as not 'elaborative' enough. The equivalent contradictory channels of legal institutions operating in the post-war period expose the problematic in the assumption of 'collective thought' at that time, and also provide the second cause to the assumed theoretical failure of post-war jurisprudence.

Fifth, there is an epistemological gap between the portrayal of the Legal Process writing by progressive intellectuals within the legal discourse, and the discussion of it by analytic historians or jurispruds outside law. While the first group is concerned with what I define as 'the progressive riddle' and constructs the 1950s political thinking as an abyss, the second is driven by a less passionate search and focus on an analytic or a positivistic quest.

Sixth, there is a singularity in the post-war moment that cannot be captured by constructing it as being equivalent to a previous transformation in law, nor as carrying some formal theory that can be 'used' today. The 'appearance' of the Materials at Harvard, in that context, and the harmonizing role of this place and time in constituting (and at the same time marking a crisis, creating a rift in) the American legal discourse holds consequences for following generations, and for understanding those who preceded them.

The chapter begins with *my* reading of the Materials in order to illustrate the above arguments. I approach the Materials and some other prominent texts of that era in a manner that can be defined as discursive or textual analysis. I try to characterize the genre of discourse they constitute without essentializing them as carrying one formal theory. The next part engages a few contemporary readers of the Materials and of the Legal Process School and tries to reconcile (and at the same time deconstruct) their counter-positions through their sort of interaction with the discursive stories I have described before.

2.2 The 'Materialization' of the Pragmatic Idea

2.2.1 Chronological Background

In the post-war era, there was a 'collective consciousness' in law. This is at least the formal narration of that time in light of progressive legal thinkers such as Morton Horwitz or Gary Peller as described in the previous chapter.[3] The incorporation of some Realists' ideas into mainstream legal thought occurred at that time through the inscription of the post-war mature American jurisprudence.

The construction of The Legal Process Materials by Hart and Sacks started with a legislation course, which Hart had taught before the war. Between 1955 and 1958, Hart and his former pupil Sacks worked on different drafts of the current Materials, arriving at the current version. The first (1955) draft was entitled *Materials for a General View of the American Legal System*. The second (1956) draft was called *The American Legal System*, and provided the name of the course Hart and Sacks gave in that year. By 1957 the manuscript had received its current name, and so did their course.[4] As Eskridge and Frickey say in the introduction to the official publication of the book in 1994, 'This remarkable course represented the most sophisticated thinking in American public law of the post-war era.'[5]

> Hart and Sacks' opus has had a great run as teaching Materials. It was the text for a popular perspectives course at the Harvard Law School for more than three decades, and dozens of other law schools offered similar courses from the Materials during this period. Thousands of law students, including five current Justices of the United States Supreme Court, studied the Materials in the classroom.[6]

2.2.2 Evolution, the Natural Foundation of Law, and Hegemonies

Underlying the Legal Process notion of 'the legal' and 'the world' are positivism, naturalism, institutional perspective, and an evolutionary image of human society. Law, in this context, is perceived as 'an ongoing, functioning

---

3 See the chapter 'The Maturing of the Pragmatic Idea in Law and Society (Or: The Fall and the Rise of Philawsophy)', part 1.2.
4 Hart and Sacks, at xxxvii.
5 Id., at liii.
6 Id.

purposive process',[7] as the preface to the Materials suggests, and it operates through institutions.

> A legal system *is* a system – a coordinated, functioning whole made up of a set of interrelated, interacting parts. The solution of specific legal problems constantly requires an understanding of the functions and interrelationships of more than one institutional process and frequently of several. Problems arising in a court call for a perceptive awareness not only of what courts are for but of what a legislature is for and sometimes also of what an administrative agency is for and of what matters can be best left to private decision.[8]

The law functions in a complex institutional system. The four institutions that constitute this system are the subject of different chapters in the Materials, and are private ordering, courts, the legislature, and the executive branch.[9] In order to solve a legal problem there is a need to understand 'the functions and interrelationships of more than one institutional process', and the Materials proceed to show the student how to do so. The metaphysics behind this project appear as soon the Materials begin in *An Introduction to the Nature and Function of Law*.[10]

> Here enters the most fundamental of the conditions of the human society. In the satisfaction of all their wants, people are continuously and inescapably dependent upon one another ... The coexistence on the face of the same planet of these ever-changing and increasing millions of people, having these wants and such abilities to satisfy the wants under these conditions of interdependence, are the basic facts of social science, and pose its basic problems.[11]

There are millions of people on this planet and their basic condition is described as interdependence. The task of the American legal scholar proceeds from this broad picture of 'law being a pervasive aspect of social science'.[12] The fundamental social questions are: how to maintain the existence of these millions of people; among the surviving, what wants should be satisfied and

---

7   Hart and Sacks, at cxxxvii.
8   Id.
9   As the *Materials* suggest, 'the institutions which can be devised for the settlement of social questions vary endlessly ... But the possible variations in particular types of procedures are endless. So also are the variations in the relationship between each time of procedure and the system as a whole.' Id., at 6.
10 This is the name of the first chapter of *The Legal Process Materials*.
11 Id., at 1–2.
12 Id.

how; which wants are to be encouraged and which discouraged.[13] This 'social science' image of law is characteristic of views prevalent in law since the Realists' critique and even before, but they do not recur in post-post-war legal thought.[14]

When the Materials say that these questions '*must* be answered – by events if not by conscious choice',[15] they seem also to refer to the international questions of the Cold War. The universal tone, which claims to reflect on problems also 'from an Olympian point of view',[16] is repeated in the Materials again and again.[17] It seems like the same spirit that inspires the depiction of the 'wrong' treatment of the social problem:

> In particular, many people have rejected the whole notion of purpose in social organization. At bottom, they have argued, the social problem is a problem simply of deciding who gets what. This view starts with the obvious fact that there is not enough in the world of all the things that people want to go around among the people who want them. The gist of the social situation is then seen baldly, as no more than a continuing struggle among conflicting claimants to get what they can. In this view, the whole apparatus of social order, law included, becomes little more than a substitute or a mask for force, providing a cover of legitimacy for the decisions that have to be made among the various contestants.[18]

The people who have rejected the whole notion of purpose in social organization do not accept the 'ultimate test of the goodness or badness of every institutional procedure'. This test is whether or not the existing institutional procedure 'helps to further the purpose of maintaining and perfecting "the conditions necessary for community life to perform its role in the complete development of man"'.[19] These people see struggle and distribution at the core of the social condition. In this context, law is becoming a substitute or a mask for force, a tool of legitimacy. If this positioning of 'the wrong' answer tries to capture Marxist ideas about force and legitimization, it certainly builds them into the particular context of the Materials. Marxists, in

---

13   Id.
14   See the discussion of Brian Tamanaha's call for a socio-legal jurisprudence in part 2.4.3.
15   Hart and Sacks, 2.
16   Id., at 67.
17   See also *A Retrospective Query* at 113, opening the discussion for diverse political and academic players, claiming to engage them all in the legal endeavor. This query is discussed in the chapter 'In Search of the Dispute: On Lawyers and Legal philawsophers at Harvard Law School', part 4.3.
18   Id., at 102.
19   Id.

this text,[20] claim a static 'pie' and for a distributive interdependence, and on that level, they receive a proper defeating answer:

> These Materials proceed upon the conviction that this is a fallacy – 'the fallacy of the static pie'. The fact – the entirely objective fact – seems to be that the pie – that is, the total of actually and potentially available satisfactions of human wants – is not static but dynamic. How to make the pie larger, not how to divide the existing pie, is the crux of the long-range and primarily significant problem.[21]

It is interesting to note that this optimistic evolutionary and progressive observation is given here, maybe for the last time, in a text that claims to provide a political philosophy, or at least a set of justifications for public decisions about distribution and social justice.[22] The a-historic scientific mode in which this text depicts 'the facts', the convictions and the conclusion, is typical of the post-war political thought.[23] There is order in law as in nature, even though the basic notion of lawmaking is settlement.

> The law which governs daily living in the United States is a single system of law: it speaks, in relation to any particular question with only one ultimately

---

20 Perhaps Realists do so as well; see Kent Roach, 'What's New and Old about Legal Process?', 47 *Univ. Toronto L.J.* 363, 378 (1995): 'In one sweep, Hart and Sacks characterize the more radical aspects of legal realism as nihilistic and lacking in a basic faith in the purposiveness of human life, if not un-American. In historical terms, the message seems to be that Depression-era concerns about scarcity and distribution of resources should be abandoned. In the expanding America of the 1950s, "the fallacy of the static pie" should be obvious to all intelligent observers. The only way that the pie could possibly get smaller is if the big one is dropped and "Armageddon" occurs. Even that horror, however, is a cause of optimism because the ability to destroy nature reveals human mastery of it and hence the ability to use technology to expand the pie. The Legal Process can neglect questions of distributive justice because of its assumption that if humans continue to cooperate, the pie will become so large that even those with the smallest pieces will be satisfied.'
21 Hart and Sacks, at 103.
22 Regarding pluralism as the prevailing mood among American scholars in the 1950s, see Sebok, *supra* note 22, 172: 'The theory of pluralism arose from the need of social scientists to reinterpret the elements of pragmatism and interest-group politics into a theory that could explain, justify, and even celebrate American democracy. The twin pillars of pluralism were value relativism and group conflict ... The fact that people differed in their fundamental views of the good meant that it would be more difficult for any one views to tyrannize the others ... The fact that individuals were molded by broad economic and social forces into groups was also a positive source of stability, because in a modern society, only through groups could individuals express their interests.'
23 Id., at 173: 'Democratic pluralism was a product not of laws but of culture.'

authoritative voice, however difficult it may be on occasion to discern in advance which of two or more conflicting voices really carries authority. In the long run and in the large , this must be so. People repeatedly subjected, like Pavlov's dogs, to two or more inconsistent sets of directions, without means of resolving the inconsistencies, could not fail in the end to react as the dogs did. The society, collectively, would suffer a nervous breakdown.[24]

There is one ultimately authoritative voice, speaking through a single system of law (in America). The fact that it is so, 'however difficult it may be on occasion to discern'. the right voice, recalls Dworkin's insistence that there is only one right answer. Still, in contrast to Dworkin, the medium of decision making is constructed at that time as entirely organic. Law functions as a control system within the body of society and can transmit signals only through a single defined mechanism, which should be located anew again in any particular decision. This unitary whole is a necessary quality of any society, which functions, as nature does, with the law as its nervous system.[25]

> Law, it must be apparent, is the inescapable context within which we all live. To be impatient with law because it sometimes fails to do its job well is no more sensible than to be impatient with air because it sometimes gets fouled. Indeed, it is less sensible. For air in its natural condition is pure and there is some justification for annoyance when it turns out to be impure. But law is the creation of human beings responding to their own natures and the conditions of their environment.[26]

The naturalism in this paragraph and throughout the epistemology of the Materials is that of classical pragmatism, which assumes science and evolution to be foundational notions. The idea of 'law being an aspect but only one aspect of the science of society'[27] and that 'lawyers need always to take account

---

24 Hart and Sacks, at 159.
25 See Sebok, *supra* note 22, at 173: 'The question still remained, however, why, in a democratic system that rejected *a priori* principles of justice, majority rule would never generate unjust (even antidemocratic) results. The pluralists' answer to this question was not that democracy could be protected from failure by laws and constitutions ... If democracies were to resist collapse into majority tyranny, it would be because of the health of the democracy's non-legal institutions.' I think the organic metaphor helps to better address the question of Sebok by pointing to the epistemic horizon of the Legal Process texts. Under Hart and Sacks' assumptions (which have their time and place constraints), it is taken for granted that law stabilizes society and its forces into a harmonious functioning.
26 *The Legal Process Materials*, *supra* note 5, 174.
27 Id., at 175.

of relevant knowledge in other branches of the sciences'[28] corresponds with this framework. Law is perceived as a 'problem solving' activity. It is an instrument for the satisfaction of basic human wants, in a society of individuals who live under conditions of interdependence. 'Law is a doing of something, a purposive activity, a continuous striving to solve the basic problems of social living.'[29]

This scientific image helps to represent what was once considered radical and destabilizing to be organic and natural. We cannot find the same appeal today for deducing the political answers from a set of assumptions about 'the world' and its resources. In negotiation studies, nevertheless, or in social psychology books, которые deal with disputes as a private matter, these modes of analysis are more prevalent.[30]

> The proposition that supply of the good things of life is not fixed but expansible holds true even of tangible satisfactions, which the exponents of the dog-eat-dog view of human existence are likely to have chiefly in mind. It is still more conspicuously true of the intangible satisfactions of life, which are intensely desired also, and all the more intensely as the more urgent of tangible needs are met.[31]

Freedom of speech is considered an 'intangible satisfaction', and together with the tangible ones can be supplied through overcoming distributive questions. The possibility of enlarging the pie derives from the knowledge that it can become smaller. 'At the extreme, mankind has presumably the capacity to destroy itself, thus leaving no pie at all for anybody.'[32] The wisdom of handling social life is to recognize that 'there *can* be enough freedom of thought and speech for everybody and enough freedom of worship ... so of friendship, peace of mind, self-respect, and the sense of participation in the life of the community ...'. The optimism in this paragraph probably applies to the white-male, prosperous community for which the authors speak, but it is also a part of enacting a hegemonic text of legal education, in the spirit of the post-war era. It is possible to use here Ernesto Laclau and Chantal

---

28   Id.
29   *The Legal Process Materials, supra* note 5, 148.
30   See the discussion of Roger Fisher's activism in preferring the integrative pole of interdependence, in the chapter 'In Search of the Dispute: On Lawyers and Legal Philawsophers at Harvard Law School'. See also Jeffrey Z. Rubin and Bert R. Brown, *The Social Psychology of Bargaining and Negotiation* (1975), 197.
31   Hart and Sacks, at 103.
32   Id.

Mouffe's[33] description of the discursive location of hegemony, in order to articulate the uniqueness of these texts.

> The concept of hegemony did not emerge to define a new type of relation in its specific identity, but to fill a hiatus that had opened in the change of historical necessity. Hegemony will allude to an absent totality, and to the diverse attempts at recomposition and rearticulation which, in overcoming this original absence, made it possible for struggles to be given a meaning and for historical forces to be endowed with full positivity ... 'Hegemony' will not be the majestic unfolding to an identity but the response to a crisis.[34]

The post-war is indeed an era which responds to 'absent totality', a crisis which necessitate a new system of symbols and practices. Within the realm of law, an important channel to 'recompose' and to 'overcome' this void, is manifested in the Legal Process materials. An adjacent general hegemonic text of that era might be the one by Morton White, which I discuss elsewhere,[35] and The Warren Court provides its own distinct track.[36] The precise discursive location of the hegemonic text is always locked, according to Laclau and Moffe, between 'something more' and 'something less'.

> Something more, inasmuch as the space of hegemony is not merely that of a localized 'unthought': it is rather a space in which bursts forth a whole conception of the social based upon an intelligibility which reduces its distinct moments to the interiority of a closed paradigm. Something less, inasmuch as the diverse surfaces of emergence of the hegemonic relation do not harmoniously come together to form a theoretical void that a new concept is required to fill.[37]

The function of the materials within this play seems to be the 'something more', which is brought by Harvard of the post-war: A 'conception of the social based upon an intelligibility which reduces its distinct moments to the interiority of a closed paradigm'. The world is built in already old-fashioned terms within the interiority of the materials and law, as part of the hegemonic structure which the post-war produces.

---

33 Ernest Laclau and Chantal Mouffe, *Hegemony & Socialist Strategy* (1985).
34 Id., at 7.
35 See the chapter 'The Maturing of The Pragmatic Idea in Law and Society (Or: The Fall, and the Rise of Philawsophy)', part 1.3.
36 I discuss later in part 2.4.3 the perceived opposition between the Legal Process jurisprudence and the Warren Court activism. The gap between them, according to my writing, is a background for later intellectual developments in law.
37 Id., at 93.

2.2.3 Institutional Settlement and the Materialization of the Functional

There is an optimistic evolutionary apprehension of the human's response to their basic interdependence, which is their original social situation. 'So recognizing, people form themselves into groups for the protection and advancement of their common interests, or they accept membership in group formed by others.'[38] Law evolves from the need to settle indeterminacies within customary peaceful patterns of understanding that emerge in little groups.

> Substantive understandings of arrangements about how the members of an interdependent community are to conduct themselves in relation to each other and to the community necessarily imply the existence of what may be called *constitutive or procedural* understandings or arrangements about how questions in connection with arrangements of both types are to be settled. The constitutive arrangements serve to establish and to govern the operation of regularly working – that is *institutionalized* – procedures for the settlement of questions of group concern. These institutionalized procedures and the constitutive arrangements establishing and governing them are obviously more fundamental than the substantive arrangements in the structure of a society, if not in the realization of its ultimate aims, since they are at once the source of the substantive arrangements and the indispensable means of making them work effectively.[39]

Substantive understandings evolve in a natural way between people and create the fundamental arrangements in the structure of society. Above them is 'procedural understanding' about how questions in connection with constitutive or procedural arrangements are to be settled. The idea that institutionalized procedures are 'more fundamental than the substantive arrangements in the structure of society' is typical of post-war political and philosophical thought, and differentiates the American 'original condition' as described in the Materials from that of European thinkers such as Holmes, Locke, or Rousseau. The primacy of process over substance is equivalent to that of experience over metaphysics, and reenacts an old American impatience with the belief in one truth. Although basically the initial picture of society is presented in positivistic terms, recalling even Hartian (H.L.A. Hart) ideas of primary and secondary rules,[40] the pragmatic 'leap' supplements the picture

---

38   Hart and Sacks., at 108.
39   Id., at 3–4.
40   See, for example, id., at 4: 'An organized society is one which has an interconnected system of procedures adequate, or claiming to be adequate, to deal with every kind of question affecting the group's internal relations, and every kind of question affecting its

with its positioning of experience and process as overcoming or evading the old questions. It is posited as evading the substance – as the only process that is worth reflection. The idea of 'institutional settlement' captures the legal pragmatic notion of experience of that time.

> Implicit in every such system of procedures is the central idea of law – an idea which can be described as *the principle of institutional settlement*. The principle builds upon the basic and inescapable facts of social living which have been stated: namely, the fact that human societies are made up of human beings striving to satisfy their respective wants under conditions of interdependence, and the fact that this common enterprise inevitably generates questions of common concern which have to be settled, one way or another, if the enterprise is to maintain itself and to continue to serve the purposes which it exists to serve. To leave decisions of these questions to the play of raw force would defeat these purposes.[41]

There is 'an enterprise' to maintain and there are 'the basic and inescapable facts' of social living. Questions that need to be settled emerge through random occurrences, from the bottom, as natural selection happens in nature, and the principle of a 'settlement' of these questions is built into their description.

The central idea of law is 'settlement' in the Legal Process era, and some fifteen years later this idea will be the most degraded and foreign to the theory of law in Owen Fiss's 'public law' writing.[42] In the meantime, the settlement notion is used, as is 'experience' in philosophical pragmatism, to overcome old questions.

> Many of the mysteries about the nature of law and of legal concepts disappear in the light of a clear understanding of the principle of institutional settlement and of the reasons which entitle it to acceptance. Thus, countless pages of paper and gallons of printer's ink have been expended in debate about whether law is something which 'is', like the data of the physical sciences, or something which involves elements of what 'ought' to be, resting upon moral or other prudential considerations.[43]

---

external relations which the group can establish competence to deal with'. Hart's idea of primary and secondary rules and their emergence in the development of societies has equivalencies with the description in the Materials. See H.L.A Hart, *The Concept of Law* (1961).

41 Hart and Sacks, at 4.
42 See the chapter 'Taking Sides: Margins and Phases of Pragmatics of Legal Process Disciples (Or: The Pragmatists that We Are)', part 3.2.
43 Id., at 5.

Overcoming the is-ought dichotomy and its 'countless', useless pages of debate is done in the name of an old, American pragmatic spirit of evasion. Instead of choosing between law being a fact or a moral judgment, when the principle of institutional settlement is plainly applicable, we first say that the law 'is' thus and so, and brush aside further discussion of what it 'ought' to be.

> Yet the 'is' is not really an 'is' but a special kind of 'ought' – a statement that, for the reasons just reviewed, a decision which is the duly arrived at result of a duly established procedure for making the decisions of that kind 'ought' to be accepted as binding upon the whole society unless and until it has been duly changed.[44]

The statute, the administrative act and the judicial decision get an 'is' only through their applied meaning in context. The 'is' is a special kind of 'ought', which brings the authors to define later 'the-law-which-is-not-but-ought-to-be' as standing in contrast to 'settled law'. The robust, almost impossible formula of hyphenated concepts as the right precise definition captures the evasive hocus-pocus mediation of that era, which claims to settle all the previous dichotomies into one ultimate, harmonious formula.[45]

This approach is optimistic, scientific, pretentious on the one hand as in the old pragmatic program of beginning from scratch, and modest when approaching the singular dispute.[46] It has the hysterical mode of Dewey in describing the world and its institutional setting, combined with the rigorous legal passion to address the manifestations of law from the inside only in their various particularities. The story of Joseph Martinelli, the hero of *The Case of the Spoiled Cantaloupes*, which is the introductory problem to the Materials,[47] illustrates this mediation. Starting with the singular event of the sale of cantaloupes on 21 June 1943, the Materials proceed with the case through its various choices and institutional debates until it reaches the

---

44 Id.
45 See also the discussion of the functional element later in this part.
46 For example, id., at 67: 'All the rest of the Materials are designed to cast light on the questions under this last subheading. The questions are put at this point to invite reflection and not with any thought that what has so far been presented makes possible a confident answer.'
47 Id., at 10: *The Significance of an Institutional System: The Case of the Spoiled Cantaloupes.* See also at 9: 'The introductory problems which follow are designed to exhibit concretely the operation of a particular system of institutional procedures in relation to a definite set of events, and to pose some characteristic questions about the appropriate scope of the principle of institutional settlement in resolving the controversies to which the events gave rise.'

Supreme Court. The idea is of a system that can be described from above and from within, upside down and inside out, the public and private compactly arranged, as well as the grand picture and the rigorous case work.[48] No lawyer can understand Martinelli's problem if that lawyer was not witness to its unfolding and to the various steps it went through until reaching its end. The modesty of following only one case and being fully reflexive regarding its particularities goes together with describing from above the whole social context in which it occurs. This can also account for my definition of this genre in the title to this chapter as *the pragmatic philosophy* (and not philawsophy) *of dispute resolution*.[49]

Karl Llewellyn, the former Realist prophet,[50] describes in 1960 in *The Common Law Tradition*[51] this double gesture as being unique to the legal discipline in comparison with other academic areas:

> The lawyer does not ask: How does an appellate tribunal arrive at *a* decision, *some* decision, *any* decision – in general, as an approximative pattern, in perhaps three, even four or seven, cases out of ten? The lawyer asks, instead: How does

---

48   See also Kent Roach, 'What's New and Old about Legal Process?', 47 *Univ. Toronto L. J.* 363, 368 (1995): 'The most striking feature of The Legal Process is its breadth and expansive understanding of the different skills that lawyers will require to serve their public and private clients. Hart encouraged his students to become "experts in the art and science of ordering human affairs" and his ambition is reflected in the gargantuan scope of *The Legal Process*. Hart and Sacks attempt to study the law as "a coordinated, functioning whole made upon a set of interrelated, interacting parts".'
49   Equivalent accounts of this era as pragmatic can be found in Garry Peller, *supra* note 2, as discussed throughout this chapter and in the chapter 'The Maturing of The Pragmatic Idea in Law and Society (Or: The Fall, and the Rise of Philawsophy)'. See also Roach, 'What's New and Old about Legal Process?', id. Roach suggests that Hart and Sacks embraced a 'pragmatist epistemology', encouraging readers to follow the pragmatic method in their dealing with legal problems, as well as in dealing with the social sciences as applied to law. Id., at 366: 'The pragmatic practice of considering a problem from different angles and perspectives was achieved by asking students to examine the problem from the perspectives of all the private decision makers, administrators, legislators, judges, and student of government who encountered the problem ... The ultimate aim of decision makers was to make sound judgments informed by experience and by all the objective data that can feasibly be assembled, but upon judgment nevertheless.' Roach acknowledges the exceptional character of his claim, considering the more prevalent view that the Legal Process emphasizes a retreat from pragmatism. Still, as external to the progressive disappointment of that era (coming from Canada), he claims that pragmatism is what emerges from the Materials.
50   See the discussion of Llewellyn in the chapter 'The Maturing of the Pragmatic Idea in Law and Society (Or: The Fall, and the Rise of Philawsophy)', part 1.4.
51   Karl N. Llewellyn, *The Common Law Tradition: Deciding Appeals* (1960).

this appellate tribunal arrive at *the particular and concrete answer* which it reaches *in the particular and concrete case?* I know of no man in the social disciplines who would dare to ask such a question. But the lawyer wants to know in order that he *may apply the knowledge in advance to a particular concrete tribunal in the next specific appeal* with which he will be concerned. In the present state of the other social disciplines or of behavioral science at large – so far as published work goes – this would be a dream-inquiry. It would be fantastic.[52]

In the 'late Llewellyn' writings, the search for the concrete and the forward-looking prediction of the next case characterizes the departure from the dangers of the 'psychologists' and 'logicians' who questioned the old belief in the way deduction and rational decision-making operate.[53] His writing depicts itself in a long tradition which, 'in spite of all such talk', promoted a 'powerful current of sound inquiry'.[54] In Llewellyn, nevertheless, the grand picture is less present, congruent with his Realist past.[55] The focus on the dispute and on the lawyer as the practical intellectual is still present in the above paragraph, and is maybe one of its late and sincere appearances.[56] According to Morton Horwitz, in the 1951 foreword to *The Bramble Bush*, Llewellyn revised and regretted his 'thirteen word' definition of law ('What these officials do about disputes is, to my mind, the law itself'), by moving to a more purposive definition: 'As early as 1940, Llewellyn has conceded that "the heart and core of jurisprudence" was the problem of ethical purpose in the law.'[57]

The opposition to Holmes and the Legal Realists is brought in the Materials, under this combination, during the discussion of the relationship of the social sciences to law.

---

52 Id., at 16.
53 Id., at 11–13.
54 Id., at 13.
55 'Llewellyn's retreat' and his moving away from the 'critical tradition of Realism' are described in Morton J. Horwitz, *The Transformation of American Law 1870–1960* (1992), 247–50. Horwitz presents the foreword to the 1951 edition of *The Bramble Bush* as apologetic. In *The Common Law Tradition*, according to Horwitz, 'Llewellyn ardently sought to emphasize the virtues of "stability", "predictability", "tradition", and the professional "craft"' (p. 250).
56 On the intellectual shift within law schools during the 1960s, which transformed them into 'law schools without law', focusing only on theory and interdisciplinary studies, see the chapter 'In Search of The Dispute: On Lawyers and Legal Philawsophers at Harvard Law School (Or: Some Private Hope and Public Irony)'. See also the discussion there of 'the lost lawyer' of Kronman, part 4.4.
57 Horwitz, *supra* note 55, at 248.

> The Materials reject the teaching of a vast body of literature which has accumulated during the last half century seeking to equate the methods of the various social sciences, and in particular of law, with the methods of the natural sciences ... In keeping this model, many social scientists and legal philosophers have tried to construct a science of society and of law based scrupulously on the 'isness' of people's behavior – of the behavior of judges, legislators, and other public officials as well as of ordinary private citizens – while at the same time rigorously separating questions of how the people ought to behave.[58]

Referring here to the empiricist inclination in Realists' thought, and coming back to Holmes as the originator of this position,[59] the authors provide their own (collective) answer to the fact-value choice. They, first of all, 'proceed upon the conviction that the science of society is essentially a judgmatical, or prudential, science demanding modes of inquiry and reflection which are sharply at variance with the procedures conventionally thought to be appropriate in the natural sciences'.[60] Then, assuming the purposive nature of human life and social organization, they perceived each decision-making experience as having been done for a purpose.

> ... how can the observer of decisions understand the actions of the decision-maker unless he takes account of these choices and tries to appraise their soundness? If he does not do this, how can he hope to predict future decisions or give any assistance in making them?[61]

Just like Roger Fisher some twenty years later,[62] the 'Process people' do not believe in the possibility of being only an observer. At their time, the observer is built in the image of the Realist or the Holmsian, who adopts a behaviorist empirical science posture to their legal and jurisprudential message. The observer is also, for Fisher, as well as for the progressive intellectuals like Grey, the one who tells the legal history, the philosopher. He is the intellectual, the theoretician, who internally digs into the body and externally defies theory. In the post-war era, in Hart and Sacks' writing, this figure does not exist. The theory is transparent and hence also practical. There is actually

---

58 Hart and Sacks, at 107–8.
59 Id., at 108: 'Closely related, in the American legal tradition, to the notion that law can somehow be drawn from the behavior patterns of the people has been the notion that ethics is a body of thought to be distinguished sharply from law.'
60 Id., at 107.
61 Id., at 108.
62 See the chapter 'In Search of the Dispute: On Lawyers and Legal Philawsophers at Harvard Law School'.

'no theory' in terms of an intriguing, fresh, and progressive call (in the theory of adjudication). There is a 'collective consciousness' – the Materials, an unpublished manuscript dealing with 'basic problems in the making and application of law' – which functions as an oral tradition for the current and coming generations. The statutory interpretation instructions in *Some Concluding Observations* in the Materials reinforce the idea that there is no interpretation without assuming a purpose, that this is the horizon of any decision-making in law, and that choosing between principles and policies can be done in a natural reasonable manner:

> In interpreting a statute a court should:
>
> 1. Decide what purpose ought to be attributed to the statute and to any subordinate provision of it which may be involved; and then
> 2. Interpret the words of the statute immediately in question so as to carry out the purpose as best as it can ...[63]

There is actually no access to the words of the statute without assuming a purpose. Sometimes it is obvious, and then the process of ascribing to it a process is unconscious. In other times, 'the words of a statute, taken in their context, serve both as guides in the attribution of general purpose and as factors limiting the particular meanings that can properly be attributed'.[64] The Fuller-H.L.A. Hart debate on vehicles in the park seems to return to this idea by insisting on the American experience of understanding only for a purpose.[65] The pragmatic, evolutionary picture of human inquiry arrives some fifty years later in the legal arena as social engineering for the sake of repeating it again and again.

What seems to happen in the Legal Process Materials is that the pragmatic problem-solving creature in philosophical pragmatism is becoming, in that

---

63 Hart and Sacks, at 1374.
64 Id., at 1375.
65 See Lon L. Fuller, 'Positivism and Fidelity to Law – A Reply to Professor Hart', 71 *Harv. L. Rev.* 630, 663 (1958): 'If the rule excluding vehicles from the parks seems easy to apply in some cases, I submit this is because we can see clearly enough what the rule is "aiming at in general" so that we know there is no need to worry about the difference between Fords and Cadillacs.' I think the linguistic wisdom that there is no meaning without a context has transformed in Fuller's above reply to Hart into the idea that the context is always a purposive one. The pragmatic anti-foundational mode, which suggests that aims themselves are always means to achieve some other ends and are never fixed, is treated through the institutional aspect of Fuller's theory and the mediating role he ascribes to adjudication as demarcating the public and the private, thus preserving a flexible mode of inquiry.

time, in Fuller's writing, the legal animal which decides only for a purpose: 'Law is the creation of human beings responding to their own natures and the conditions of their environment.'[66] The pragmatic idea that 'matter and form are fused and refused through problem solving innovation'[67] is translated in law into the idea that decisions are always instrumental.

Beyond the rules there are principles and policies, but as in the Holmsian legacy it is not even they that decide the case. Substituting the obscure slogan of 'the life of the law' as experience, and the prediction or commandment to anticipate the moment of decision, is the idea of process as a valid way to cover each choice and indeterminacy.

> Insistence on the distinction between law and morals can at times be understood as an expression, in substance, of the principle of institutional settlement. That principle requires that a decision which is the due result of duly established procedures be accepted whether it is right or wrong – at least for the time being. Thus, it seems to call for a distinction between settled law and the law-that-is-not-but-ought-to-be.[68]

A decision which is the due result of duly established procedures should be accepted whether it is right or wrong. In the texts of Fuller, who probably stands behind these ideas, there is still a realm of morals, one which is natural and beyond the pragmatic.[69] In Hart and Sacks, there is no need for such an external moral realm. Although the above quote is part of the post-war reaction and the actual resistance to the pragmatic formal morality,[70] it is a repetition of an old American-pragmatic gesture, combined with a fresh vision of a pluralist democracy.[71] What is phrased here in law is not a post-modern insight but the very inscription of a genre of American modernity. In law, there is only an ongoing process of decision making, of settling and resettling. This process substitutes the old notion of experience in Holmes and the idea of 'the business of the law' in Llewellyn. It applies, at this era, to the whole institutional system of law.

---

66 Id., at 174.
67 See the chapter 'The Maturing of the Pragmatic Idea in Law and Society (Or: The Fall, and the Rise of Philawsophy)', part 1.2.
68 Hart and Sacks, at 109.
69 See Lon Fuller, *The Morality of Law* (1964).
70 See also the discussion of Holmes and the shifting evaluation of him through the years, in the chapter 'The Maturing of the Pragmatic Idea in Law and Society (Or: The Fall, and the Rise of Philawsophy)', part 1.3.
71 See the discussion of pluralism above, *supra* note 22.

Yet it is important to see that this distinction – even in this situation, in which a duly made settlement is in question – is not in a just sense a distinction between law and morals. It is a distinction rather between one aspect of morals in relation to law and another. For the proposition that settled law should be respected, until it is duly changed – that a decision is in some sense 'right' simply because it has been duly made – is itself an ethical concept, resting on the recognition that defiance of institutional settlements touches or may touch the very foundation of civil order, and that without civil order, morality and justice in anybody's view of them are impossible.[72]

There is a circularity in this argument, namely: Settled law should be respected as an ethical command, resting on the recognition that no ethics can be possible without the founding idea of institutional settlement.[73] In other words, the principle of institutional settlement both derives from ... and predetermines the ... idea of justice.[74] There is, conceptually, no justice before there is institutional settlement, and at the same time it is justice to accept the idea of institutional settlement.[75] Institutional settlement, actually, *is* justice,

---

72 Hart and Sacks, at 109.
73 For another version of the circularity in their notion of institutional settlement see Sebok, *supra* note 22, at 132: 'The separation of law and morality demanded by the principle of institutional settlement entails that Hart and Sacks wanted to avoid the natural law option. In a deft move that navigated between utilitarianism and natural law, their definition of a valid human want ultimately referred back to the principle of institutional settlement ... Hart and Sacks seem to be saying that in order to know whether a human want is a *valid* human want, we must evaluate it according to a test generated by the "procedure of institutional settlement". Yet we originally wanted to know what was a valid human want in order to determine what sort of social processes were justified under the principle of institutional settlement. *Their definition of the principle of institutional settlement appears circular*' (my emphasis – M.A.). I think the circularity I describe differs from that of Sebok due to our conflicting perspectives. Sebok, as I show later, belongs to the analytic camp, and since his project is reviving positivism through the rereading of the Legal Process, he wants to save Hart and Sacks from empty circularity by showing how we do find valid human wants. For me, in contrast, the empty circularity is a mobilizing force of the discourse, and important for the understanding of the notion of 'justice' itself at that era.
74 In contrast see Sebok, *supra* note 22., at 133: 'Therefore, under my analysis, the principle of institutional settlement was not defended by Hart and Sacks on the basis that it would necessarily produce just results. It was defended on the basis that it would help the majority produce the results that the majority would prefer. It was a test of technical competence.'
75 Sebok perceives the principle as 'the key to the mystery concerning Hart and Sacks, Fuller, and legal positivism', *supra* note 22, at 169. He gives it a positivistic interpretation, and claims they used the concept of 'due result' as a 'proxy for a social fact such as a majority preference', *supra* note 22, at 168. This idea seems to impose a formal rigid 'reference' on a notion that claims to be 'both and neither', obscure for itself, evasive, like the pragmatic formula itself. See also the response of Brian Leiter to Sebok, part 2.4.3.

in this context, but why? In a discourse of law that assumes no metaphysics, the answer seems to go back to the pragmatic ideas prevalent at the time of the Materials. The functional approach to law seems to go together with the post-post-war declaration that 'we are all Realists now',[76] and with the way the critical aspect of the choice between policies and principles is silenced in the Materials through the image of society as endless settlements that can be harmonized. In the post-war era, the indeterminacy is not obscure as in the time of Holmes, or inviting the political choice, as in the Realists' writing. It is manageable and is the state of nature in Hart and Sacks' time. It is manifested in the idea of institutional settlement, which is equivalent to the idea of justice itself. In the more internal debate of contract law, in the core of the 'real' legal texts, this materialization of the pragmatic idea is manifested in Fuller and Perdue's celebrated article *The Reliance Interest in Contract Damages*,[77] published in 1936. Morton Horwitz writes that this article 'remains perhaps the single most influential piece of Realist-doctrinal work, though it was written by a scholar whose own jurisprudential work had already begun to target Legal Realism'.[78] An article that opens by declaring that 'the proposition that legal rules can be understood only with reference to the purposes they serve would today scarcely be regarded as an exciting truth ...'.[79] ends with a suggestion to reform the textbooks to acknowledge the interest-based background of conferring damages instead of the 'all or nothing' decision.[80] Fuller's 1942 article *Consideration and Form*[81] is a more elaborate manifestation of the same 'internal' wisdom. Duncan Kennedy describes it as moving us towards a model of 'conflicting considerations' consciousness, i.e., to the understanding 'that each and every one of the valid legal norms that makes up our legal system (including private, public, and international

---

76 See, for example, Laura Kalman, *Legal Realism at Yale 1927–1960* (1986), 229. 'The statement has been made so frequently that it has become a truism to refer to it as a truism'. See also John Henry Schlegel, *American Legal Realism and Empirical Social Sciences* (1995) 2: '... more important than the errors embedded in the common understanding of Realism is the fact that each is invariably accompanied by the implicit fatherly assertion, "We are all Realists now; don't worry about these questions".'
77 Fuller and Perdue, 'The Reliance Interest in Contract Damages' (pts 1 and 2) 46 *Yale L.J.* 52, 373 (1936–7).
78 Horwitz, supra note 55, at 184.
79 Fuller and Perdue, *supra* note 77, at 52.
80 Id., at 418.
81 Lon Fuller, 'Consideration and Form', *Colum. L. Rev.* 799 (1941).

law) *can be understood* ... as representing a choice in the colloquial lawyers' sense of a "policy question".[82]

Fuller's private law writing is a paradigm for understanding the claim that 'we are all Realists now',[83] which is actually also the claim that we are all legal pragmatists now. Horwitz presents Fuller's doctrinal internal message as opposing his political attack on Realists.

> Fuller's strategy of disaggregating and contextualizing the question of contract damages, as well as the consequentialist policy orientation he brought to the question, were part of a generational revolt against formalism that was still capable of producing revolutionary technical insights whose political insights he may never have realized.[84]

Fuller is read from a progressive point of view, assuming that an anti-formalist mode necessarily carries political-leftist insights. Coming back to the Materials, we can definitely see that the mode once considered anti-formalist can be served through a conservative, stabilizing, and harmonious story. Still, the contradictory character of Fuller's writing is worth further reflection. It can be examined from an equivalent angle: that of his jurisprudential writing against the private law writing. James Boyle describes this private-public split in Fuller in the following way:

> Describing the contracts in private law, Fuller gave an account that owed a great deal to legal realism, particularly in the way that it attacked formalistic criteria of enforceability. Where the classicists stressed form and consideration as theoretical a prioris, Fuller subjected those ideas to functional scrutiny, decried the undervaluation of the reliance principle, and found some reasons to enforceability in relative and contingent community norms ... he portrays the formal requirements of contract as being in dialectical, productive tension with their functional goals; and he denies that the rules of contract law are somehow immanent within the very definition of a contract ... In his more general

---

[82] Duncan Kennedy, 'From the Will Theory to the Principle of Private Autonomy: Lon Fuller's Consideration and Form', 100 *Colum L. Rev* 94 (2000). For the discussion of this reading of Fuller and the pragmatism of law or the genre of discourse which characterizes Fuller and Kennedy as well, see the chapter 'The Maturing of the Pragmatic Idea in Law and Society (Or: The Fall, and the Rise of Philawsophy)', part 1.5.

[83] See also the description of Kennedy, id., at 79, of the *Reliance* article, agreeing with Todd Rakoff that 'the whole idea is to create a series of solutions, each motivated by a series of purposes, differentially applicable to a series of situations, in a kind of declining order of promissee appealingness and promisor nastiness'.

[84] Horwitz, *supra* note 78, at 184.

jurisprudential writing, however, when Fuller describes the 'morality that makes law possible', he has in mind a set of formal criteria that *define*, or perhaps it would be better to say *are deduced* from, the very meaning of law ... it seems like Fuller thought he could deduce his eight formal and necessary principles of legality from the social contract. Yet the vision he gives of the *social* contract seems to conflict with his vision of a *private* contract. In the latter case Fuller writes more like a Realist, in the former, more like a formalist.[85]

'Fuller, the early contracts theorist, apparently undermines the claims made by Fuller, the later jurisprud',[86] according to Boyle, and he continues to explain this discrepancy by showing its relation to Fuller's very definition of law: 'The very definition of law includes certain uncontentious purposes, and achievement of those purposes constitutes the good.'[87] This functional definition, according to Boyle (who cites Alasdair Macintyre), pretends to resolve the fact-value problem, but actually is bounded in its own fallacy – the functional one.

> Any argument which moves from premises which assert that the appropriate criteria are satisfied to a conclusion which asserts that 'This is a good such-and-such', where 'such-and-such' picks out an item specified by a functional concept, will be a valid argument which moves from the factual premises to an evaluative conclusions. Thus, we may safely assert that, if some amended version of the 'No "ought" conclusion from "is" premises' principle is to hold good, it must exclude arguments involving functional concepts from its scope.[88]

Fuller's presumption of the functional story enables him, in other words, to overcome the basic problematic of deducing any moral obligation from the social fact. The problematic in this 'logical' sequence is exactly the initial stage of asserting the functional: the norms of the 'proper function' of the concepts are not built into them. They dissolve back 'into contingent facts and contentious concepts'.[89] As Doyle says, 'The only way that arguments like this can survive is to pick implicit values that are either vague enough or reassuringly familiar enough to survive prolonged scrutiny.'[90] My claim is

---

85 James Boyle, 'Legal Realism and the Social Contract: Fuller's Public Jurisprudence of Form, Private Jurisprudence of Substance', 78 *Cornell L. Rev.* 371, 372 (1993).
86 Id., at 373.
87 Id., at 396.
88 Id., at 396, quoted from MacIntyre.
89 Id., at 397.
90 Id.

that in the post-war era, the vague reassuring values that provided the foundational story for the legal universe were the pragmatic ones. To summarize the above sequence, the constitutive elements for today's 'legal consciousness' that appear in the private law writing of Fuller and are described by Horwitz, Kennedy, and Doyle go together with the functional dogma, or axiom, which is actually the pragmatism of the post-war period. Fuller in *Consideration and Form* promotes the idea that there is purpose in law in general by assuming the transparency of the functional as defining the operation of the legal. Hart and Sacks transcribe this transparency in their Materials.

2.2.4 Language as an Indexing Device and the Example of Hohfeld

The notion of language in the Materials emphasizes again the way in which a naturalistic scientific posture can restructure ideas in the post-World War II era that were (and will be) considered radical and rebellious into a constructive picture.

> General arrangements have to be expressed in words. The way in which such arrangements work is a special phase of the way in which language works. If law is to be understood language must be also.[91]

The Materials proceed upon the idea that language is a representation of experience.

> The basis of language is the fact that people do not think solely in terms of physical phenomena which are present immediately to the senses, and which can be designated simply by pointing to them. What they do is to use agreed symbols, or *signs*, to represent these phenomena and think in terms of them. They do the same thing with respect to phenomena which are not physical. When the signs so used are verbal, language begins.[92]

There are '*indexical* signs', like names, which represent one instance of experience. There are *characterizing* signs or *abstractions*, which 'stand not for any particular instance of experience but for an idea – an idea that there *are* certain similarities among an indefinite number of a certain variety of instances of experience'.[93] 'Signs, whether indexical or abstract, have the

---

91 Hart and Sacks, at 114.
92 Id.
93 Id., at 115.

great virtue of making possible thought and speech about things which are not immediately present to the senses, and indeed which may not even be in existence.'[94] Language as a representational form is incapable of mastering and capturing the reality. Nature and society are in a flux that has a natural existence. 'There are more ideas in the world to be expressed than there are words in any language in which to express them.'[95]

This notion of language was described some years before by Ludwig Wittgenstein in his *Philosophical Investigations*[96] as 'a primitive idea of the way language functions'.[97] Instead of this idea of representation, he suggests we think of the whole process of using words as a language game. 'Speaking of language is part of an activity or of a form of life.'[98] 'To imagine a language means to imagine a form of life.'[99] Over a long, fragmentary reflection, Wittgenstein problematizes the idea of indexing devices,[100] abstractions, and provides a complex fragile picture of language as a game that we play, that plays us. He also gives another angle from which to examine the language game and form of life of the Materials.

Considering the philosophical inquiries of Wittgenstein, Hart and Sacks' ideas of language seem simplistic and already outdated at the time the Materials

---

94 Id.
95 Id., at 1124. See also Henry Hart, 'Semantics and The Law', Harvard Special Collection, Box 28-9: 'Those signs which men use to communicate one with another, and as instruments of thought, occupy a peculiar place. It is convenient to group these under a distinctive name; for words, arrangements of words, images, gestures, and such representations as drawing or mimetic sounds we use the terms symbol ... the connection between the word and the thing is only through the thought.'
96 *Wittgenstein, Philosophical Investigations* (3rd edn, 1958). The first part of the book, from which the quotation is taken, was complete by 1945, according to the editor's note in the preface.
97 Id., at 3. Referring to Augustin's confession he summarizes this view (p. 2): 'These words, it seems to me, give us a particular picture of the essence of human language. It is this: the individual words in language name objects – sentences are combinations of such names. In this picture of language we find the roots of the following idea: Every words has a meaning. This meaning is correlated with the word. It is the object for which the word stands.'
98 Id., at 11.
99 Id., at 8.
100 There is a long discussion in the book about the idea of naming. For example, there is the 'language game of inventing a name for something' (id., at 13). 'Naming appears as a *queer* connexion (*sic*) of a word with an object' (id., at 19). And finally: '"A *name* signifies only what is an element of reality. What cannot be destroyed; what remains the same in all changes". – But what is that? – Why, it swam before our minds as we say the sentence' (id. at 29).

are written,[101] and it might be the legal academic framework that enables this home-made 'common sense' philosophy to overcome in a few pages some thousands of pages and years of philosophical debates about language, nominalism, abstractions and names. Still, there is a certain form of life in them that can be read today in their description of how law and language function.

> Legal language differs from ordinary language in that it is concerned predominantly not with describing human experience or evoking emotion about it but with controlling it in the future. When words are used to give authoritative directions about future conduct, the difficulties which result from the imperfect patterning of experience, from its enormous complexity, and from the inability of people to agree in their analysis of it are vastly accentuated.[102]

If legal language is a kind of language game, the Materials present it as a purposive one. Although it has other possible characteristics such as normative, authoritative, prescriptive, distributive, corrective, the choice of the Materials goes back to the pragmatic translation of philosophy into law (and there is certainly no Freud in these texts). Overall, the Materials posit a picture of reality in flux towards an end that can never be captured. The Hohfeldian legacy seems to be rewritten here in order to reinforce this view:

> A welter of jurisprudential discussion has raged about the nature of 'rights' and 'duties' and other such concepts. In the view of these Materials, the matter is much simpler than it has been made to appear.[103]

There are times and places when things are much more complex than they appear and there is a time when they are much simpler (as in the negotiation writings of today). In the post-war period, they seem to be much more simple. (This is a mode very different from the obscure and theoretical

---

101 There is, nevertheless, a reference in the *Materials* to H.L.A. Hart, who takes Wittgenstein's idea of a game, and imports it into law. The authors say the argument of H.L.A. Hart 'seems unduly labored, and in strictness to be mistaken'. There is not an 'intrinsic futility in the attempted mode of elucidation'. There is no need of 'truth conditions' and procedural directions for finding them. 'An accurate specification of the genus – namely, characteristic positions in relation to authoritative directive arrangements – will serve the same purpose of avoiding metaphysical pitfalls as his own more elaborate method of elucidation'; Hart and Sacks, at 129.
102 Id., at 117.
103 Id., at 128.

pragmatism of law, as promoted by Holmes and the Realists.) The Materials update the terminology of Hohfeld with the idea of institutional settlement.

> Statements about legal 'duties' and 'rights' and the like, in other words, assume the existence not only of directive arrangements but of a legal system which is competent and prepared to determine what asserted arrangements are and what are not authoritative, and to act on the basis of the determination. *They are corollaries and expressions of the principle of institutional settlement and of the system of procedures through which the principle is carried out*[104] (my emphasis – M.A.).

The 'provocation of thought' which Hohfeld provided with 'eight fundamental legal conceptions', which he called 'the lowest common denominators of the law',[105] is transformed in the Materials into three 'positions of a recurring type which people have in the sphere of primary private activity as a result of the directions which are given them in self-applying arrangements'.[106] There are primary private duties, liberties, and powers, and the other concepts of Hohfeld are rejected as only occasionally relevant (disabilities), or dangerously confusing between a primary and remedial claim (rights, no-rights, liabilities, and immunities).[107] The 'simplification' procedure is done in the name of the same scorn of the behaviorist-Holmsian notion of the law.[108] While Holmes and Hohfeld kept the obscurity of what the law is by studying its operation in fact as retrospectively transforming its essence, Hart, Sacks, and Fuller leave no philosophical knots or obscure formulas in this matter.

> Law is the process of purposeful pursuit of social ends. The purposes of law are not expressed in the sanctions which it is feasible or expedient to impose. They are expressed in the primary provisions of general directive arrangements, and in the more nearly ultimate conditions which those conditions provisions are designed to foster.[109]

It is not the life of the law that is at stake here. It is not the body of current legal thought and doctrine that is analyzed in pragmatic tools. It is a grand

---

104 Id., at 128–9.
105 Id., at 127, footnote 4.
106 Id., at 130.
107 Id, at 135–6.
108 See *supra* note to text 58–63.
109 Id., at 136.

picture of law that is from the beginning pragmatic, like generalities in philosophy, and needs to serve us to reach some goals. Still, the goals themselves, as always in the pragmatic lesson, are not for themselves. They are meant only to become means again in an endless settlement of society.

2.2.5 The Social Sciences and The Grand Pyramid of Legal Order

The prevalence of science as the paradigm for objectivity and as the ultimate theoretical subtext is brought up and stressed in many places in the Materials. The whole project to deal with law in all its institutional manifestations has a scientific pretension, and the authors strive to show that, although methods of the natural sciences do not apply here,[110] science is still at stake, a distinct genre of which applies to societies.

> But does it follow from this that the body of knowledge about society is unworthy of the name science – that it is not a cognizable body of knowledge, capable of helping man to improve his condition on the face of the globe? The answer here ventured is no. What follows, only, is that the conclusions of the science must depend ultimately upon *judgment* – upon judgment informed by experience and by all the objective data that can feasibly be assembled, but upon judgment nevertheless.[111]

There is an effort to use the body of knowledge of the social sciences to help man 'to improve his condition on the face of the globe'. The functional approach and the engineering pathos involve an element of judgment, which is an integral part for the understanding of the kind of science that law is.

> The science of society builds upon a vast reservoir of human experience and of human reflection about the experience. This reflection makes plain that what is involved is a process of interaction between social ends and social means.[112]

---

110 Hart and Sacks, at 110: 'It is suggested that the science of society cannot proceed by the experimental methods of the natural sciences, because it cannot control its experiments. Nor can the science content itself simply with the observation and analysis of human behavior in the past and present (referring here again to the Realist empiricist creed – M.A.), because, however informative, the results of these are bound to be inconclusive. The science must depend heavily upon ethical and hence disputable considerations.'
111 Id., at 110.
112 Id., at 111.

A problem of institutional decision represents a science of 'Where-do-we-go-from-here?' though a major difference between the 'collective consciousness' of the 1950s and that of the 1960s and beyond is that after the post-war era, the label 'science' itself is not enough to provide the objective foundation that is always searched for.[113] It cannot suffice under humanist and intellectual perspectives. The more literary interpretive subtext, as in Dworkin's writing, which is described elsewhere,[114] is becoming one offer of a foundation, while the scientific mode prevails only in particular schools of thought among the diversity which emerges.[115] The social sciences, which remain scientific and a-historic in their posture, are no longer an agreeable foundation in law.

In a speech to the first-year class of 1948, Henry Hart explains this conception of law in relation to the social sciences:

> Law is a part of the grand body of knowledge which deals with every aspect of man in society. Law, in other words, is a social science. But what distinguishes law from the other social sciences? For me a good short answer is that law is *applied* social science. Or, in a happier phrase of Dean Pound's, it is a social engineering. Both those answers are inexact, but no more so than any short answer must be.[116]

Coming back to the Materials, the mediation of the social sciences with law seems to go back to the old Holmsian aphorism, 'to be master of any branch of knowledge, you must master those which lie next to it; and thus to know anything you must know all'.[117]

> Law being involved in every social relation, it is in some sense an element of every other social science as in some sense every other social science is an element of law.[118]

---

113 See the chapter, 'In Search of the Dispute: On Lawyers and Legal Philawsophers at Harvard Law School (Or: Some Private Hope and Public Irony)'.
114 Id.
115 See the discussion of Richard Posner in the chapter 'Taking Sides: Margins and Phases of Pragmatism of Legal Process Disciples (Or: The Pragmatists that We Are)', part 3.3.
116 Henry Hart, Harvard special collection, Box 22–10: Speech to the first-year class of 1948: 'How to go about the job of studying law'.
117 Julius J. Marke, *The Holmes Reader* (1955), 278.
118 Hart and Sacks, at 174.

In the post-war era, the mediation between all the sciences in the concrete case seems much more possible than before or after that time.[119] The functional framework, again, works here as the mediating device.

> The beginning of wisdom for the social scientist, therefore, is to seek an understanding of the relevant aspects of the institutional system within which the subject of his inquiry is located. He needs to know both the presently fixed limitations of the system and its existing leeways. He will be helped by the sense of the respects in which existing procedures might be modified to make them serve their purposes more effectively.[120]

In contrast to the Realists' emphasis on the social sciences and their study, or to Jerome Frank's notion of lawyer schools, where the effort is to intellectualize the dispute and learn humanist sciences in order to understand its context,[121] the social science emphasis is limited in the 'private ordering' chapter of the Materials to economy and to the technocracy of the dispute. 'Law, it must be apparent, is the inescapable context within which we all live,'[122] and the effort is to present the world through legal lenses. The impossible but crucial task to study all in order to know all and vice versa (to be external and internal at once), is limited in the Materials to the phrasing of two core skills that any American lawyer should have: first, 'skill in the framing of directive arrangements of all kinds, both official and private, and secondly, of skill in their application'.[123]

The bottom-to-top mode of the process of jurisprudence, which starts with 'social reality' and builds the legal as emerging within it, is well reflected in Hart and Sacks' Grand Pyramid of legal norms as described in the Materials. The image of this pyramid of legal norms and its inverse character, in comparison to the European Hans Kelsen's pyramid of norms, illustrates well the pragmatism implied in Hart and Sacks' view.

> The overwhelming proportion of the things which happen and do not happen in American society pass without any later question. Many of these acts and

---

119 See the discussion of the 'query' on page 113 to the Materials, in the chapter 'In Search of the Dispute: On Lawyers and Legal Philawsophers at Harvard Law School(Or: Some Private Hope and Public Irony)', part 4.3.
120 Hart and Sacks, at 111.
121 See the chapter 'In Search of the Dispute: On Lawyers and Legal Philawsophers at Harvard Law School (Or: Some Private Hope and Public Irony)', part 4.4.
122 Hart and Sacks, at 174.
123 Id., at 175.

omissions are the results of decisions which people make in the exercise of a private discretion, accorded to them by official recognition of a private liberty. Still others are in conformity, conscious or unconscious, with officially formulated arrangements conferring private powers or declaring private duties. The remainder are in violation, likewise conscious or unconscious, of such arrangements.[124]

The bottom layer of the Great Pyramid of legal order consists of these 'billions upon billions of events and non-events' which 'stir no later question'.[125] This is society in flux as in Llewellyn's writing, and like reality and nature in flux long ago in Emersonian writing. In the post-war era, this image of an uninterrupted natural interaction between individuals also serves the ideological project of defining capitalism and liberalism in the face of communism and to rewrite the public-private dichotomy in this context.

> The thesis that private ordering is the primary process of social adjustment, in the dynamics of a legal system, has already been several times stated ... The problems which private orderers are able to solve never reach officials at all ... On occasion, of course, social problems do have their origin in an enterprise which is largely or wholly governmental. The Pharaoh may decide to build a pyramid, the Kaiser to launch a war, the Politburo to promulgate a five-year plan, or the United States to build an atomic pile.[126]

Pharaoh, the Kaiser, the Politburo, and the United States appear here on the same line as representing originators of social problems that, on occasion, do emerge from some public decision. The effort to draw the broad, a-historic picture of the great system is typical of that writing, and the idea of the ordinary bottom layer is reinforced in other places as the only natural, true description of what the law is.

> Historically, the law begins and has to begin at the grass roots. Currently and continuously in the continuous current of time the same thing is true. For the function of law is the function of settling the problems of people who are living together in a condition of interdependence ... Governmental action may and constantly does alter the conditions of collaboration among the people in a society. So doing, it may change the nature of the problems pressing for solution, solving some, modifying others, and creating still others. But what the

---

124 Id., at 286.
125 Id.
126 Id., at 161.

government never can do, whatever techniques or legislation it employs, is to change the way in which the problems keep coming to it, emerging at the level of private activity with the gloss of private adjustments and maladjustments already put upon them. This is a fact of social dynamics which not even the masters of Soviet Russia may escape.[127]

The emergence from the private and the bottom layer as the founding base is a social fact,[128] a historical description (historically, law 'has to begin at the grass roots'), and the problems keep emerging from the ground, whatever top-to-bottom arrangement the government will try to enforce.[129] This is a fact of social dynamics that the masters of Soviet Russia must accept, but this is, of course, an American picture of public-private and of the capitalism of that time. The basic 'fact' at stake here, which the quote suggests, already contains ideological motives. It has a history, an origin and an end (in all senses). The previous title of the Materials, *The American Legal System*, as described above,[130] is another indication for the aspiration of the authors to provide the entire broad picture through the local American perspective.

Reflecting on Kelsen's project of building a pyramid of norms can sharpen the cultural background of this description. In Kelsen's *Pure Theory of Law*,[131] the effort is to remain 'purely' within the realm of the norms, to understand their internal logic. Borrowing the purity idea (probably from Kant and his 'Critique of Pure Reason'), and reflecting the logical positivism of the Vienna circle to which he once belonged, Kelsen is interested in describing the unity of the legal order, not through the grass roots, but through the grand norm.

> The norm which represents the reason for the validity of another norm is called, as we have said, the 'higher' norm. But the search for the reason of a norm's validity cannot go on indefinitely like the search for the cause of an effect. It must end with a norm, which, as the last and highest, is presupposed. It must be

---

127 Id. at 159.
128 See Sebok, *supra* note 22 at 175: 'The political culture to which the pluralists referred was a contingent social fact that they believed existed in the United States and could be developed elsewhere.'
129 Id., at 173: 'Democratic pluralism was a product not of laws but of culture ... A shared culture enabled Americans to "combat the weaknesses of human nature and to correct the natural defects of democracy". William Kornhauser argued that in America, "intermediate organizations" made it difficult for elites to control any large portion of the non-elite population, thus preventing the sort of antidemocratic politics of mass culture that occurred in both Germany and Russia.'
130 See *supra* text to note 4.
131 Hans Kelsen, *Pure Theory of Law* (Max Knight, trans., 1960, 1978 ed.), 1934.

presupposed, because it cannot be 'posited', that is to say: created, by an authority whose competence would have to rest on still a higher norm ... The basic norm is the common source for the validity of all norms that belong to the same order – it is their common reason of validity. The fact that a certain norm belongs to a certain order is based on the circumstance that its last order of validity is the basic norm of this order.[132]

Norms are classified in the pyramid according to their place relative to a hypothetical, basic norm. Each norm derives its validity from a higher one, and the highest of all norms is presupposed. The metaphysical impulse to draw, in analytic tools, the science of law is accompanied by a scientific positivistic posture to describe law without any interference of values.[133] The post-war project of Hart and Sacks differs from this effort in a few ways: first, in its self-presentation, not as a theory, but as working materials[134] and a collective consciousness, it avoids the question of what is a jurisprudential text.[135] Second, in their insistence on the robust formula of 'is-ought' and in refuting Kelsen's sharp dichotomy between the normative and the natural, they provide a picture of law that is both natural and normative, in an evolutionary purposive universe. Third, in following their American inheritance of scorn for metaphysics and embrace of the ordinary, they turn the pyramid upside down, or actually begin from the bottom layer as an ideological declaration. This is the place where people settle and resettle by themselves. At the foundation of the pyramid stand all the cases that get settled

---

132 Id., at 195.
133 See for example id., at 1: 'The Pure Theory of Law is a theory of positive law. It is a theory of positive law in general, not of a specific legal order ... As a theory, its exclusive purpose is to know and to describe its object. The theory attempts to answer the question what and how the law *is*, not how it ought to be. It is a science of law (jurisprudence), not legal politics.'
134 See also Vincent A. Wellman, 'Dworkin and The Legal Process Tradition: The Legacy of Hart and Sacks', 29 *Arizona L. Rev.* 413, 417 (1987): 'Hart and Sacks' views on the nature of law and the proper role of the judiciary are neither systematically expressed nor rigorously defended. In many respects, their argument follows the traditional methodology of the common law: they move from example to example, articulating their general propositions only in the context of particular problems. The reader can discern the contours of their theory only after wrestling with the series of cases and questions which have been provided.'
135 See the discussion of the jurisprudential significance of the Materials above, part 2.4.3, and also Dworkin's criticism of Hart and Sacks as failing to account for what it is to follow a rule, in the chapter In search of 'The Dispute: On Lawyers and Legal Philawsophers at Harvard Law School (Or: Some Private Hope and Public Irony)', part 4.3.

by private ordering and do not reach the courts at all. At this private level, people interact freely, as in a state of nature. Going up through the pyramid of norms implies that more judicial intervention has been needed, that more problems have required settlement, but it does not imply anything about the substantial absolute importance of one rule or another which the pragmatic pyramid handles. The hierarchy is based only on the challenges that the rule has met. The singular genealogy of the ordinary case from its experience in reality until its inscription in appeal court opinions is a central focus of the professional jurist. Through their harmonious depiction of the private and public and their repetition of the idea of institutional settlement, they reinforce the view of a pleasant and compact social life, founded on a private sphere of private autonomy, private ordering and interdependence, that is, in a constant state of settling and resettling.

This difference between Kelsen and Hart and Sacks can recall the impulse toward metaphysics against the impulse toward the ordinary, as described by Cavell earlier,[136] but it is also actually marking two diverse notions of law. According to Kelsen, law is a distinct, linguistic genre that needs to be understood in its unique characteristics. In Hart and Sacks' text, law is a functional directive in an assumed natural world, but the crux of the theory's work is to capture its interaction with this world, of the places where the system of settlement was operated. This capturing is the pragmatic impulse, and its impossibility is covered in the post-war era by the idea of society as endless settling and resettling.

From another angle, there is an equivalency between the two (1930s) positivist impulses – that of Kelsen and that of the Legal Realists – in defining law as a science, and the description of its conditions in their purity. While Kelsen tries to do so through the differentiation of the domain of norms, the Realists choose to do so through the empirical sciences' emphasis on the facts of the dispute being resolved.[137] While the first project is highly metaphysical or theoretical and its political motivation seems to arrive from an analytical trend in philosophy, the second project is part of a rebellious intellectual mood in law, which has a political flavor, and does not have an analytical project or a pyramid at stake. The Hart and Sacks pyramid takes the positivist impulse

---

[136] See the chapter 'The Maturing of the Pragmatic Idea in Law and Society: Or, The Fall, and the Rise of Philawsophy', part 1.2.

[137] For an account of Fuller's writing opposing the Realists as being positivist by perceiving law as fact through social science methods, see Duncan Kennedy, 'Lon Fuller's Consideration and Form', *supra* note 82, at 26–7. See also the discussion of Schlegel's position regarding the Realists, later on part 2.4.3.

of the Realists and builds it into a new unifying 'story' – that of society in evolution and of law as a major tool of its coordination. This explains why it is more accurate to say that a pragmatic child is born in these Materials, because the old pragmatic story is materializing here in a different context. The instrumental quality of law as its ultimate discursive quality is rewritten at this moment.

2.2.6 Private Ordering

The place of private ordering in the Materials, which is actually also the place of what is equivalent to negotiation studies of today,[138] is very social; it is the pre-condition of the social organization and stability at that time. Accordingly, the private ordering chapter does not deal with skills and negotiation principles as it would today,[139] but illustrates more the play of lawyers 'in the shadow of the law', and its many implications on the law itself. The two questions which the chapter raises serve as an example:

> [T]he Materials are designed to invite reflection about ... 1. What is the role in fact of private decision in the total direction of American society? 2. What is its optimum role? What are its characteristic advantages and disadvantages? How can private ordering be best regulated so as to make the most of its virtues while curbing its abuses? What are the principle techniques for doing this?[140]

It is crucial not to be deceived by the invitation for reflection and the open thematic, and to ascribe some skepticism or what is considered today post-modernism to the texts at stake. It is modernism in its American peak, aiming to mediate the private and the public and to educate the 'lost lawyer' (of today) in Kronman's call.[141]

---

138 See the chapter 'In Search of the Dispute: On Lawyers and Legal Philawsophers at Harvard Law School (Or: Some Private Hope and Public Irony)', part 4.4, and the suggestion of Albert Sacks that the *Legal Process Materials* are the first place wherein law students were exposed to negotiation studies.
139 See the discussion of Mnookin's book Beyond Winning and his image of the lawyer as a problem solver in the chapter 'In Search of the Dispute: On Lawyers and Legal Philawsophers at Harvard Law School (Or: Some Private Hope and Public Irony)'. Mnookin revitalizes the notion of 'private ordering' in his article 'Bargaining in The Shadow of The Law: The Case of Divorce', while referring directly to The Legal Process writing.
140 Hart and Sacks, at 186.
141 See the discussion of Kronman's claim in the chapter 'In Search of the Dispute: On Lawyers and Legal Philawsophers at Harvard Law School (Or: Some Private Hope and Public Irony)', part 4.4.

> In carrying out his work as law-maker, the lawyer is at once the architect and the builder of human relationships. He draws on his legal learning for knowledge of the legal tools and Materials he can use and their capacity to bear loads and withstand stresses ...[142]

The lawyer is the architect and builder of human relationship, and this central role is a very important social one. His job (not yet 'her' job at the time of the writing of the Materials) is not only the handling of the particular dispute, but of reinforcing the ideology of harmony and cooperation in the American society (the lawyer as statesman, combined with the lawyer as engineer, as I describe elsewhere[143]). The following 1952 call for more emphasis on the lawyer's role can be inserted into the current negotiation wave, which calls us back to the truth of 'real world' interactions.

> Books and articles have been and are continuing to be written about the judicial process, the legislative process, the administrative process. But I suspect the first book has yet to be written about the process whereby a couple of lawyers bring two militantly hostile parties together in an office, adjudicate their disputes, draw a decree or statute called a contract to govern their conduct for the next ten years, and thereafter administer the law they have written in a way that will sensibly and faithfully carry out the legislative intent.[144]

It took more than two decades until such books began to be written in law. Still, they wear quite a different mode than the Materials. It is interesting to mention that in the editors' note to the above-cited call for dispute resolution emphasis, they ask: 'Why "militantly hostile?" Isn't the point just as good, or better, when the parties to begin with are friendly?'[145] This is the post-war optimism that still echoes today in negotiation studies. If there is a choice to present parties as hostile or friendly, let us look at the bright side.

There is a 'multifariousness of questions and possible solutions which is characteristic of all legal problems arising at the stage of initial formulation of an arrangement'.[146] 'This multifariousness is to be contrasted with the relatively sharp focus of the questions characteristically presented in appellate

---

[142] Hart and Sacks, at 188, cited from Cavers, 'Legal Education and Lawyer-Made Law', 54 *W. Va. L. Rev.* 177 (1952).

[143] See the discussion of Kronman's ideas in the chapter 'In Search of The Dispute: On lawyers and Legal Philawsophers an Harvard Law School (Or: some Private Hope and Public Irony)', part 4.4.

[144] Hart and Sacks, at 188.

[145] Id.

[146] Id., at 189.

litigation.'[147] It is a focus on the ordinary, and a claim which recalls the Jerome Frank plea for a lawyers school.[148] Still, the extent of the appeal is limited to a very technical and non-intellectual occupation with the dispute, and it is sometimes embedded in an explicit ideological program. In *The Case of the Jittery Landlady,* the aim is '... to provide a test of one of the editors' general theses – namely, that there *are* types of matters, of which the editors believe this to be one, which ought to be left primarily to private decision rather than being taken over by some officially manned procedure of decision'.[149] In other cases, it is more the thinking of the big problems in context that is at stake, either with 'private decision makers with officials looking over their shoulders',[150] or with assignments of powers in case of federal regulations.[151]

The alternatives to adjudication – arbitration and what is called 'settlement of internal disputes by private groups'[152] – are dealt with as one section within the private ordering chapter, under the title *Remedial Activity*.[153] It is within the third layer of the 'Grand Pyramid of Legal Order' that these processes are located. They are just above the second layer, where all the 'trouble cases' are located, 'situations in which established general arrangements are claimed to be violated',[154] but nothing formal is done to settle them. And they are below the fourth layer, where cases are 'instituted in courts or in other tribunals endowed with powers of formal adjudication'.[155] The third layer is where cases are settled privately, standing between the extreme private and the preliminary public. In the *Courts and the Common Law* chapter, this hierarchy is translated into the role of reason in the social ordering. The bottom layer of the pyramid seems to contain, under the analysis in the *Note on the Problems Appropriate for Adjudication,* two kinds of social interaction that are not susceptible to reason. The first group consists of disputes that depend on the principle of reciprocity.

> To the extent that the resolution of the dispute depends essentially upon what Professor Fuller calls the principle of order by reciprocity, as distinguished from

---

147 Id.
148 See the chapter 'In Search of the Dispute: On Lawyers and Legal Philawsophers at Harvard Law School (Or: Some Private Hope and Public Irony)', part 4.4.
149 Hart and Sacks, at 189.
150 Id., at 209.
151 Id., at 240.
152 Id., at 331.
153 Id., at 286.
154 Id., at 286.
155 Id., at 287.

the principle of order through common ends (including the maintenance of a regime of reciprocity), the method of adjudication operates to eliminate the best judges of a satisfactory exchange – namely, the parties to the exchange themselves – from any effective share in the decision.

For these kinds of disputes, negotiation is the proper method, and the praise of its efficiency recalls with contemporary promotion of that field and its promises.[156]

> In achieving an agreement among disputants, experience seems to show that the most fruitful method, generally speaking, is that of negotiation. Negotiation is informal and flexible in its procedure whereas the procedure of adjudication is formal and rigid. Negotiation is far better adapted than adjudication to securing the pre-condition of a satisfactory agreement – namely, a sympathetic understanding of the other party's point of view.[157]

At this level, 'when negotiation at first fails, but agreement is still to be desired, the most effective form of interposition by a third party is usually the procedure of mediation'.[158]

The second group consists of the most public decisions that are neither susceptible to reason nor to the reciprocity principle:

> For disputes which are not susceptible of solution by reasoning from generally applicable criteria of decision and which fail to yield to efforts to secure agreement among the contestants through negotiation or mediation, modern democratic societies provide the last-ditch solution of a majority vote.[159]

The public-private knot of that time that goes together with the location of negotiation and mediation at the exclusive private level conveys a bottom layer of natural interactions, where both the most private and the most public questions are settled in institutions that are not adjudicative. Adjudication occupies the place of reason, which navigates and handles these parallel orderings, without intruding to their respective realms or to the 'substance' of

---

156 See also Roach, *supra* note 48, at 372–3: 'Hart and Sack's defense of private ordering resembles contemporaneous advocacy of ADR. This includes not only praise for the speed and flexibility of negotiation, but also the tendency to subject adjudication to cost-benefit analysis without being concerned that private solutions may only duplicate existing power distributions.'
157 Hart and Sacks, at 645.
158 Id.
159 Id., at 645.

their determinations. The belief that there is a way to 'describe' the basic forces in society in this natural way, and that there is a way to maintain the balance between them by using adjudication and its 'reason', establishes and at the same time reinforces a very central role for 'the reason of law' as the ultimate engineering force of society. This role keeps echoing in contemporary writing, where the public-private 'description' of the Materials is no longer assumed.[160] It is interesting to examine the ADR movement as challenging this hegemony while using, in a sense, a terminology not so different from that of the Materials.[161]

In a contemporary context, it seems that the above demarcation between alternatives and the core is impossible. The ADR is both at the higher level of the institutional formal public system of dispute resolution, and at the other pole of private ordering where the dispute is studied as a program to engineer, with no value (or 'public') problematic aspects. Its call can be considered radical by questioning *any* pretension to address the great, grand questions by any 'grand style' of reason. The current move from 'alternatives' (to adjudication) to a 'dispute resolution design' for each problem, and to a multi-door courthouse, is another manifestation of the fact that the 'public' today is administered using a different grid. It suggests that there is always only the private singular dispute with its particular sequence of unfolding, according to 'social' principles, and the effort to address it exclusively in one scheme or method is itself a fallacy, that of the static pie, or simply of generalizing.

2.3 Reasoned Elaboration and the Theory of Adjudication

Another central notion that seizes the obscure happening in the process of decision making is that of reasoned elaboration. The organic metaphor of settling law in a scientific way is captured in the Materials through the notion of reasoned elaboration, and also formally frames the legal world of the post-war era: rules, standards, policies, principles.

---

160 See, for example, the discussion of Owen Fiss's notion of adjudication in the chapter 'Taking Sides: Margins and Phases of Pragmatism of Legal Process Disciples (Or: The Pragmatists that We Are)'. Although Fiss promotes a notion of adjudication which stands in opposition to Fuller's definition, and is hostile to its notion of settlement, he is actually affected and conditioned by the Materials' construction of the judge as the ultimate social engineer.

161 See the chapter 'In Search of the Dispute: On Lawyers and Legal Philawsophers at Harvard Law School (Or: Some Private Hope and Public Irony)'.

> In the narrow and technical sense in which the term is here used, a rule may be defined as a legal direction which requires for its application nothing more than a determination of the happening or non-happening of physical or mental events – that is, determination of *fact* ...[162]
>
> Unlike a rule, the application of a standard requires something more than the determination merely of the happenings or non-happenings of physical or mental events. It requires a comparison of the quality or tendency of what happened in the particular instance with what is believed to be the quality or tendency of happenings in like situations.[163]
>
> A *policy* is simply a statement of objectives ... a *principle* also describes a result to be achieved. But it differs in that it asserts that the result *ought* to be achieved and includes, either expressly or by reference to well understood bodies of thought, a statement of the *reasons why* it should be achieved.[164]

Some twenty years later, Ronald Dworkin will describe this structure of principles and policies beyond the rules as a common-sense understanding of any lawyer.[165] Some forty years later, Duncan Kennedy will use this framework to build his *semiotic of legal argument*.[166] At this time, these notions function as an 'indexing device' (coming back to the Holmsian notion of decision making) to delineate the legal universe. A rule requires a determination of facts in 'reality'; a standard requires a more statistical consideration and an

---

162 Id., at 139.
163 Id., at 140.
164 Id., at 141-142.
165 See Ronald Dworkin, *Taking Rights Seriously* (1977) 22: 'I call a "policy" that kind of standard that sets out a goal to be reached, generally an improvement in some economic, political, or social feature of the community ... I call a "principle" a standard that is to be observed, not because it will advance or secure an economic, political or social situation deemed desirable, but because it is a requirement of justice or fairness or some other dimension of morality.' See also the chapter 'In Search of the Dispute: on Lawyers and Legal Philawsophers at Harvard Law School (Or: Some Private hope and Public Irony)', Part 4.3.
   For a discussion of the similarity between Dworkin's theory of adjudication and that of The Legal Process, see Wellmam, *Dworkin and The Legal Process*, *supra* note 134, at 421–8. Wellman analyzes the similarity and difference between the definitions of principles and policies in Hart and Sacks and Dworkin. He describes the definition of principles by Dworkin as 'more rich' than in the Materials, including elements of morality: justice, fairness, etc.
166 See the chapter 'The Maturing of the Pragmatic Idea in Law and Society (Or: The Fall, and the Rise of Philawsophy)', Part 1.5.

evaluation that goes beyond the bare facts. Principles and policies are 'on a much higher level of abstraction'.[167]

> A policy leaves to the addressee the entire job of figuring out how the stated objective is to be achieved, save only as the policy may be limited by rules and standards, which mark the outer bounds of permissible choice. A principle gives the addressee only the additional help of a reason for what he is to try to do.[168]

It is upon the image of society in a flux, and the evolutionary spirit of interdependence as the basic real condition of the human animal, that this hierarchy of rules and standards, policies and principles is built. Upon the assumption of the purposiveness of law as the fundamental natural condition, the 'reasoned elaboration' idea enters as the navigating force of the decision process in the legal universe. There is not a merely obsessive commandment to predict the moment after the decision, nor a vague call to do the work and endure the life of the law. The absorption of some of the Realists' ideas and the unified voice of the 1950s present the judicial work as theoretically transparent within the pragmatic collective picture of the world. There is now a constructive narrative for the discretional operation of the judge. Reasoned elaboration is a type of power given to an official who is obliged to first 'resolve the issue before him on the assumption that the answer will be the same in all like cases'.[169] Second, there is also an obligation to respect the position of the legislator (or another rule maker) in the legal system, and hence to think in terms of 'ought'. Instead of perceiving the kind of discretion that operates here as indeterminate or arbitrary, the Materials depict it as the mediating, stabilizing force of the system.

> [M]any of the questions arising out of general directive arrangements *can* be left to be worked out by the process of reasoned elaboration. In the difficult and delicate enterprise of trying to control the future, choice does not have to be made between the rigors of a perfected rule, on the one hand, and the looseness of unbuttoned discretion, on the other.[170]

Between a perfected rule on the one hand and a loose 'unbuttoned' discretion on the other stands 'reasoned elaboration', a process which goes

---

167   Hart and Sacks, at 142.
168   Id., at 142.
169   Id., at 143.
170   Id., at 144.

back to Holmes's 'obscure' notion, but in this stage and time does not seem obscure anymore (or yet). Rationality itself is depicted as mediating principles and policies through the process of applying a rule.

> The technique of reasoned elaboration which courts pursue or ought to pursue in the effort to arrive at decisions according to law defies any facile generalization which will convey in itself a working understanding. These Materials seek mainly to arrive at such an understanding by grappling with a series of concrete problems of decision of the type of *The Case of the Spoiled Cantaloupes* and of *The Case of the Spoiled Heir*.[171]

There is an experience of the concrete which defies any 'facile generalization', and there is a 'working understanding' which is learned through the concrete problems which are discussed in the course. The optimism and the harmony which characterize this process are probably inspired by the post-war American 'maturing of collective thought' assumption of Henry Hart,[172] an ideological and Harvard-centered idea that if only judges sit together to reflect on the perplexity of principles and policies, the right settling answer will arrive.

Fuller's differentiation between organization for social aims and reciprocity in his then-unpublished article *The Forms and Limits of Adjudication* illustrates the 'rational' element in the reasoned elaboration formula.

> In my opinion, there are two fundamental forms of social order: order through reciprocity and order through common ends. These represent two forms of human association which are capable of enriching the lives of all the participants ...[173]

Based again on the evolutionary image of society, where social arrangements are created in a friendly manner under the conditions of interdependence, these two organizations that Fuller depicts, which were dealt before in their appearance in Hart and Sacks texts,[174] reinforce the public-private dichotomy in the Grand Pyramid above, and in American grassroots ideology, as already discussed. They also capture the notion of reason in adjudication of that era, that is, being governed by norms in contrast to

---

171 Id., at 146.
172 See the discussion of this notion in relation to The Warren Court, and the counter-evidence from that time in part 2.4.2 later.
173 Id., at 402.
174 See part 2.2.6.

fiat.[175] We should not accept 'the fallacy of the static pie', and instead we must assume that the 'two fundamental forms of social order ... are capable of enriching the lives of all the participants'.[176] Adjudication can function well as long as it can elaborate principles, policies, and rules to promote these two forms of social ordering.

> I submit that adjudication can remain rational only so long as it can be meaningfully related to these two basic forms of social order. The objective of maintaining a regime of reciprocity is something that can give adjudication rationality, even though the demands of that regime in particular cases are not obvious in advance, and the rules by which these demands are met may seem unfamiliar when enunciated. In a similar way, the effectuation of shared purposes presents adjudication with a rational task, even though it may be necessary to work out case by case what is demanded by these purposes in particular situations. It will be observed that in both cases adjudication requires shared objectives, except that in the first instance the objective is that of maintaining a regime of reciprocity.[177]

When judges operate discretion, they are trying to promote these two forms of social order, working on a level which is beyond the rules – at the level of society that the rules are supposed to handle. 'The method of adjudication is well suited only for the settlements of disputes which are susceptible to solution by reasoning from general applicable criteria of decision,'[178] and this reasoning is done from the basic principles of social order. As Hart and Sacks say:

> If a claimant comes before a court of general jurisdiction with jurisdiction also over the person of the defendant and asks for a remedy of a type which the court is empowered to give, the dispute, it seems, must always be adjudicable. For either there is some previously formulated settlement affirming or denying the right to the remedy or there is not. If there is, the question of the claimant's

---

175 Sebok, *supra* note 22, at 162: 'Fuller phrased this contrast differently at different points in his career, but the dichotomy always indicated the same stark choices: between reason and fiat, adjudication and arbitration, law and "managerial discretion". In each of the second terms, the regime described is one in which no one's conduct – neither the commander's nor the subject's – is governed by a norm. Just as the commander cannot look to past decisions as reasons for how to decide in the future, the subject cannot conform his or her behavior to meet the commander's "norm".'
176 Id.
177 Id.
178 Id., at 646.

right, of course, can be determined by conventional processes of judicial reasoning. If there is not, then, it is suggested, the only difference is that reasoning must probe more deeply to the basic postulates of the social order – to the rational implications of the 'shared purposes' of the members of the society of which Professor Fuller speaks. *A reasoned answer to the question whether those implications do or do not justify the asserted right will always be possible. Within the limits fixed by established remedies, in other words, the common law provides a comprehensive, underlying body of law adequate for the resolution of all the disputes that may arise within the social order*[179] (my emphasis – M.A.).

The 'either-or' initial presentation continues with the idea that for every unsettled question, we must 'probe more deeply' and reach 'the basic postulates of the social order'. There, where those basic postulates are, we can find the 'shared purposes of the members of the society', and by working with them a reasoned answer 'will always be possible'. The common law provides a body of law for 'all the disputes that may arise within the social order'. The idea that we can touch the basic postulates, resolve all the disputes, expose the shared purposes, and operate within our remedies will be discussed later in light of the Brown decision and the perceived challenge it made to that view.[180] From today's perspective, it seems much more reasonable to describe the 'polycentric' exception of Fuller[181] as conditioning the basic postulate of the social order.

The peaceful expression of settlement is well understood when the role of a judge is posited as coordinating the natural forms of social ordering that enable enrichment and progress. The official role of courts as settling disputes derives from the founding assumption of natural organizations that need to be handled rationally. The common law tradition helps to reinforce this notion of a delicate craft as carrying a promise and a life of its own.

---

179 Id., at 647.
180 See part 2.4.3.
181 The limits of adjudication, according to Fuller, are determined by the level in which the rights of the individuals to participate in the process are preserved, and this is why polycentric, or 'many-centered', problems are not suitable for adjudication. Multiple repercussions might result from any decision regarding just one of the issues. 'Each crossing of strands is a distinct center for distributing tensions.' See the discussion of this notion in the chapter 'Taking Sides: Margins and Phases of Pragmatics of Legal Process Disciples (Or: The Pragmatists that We Are)', part 3.2. See also Hart and Sacks, at 647: 'A problem is "polycentric" when it involves a complex of decisions, judgment upon each of which depends upon the judgment to be made upon each of the others. Such problems characteristically present so many variables as to require handling by the method either of *ad hoc* discretion or of negotiation or of legislation.'

[T]he development of a body of decisional law is only a byproduct of the judicial process. The basic function of law is only a byproduct of the judicial process. *The basic function of courts is the function of adjudication – or, more accurately, the function of settling disputes by the method of adjudication*[182] (my emphasis – M.A.).

The decision of the judge is considered 'bringing to a peaceable conclusion the particular disputes which the courts actually settle'.[183] Since the whole grand social apparatus is functioning in harmony, the dispute is handled as a matter of natural order, which lacks any aspect of force or violence. Adjudication is at once settling the dispute and settling the law.[184] It is not only that the dispute settlement function is an integral function of courts (which will be conceptually denied some twenty years later), but the discretional element in law, which is the violent potential of any decision making, is posited as a dispute settlement itself. Duncan Kennedy describes this belief in harmony and evolution as emerging also from Rene Demogue's 1911 writing, which influenced Fuller in his *Consideration and Form* article:

Compromise, Not Logical Synthesis, the Goal of Juridical Effort. May we hope that the human brain will one day be strong enough to unite in one harmonious synthesis the elements on which law depends? I do not believe that it is possible. We can make fortunate reconciliations – an effort which is even facilitated by the shut-in character of every society; but we must be conscious of their imperfection… Law can perfect its technique, that is to say its methods of perfectly attaining an end, or even several ends simultaneously. This is the only side on which it is certain that progress is possible.[185]

The modest tone above, and the writing in favor of compromise, might have influenced private law development as Kennedy suggests, and enhanced a complex understanding of 'conflicting considerations'. In the *Legal Process Materials*, however, there is another tone and operation of the same idea of compromise and settlement. The lack of any pretense of being rigorously academic and the spirit of the era allow the authors to announce firmly that the dispute and the law *are* settled. This is the way it is, not a compromise, but as a picture of the legal world through an American lens in the post-war period. The court is the 'happy harmonizer', as pragmatism once was, but the world

---

182 Hart and Sacks, at 342.
183 Id.
184 Id., at 640.
185 From Kennedy, 'Lon Fuller's Consideration and Form', *supra* note 82, at 22–3.

in which it operates is much more complex, much more sophisticated in the Legal Process era. It is a world – a body – that will be endorsed faithfully in its materiality by coming generations, even if its ideology and epistemology will be scorned.

The discussion of the relation between fact and value is another example of the way the critical knot of the Realists' message is evaded, through the pragmatic tone and the idea of elaboration. The authors declare that 'in a more spacious view of the Legal Process than these Materials have taken, it would be appropriate at this point to present a problem dealing with the modes by which the courts ascertain the historical facts of a litigation which pose the legal problems for decisions'.[186] They mention Jerome Frank as being interested in these questions,[187] but choose not to try and answer them. They see this inquiry as not strictly relevant to the main theme of the Materials, which concerns basic problems in the development of law. The many ways in which perceptions are affected by idiosyncratic factors and the many laws (cultural, social) through which a factual 'happening' is framed and transformed are not of their interest (the colorful theater of the ordinary, of experience). The complexity they choose to focus on is the circular relationship between facts and the legal rules that are supposed to apply to them. Instead of asking, 'Is this a question of law or of fact?' one should acknowledge the indeterminacy (or actually, perhaps the interdependence) of the dichotomy itself.

> ... [W]ith respect to a question which is posed *initially* as a question of law application – *e.g.,* is a game with these features a lottery or not a lottery? – the answer, whether it be 'law' or 'fact' cannot be derived from the inherent characteristics of the question .... To ask whether the initial question of law application 'is' a question of law or fact is to conceal crucial issues of policy as to whether this further elaboration (the elaboration of the governing general proposition 'lottery' in this case – M.A.) will take place. The real problem about such questions is not whether they *are* questions of law or fact but rather whether they *ought to be treated* as law or fact.[188]

There is a judgmatical aspect in determining the facts when the ultimate question is one of applying the law: the elaboration of law according to principles and policies serves to determine the facts, and that is how the 'ought'

---

186 Id., at 344.
187 Id.
188 Id., at 352.

element conditions the delineation between law and fact. The facts are sometimes determined according to the elaboration of law that applies to them. There is also a dependency 'on the governing institutional arrangements (a) as to who decides it, and (b) as to whether the decision will be significant for all other like cases or only for the case in hand'.[189] The crucial message in this context is to avoid the hard questions of 'reality' and its perceptions (the Jerome Frank business) by providing a complex picture of facts, legal rules, and institutional arrangements that is nevertheless manageable (and given to generalization) due to the circularity it establishes. The idea that the judge 'elaborates', and that the rich description of the conditions of this activity are essential to the demarcation of fact and value, assume the naturalness and the organic character of discretion in law.

2.4 Why Couldn't Henry Hart Speak?, and the Many Faces of Retrospection

2.4.1 *The Next Generation, and the 'No-voice' Metaphor*

My effort to posit the post-war time as a constitutive moment focused until now on the reading of the Materials in terms of the texts and discourses operating before that era and within it.[190] Legal scholars in the 1950s constructed a manuscript without a primarily theoretical pretension in the form of course Materials, an amalgam of ideas from philosophy and law since the turn of the century, to produce the canonical manifesto of the American legal system. As already mentioned, while this text was written, the ideas themselves – evolution of the social, pragmatism, the is-ought problematic – were already theoretically outdated, and that is how, beside the sophisticated appealing 'internal' lesson of the body of the law as rules, principles, and policies, and that of an institutional perspective, the theoretical message of this school remained ambiguous. Had it meant to produce a theory? Was it a jurisprudence of process? What is the significance of defining the school as theoretical or not? What is its relationship with theories which succeeded it? One preliminary answer of contemporary discourse to these questions is that

---

189 Id.
190 There were a few exceptions to this 'pure' presentation in the first part of this chapter when the writing of Duncan Kennedy, Morton Horwitz, or Robert Doyle was brought forward, and they were all related to examining the 'Realist-pragmatic' message against the 'formalist-contractarian' one.

there is no one right answer. Since the 1970s, there have been many legal histories, no longer a collective consciousness or a unifying evolutionary story. There is an interpretive turn in progressive legal thought, an economical turn in conservative thought; there is an analytical branch, still faithful to British sentiments, which sometimes claims for veto power to define 'the theory of law' (or the jurisprudential question); and there are still marginal scholars who call for natural law or a literary perspective. There are many schools and movements, children and grandchildren, defined as dead or claiming to live. The legal academy is modernity itself: diverse, colorful, refusing to be captured by one voice.

Within this diversity, however, there is hierarchy, there are role assignments, hegemonies and complex relations between internals and externals, core and periphery. A guiding power in reflection is given in that context to the so-called progressive intellectuals in the legal academy, and *their* point of view in depicting the post-war era informs a crisis, and an experience of the loss of parental authority. The image of Henry Hart illustrates this rupture in its most symbolic appearance. Hart served as a law professor at Harvard during the years following the publication of the Materials, and was famous for his interest in providing a theoretical base for The Legal Process approach. For many years, he was preoccupied with the jurisprudential consequences of such an approach. Rumor had it that he was working on a jurisprudence book, and was supposed to present its outline at the third of the prestigious 'Holmes Lectures' series, which he gave in 1958 at Harvard. During the third lecture, when the time arrived for the promised theory to be told, 'he announced that, upon further reflection, his planned resolution of the problems did not work. Having said that, he sat down before a stunned audience'.[191] This projection of failure is repeated in another historical description wherein Hart, upon reflection in front of a class, gives up his intellectual weapons and chooses not to attack an activist ruling of the Supreme Court. Instead, after a few minutes of his students' 'breathless' silence, Hart says: 'Sometimes, sometimes, you just have to do the right thing.'[192]

---

[191] Id., at xcviii.

[192] Id., at cxiii. This occurred when Hart 'taught "Federal Courts" for the last time, during the Spring term of 1965' and brought into the class the Supreme Court's opinion in *Hamm v. City of Rock Hill*. 'The Court applied the just-enacted Civil Rights act of 1964 to abate Southern prosecutions of sit-in demonstrators. Hart stated the facts and relevant authorities, including a federal statute creating a presumption against finding abatement for prosecution by new statutes. It was apparent from the professor's statement of the case and the authorities that the decision was about to be analytically dissected.'

The image of Hart, standing mute before a stunned audience, the image of the silent students watching the giving up of intellectual weapons are characteristic of the experience of the 1960s generation. Henry Hart could not speak, probably because the post-war era, with its optimism, collective spirit, and national pride, is perceived as blind in the eyes of the new generations of intellectuals. Albert Sacks, his younger co-author, is also famous for his 'curious refusal to resume work on their unfinished yet widely accepted theory'.[193] While Hart is described as 'the most creative law teacher of his time', Sacks 'played the solid and excruciatingly thorough partner'.[194] The perceived inability to raise the Materials to a level of a 'theory', of a jurisprudence, is actually a common judgment among all the diverse schools in contemporary discourse.[195] Hart and Sacks are frequently regarded as 'figures only of their time',[196] and though they had some other theoretical writing,[197] the common

---

193 Sebok, *supra* note 22, n95. See also J.D. Hyman, 'Constitutional Jurisprudence and the Teaching of Constitutional Law', 28 *Stan L. Rev.* 1271, 1286 n70 (1976): 'If Dean Sacks could be persuaded to abandon his less important duties at Harvard to complete the book and see it into print, I would be prepared to argue that it was a denial of the equal protection of the laws to confer a law degree on a student who has not been exposed to it.'
   It is interesting to note that Sebok, who cites Hyman as an evidence for the 'theory lack' in Hart and Sacks, probably gives a new reading to the 1976 more 'practical' call to publish the book, which Hyman considers 'the most influential book not produced in movable type since Gutenberg'. Sebok builds on this lack he reads (as I do) and continues to say that: 'The purpose of this book is, in one sense, an attempt to make an argument that Hart and Sacks could have made but did not make.' Id.
194 Norman Dorsen, 'In Memoriam: Albert M. Sacks', 105 *Harv. L. Rev.* 1, 14 (1991): 'Whatever one may think of its philosophy, The Legal Process was a germinal work; countless judges and lawyers remote from academic discourse "moved to the measure of its thought". That it was such a work must be attributed in the first instance to Henry Hart, the most creative law teacher of his time. Hart added to his own stature even further by selecting the ideal colleague with whom to produce The Legal Process. They reversed the usual relationship between youth and age: Al Sacks played the thoroughly and excruciatingly thorough partner; he personally typified the Legal Process virtues of fairness, balance, and propriety. He was the perfect counterpoint to his more volatile and pyrotechnic senior.'
195 See Sebok, *supra* note 22, at 113: 'It seems commonly assumed by those who study constitutional law or jurisprudence that the Legal Process school did not possess a legal theory of great sophistication.' See also Wellman, *Dworkin and The Legal Process, supra* note 165, at 145: 'Philosophers writing on current issues of legal theory seem generally unaware of *The Legal Process* and its importance in shaping a generation of legal scholarship.'
196 Wellman, *Dworkin and The Legal Process, supra* note 165, at 415.
197 Id., at 416, footnote 25, and also Sebok, *supra* note 22, at 113–19, where he tries to revive the neglected jurisprudence of Henry Hart by analyzing his 1951 Holmes' *Positivism* article.

opinion is that 'their manuscript was not only the foundation of their contribution, it was their only joint foray into the problems of law and judging'.[198] The following discussion aims to illustrate the multifarious narrations of the post-war era's Legal Process product, looking through progressive eyes, and through the eyes of others, while trying to keep my textual reading of the previous part as the guiding analytic tool.

2.4.2 Reasoned Elaboration and the End of Reason[199]

Anthony Sebok describes 'the theory of reasoned elaboration'[200] as built in stages, culminating in Hart's famous 1959 Foreword to *Harvard Law Review*. He perceives the history of the foreword to the annual Supreme Court survey as a 'useful lens through which to chart the development of reasoned elaboration as a critical institution'.[201]

> The first stage ... concerned the question of 'political' judging: The problem with adjudication based on political reasons was that such a decision cannot produce useful legal reasons ... the second stage of the development of reasoned elaboration began in 1955 and focused on the court's denial of *certiorari* in clearly ripe but controversial cases ... The third stage of the development of reasoned elaboration was found in Ernest Brown's attack in 1958 on the Supreme Court's practice of reversing lower court opinion through *per curiam* opinions ... To put it bluntly, he was worried that the court's newfound taste for *per curiam* reversals was evidence of the Court's declining abilities.[202]

---

198 Wellman, *Dworkin and The Legal Process*, supra note 165, at 416.
199 The title suggests at first an inquiry into the purposive orientation of the 'reasoned elaboration' notion. Additionally it refers to the goal of using reason in general in that era in law, discussing the political motivation of this project in the face of the Warren court. Finally, it recalls *The End of Reason* of Max Horkeimer, whom at the same era was writing about the 'progress of reason that leads to its self-destruction'. See Duncan Kennedy, 'Lon Fuller's Consideration and Form', *supra* note 82, at 6, presenting Horkheimer and Fuller as characters from different worlds.
200 Id., at 122.
201 Id., at 120: 'The foreword was first published in 1951 and served as simply what its title promised: a short introduction written by a member of the faculty to the student-written summary of important Supreme Court decisions of the previous year. The forward eventually evolved into an institution in its own right, in which a major scholar not only reviewed the past year but also took the opportunity to set out a substantive theory of constitutional law.'
202 Id., at 123–5.

In an era in which the Warren Court gives its progressive decisions, which Morton Horwitz describes as 'having initiated a unique and revolutionary chapter in American constitutional history',[203] the scholars at Harvard are worried that the court's performance is too political and describe it as having poor scores when 'measured on the scale of its mastery of legal reasoning'.[204]

> In the 1954 Foreword, Albert Sacks praised the Warren Court's desegregation cases but focused most of his attention on the Court's use of 'summary opinions' to dispose of some of the year's most difficult legal issues.[205]

As Garry Peller claims later, the people at stake are liberals, and understand themselves as progressives.[206] Still, they perceive a conceptual problematic in the ruling of the Supreme Court, and try to promote their own theory about how the Court should decide cases. 'The theory of reasoned elaboration received its fullest statement in two articles written by men who would come to symbolize the Legal Process movement.'[207] The first was Alexander Bickel; in his 1957 foreword, Bickel and Wellington criticized the Court as producing a 'sweeping dogmatic statement' in the *Lincoln Mills* case.[208] The second was Henry Hart in his 1959 foreword, wherein he criticized the Supreme Court for being too busy to review and debate the opinions of the various justices.

> Hart was assuming, of course, that legal reasoning is a bit like shooting at a target: The more people and more attempts there are, the greater the likelihood of hitting the 'right' answer. Hart based this assumption on the phenomenon he called the 'maturing of collective thought':

> Ideas which will stand the test of time as instruments for the solution of hard problems do not come ... with dependability to any single individual even in much longer periods of study and reflection. Such ideas have ordinarily to be hammered out by a process of collective deliberation of individuals, gifted or otherwise, who recognize that the wisdom of all, if it is successfully pooled, will usually transcend the wisdom of any.[209]

---

203 Horwitz, *The Warren Court*, *supra* note 240, at 3.
204 Sebok, *supra* note 22, at 122.
205 Id., at 123.
206 See part 2.4.3 above.
207 Sebok, *supra* note 22, at 125.
208 Id.
209 Id., at 126.

The expression 'maturing of collective thought' which opened the chapter and marks the 1950s jurisprudence, at least through some lenses,[210] is born here in Hart's writing, within the mode of an opposition to an activist court that does not reflect the majority opinion. Good and right decisions in law should follow the polls, the statistics, and emerge from bottom to top in a reasoned process of balancing and harmonizing.[211] 'The right answer would win not only more of the Court, but of the legal community and the nation as well.'[212] It should be settling. 'The fundamental proposition suggested by each succeeding set of forewords was that a judgment accompanied by a reasoned justification – whatever its political outcome – was better than a judgment alone even if it reflected the "right" result.'[213]

> Thus, reasoned elaboration was a theory of adjudication in which reason served three functions: It controlled political willfulness, it provided the public with principles around which action could be planned, and it helped increase the likelihood of the right outcome.[214]

Eskridge and Frickey describe the emergence of this notion as responding to law's purposiveness.

> Law's purposiveness inspires Hart and Sacks' theory of 'reasoned elaboration'. Acknowledging that general directives often do not transparently tell officials and citizens what to do in specific situations, Hart and Sacks nevertheless dispute the Realist claims that the official simply imposes a political interpretation on the general directive and that law is a prediction of how the official will exercise his discretion. To the contrary, an official applying a 'general directive arrangement' must 'elaborate the arrangement in a way which is consistent with the other established application of it' and 'must do so in a way which best serves the principles and policies it expresses'.[215]

---

210 See part 2.4.3 above.
211 See also Henry Hart, 'Foreword: The Time Chart of the Justices: The Supreme Court 1958 Term', 73 *Harv. L. Rev.* 84, 99 (1959): 'Only opinions which are grounded in reason and not on mere fiat or precedent can do the job which the Supreme Court of the United States has to do ... only opinions of this kind can carry the weight which has to be carried by the opinions of a tribunal which, after all, does not in the end have the power either in theory or in practice to ram its own personal preferences down other people's throats.'
212 Id.
213 Id., at 156.
214 Id., at 127.
215 Id., at xcii.

This mediation they describe between the political and the deductive, the Realist and the formalist, parallels that of Edward White in his article *The Evolution of Reasoned Elaboration: Jurisprudential Criticism and Social Change*.[216]

> The view of the Article is that Reasoned Elaboration emerged in the late 1930s and early 1940s when certain social experiences – particularly the threat of totalitarianism and the circumstances surrounding the Court-packing crisis of 1937 – generated overwhelming academic hostility to jurisprudential Realism.[217]

He goes on to describe the emergence of the principle in the following way:

> As legal scholars of the 1950s grew increasingly convinced of the importance of judicial rationalization, they came to criticize its contemporary manifestations and to formulate a new set of ideals and standards for judicial decision making. Reasoned Elaboration, a catch phrase coined by Henry Hart and Albert Sacks in 1958, came to summarize those ideals and standards. The phrase, as applied to the Supreme Court, demanded, first, that judges give reasons for their decisions; second, that the reasons be set forth in a detailed and coherent manner; third, that they exemplify what Hart called 'the maturing of collective thought'; and fourth, that the Court adequately demonstrate that its decisions, in the area of constitutional law, were vehicles for the expression of the ultimate social preferences of contemporary society.[218]

We can find here again the stigmatized basic ideology of that era: the assumption of a collective consciousness, the ability to access 'ultimate social preferences', the organizing glue of pragmatism and experience.

A more contextual notion of this concept, accounting for its use as determining institutional competence, is given by Peller in his *Neutral Principles* article:

> 'Reasoned elaboration' referred to a sense of craft within which the judiciary could elaborate principles and policies contained within precedent and legislation to reach a reasoned, if not analytically determined, result in particular cases. In general, if an issue was capable of a reasoned resolution, the judiciary had jurisdiction to decide the issue so long as the legislature had not already spoken.

---

216 G. Edward White, 'The Evolution of Reasoned Elaboration: Jurisprudential Criticism and Social Change', 59 *VA L. Rev.* (1973) 279.
217 Id., at 279.
218 Id., at 286.

On the other hand, if an issue was not capable of 'reasoned elaboration' that is, if it involved mere 'preference' or 'sheer guesswork', then it was beyond the competence of the judiciary and therefore outside the functional jurisdiction of the courts.[219]

The new rationalists in law believed that 'law's rationality is informed by an organic relationship among legal rules, social policies, and ethical principles'.[220] (They disputed the Realist claims that 'the official simply imposes a political interpretation on the general directive and that law is a prediction of how the official will exercise his discretion'.[221]) 'A judge interpreting a statute must first identify the purpose of the statute, what policy or principles it embodies, and then should reason toward the interpretation most consistent with that policy or principle.'[222] Hart and Sacks assumed that for every judicial problem there was an ultimately 'reasonable' solution, reasonable in terms of the value preferences of American society at a particular point in time. This solution could be reached, despite human frailties, if judges 'would take the time and effort to discuss openly their view of cases, compare them with the views of other colleagues, and articulate as fully as possible the general areas of ultimate concordance'.[223] They focus on 'institutional competence' as the basis for the distribution of legal tasks among various legal actors, and in adjudication, this principle implies that judges are competent to decide cases where 'reasoned elaboration' is possible.

> Thus, reasoned elaboration was a theory of adjudication in which reason served three functions: It controlled political willfulness, it provided the public with principles around which action could be planned, and it helped increase the likelihood of the right outcome.[224]

Between the lines of these historical narrations we can trace the 'non-collective' pole of the expression 'maturing of collective thought'. Its birth, as well as its development and later depiction, are part of a response to a judicial phenomenon which has not yet won its theoretical establishment. It is actually a lesson taught to a Court that is assumed not to operate its 'collective thought' properly at all.

---

219 Peller, *supra* note 2., at 595.
220 *The Legal Process*, *supra* note 5, lxiii.
221 Id., at xcii.
222 Id.
223 White, *supra* note 216, at 287–8.
224 Sebok, *supra* note 22, at 127.

In an interesting reverse on the Holmsian legacy, Hart announces what he perceives as the contemporary call: '... the time must come when it is understood again, inside the profession as well as outside, that reason is the life of the law'.[225] The life of the law has been reason all along, not experience, says Hart, and there is here indeed 'faith in reason', but also a certain kind of reason, in order to support a certain project.[226] The political and cultural climate of the 1950s produces a discourse of law where the grand hysterical narrative (of reason or the new beginning of the style of reason that the Americans suggest, of a pragmatic reasoning of settlement) is intertwined with the hard professional work of the legal scholar. At the same time, the emergence of the 'reasoned elaboration' notion is a reaction to the 'political' and 'immature' manner in which the Warren Court gives its decisions in that era.

The apparent uniformity, accordingly, is not at all neat at that time. While Harvard produces a unifying conservative call, in other places there are still Realists, activist progressives, and other groups that refuse to join the celebration. The 1960 Thurman Arnold's *Professor Hart's Theology*[227] seems to illustrate this point:

> Professor Hart seems to think that reason would replace the conflicting views now present on the court if the court had more time for 'the maturing of collective thought'. There is no such process as this, and there never has been; men of positive views are only hardened in those views by such conferences. There is no possibility that I could pool my wisdom with Professor Hart's so that the wisdom of both of us, 'successfully pooled', would 'transcend the wisdom of' either of us. The reason is that I do not think his wisdom is real wisdom, and I am sure that he has the same opinion of mine. To lock the two of us in a room until I came to agree with the theology of Professor Hart by the process of the 'maturing' of our 'collective thought' would be to impose a life sentence on both of us without due process of law.[228]

Arnold, writing only one year after Hart's article, perceives no 'collective consciousness' at hand, and does not accept the optimistic assumption that waiting for a consensus to emerge or 'elaborating' through more legal sources will produce more just decisions. He describes Hart's article as 'a whole series of similar pompous generalizations dropped on the Court from the height of

---

225 Henry Hart, *The Time Chart Of The Justices*, supra note 225, at 1300.
226 See the discussion of Daxbury and Sebok later, part 2.4.3.
227 Thurman Arnold, 'Professor Hart's Theology', 73 *Harv. L. Rev.* (1960) 1298.
228 Id., at 1312.

Olympus'.[229] Olympus at that time is Harvard, and in its iconic role as representing the American, the message it emanates is of peaceful reasoned deliberation. As Erwin Griswold responded to Judge Arnold's critique in the following year's foreword, 'To me, "the maturing of collective thought" is a profound reality.'[230] This indeed might be the 'profound reality' at Harvard, in some sense, until today.[231] In a contemporary negotiation workshop at Harvard Law School, we can find the same spirit today, referring to feelings, interests and relationships. Instead of the idea of 'reasoned elaboration' there are the ideas of 'brainstorming', 'win-win', and 'expanding the pie'. 'Neutral principles' are also back again within this engagement.[232] It is not the truth-value of Arnold's article, Hart's writing, Griswold or Mnookin's call that matter. It is the context: the time, the place, the addressee, the pretension. Hart's text tries to be theoretical, academic, aimed towards constitutional law and the highest public debates. Negotiation texts try to stay at the level of practical advice, skills teaching, and overcoming the big public questions through the technology of dispute resolution.[233]

Coming back to Arnold, his call to break the charts and to demystify the theology seems almost prophetic when we read it from today's perspective:

> It is highly probable that if the Supreme Court were selected from a single law school whose faculty was recruited from like minded dialecticians, the decisions of the Court would more closely conform to a uniform and less Realistic set of standards. This, I take it, is the ideal of Professor Hart. It would be unfortunate indeed if that ideal were even partially realized ... But fortunately for the nation in time of changes, the present court is composed of men of widely differing experience representing many facets of American thought ... But it is these very conflicts of which Professor Hart complains that are making the court responsive to the demands of a rapidly changing economy ... When these conflicts are all resolved – when the members of the Court by the process of

---

229 Id., at 1299.
230 See Sebok, *supra* note 22, at 128: 'Griswold's response was more a rebuke than a rebuttal: he seemed to regard Arnold with the same condescension with which the Realists once dismissed Langdell and Beale.'
231 See the discussion later, infra text to , and also the chapter 'In Search of The Dispute: On Lawyers and Legal Philawsophers at Harvard Law School (Or: Some Private Hope and Public Irony)'.
232 See the discussion of Wechsler's article in part 2.4.3 above.
233 See the discussion of the relation between the Legal Process scholarship and the dispute resolution discourse in the chapter 'In Search of the Dispute: On Lawyers and Legal Philawsophers at Harvard Law School (Or: Some Public Hope and Public Irony)'.

maturing of collective thought all think alike – then and then only will it be appropriate to begin to worry about the future of the court.[234]

The Supreme Court at that time is not selected from the same law school. It is, in Horwitz's words, 'the first Supreme Court in American history to champion the legal position of the underdog and the outsider in American society. Studying the biographies of the legal justices, one is immediately struck by the extent to which they were themselves outsiders.'[235] When jurisprudential theories finally emerge during the late 1960s and 1970s to account for such a progressive Court,[236] the Court indeed transforms again, as Arnold offers, and might suffer from 'a collective thought' at last. Coming back to the 1950s, the independent direction the Warren Court took at the time of the development of the idea of reasoned elaboration has its own mode of reason, at that time still not articulated in theoretical terms.

2.4.3 The Warren Court and the Metaphysics of Externals

There is a perceived gap between the progressiveness of the Warren court and the conservative approach of the Legal Process scholars that this section will seek to explore and question. Within the history or storytelling of the Legal Process era, there seem to be at least two groups that try to provide their evaluation of the intellectual contribution of legal scholarship at that time. The first is that of progressive legal historians, who grief the loss of progressivism at that era. They usually depict this era as having no theory, no passion, and I present them as providing the hegemonic narrative of legal history. The second is some other intellectuals, the externals in my framework, and I include here by way of example two groups: first, British-oriented positivists who engage in analytical jurisprudential debates about sources of law and the separation of law and morals, while trying to catalogue the jurisprudence of that era as formalist, positivist, realist or non positivist; second, historians who touch this era as part of a story about the relation of the social sciences and law.

Beginning with the progressives, Herbert Wechsler's article *Toward Neutral Principles of Constitutional Law* is a central theme in this part. While Hart and Sacks are perceived as failing in producing a theory, and are

---

234 Arnold, *supra* note 227, at 1313–14.
235 Morton J. Horwitz, *The Warren Court and the Pursuit of Justice* (1998), 13.
236 See the chapter 'Taking Sides: Margins and Phases of Pragmatics of Legal Process Disciples (Or: the Pragmatists That We Are)'.

considered indifferent to the *Brown* decision or even silent supporters of it,[237] Wechsler, who is considered a Legal Process scholar, *is* assumed to produce a theory, and a very controversial one. Sebok calls it 'an infamous symbol of the legal process schools' hostility to civil rights',[238] and characterizes four types of response to it in his article: Realist, internal, conservative, and fundamental rights school (or liberal).[239] In my reading, two responses will be characterized: the progressive internals, and the analytic or a-historic externals (where I locate Sebok too). Later, in another part, a third position, that of Duncan Kennedy in 1970, will be examined in its singularity.

A basic claim I try to prove throughout the following exposition is that the externals are unable to perceive the gap, or the theoretical vacuum, that the 1950s created for the generation that followed. This gap can be traced between two descriptions by Morton Horwitz of that time.

By the end of the nineteenth century, then, the Civil War Amendments had been interpreted to give almost no special constitutional protections to the former slaves, who were originally thought to be their principal beneficiaries. And despite the fifteenth amendment, which barred racial discrimination in voting, by the turn of the century virtually all southern blacks had been disenfranchised.

By the time *Plessy* was decided, the Supreme Court justices had themselves come to absorb and endorse the post-1877 political realities, which conceded to Southern whites a free hand in reestablishing and maintaining what would come to be romanticized as the 'Southern way of life'.[240]

---

[237] Hart and Sacks have not included the *Brown* decision in their Materials and were considered suspicious toward that decision, though in their personal life, they are described as 'liberal'. See Norman Dorsen, *In Memoriam*, supra note 194, at 11–13. See also Eskridge and Peller, *Introduction to Hart and Sacks*, at cvi–cvii. They say that omitting 'neither a problem nor any discussion of courts challenges to racial discrimination' is ironic. This is in light of 'Hart's stated "bias in favor of a representative variety of subject matter" in teaching Materials. It is downright mysterious, in light of the co-authors' strong personal interest in civil rights. Albert and Sadelle Sacks both served on the Governor's Civil Rights Commission in Massachusetts and joined Dr. Martin Luther King Jr.'s 1963 March on Washington. Hart was also committed to the principle of civil rights and to the practice of integration. For example, he was one of the few Harvard faculty members living in Cambridge who sent his child to the integrated public schools.'

[238] Sebok, *supra* note 22, at 180: 'The essay prejudiced an entire generation of liberal scholars to the point where few chose to look past Wechsler's presentation of reasoned elaboration before rejecting the project out of hand.'

[239] Id., at 183. 'Because he was seen as applying Hart and Sacks' principles, Wechsler was seen as speaking for the Legal Process school.'

[240] Horwitz, *The Warren Court*, supra note 235, at 17.

As World War II ended, something new and intangible had clearly begun to transform the atmosphere of American race relations. Whether the courage and loyalty of African American troops who fought against Hitler in segregated army units touched the American conscience; or whether Hitler's mass murder of European Jews had finally demonstrated where racist laws might lead; or whether black soldiers, having experienced interracial European societies at first hand, returned home unwilling to accept traditional race relations; or whether American politics was beginning to register the effects of a massive migration of five million disenfranchised Southern blacks to Northern cities, where they were often in a position to tip the balance in closely contested presidential elections – whatever the precise explanation, there clearly appeared a new determination among blacks and some whites in post-war America to end institutionalized racism.[241]

And on the other hand:

> From the perspective of a generation later, Wechsler's difficulties in holding racially discriminatory statutes unconstitutional have that inaccessible quality of ancient structures of understanding derived from a time when a fundamentally different moral order seemed to prevail with assurance. Indeed, his conclusion that 'the question posed by state-enforced segregation is not one of discrimination at all' seems positively astonishing. Was there something about neutral principles that produced such a startling conclusion?[242]

The Warren Court ruling in the desegregation cases is described, from a 1998 perspective, as producing the *obvious*: it is the coming to substantial terms with the Civil War. World War II provides new reasons and fresh collective thought to redefine the position of black people in American society. The opposition to the Brown decision, manifested by Wechsler's *neutral principles* in the above paragraph, according to Horwitz represents the other side of the story which is the *pathetic*. It is even harder today to access the logic behind the following astonishing questions of Wechsler:

> In the context of a charge that segregation *with equal facilities* is a denial of equality, is there not a point in *Plessy* in the statement that if 'enforced separation stamps the colored race with a badge of inferiority' it is solely because its members choose 'to put that construction upon it'? Does enforced separation of

---

241 Id., at 18.
242 Morton Horwitz, *The Transformation of American Law 1870–1960: The Crisis of Legal Orthodoxy* 267 (1992).

the sexes discriminate against females merely because it may be the females who resent it and it is imposed by judgments predominantly male?[243]

Wechsler's logic, from a contemporary point of view, indeed seems pathetic, having an 'inaccessible quality of ancient structures of understanding'. Garry Peller shares the same pain when he posits the guiding questions to his article, *Neutral Principles in the 1950s*.

> In the context of the racial and sexual domination that marked everyday life in the United States in the 1950s, how could Wechsler, an eminent and sophisticated lawyer and scholar, find it plausible to think that, assuming 'equal facility', any inequality flowing from the 'enforced separation' of American racial apartheid might be 'solely' in the minds of blacks who 'choose' to 'put that construction upon it', or that the inequality of gender roles was not manifest in 'female who resents it'? From what perspective could it seem coherent to assume that racial segregation in public schools was not part of a broad structure of social inequality? In what conception of the world was the distribution of wealth, jobs, political power, intellectual prestige, educational opportunity, housing and social status that continues to reflect the objective face of institutionalized American racism irrelevant to the question of equality in public education?[244]

The puzzling of Peller, combined with the wonder of Horwitz, emphasizes the intellectual rapture conditioning the scholarship after the 1950s. This is the progressive riddle. Contemporary progressive intellectuals in law construct a conceptual abyss between the jurisprudence and the political theory of that time, and between their own. The phenomenon they try to narrate is the academic response to the event of *Brown v. Board of Education*.[245] It is not only Wechsler at stake here. The 'collective' response to *Brown* was critical,[246] and as Horwitz adds in a footnote, 'One is surprised to learn how late it was that legal academics actually thought to defend the *Brown* decision.'[247] Peller gives more cultural background regarding this phenomenon.

> [I]n terms of the American intellectual discourse of the 1950s, Wechsler was part of a community of white, male legal scholars who actually represented a

---

243 Herbert Wechsler, 'Toward Neutral Principles of Constitutional Law', 73 *Harv. L. Rev.* 1 (1959).
244 Peller, *supra* note 2, at 562.
245 *Brown v. Board of Education*, 347 U.S. 483 (1954) (*Brown I*); *Brown v. Board of Education*, 349 U.S. 294 (1955) (*Brown II*).
246 Horwitz, *The Transformation, supra* note 242, at 258.
247 Id., at 340.

liberal and progressive force in Academia ... Speaking the rhetoric of institutional legitimacy, a significant number of northeastern, white, liberal lawyers joined with white, southern, never-say-die segregationists in questioning the Court's authority and legitimacy in *Brown*.[248]

How could progressive white Northeastern lawyers be so theoretically blind to perceiving the justice in *Brown?* What ancient logic did they use to reach their conservative conclusions? Part of the depiction of the 1950s enigmatic conservative shadow is the rereading of the Realists as having the right progressive mood.[249]

Coming back to the 'obvious political truth' of *Brown*, there is a contextual comment to give from today's perspective: the progressive updated activism that is the other pole of the assumed conservative jurisprudence of the Legal Process can be seen as a beginning of the application of a basic, almost trivial, modernist assumption in favor of equality and freedom. This application, with all its innovation, has not yet managed to 'solve' the 'institutionalized racism'[250] in America. De facto segregation actually exists until today,[251] not only in Southern states, but in Northeastern places as well. A closer examination might suggest that the progressive impulse is itself a construction within the discursive practice of law and its theory. Since in the post-war era there is a perceived gap between the mainstream theoretical discourse, represented by Harvard, and the activist approach of the Warren court, the progressive reader will interpret the glorious text of Harvard as theoretically dead. The jurisprudence

---

248 Peller, *supra* note 2, at 563.
249 See Horwitz, *The Warren Court, supra* note 240, at 114, referring to the 'legal consciousness' of the Warren Court: 'Despite the varying origins of their political progressivism, the Warren Court liberals shared a vision of law that the Legal Realists of the 1920s and 1930s had incorporated into New Deal legal consciousness. Justice Brennan summarizes that view: "The genius of the Constitution", he wrote, "rests not in any static meaning it might have had in a world that is dead and gone, but in the adaptability of its great principles to cope with current problems and current needs".' See also the discussion of the characterization of the Realists as progressives by Horwitz in the chapter 'The Maturing of the Pragmatic Idea in Law and Society (Or: The Fall, and the Rise of Philawsophy)', part 1.3.
250 See, for example, Stephen Therstorm and Abigail Thernston, *America in Black and White: One Nation Indivisible* (1997).
251 A contemporary report on the condition of education in America will say that (*The New York Times*): 'The trends of subordination, white flight, industrial ennui have combined to keep minority students in poorer districts, in schools with fewer expectations for their students' achievements, in communities that are nurseries for failure'. See also Gerald N. Rosenberg, *The Hollow Hope: Can Courts Bring About Social Change?* (1993). Rosenberg discusses the effects of *Brown* until the 1970s in comparison with legislative acts.

of that era is hence proceduralist and conservative, and its basic and traditional focus on dispute resolution disappears as a theoretical interest after that time.

From another angle, the contradictory theoretical message of both institutions (the Court and the academy) can be perceived as two channels through which to deal with the same questions. The same effort to come to terms with the American modernity is done through a pragmatic jurisprudence and a structural reform, and is supported by different institutions, and through concern for diverse social actors – the court of the poor and weak, the law school of the rich and dominant. Actually, it is more accurate to say that two equivalent and contradicting social modes are crystallized at this time through different channels.[252] My focus, as part of my academic location, remains upon the law school and its intellectual surroundings.

The mediation or the reaction in 1950s thought is described in Peller, as well as in Horwitz, as the intellectual response to World War II.

> American legal thought after World War II shared a strikingly similar agenda with many other areas of social thought. There was more similarity of approach between the different branches of thought during this period than at any time since the decade before the First World War... much of post-war American legal thought was obsessed with identifying the 'lessons' to be learned from the spread of totalitarianism. While one school of thought, mainly Catholic, sought to blame moral relativism for the spread of a 'might makes right' philosophy, others wished to show instead that an absolutist mindset was actually more conductive to the growth of totalitarianism.[253]

The two responses Horwitz describes – the moralistic absolutist school against the anti-absolutist one – are described in Gary Peller's article as the traditionalists against the pragmatists, substituting for the pre-war debate between the traditionalists and the modernists (Realists). Peller actually describes the pragmatist solution as overcoming the choice between the modernists and the traditionalists.

> Dewey brilliantly turned the relativist and instrumental premises of the modernists into a virtue rather than a vice. According to Dewey, value-relativism did not lead to condoning the fascists. Quite the opposite. It was philosophical absolutism, the arrogance that one has the true vision of things, that supported

---

252 A description of the cultural background and the vision of Democracy that the Warren Court has been represented in his ruling can be found in Horwitz, *The Warren Court*, *supra* note 240, at 31–51, 74–99. See also the discussion of hegemonies above, part 2.2.2.
253 Horwitz, *The Transformation*, *supra* note 55, at 250.

the fascists' notion that they could legitimately impose their vision on others. The social science approach, the functionalist methodological focus, and the pragmatic epistemology all shared a relativism about ultimate truth and an agnosticism about ends. Values and ends were outside the realm of knowledge.[254]

Peller explains how this insistence on the distinction between fact and value 'actually carried within itself an intermediate kind of normative premise: the commitment that an open, democratic society was superior to a closed totalitarian one'.[255] Dewey made this distinction 'the main feature of a discursive peace treaty that divided up the territories of intellectual and political life into a realm of instrumental reason and a realm of irreducible value conflict'.[256] 'His defense of pragmatism (in response to the traditionalists' post-war accusations of relativism and fascism[257] – M.A.) was echoed in the way that the modernists would be institutionalized within each particular field of the humanities and social sciences, including law.'[258]

> The humanist pragmatism that Dewey advocated was more than a philosophical position. In the period immediately after the Second World War, it became the cultural framework that defined for mainstream American intellectuals their roles as intellectuals and, more generally, their conception of the difference between freedom and domination.

This 'cultural framework' or 'discursive peace treaty' of the 1950s is translated in law, according to Peller, into the process/substance distinction:

> Just as the fact/value distinction served as a territorial truce line in the more general intellectual conflict, so Hart and Sacks were sure that the process/substance distinction was the geographic foundation for a pluralist tolerance of both the traditionalists and the Realist vision of law. Just as Dewey had rendered the modernist relativism acceptable by limiting it to the priorities of ends and values, so the fifties legal scholars made legal realism acceptable by editing out its most radical implications, by domesticating the Realist critique to the realm of substance.[259]

---

254 Peller, *supra* note 2, at 584.
255 Id.
256 Id.
257 See also Horwitz, *The Transformation*, *supra* note 55, at 248: 'Amid the resulting "intensity and extremism of debate", it has become common to "charge realism with everything from atheism to communism to nihilism".'
258 Peller, *supra* note 2, at 583.
259 Id., at 589.

The fifties' scholars have domesticated the Realist critique 'to the realm of substance' and have depicted the settling process as able to overcome its danger. Whether this exact discursive conversion has occurred,[260] or another kind of mediating or reconciling of past polarities (like the is-ought, fact-value, political and reasonable, integrative and distributive, which I discuss in the first part of this chapter), what Peller describes is an intellectual mode that is more than the adoption of one theory or another. It is a mainstream intellectual consensus to speak in a mediating voice, to harmonize and not be dogmatic, to restate the American (while believing that things are much more simple than they appear(ed)), and in my reading, stating the pragmatic. Dewey is this time the collaborator from philosophy to reconcile the tensions in law between old common law and modern-pragmatic realism. Dewey's 'return' provides the philosophical overview, the grand picture, the one that the discourse of law has not formally phrased before (and will not do after). The generation of scholars is of the children who went to progressive schools, grew up and matured, and were then at a point of giving a mediating picture of society. The Legal Process moment is a manifestation of a space where the philosophical-general and the legal are assumed to be speaking in the same voice in law. There are no more complementary discourses adjacent to one another; the picture is a whole. The 'domestication' which Peller describes 'of the Realists' critique to the realm of substance[261] is actually the giving up of what was considered uniquely legal, i.e., the obscurities, the irony, the obsession with the criteria, the man-like work of the law. It is also the giving up of political passion, that of the progressive. Within the theoretical discourse of law, it is the merging point between the social-sciences orientation that law will not have again (the positivist-scientific reading of the Realists), of law as a bundle of facts to investigate, and the philawsophy passion that it will have from now on, of living within generalities. It is a textual moment that was not officially published for many years, but it continues to affect the conditioning

---

260 Id.: 'Through the distinction between process and substance, the fifties theorists could walk a pluralist middle ground between the traditionalist belief in ethical objectivity and the Realist implication of relativism. On the one hand, the principle of institutional settlement reflected the acknowledgement that, as the Realists has suggested, there was no a priori, transcendental content to law. In terms of substance, there was only the positive fact that a particular decision had been made by a particular institution. The relativity of a value premise of modernism would be taken to mean that the identification of legitimate legal decisions could not turn on a substantive theory because any such theory would encompass value judgments ... On the other hand, the traditionalist identification of law with value-free neutral principles was rejected in the conviction that, in the realm of procedure, neutral, value-free reasoning was possible.'
261 Id., at 589.

of the intellectual legal subject of today. As Peller says, 'The great significance of the Legal Process text lay in the possibility it held out that a seamless, symmetrical, and comprehensive vision of American law was still possible, regardless of the disintegration of the grand nineteenth-century models under the modernist and Realist attacks.'[262] Actually, this vision he posits as 'still' possible produces a constitutive moment from which it is 'already' impossible.[263] Eskridge and Frickey say 'They had the misfortune to pen their classic works just as these assumptions (the belief in 'the greatness of America', in 'incremental change through the duly established procedures' the consensus – M.A.) were called into question.'[264] Actually it seems that this was their fortune and misfortune. This was the moment for writing the classic, which was actually already common sense, already in opposition to new waves, to counter forces. Eskridge and Frickey describe the contradicting forces as suggesting 'social justice' and 'human dignity' ideas that could not go together with the instrumentalism in the Materials:

> The better criticism is that Hart and Sacks' views about *Brown* were 'unworldly', but not in the sense Hart contemplated. Under this critique, Hart and Sacks were insufficiently cognizant of the deeply rooted social subordination that apartheid supported and of the ramifications that *Brown* might have for doctrinal issues in public law. Moreover, to the extent that Hart and Sacks aspired to 'worldly' understandings, it was a means-oriented instrumentalism which offered few insights about social justice. The most persuasive response to Wechsler ... contrasted our country's history of racial subordination and bigotry with conceptions of human dignity and equal citizenship that were hard to translate into the instrumentalism that dominated The Legal Process.[265]

Being 'unworldly' in the above description seems to be equivalent to holding the wrong political opinions, supported by the outdated theory. But actually, it is also a matter of a younger generation wondering how their parents cannot see what they themselves see so clearly. 'The most persuasive response to Wechsler' they describe in the paragraph above refers to Charles L. Black Jr's article *The Lawfulness of the Segregation Decisions*.[266] Black, a

---

262 Id., at 598.
263 See the chapter 'Taking Sides: Margins and Phases of Pragmatics of 'Legal Process' Disciples (Or: The Pragmatists That We Are)'.
264 Eskrdige and Frickey, Hart and Sacks, at cxiii.
265 Id., at cx.
266 Charles L. Black, Jr, 'The Lawfulness of The Segregation Decision', 69 *Yale L.J.* (1960) 421.

jurisprudence professor at Yale, writes what he defines as a very 'simplistic' argument in favor of the Court's ruling. His different perspective as one who 'was raised in the South, in a Texas city where the pattern of segregation was firmly fixed',[267] makes him present the 'history' of segregation and of the Southern 'reality' as an obvious 'massive intentional disadvantaging of the Negro race, as such, by state law'.[268] He and Wechsler seem to see in 1960 two versions of reality, which can be reflected in his following urgent call (which is always the gesture in law) to leave the metaphysics and come back to the concrete.

> I think that some of the artificial mist of puzzlement called into being around this question originates in a single fundamental mistake. The issue is seen in terms of what might be called the metaphysics of sociology: 'Must Segregation Amount to Discrimination?' That is an interesting question; someday the methods of sociology may be adequate to answering it. But it is not our question. Our question is whether discrimination inheres in that segregation which is imposed by law in the twentieth century in certain specific states in the American Union. And that question has meaning and can find an answer only on the ground of history and of common knowledge about the facts of life in the times and places aforesaid.[269]

Reading this call from today's perspective, it seems clear that the methods of sociology will never be adequate to answer the metaphysics. There will always be another segregation between black and white, poor and rich, Western and third world, de facto or by law, and some combination of them. The claim of Black himself in the opening and ending of his article to show that 'the judgments, in law and in fact, are right and true as any that ever was uttered',[270] is itself an acceptance of 'the metaphysics of the concrete' that he suggests, from his perspective. It is not just instrumentalism that stands between Black and Hart and Sacks, as Eskridge and Frickey might suggest above. The whole picture of society is built in Hart and Sacks as a grand story, written in Boston, and blind to what Black describes so clearly as a 'functioning complex' of racism and segregation. Society is depicted as being in harmony with law, merging the diverse pragmatic sensitivities, and through this vision radical social reforms seem to undermine the Grand Pyramid's bottom layer. What can be seen from one place or time cannot be seen from another, and the progressive

---

267 Id., at 424.
268 Id., at 421.
269 Id., at 427.
270 Id., at 430.

riddle can perhaps be translated here and now into the question, how can we be responsible today for what we do not see? How can we defer the generalities and the grand theories in favor of a meaningful healing intervention?

The ambivalence towards the post-war era and the Materials is hence prevalent among contemporary intellectual jurists. On the one hand, they have an immense educational influence in framing the legal universe and setting its professional discipline. On the other hand, 'at the very time when Hart and Sacks were drafting the Materials ... (their – M.A.) assumptions were being called into question by a new generation, whose attention was focused upon *Brown v. Board of Education*. More intellectuals in this next generation saw social goals in non-utilitarian terms, valued equality as a higher priority than liberty, and were suspicious of the state.'[271]

Eskridge and Frickey explain their personal involvement in the intellectual journey of editing the Materials by acknowledging that 'this project has connected us with perhaps the greatest generation of this American century – men and women who triumphed over the Depression, won World War II, and built a thriving post-war society. Although never published, "The Legal Process" provided the name and much of the substance to the sophisticated jurisprudential approach of that generation.'[272]

> One need not to think that The Legal Process is 'the most influential book not produced in movable type since Gutenberg' to believe that these are exceptional teaching Materials indeed, for they touched and influenced a generation of legal scholars and judges.[273]

This account suggests that the Materials functioned as an oral tradition among the editors' generation of legal scholars.[274] I would suggest that the delay in publication is part of the perceived dissonance between the professional disciplining quality of the Materials[275] with their mediation of

---

271 Eskridge and Frickey, Hart and Sacks, at liv.
272 Arnold, supra note 227, at xiii.
273 Id.
274 See also id., lii: 'The Materials also occupy a place of substantial importance in the history of American jurisprudence, for they provided the name, the agenda, and much of the analytical structure for a generation of legal thought – the "Legal Process school".'
275 See also Peller, *supra* note 2, at 571: 'If professional acceptance is the criterion, the fifties writers were incredibly successful. For nearly two decades, the process approach went virtually unchallenged in the world of legal scholarship. The premises of process theory became the background assumptions for a whole generation of scholars who believed the basic message that it was possible to talk about legal issues in neutral, apolitical ways, and that ideology was outside the realm of their legal discourse.'

the two genres of pragmatism that existed prior to them, and the perceived theoretical failure of the Materials in terms of the political agenda they promoted and of their scientific foundational meta-text. The decline of a theory, under these terms, is related to its becoming a common-sense-like text, a transparent contextualization of the legal scholar. As Peller says, 'Even today, when it is clear that any consensus that might have once existed as to the appropriate framework for legal theory has disintegrated, the process approach continues to form the background assumptions for the most centrist legal scholars who take the institutional focus of process theory as their starting point.'[276] The other group of history tellers of that era does not operate from the inside. Since they define their interest as purely academic, they lack the philawsophical pathos of the narrators in law, and the epistemological gap or intellectual rapture does not condition their discourse.

Anthony Sebok's writing, which I would like to analyze, is the first example of such a narration. He also produced the most elaborate effort to capture the Legal Process jurisprudence. In his book *Legal Positivism in American Jurisprudence*,[277] he tries to prove his thesis that the Legal Process school shared the basic positivist tenets, and that contemporary 'soft' theories of positivism can redeem the conservative image of the school and of positivism altogether. In a tradition that I perceive to be 'English', he gives an analytic account of the idea of reasoned elaboration and institutional settlement, and explores their deviation from Fuller's notion of natural law on the one hand, and their affiliation with positivism's basic maxims on the other. He suggests that it is Wechsler's article that is to blame for the notorious image of the Legal Process School as conservative, and tries to explain in a formal way, however conceptually, that Wechsler's conclusion is not necessary. In contrast to Peller, who reaches the same conclusion[278] but continues to explain the

---

276 Id. For an overview of the new Legal Process writing in contemporary discourse, see Edward L. Rubin, *Institutional Analysis and The New Legal Process*, *Wisconsin L. Rev.* 463 (1995). (It describes Komesar's ambition to articulate a new Legal Process synthesis, by integrating law and economics into institutional competence analysis that characterizes Legal Process.) See also Kent Roach, *What's New and Old about Legal Process*, *supra* note 46, at 389–4.

277 Sebok, *supra* note 22.

278 See Peller, *supra* note 2, at 619: 'In short, there was nothing historically or analytically determined about the structure of the legal rhetoric that the fifties writers constructed. In terms of the intellectual context in which they found themselves, there were alternatives that included the possibility of continuing the Realist and modernist critique of authority or the possibility of pursuing an objective theory of social justice based on the primacy of the group and the community.'

'arbitrary' choice as part of a 'collective consciousness' or a cultural background of the 1950s, Sebok constructs it as a mistake which can be corrected. The 'soft positivism' he suggests as a liberal justification of *Brown* is actually also a call to embrace 'a theory of legal positivism that takes moral principles seriously'.[279]

From an internal, intellectual point of view, this call by Sebok is empty, together with his effort to 'amend' the misconception Wechsler has created. The pure non-contextual manner, combined with the detachment of an analytical discussion that assumes a metaphysical essence to the notions at stake (positivism, formalism, realism) is reflected also in a review of his book by Brian Leiter. As Leiter shows in his criticism of Sebok,[280] there is something deeply non-positivistic in the Legal Process theory even if it does not contain the natural law ideas. On the other hand, there is something deeply positivist in the legal Realist tradition, which Sebok tries to locate as skeptical.[281]

From a third point of view, there is actually another narrative, which I try to present throughout my writing, in which the pragmatism of law (or the American discursive legal genre) unfolds in a few stages, first through the rebellious act of the Realists, reclaiming Holmes in their insistence on the rigorous study of law through methods of the social sciences and the prediction theory. Then there is the Legal Process moment where the backward-looking of the social-scientist Realists is switched for the pragmatic purposive decision maker who looks forward in his social-engineering pathos. The difficulty in describing this mode as positivist is indeed related, in my view, to what Leiter defines as the 'purposive' element.

> The real worry, in short, is that the Legal Process theory of adjudication as 'reasoned elaboration' involves an essentially anti-positivist view of law, because it makes morality a criterion of legality by its emphasis on 'purposive' interpretation. 'Reasoned elaboration', according to Hart and Sacks, requires judges to make decisions that are *consistent* and that reflect the *purpose* of the laws they are asked to interpret ... According to Sebok, 'consistency and purpose ... were essential features of a legal system' for Legal Process. Thus, it follows that 'there are norms embedded in the law for judges to discover', where that discovery is effected by looking to the underlying purpose of the law while, all the time, making the present decision consistent with those that preceded it.[282]

---

279 Sebok, Preface to the book, *supra* note 22.
280 Brian Leiter, 'Positivism, Formalism, Realism', 99 *Colum L. Rev.* 1138 (1999).
281 See the discussion above of the Realists and Kelsen as sharing an equivalent project, part 2.2.5.
282 Id., at 1157.

The essential 'anti-positivist view of law' that the Legal Process theory promotes is, according to Leiter, rooted in their demand that the purposive judgment and the consistency test be criteria of legality. In contrast to Sebok, who posits the 'institutional settlement' notion as the key to understanding Hart and Sacks as accepting the positivist tenet of the separation of law and morals,[283] Letiter claims that this notion is 'a procedural requirement for the *legitimacy* of law',[284] and does not determine positivist characterization. Leiter points to the similarity between this view of adjudication and that of Ronald Dworkin[285] in order to emphasize its non-positivistic character. I think the non-positivism of Dworkin and that of Hart and Sacks are different from one another due to their historical intellectual context, and because formal characterization of them (as Leiter does) without any historical context of their emergence is rendered meaningless, or at least is lacking.[286] What they do share, in my view, which also accounts for the problematic in Sebok's theory, is that they take the pragmatic story of law for granted. Dworkin opposes the Legal Process, but accepts Hart and Sacks' basic pragmatic drawing of the legal universe. There are policies, principles, and rules, and there is the mystery of decision making which navigates among them, settling and resettling. Hart and Sacks tell the story of law as a functional entity through the delayed (for fifty years) repetition of the pragmatic story, in its accommodated rebirth in the legal sphere. Sebok in his analytic march, as well as his critic Leiter, neglect an old pragmatic wisdom that says it is not the metaphysics (of positivism) that is at stake, but it is its unfolding through history, its uses and abuses, its play. When Sebok refers to Peller he gives the following remark:

> I think that Peller's conclusion is too sweeping. As the foregoing discussion shows, Hart and Sacks, like Fuller, were less concerned about the specific political consequences of applying their theory of the Legal Process than they were about ensuring that the law did not mistreat complex social problems *either* by forcing them into an adjudicative process when they were not susceptible to

---

283 Sebok, *supra* note 22, at 130, 169.
284 Leiter, *supra* note 280, at 1156.
285 See id., at 1157: 'In identifying the jurisprudential view with which this picture of adjudication most clearly resonates, it would seem bizarre to single out positivism. For the conception of law as integrity of Ronald Dworkin – positivism's arch-opponent – echoes Legal Process note to note.' On the relation of the process theory and the jurisprudence of Dworkin, see the chapter 'In Search of the Dispute: On Lawyers and Legal Philawsophers at Harvard Law School (Or: Some Private Hope and Public Irony)'.
286 Regarding the different modes of pragmatism that Dworkin and the Legal Process present, see part 4.3.

rational analysis or (if one of the problems was susceptible to rational analysis) through the application of a Legal Process that was insufficiently adjudicative.[287]

In a formal manner, Hart and Sacks' theory could have supported a progressive ruling as well as a conservative one. Their focus was not political but academic; theoretical and not practical; providing the big picture and not getting into details: interested in form and not substance. All these negations suggest that there is, indeed, a valid separation that enables these dichotomies to exist independently. What I have thus far argued is that in the post-war era, in the intellectual discourse of law, these oppositions collapse to produce a jurisprudence which is both and neither practical and/or theoretical, giving the big picture and the small details as well, political and academic at once. Before and after this time, the discourse indeed unfolds according to these categories,[288] but the secret of the post-war era, or the plain flag of it, lies in the discursive vacuum it creates in terms of the outside (of politics) and the inside (of law).

Actually, from another perspective, it seems that Sebok, and Peller do not share the same notions of history and language.[289]

The second example of narration of that era belongs less to the analytic tradition that tries to examine the classic jurisprudential questions, but to the social scientists or their historians, who try to examine the role and the history of this interest within law. They are the second kind of 'externals' I would like to examine in order to grasp the gap between them and the progressives. In her book *Legal Realism at Yale 1927–1960*,[290] Laura Kalman describes the way in which the Hart and Sacks endeavor was perceived in Yale during the 1940s and 1950s.

Although the jurisprudence Hart and Sacks proposed may have entailed a short–term capitulation to the politics of status quo, it was not political conservativism as much as a reaction against legal realism that motivated Hart, Sacks and other members of the Legal Process school. As Bruce Ackerman put it: 'No longer did the best minds seek either to refine classical

---

287 Sebok, *supra* note 22, at 153.
288 All my other chapters discuss manifestations in time and place of the categories above. At the beginning they exist in relation to the philosophical discourse, than in relation to the inner discourse of progressives in the post-World War I era in law, then in disciples of the Legal Process, and finally in contemporary Harvard.
289 See the discussion of 'progressive miss-communications', part 4.5, in the chapter 'In Search of the Dispute: On Lawyers and Legal Philawsophers at Harvard Law School (Or: Some Private Hope and Public Irony)'.
290 Kalman, *supra* note 76.

legal science or to rebel against it. Instead the fundamental problem was defined in terms of the issue left unresolved by legal Realism: once it is perceived that the substantive legal tradition speaks ambiguously for the resolution of a hard case, is there anything a lawyer can do to define a proper decision? For the process jurisprudents there was. Recognizing the truth of realism, recognizing that judicial decisions were inherently idiosyncratic, they attempted to take as many decisions away from the judicial branch as possible and to remind judges of their duty to decide cases by "impersonal and durable principles", which Langdell himself might have declared.'[291]

Hart and Sacks recognized the truth of Realism, according to Kalman, and accommodated it through the institutional restraint they imposed on judges, and the neutral formal principles they were claiming for. 'Old Yale Realists ridiculed the processors' search objectivity'.[292] They called it an 'ostrich approach' and claimed that they were developing 'a new mythology of the judicial process to replace the myth destroyed by the Realists'.[293] At the same time, they were developing a 'Realist' curriculum at Yale, as Kalman describes, rich with applications of social sciences, and combining the reflection on a legal problem through a broad context. Yale law professors were also much more political in the 'Red Scare' era, and are described by Kalman as stepping in 'where practitioners feared to tread'.[294] These 'Realists of the 1940s and 1950s, according to Kalman, did what the Realists of the 1920s and 1930s had wanted to do',[295] and were putting together social science and law in a developed and extensive manner, but their contribution to the educational curriculum was minor and they were conquered by Harvard's new formalism.[296]

---

291   Id., at 223.
292   Id.
293   Id.
294   Id., at 194: 'The Red Scare, which continued to grip the country during the early 1950s, posed a particular challenge to the legal profession. The communists whom witch-hunters searched out needed attorneys to defend them, and it soon became apparent that attorneys who represented accused communists were jeopardizing their careers ... Tenured Yale law professors stepped in where practitioners feared to tread. A. Withney Griswold, a historian who had become president of Yale in 1950, could do little to curb them. Because their livelihood was guaranteed, Griswold's hands were tied when "Fred the Red" Rodell glorified the Black and Douglas dissents in *Dennis,* Fowler Harper wrote of lawyers' troubles in political trials and told the General Foundation of Women's clubs that communists should be permitted to teach in American colleges and universities, and "Tommy the Commie" Emerson defended accused communists in courts.'
295   Id., at 230.
296   Kalman describes Harvard's process orientation as returning to the Landellian tradition, and perceives the school as remaining a 'trade school' all the way. See also id., 218:

Kalman concludes by offering a correspondence between the political and the theoretical sequences within the legal discourse.

> In many ways, legal realism was very much like its contemporary, the New Deal. Although it seemed revolutionary to those who lived through it, it was not. By 1960, it had become clear that the United States had accepted the welfare state that had originated with the New Deal. So too, it had become clear that many at Harvard and Yale Law Schools had accepted a large part of legal realism. Yet change had not caused a revolution in either case. Intellectually, realism had not proved significant; pedagogically, it had not fulfilled its promise. The New Deal had preserved the country Americans knew in the darkest days of 1931. Legal realism had preserved the legal education Christopher Columbus Langdell had created in 1870 by reforming it.[297]

Kalman's description above of the Harvardization of the Yale approach depicts both a reaction and transgression, which resulted in coming back to the Landellian education system. Although the introduction to The Legal Process Materials might support her position, when the authors claim that 'the essential method, it will be seen, is nothing more than an application of the method of teaching law first popularized by Christopher Columbus Langdell',[298] still her view that 'intellectually, realism had not proved significant' does not seem convincing. Throughout her book, she describes Realism solely to be the application of social sciences as the guiding educational method in law. If realism is indeed the application and study of social sciences through the functional perspective as narrated in her book, then she might be right; but this emphasis is only one aspect of how the Realists operated in law.

The same pain of Kalman, regarding the decline of the call to link social sciences with the study of law, appears in Brian Tamanaha's book: *Realistic Socio-Legal Theory: Pragmatism and a Social Theory of Law*.[299] In 1997, Tamanah describes 'the problematic state of socio-legal studies',[300] by pointing

---

'Although Harvard law professors made overtures to the social sciences during the 1950s, they never seemed as enraptured with them as their Yale counterparts. Until the 1960s, the Harvard Law School faculty never included an economist such as Hamilton, a philosopher such as Northrop, or a political scientist such as Lasswell. Yet Harvard had certainly moved closer to the Yale approach than it had ever been willing to go in the 1930s.'

297 Id., at 231.
298 Hart and Sacks, at cxxxix.
299 Brian Z. Tamanaha, *Realistic Socio-Legal Theory: Pragmatism and a Social Theory of Law* (1997).
300 This is the title of his introduction. See id., at 1.

to the undeveloped state of this discourse within law and to the current politicization of the legal discourse which is characterized by him as 'a plethora of competing approaches, each representing a particular normative or interest group perspective, each arguing that law should serve the interest they tout'.[301] This development is presented by him as related to the problem of 'postmodernism',[302] which has produced a 'short-term transition in US legal theory', that of 'the seemingly overnight convergence upon pragmatic philosophy of many of these competing jurisprudential schools'.[303] The 'long-term transition', which Tamanaha hopes to continue, 'has been ongoing for almost a century, and was notably instigated by Oliver Wendell Holmes'.[304] 'The change wrought by Holmes, which was carried through by Roscoe Pound and the Legal Realists, was to render law and legal theory increasingly instrumental-oriented.'[305] His thesis is that 'the role of Realistic socio-legal theory in the context of postmodern jurisprudence is to be a non-political source of knowledge about the nature, function, and effects of legal phenomena'.[306]

But Tamanaha and Kalman, just like Sebok and Leiter before, use a positivist analytic approach for their academic endeavor, switching the focus on positivism for the search for a social science emphasis. The history of

---

301 Id., at 7.
302 Id., at 5: 'Postmodernism apparently destabilizes all the core certainties of our existence – truth, reality, meaning, the world out there. It unceremoniously dumps the notion of objectivity, and the fact-value distinction and reason itself into the rubbish bin of no longer believable Enlightenment illusions. The pessimistic postmodern vision harkens back to the Tower of Babel: an anarchic clash of incommensurable perspectives, each bearing its own standards of reason and right, impervious to criticism from others ....'
303 Id., at 7.
304 Id., at 6.
305 Id., at 6–7.
306 Id., at 8. For a more skeptical view towards this goal from another supporter of the social sciences in law, see Shlegel, *supra* note 76, at 256–7. Schlegel says he hopes his study of the Realists and what they did has convinced his readers that there is not an apparent way today 'to put empirical social sciences in the center of the law school world ... Professional identities are strong things. Though the tall-grass prairie is almost all gone, we still forge the law professors alone in a room with 80 to 100 recalcitrant twenty-two-years-olds who bring with them the cultural understanding that law is about rules and who gets a pile of appellate cases to chew on. The centrality of that experience of the notion of law as rule is overwhelming as the smell of limburger cheese. Until some genius comes up with some reason for seeing law as something else, matches it with an appropriate professional identity, and sells it in a culture where currently the only alternative of law available is that of the rule of law's evil twin brother – law as who you know – until one takes the "and" out of "law and ..." there is no point in talking.'

legal thought since Holmes, including the Legal Process moment, is narrated by them thereupon according to the advance of this scientific notion of the law. They actually continue the Realists' tradition, but from the outside.[307] John Henry Schlegel represents the same interest when he posits the basic question that guides his book *American Legal Realism and Empirical Social Sciences?*[308]

> Why did law not become a scientific study, in the twentieth-century sense of science as an empirical inquiry into a world 'out there', as did all other disciplines in American academic life that formed the late nineteenth and early twentieth centuries?[309]

The basic problem in the history-telling of the Realists' tradition lies, according to Schlegel, in the initial claim for the movement to carry a jurisprudence. Llewellyn begins this unnecessary theoretical pretension[310] and 'thereafter, it was all downhill'.[311] Actually Schlegel, in his social science mode, repeats the Realist gesture of caring only for what the 'officials do in fact', by insisting upon pointing it back against them, focusing only on what *the Realists did in fact*. Kalman as well as Horwitz, Twinning as well as Purcell are wrong according to Schlegel when they portray a theory (or a jurisprudence) in places where there were only individuals doing their work, which is, in Schlegel's case, applying methods of the social sciences into law. Schlegel opposes the whole notion of intellectual history in general and of Realism as a theory in particular, but in doing so, he neglects his own perspective of a believer in social science methods, and in their legitimacy as a foundational text for his whole intellectual endeavor. He defines Realists according to what 'they did', while assuming that what 'they did' has a quality of direct accessibility to a laboratory study, possesses a distinct entity in relation to what 'they said they did' (the jurisprudence they promoted, the theory they

---

307 See the discussion above, part 2.2.5 of the relation between the two kinds of positivism which Kelsen and the Realists suggest.
308 Schlegel, *American Legal Realism, supra* note 76.
309 Id., at 1.
310 Id., at 2: Both common understanding of Realism and the fatherly assertion of our having absorbed the lessons taught by Realism are founded on the understanding that Realism *is* a jurisprudence rather than that the Realists *had* (or shared, not the same thing) a jurisprudence. Such has been the assumption since the 1930s, indeed since the famous Llewellyn-Pound exchange about Realism. Here Llewellyn made the first misstep, at least for someone who believed that Realism was a 'technology' and not a 'philosophy'.
311 Id. at 3.

called for), and has a presence 'for itself' without all the supplementary narration of Purcell, Kalman, or Horwitz. His choice to rewrite history is, of course, appealing, and there is something enlightening in exposing the ideological biases in writing a heroic history of the Realists as progressives[312] or prophets of education. Still, there is not a straightforward way to approach the concept 'acts for themselves' without already having adopted a perspective: about science, history, and even theory. For Schlegel, the contours of his perspective are quite explicit: the *scientific* is the 'empirical inquiry into a world "out there"', and not accepting the assertion that 'the law library was the professor's laboratory';[313] the right way to write *history* is to examine the individual intellectuals or other people that are at stake, and not their general ideas;[314] as to his idea of the *theory* of law, let the jurispruds discuss 'Realism as jurisprudence, timeless answers to what are taken as timeless questions'.[315] While he mourns the fact that real Realists like Moore and Cook have 'caught one such phantasm (of providing a theoretical base – M.A.) and it changed his life',[316] he ignores the fact that we all do so, following a phantasm, changing our life accordingly, just as his belief in his own notion of the social sciences and the scientific in general.

It turns out that the Realists' positivist emphasis on the social sciences could not operate without a jurisprudential internal operation. To write a history which skips this 'secondary' residue is to miss some of the mobilizing forces of the 'scientific' action 'itself'. The problem with law compared to other social sciences that were institutionalized since the end of the nineteenth century is that, as Schlegel says, 'Law already saw itself as practicing a science, "legal science".'[317] The 'rational ordering' that was perceived to be the quality

---

312 Id., at 5–7: Regarding Morton Horwitz, he says 'Horwitz wished to tell the story of the shift in the legal thought from the nineteenth-century "formalism" to something he first called "instrumentalism" but later slipped into calling "realism". The generality of these conceptions, and their rootedness in the idea that what he was attempting to describe is a jurisprudence, allowed Horwitz, like Kalman, to assemble a quite diverse group of scholars and permitted him to assert that they belonged together. But unlike Kalman or Purcell, Horwitz used this freedom to assemble a cast that included not only all the suspects usually seen as Realists but ... indeed, almost any legal academic vaguely related to legal reform between 1920 and the 1960, except for Pound'. Id., at 7. See also the discussion of Horwitz' definition of the Realists in the chapter 'The Maturing of the Pragmatic Idea in Law and Society (Or: The Fall, and the Rise of Philawsophy)'.
313 Id., at 1.
314 Id., at 12.
315 Id., at 4.
316 Id., at 254.
317 Id., at 1.

of legal science prevailed in legal studies until the Realists' arrival. In Schlegel's story, the Realists offer unification with other American social sciences, hence offering, as I claim, the American in law. But the rational old pathos had not disappeared from law by the time the Realists arrived, nor 'came back' in a simple way after they vanished.[318] The rational as the ironic intellectual living within law is, according to my narration, a living legend of the Realists' call, as perceived from a year-2000 perspective, while reading again the 'origin'. From that angle, the Legal Process moment, whether it is a moment of reaction and repression of the 'true' social sciences emphasis, and whether it is the last moment of the incorporation of this appeal,[319] is a time where irony, which has also a political passion, is dropped, and a little American child is claiming itself out in Harvard. From today's perspective, his body seems to prevail and his spirit is a matter of multifarious perspectives. Seen through progressive eyes, he had no spirit at all.

An equivalent account of the hierarchy between social science and law appears in Neil Daxbury's article 'Faith in Reason: The Process Tradition in American Jurisprudence'.[320] Duxbury (like Tamanaha) seems to stand for an English positivist tradition which tries to re-present (recreate) American legal scholars as eternal believers in reason, which is neither deductive nor intuitive, but scientific and based on the social sciences and the animation of principle.

In fact, realism was a rather half-hearted and largely unsuccessful attack on formalism. Indeed, post-Realist commentators have tended to find in the literature of realism a 'radical' impetus which was neither as pronounced nor

---

318 This is not the claim of Schlegel either, who perceives the Realists not as a counter 'theory' to the rational, as I said before. He acknowledges the fact that since the beginning, the professionalization in law took a different path from pursuing the purely scientific. See Schlegel, id., at 253: '... as part of that process of professionalization, the law teachers came to agree on a subject matter for their science. It was to be largely private, common law embraced as a scientific – that is, a rationally ordered and justified – system. Put slightly differently, although there may have been a great deal of talk about teaching people to think like a lawyer, whatever that might be, the real subject matter was going to be law as rule, the rules of law. Law professors were not going to teach the other sciences; they were not going to teach about law; they were going to teach law.'
319 See also the discussion above in part 2.2.5. Schlegel describes the decline of the social sciences emphasis during the 1960s, as part of a sociological and a professional identity transformation that occurred, and also as accidental. See Schlegel, *supra* note 76, id., at 211: 'It was as if someone had invented the square wheel; some movement of the horse cart was possible, but not much'. In 251 he summarizes the 'team's overall performance as "one hit, no runs, innumerable errors".'
320 Neil Duxbury, 'Faith in Reason: The Process Tradition in American Jurisprudence', 15 *Cardozo Law Rev.* (1993) 601.

as sincere as is commonly believed. Part of my objective here is to dispel another common misconception about American jurisprudence, that the field of American legal thought traditionally labeled 'process' jurisprudence, emerged as a post-war response to legal realism. I hope to show that such an assumption is incorrect. Certainly process jurisprudence began to flourish once the mood of realism began to wane, but that did not mark the birth of the process perspective. Historically, the process oriented approach to the study of law parallels, if not precedes, legal realism itself.[321]

Daxbury attempts to dispel the misconception about American jurisprudence, that the 'process' jurisprudence emerged as a post-war response to Realism.[322] He claims that, historically, the process-oriented approach to the study of law parallels, if not precedes, legal Realism itself.[323] Process jurisprudence exemplifies the emergence of reason as the dominant and ideological theoretical motif in American legal thought. It is not deductive logic on the one hand, and not intuition on the other.

The process approach, according to Daxbury, is an attitude. It is a low-key style which 'tended to bubble to the surface of, rather than to dominate, the works of those who shared it',[324] who preceded the appearance of The Legal Process Materials, according to Daxbury.[325] They worked much more on the internal discourse of law, rather than on the social sciences, though they did assume that the adoption of social sciences would normally prove enlightening. Daxbury gives a rich analysis of process themes in Chipman Gray, Roscoe Pound, Cardozo, Dickinson, and especially Fuller. He claims that 'Fuller's voice can be heard throughout the Legal Process Materials',[326] and insists on ignoring the Realists as a significant distinct contribution that is mediated there, as well as the deviations from Fuller. In general, Daxbury provides an account of another external (British again) who does not see the American quality of the Materials, and narrates his notion of reason (his faith in reason) to exclude what he perceives as its challengers (the Realists).

---

321 Id., at 602.
322 Eskridge and Frickey, Peller, and Horwitz seem all to share that view. See also Jan Vetter, 'Post-War Legal Scholarship on Judicial Decision Making', *J. Legal Educ.*, 412.
323 He claims that the vocabulary of process was already emerging during Langdell's era. The case method and the dialectic technique of study exemplify this idea. Id., at 608: 'This was the kind of education that a few generations ago was called the education of a gentleman.'
324 Id., at 604.
325 For a similar idea see Schlegel, *supra* note 76, at 7–8, as discussed also later, part 2.4.4.
326 Id., at 633.

Like Kalman, but with a different emphasis and tone, Daxbury claims that process jurisprudence is a return to the Langdellian notion of reason and authority. His argument also parallels that of Sebok, who claims a positivist revival of the Legal Process wisdom.[327] Daxbury's offer is a bit different from that of Kalman and Tamanaha in his hostility towards the Realists and in his account of what preceded or followed them, but basically they, together with Sebok, share the same view of the life of the law – they do not believe in it. They cannot occupy the American intellectual position of working and living within law, while taking a partly ironic peek at the 'outside'.[328] They have not graduated 'the interpretive' turn, in and outside law;[329] they do not share the megalomaniac impulse in law to provide the grand philosophical truth. Their analytic approach is in a way a-historic, and hence fails to see the unique construction of the 1950s in its intellectual context.

2.4.4 Recurrence and Singularities in Theories of Adjudication

From another angle, there is a way to read an intermediate position between the externals and the progressive internals. There is an analytic mode combined with social sensitivities that I will try to trace in Duncan Kennedy's 1970

---

327 See also Sebok, *supra* note 22, at 159: 'Not only was Hart and Sacks' theory fundamentally continuous with classical positivism, but their theory improved upon Langdellian formalism. Hart and Sacks took seriously, in a way that the formalist did not, the role of discretion in the application of rules.'

328 See also Roach, *supra* note 49, at 365. Roach explains his sympathy for the Materials, and his characterization of them as pragmatic, as being driven by his being external to the discourse, that of the intellectuals who mourns the 'progressive riddle' (in my terms), and in general the American play of politics and law, himself having been educated in Canada. Referring to the *Brown* problematic he says: 'For most American intellectuals there was one right answer to these moral issues, and the Legal Process tradition failed to embrace it. The defining political issues in Canada have generally been less dramatic, more morally ambiguous, and thus more suited to pragmatic compromise and deference to established institutions and procedures.'

329 It is interesting to note that in Sebok, for example, 'interpretivism' is defined in analytical terms and characterizes the conservative response to Wechsler. See Sebok, *supra* note 22, at 202–3: 'The view that legal meaning relied upon empirical, not moral, judgment came to be known as interpretivism ... Because laws must ultimately refer to empirically verifiable terms, the moral terms found in the law must refer to empirically verifiable events, which in the case of normative terms could mean only the intentions of the authors of those terms ... As a result of the conservative critics' rejection of Hart and Sacks' idea that legal principles could express moral principles, interpretivism has become the modern face of legal positivism.'

article 'Utopian Rationalism in American Legal Thought'.[330] As a student who was partly brought up on the Materials, and as a 1960s leftist legal intellectual, Kennedy represents another view on the historical location of The Legal Process. His iconic prophetic position in the academic discourse, which I try to characterize elsewhere,[331] makes his writing a significant event in the story of the decline of the Legal Process jurisprudence. Eskridge and Frickey describe it as follows:

> In a 1970 student paper for Wellington (at Yale university, the Other of Harvard – M.A.), Duncan Kennedy argued that this theory of adjudication (the one that claims to different professional capacities of the court and the legislator – M.A.) is incoherent. Reasoning from principles, attributed purposes, or established rules that Hart and Sacks considered characteristic of adjudication is not different in practice from reasoning from ideologically motivated policies, constructed purposes, or general standards that Hart and Sacks considered characteristic of political decision making by legislatures or agencies.

I think they extract a very narrow argument from the elaboration in the paper. Actually, they seem to focus on the challenge to the institutional capacity following their general observation that this was the inherent problem in the Legal Process 'public' legacy. But it seems that Kennedy claims much more, and I would like to examine his historical account of Hart and Sacks regarding a theory of adjudication. Kennedy offers a narration that I call 'recurrence', and my response to it is that it lacks singularity in the phenomenon he describes, which is its American moment (of the post-war).

Throughout the article, Kennedy examines the Legal Process phenomenon in its characteristic as 'utopian rationalism in American legal thought'. In an analytic mode that accepts the basic terms of the picture drawn by Hart and Sacks,[332] but questions its operative or conceptual validity, Kennedy shows at first that in order to fulfill the institutional-competence ideal of Hart and Sacks, one has to adopt their optimistic picture of American society:

---

330 Duncan Kennedy, 'Utopian Rationalism in American Legal Thought', manuscript June 1970 (unpublished, in file with the author).
331 See my discussion of Kennedy's location in the lineage: Holmes, Llewellyn, Kennedy, in the chapter 'The Maturing of the Pragmatic Idea in Law and Society (Or: the Fall, and the Rise of Philawsophy)', part 1.5.
332 See, for example, *supra* note 330, at 2: 'I will try to lay out in some detail the logical structure of the Hart and Sacks theory', and also later when he draws his planner's legal system.

It has already been pointed out that The Legal Process is an ambiguous mixture of utopian social theory and description of social reality ... A planner capable of crediting this quotation (of Hart and Sacks, describing the American society – M.A.) as an accurate description of the social situation he confronted (and one may ask whether anyone but a fool could so credit it, or could have credited it in 1957, 1937, 1917 or 1897) would have little difficulty in resolving the final question raised in this section. He would institute forthwith a rule of jurisdiction forbidding courts to perform legislative (or administrative or private ordering) functions, and secure, perhaps by constitutional provision, the elaborative adjudicative function from legislative interference. The short form of specialization would be clearly optimal and nothing short of it acceptable.[333]

But Kennedy holds different views, and his question as to whether anyone but a fool could do differently goes together with his later conclusion that 'like the neo-classical economists who elaborated the concept of "perfect competition", Hart and Sacks base their system on utopia'.[334] When describing their notion of 'reasoned elaboration' he excludes two possible meanings of certainty that it implies:

They do not mean to suggest that reasoned elaboration provides 'answers' to uncertainties in the same manner that logico-deductive method provides answers in mathematics or symbolic logic. The complexity of the social reality with which the planner must deal, and the consequent imprecision in the process of formation of concepts and premises for argument, are fully apparent to them: they are enthusiastic participants in the 'revolt against formalism' and 'mechanical jurisprudence'.

On the other hand, they are equally opposed to the notion that certainty can be reduced to a 'high probability that courts will decide a particular question in a particular way'.[335]

Hart and Sacks have already incorporated 'the revolt against formalism' and do not fail to believe in the simple idea of deduction. On the other hand, they do not perceive the certainty of decision as based on statistics. Instead 'their method is to be applied self-consciously by judges and critics striving to find *the* right answer in the particular case'.[336]

---

333 Id., at III 24–5.
334 Id., at III 35.
335 Id., at 39–40.
336 Id., at III 40.

Its utility depends not on statistical regularity in results, but on the conviction of the planner and the participants that one can reach right answers sufficiently often to make it legitimate to use the method to police the borders of institutional domains. Hart and Sacks are above all leaders in the 'revolt against Realism'.[337]

The effort to find *the* right answer without accepting the formalist notion is based on a 'conviction' that this can be done and is at once a revolt against formalism and Realism. Kennedy shows the difficulties of such a conviction even if one accepts Hart and Sacks' optimistic view of society. The system lacks coherence and is full of contradictory principles and policies. The contradictions and inconsistencies can be observed between different fields of law, and within each field and doctrine. He claims that 'the ambiguities and inconsistencies of their theory of institutions' permit us two 'mutually incompatible subtheories of the judicial role'[338] – passive and active. When asking what makes Hart and Sacks provide a notion – reasoned elaboration – is consistent with these opposite modes, he says:

> It is possible that they are simply 'pragmatists', ambivalent about the workings of the society and the coherence of the law, responding idiosyncratically according to the emotions evoked by the particular case, but altogether unwilling to accept the cosmic *angst* an admission of freedom would entail. And then it is possible that the logical inconsistency, the naiveté, the incoherence of their theory of the Legal Process is irrelevant: what matters is the *cases*, for if we analyze them with sufficient skill we will discover the cognitive keying system which turn these consummate judges first to the activists, then to the pacifist model. In short, behind all the indeterminate talk of Reason we will find the 'real' theory, which *is* the legal mentality.

Kennedy calls 'pragmatism' to the low-key mode of deciding cases, and after rejecting their 'grand program' (which is another pole of pragmatism, in a way[339]), he suggests the psychoanalytic text, or idiosyncrasy in general, as their true meta-text. This suggestion seems to go back to the Realists, and I think is part of 'the right place' that Kennedy believes to exist – the place of the rebel, the faultfinder – but he continues to locate the belief in reasoned elaboration in the legal historical context. He shows that regardless of the logical inconsistency and the indeterminacy of the method, it is a repetition

---

337 Id.
338 Id., at III 49.
339 See *supra* text to footnote, regarding the mediation that occurs in the Legal Process Materials.

of a familiar pattern in legal thought.

> The new system represents a structural transformation of the nineteenth century solution, preserving the most important distinguishing characteristics of utopian rationalist thought. These are:
> I. The development through Reason and factual analysis of a method of analysis of social life which will:
>   i) generate a complete body of substantive rules of law for private orderers and officials, and
>   ii) control the judge in his law-making function (thus justifying his independence) so that
> II. conflict and change are controlled through coercion, and
> III. a (stable or dynamic) equilibrium is created in which free (arbitrary) private action maximizes 'progress'.[340]

There is a different lesson to learn from Kennedy here, in terms of the analytic external narrators discussed above, and in terms of the internal progressives as well. In contrast to the Peller, Eskridge, and Frickey idea, which perceives the Legal Process as an incorporation of the Realists' sophistication, the Materials are posited as revolting against their claims and as embedding only the general (outside law? As described in Morton White's famous book I discuss elsewhere[341]) revolt against formalism. There is some similarity with Daxbury's argument, which describes continuity from Langdell to the Legal Process, as one long 'faith in reason', but in contrast to Daxbury, the emphasis is on 'a structural transformation'. Hart and Sacks' claim is the recurrence of the analytical jurists' claim and the formalist posture in a different costume. His analysis is not a-historical and analytic as is Daxbury's, who tries to explore the eternal notion of decision making in law, and to promote a universal notion of 'reason'. His claim is instead that the harmony and order that Hart and Sacks offer are a repetition of an old gesture and are part of the Zeitgeist.

> Utopian rationalism flowers *between* crises, not within them. Its apostles emerge at times when, as in the 1950s, 1870s and 1760s it is possible for very intelligent men to believe that all the big problems of social organization have been settled, and that no one cares desperately about the smaller problems they set out to solve.[342]

---

340 Kennedy, 'Utopian Rationalism', *supra* note 330, at IV 29.
341 See the chapter 'The Maturing of the Pragmatic Idea in Law and Society (Or: The Fall, and the Rise of Philawsophy)'.
342 Kennedy, 'Utopian Rationalism', *supra* note 330, at IV 41.

Utopian rationalist systems based on maximization through free arbitrary private action must have to a particularly striking degree what I have been calling a formal element, and the tension between legality and equity is correspondingly pronounced.[343]

Bentham in relation to Blackstone, and the Realists in relation to the formalists, have made the same gesture of challenging the existing theory of adjudication and picture of society. Actually, Kennedy draws a figure of transformation where utopian rationalist thought is always located in the mainstream, where on the sides there are the rebellious actors trying to show the illusive elements in the harmonizing story. The opposition, though, can be heard only in crisis times.[344]

We can read the same idea in Schlegel, when he criticizes Horwitz for his portrayal of the Realists.[345]

> What is important is to see that Horwitz's failure to attend to social relationships between scholars as a delimiting factor in understanding what Realism was and who the Realists were blinded him to what I think is a significant observation that might have been derived from his work – namely, that there were two groups that worked for legal reform in the interwar years, one of which was largely centered in the usual group of Realists, and another, centered around Pound and Frankfurter. A significant part of the criticism of Realism in the 1930s was offered by this second group ... if seen as unified, this criticism might represent objections to substantive positions that were felt to undermine reform or objections to a new and noisy claimant to the title of 'progressive', depending on one's perspective, and in either case might offer clues *to the origins of the 'so-called Legal Process' school of the post-war generation* (my emphasis – M.A.).[346]

Schlegel suggests seeing the Legal Process as a phenomenon that has matured beside the Realists' appearance. There was always a mainstream position that held utopian professional ideas about decision-making. Maybe

---

343 Id., at IV 42.
344 From the perspective of a new millennium, compared to the 1970s, it seems Kennedy represents modernism in law, which means: a fundamental crisis, multifarious lenses, a thin area of utopia in public law scholarship and a large penumbra of contradicting views. It is hard to prophesy and maybe impossible, but an analytic or a process utopia prevailing in law seems today very improbable. The fundamental mode (like the contradiction of Kennedy himself) is that of crisis.
345 See the discussion above, part 2.4.3.
346 Schlegel, *supra* note 76, at 8.

there is always such a position. The play between the picture it holds of the world, society, and legal decision-making against that of its oppositional group is actually the 'reality text' of that time. Seen from another angle, what is the play in the legal academic discourse of today? Is there a point in my claim in another chapter[347] that in Harvard, in its iconic role, the boundaries between the practical and the theoretical (and the 'public-private', the old cherished target of pragmatism is definitely at play here) are drawn in a complementary manner? Is it true that between completely incommensurable discourses today, we can discern a 'reality text', a taste, a place where we can sense where the critique is going (meaning: nowhere)? And from the other side, where do the 'practical' energies go? Is it true that we can still find the spirit and style of the 1950s discourse in some (partly legal) areas, such as dispute resolution, that are the most crucial for 'real' problems, like peace, poverty, development, and so forth? Can we sense the reality in this play, or the current 'American', by enduring the split, mapping it, describing the intercourse of the discourses at stake? Isn't it again, at Harvard of today, a certain kind of 'utopian rationalism?'.

What I think is missing from Kennedy's description of the post-war play as a repetition of a few previous ones is the acknowledgment that it is not the abstract notion of 'utopian rationalism' that recurs here. It is the singularity of its garb as the pragmatist American picture of society that makes this Legal Process text so constitutive and influential in contemporary consciousness: The image of society as being in a constant movement of maximization, the idea of problem solving, of purposiveness as an ultimate perspective, all of them not necessarily more 'rationalistic' than the Realists' idea of the social sciences before. Each theory has its own kind of reason. Even Kennedy's portrayal of reasoned elaboration looking for *the* right answer ignores the emergence of this notion as part of a response to the Court, as I described above, based on the idea of a 'maturing of collective thought'. There was a 'soft' quality to the 'conviction' he describes, and it is the pragmatic organic story of settling and resettling.[348] Henry Hart might truly believe that if only the Court will give a more elaborate opinion and discuss the problems among

---

347 See the chapter 'In Search of the Dispute: On Lawyers and Legal Philawsophers at Harvard Law School (Or: Some Private Hope and Public Irony)'.
348 See, for example, Sebok, *supra* note 22, at 177, describing the 'flip' in their thinking about discretion. 'They argued that law is a good thing precisely because (not in spite of) the fact that it is a mechanism for harnessing discretion: Discretion is a vehicle of good far more than evil; it is the only means by which the intelligence and good will of society can be brought to bear directly upon the solution of hitherto unsolved problems.' See also *supra* text to 183n–184n above.

its members, a more elaborate solution will emerge. In that sense, there was a 'statistic' validation claim in Hart's call.[349] It is not necessarily 'rationalism' per se, but it is rationalism in its American official legal version of the post-war period. Kennedy himself might repeat, in his role as a Crit scholar, an old Benthamite or a Realist operation, but its location after the constitutive moment of the 1950s suggests that 'the next step' will have its own singularity, its own proper name. It seems that his fascination with mapping and of performing the delicate rigorous work on the legal body makes his perception of the Legal Process much less concerned with the 'progressive riddle' that occupies Horwitz and Peller. He is not astonished by the 'dark' logic of Wechlsler. In his historical legal writing, he is not committed to the interpretive turn as an epistemological precondition. In contrast to his story of recurrence, I would like to stress the singularity of the post-war moment. Coming back to the future from that moment on, and continuing on toward the past, can never be the same.

---

349 See also Sebok, *supra* note 22, at 125: 'The Court was too busy, argued Hart, and therefore no longer took the time to review and debate the opinions of the various justices. Hart saw a relationship between the rise in summary and vacuous opinions and the rise in individual dissents and fragmented majorities. He argued that, had the Court more time to deliberate and reflect, *and* if all nine justices were to reflect fully on each issue, the Court would have produced more carefully reasoned opinions *and* there would have been greater unanimity among the nine justices. *Hart was assuming, of course, that legal reasoning is a bit like shooting at a target: the more people and more attempts there are, the greater the likelihood of hitting on the "right" answer*' (my emphasis – M.A.).

Chapter 3

Taking Sides: Margins and Phases of Pragmatics of Legal Process Disciples (Or: The Pragmatists That We Are)

3.1   The 'Next Step': Trajectories and Resistances

The era that began in the 1960s and continues today is characterized by an epistemological crisis. There is no longer an acceptable meta-discourse that determines what is law. From another direction, there is a rich discourse about what is law, a meta-discourse which has not existed before, and thus, there is not a consensual representation of what was obvious and common sense-like before. There are many perceptions of law, many histories; there are many 'law and ...' trends, and the flourishing of the meta-discourse about what *is* law is becoming a primary intellectual affair. Some call this era 'postmodern', but this labeling usually already assumes a way to remain 'modern' without confronting the many problematics and contradictions in the liberal discourse, and in modernity itself. It assumes an era where modernism was 'ruling' with no reservations, as in the 1950s, but this depiction of the 'origin', as always, and as already shown in the previous chapter,[1] is itself a matter of having a perspective and a location within the intellectual realm of today. This chapter seeks to map briefly, and by way of examples, three diverse responses to the 1950s jurisprudence, and through the examples to delineate also the loss of the theoretical interest in the dispute and in the public notion of settlement.

The three figures this chapter examines represent the right, center and left as considered in the legal academy. Owen Fiss represents the mainstream legal scholarship of public law, and the Yale position in the legal discourse. Richard Posner represents the right, through his Law and Economics approach and the Chicago school. Roberto Unger represents the left and the flow from the discourse of law altogether into the realm of politics and of radical social engineering. Their writing will be examined by way of examples to illustrate

---

1   See the chapter 'Settled Law and the Law-That-Is-Not-But-Ought-To-Be: Hart and Sacks and the Pragmatic Philosophy of Dispute Resolution (Or: Why Couldn't Henry Hart Speak?)', part 2.4.

the discursive relationship it has towards the Legal Process writing. My claim is that, as disciples of this constitutive text, and as the next generation in law, their writing can be read as resisting the text, while still maintaining some of its characteristics. Three contemporary theories of adjudication will emerge from this discussion.

A basic lesson I would like to draw from the interaction of the texts I suggest here is the non-contemporaneous character of the discourses that surround us nowadays. The play of theories and schools is sometimes created through an interaction of genres of discourses which belong in different scales of time. The economical discourse, for example, may assume a classic individual of the eighteenth century and the scientific credibility of the beginning of the same century, while speaking in the most updated contemporary terms and dealing with current sophisticated problems. The critical discourse may incorporate the Marxist critique or adopt the most abstract up-to-date theoretical account of the law, while still accepting some problematic assumptions of its economic brother. The critical discourse, in the following engagement, claims to oversee the other two discourses and to overcome them and the public law discourse claims to mediate both the critical and the economical. Actually, what will emerge from their intercourse is a possible counter-projection, re-reading and overcoming, and an ongoing process of incommensurable interactions wherein providing a theory immediately falls back to defending a sheltered location within the discourse. I am less interested in the question of who is right than in the questions of what is the play of these gaps, what is their map. In the interaction between Unger and Posner, and also among Unger's texts themselves, I will trace the distinct genres of discourse I have delineated in the first chapter and will describe a call for a new professional identity, or what might be named a 'loss of faith'. In the discussion of Owen Fiss's writing, I describe a narrow 'new legal process' canonical center, and an institutional academic setting which enables detachment and projection of the dispute resolution discourse in light of the reaction to 1950s jurisprudence.

In contrast to Dworkin, whom I discuss elsewhere[2] and who reiterates the old legacy of Holmes in contemporary terms, and in contrast to Duncan Kennedy, who preserves that legacy in his actual writing,[3] the three individuals in this chapter provide a grand picture of what is law. While the professional

---

2 See the chapter 'In Search of the Dispute: On Lawyers and Legal Philawsophers at Harvard Law School (Or: Some Private Hope and Public Irony)'.
3 See the chapter 'The Maturing of the Pragmatic Idea in Law and Society (Or: The Fall, and the Rise of Philawsophy)'.

investment, which Dworkin and Kennedy describe and perform, respectively, does not need a grand meta-theory, just as in Holmes' time, and *The Critique of Adjudication* may stay eclectic, Unger tries to get *Democracy Realized*, and both Fiss and Unger give a comprehensive view of what it is to adjudicate. Instead of trying to judge the diverse accounts they offer, I will try to trace them through their play with the Legal Process text, and in Fiss also through his interaction with another 'practical' trajectory of that text, which is the ADR movement.

The term 'resistance' in my text emblematizes the rebellious act that conditions the need of the next generation to transform and overcome, and in some sense to forget, its constitutive text, as well as the educational message upon which it was brought. At the same time, it is an acceptance of the basic terms of the debate, and of the irresistible object, as part of accepting history, as part of belonging to a discourse and to a context that fixes the boundaries of any possible leap. As in psychoanalysis (under some interpretations), my interest is not in 'total neutrality substituting an unveiled truth for what resists it'.[4] It is rather in preserving the knot, as 'the very place where the analysis must come to a halt ... must be left in obscurity'.[5] Pragmatism will again become a fertile source and a discursive knot, for the understanding of the operation of the following diverse responses.

3.2 Settlement Aversion: Owen Fiss and the 'Public Law' Discourse (Or: What Happened to Old Martinelli?)

At the center of the theoretical map, resisting and at the same time continuing the Legal Process jurisprudence, public law scholarship can be located. In Owen Fiss's writing, I would like to trace the mechanism of denial and repression as the main device used to cope with the 1950s jurisprudence.

In their article *The New Public Law Movement: Moderation as a Postmodern Cultural Form*,[6] Eskridge and Peller claim that the new public

---

4   Jacques Derrida, *Resistances of Psychoanalysis* (Peggy Kammuf, Pascal-Ann Brault and Michael Naaf trans., 1998), 1996, 17.
5   Id. at 15. See also at 10: 'A resistance might be something other than a resistance full of meaning to an analysis full of meaning. Even if it is definitive, resistance belongs, along with what it resists, to the order of sense, of a sense whose secret is only the hidden secret, the dissimulated meaning, the veiled truth: to be interpreted, analyzed, made explicit, explain.'
6   William N. Eskridge, Jr and Gary Peller, 'The New Public Law Movement: Moderation as a Postmodern Cultural Form', 89 *Mich. Law Rev.* 707 (1991).

law scholarship both continues and dramatically reforms the Legal Process approach.[7] On the one hand, they share with the Legal Process tradition the idea that justice resides in process: 'The legal process focus on institutional relationship, the process of lawmaking, and an overriding standard of purposive coherence continues to dominate public law scholarship.'[8] On the other hand, there is the conviction that all decision-making is ultimately normative. This view presents 'the politics of legal scholarship' as the centrist position re-emergence of the Legal Process orientation in 'new public law' costume.

> The generation of scholars that followed the legal process founders was molded by the civil rights movement and by the critique of the political theory underlying the legal process philosophy ... The key intellectual moves include an antipluralism which rejects the idea that political preferences are exogenous to politics; an embrace of the normativity of law, i.e., that law's legitimacy depends upon substantive justice and procedural correctness; an a practical reasoning which seeks to reconcile colliding community norms through dialogue and reconciliation.[9]

The public law scholarship is the centrist position re-emergence of the legal process orientation, and it is assumed to mediate between Critical Legal Studies claims from the left and the Law and Economics from the right.[10] The movement is 'tilted toward the left',[11] and actually Eskridge and Peller describe it as constituting a 'genre of legal thought' which has a postmodern cultural situation.

> The 'center' chosen by the New Public Law is a distinctively *postmodern* center; the New Public Law is one manifestation of a new quasi-cultural social form that is associated with the appearance of postmodernism as a presence in American intellectual life. In other words, the postmodernism condition is

---

7   Id., at 762.
8   Id., at 708.
9   Id., at 709.
10 Id. 'On the right is the Chicago School law-and-economics movement, which takes as its starting point the legitimacy of our pluralist political system and the socioeconomic status quo and focuses on the comprehensive efficiency of different legal rules.' Id., at 725.
    'On the left, CLS scholars criticized process ideology for its tendency to depoliticize social issues by channeling inquiry into procedural discourse and challenged the normative prong of process theory by arguing that the ethical bases for deference under the principle of institutional settlement were just as controversial as substantive decision making and in any event they were analytically inseparable.' Id., at 725–6.
11 Id: 'A great part of the attraction of the movement relates to the fact that it is generally tilted toward the left in terms of its intellectual positions.'

constituted, not by its radical avant-garde – CLS in law, for example, or deconstruction in literary criticism – but also by a particular, recognizable attempt to moderate and stabilize, to constitute a center sophisticated enough to comprehend the postmodern stance but nevertheless reformist enough to believe that it doesn't make all that much difference after all.[12]

The centrist position is assumed to be sophisticated enough 'to comprehend the postmodern stance', but nevertheless is reformist enough to believe that 'it doesn't make all that much difference after all'. Its basic notion of normativity is that first, law is contextual; it cannot be separated from society, its values, and its socioeconomic structure. Second, law is defining; it helps shape society, its values, its socioeconomic structure. Third, law is interpretive; it is the result of a dynamic process by which the perspectives of an interpreter and a text merge to yield an interpretation.[13]

The public law movement makes many claims about law. Law is normative and interpretive; it is formative and contextual; it is transformative and a type of practical reasoning. As in the Legal Process era, but this time through texts of distinct authors and not through 'basic problems in the making and application of law', in the Legal Process text, there is an effort to give the grand mediating picture of adjudication and its role in society. The resistance to the post-war era's 'collective thought' and the opposition it produces are manifested in a few ways. First, the political progressive pathos is back to redeem the discourse of law from the conservativism of the 1950s. The public law scholars are considered leftists, but 'not too extreme'. Their personal profile, which Eskridge and Peller portray, describes a public law scholar who joins the law school both to fulfill his social ideals and out of admiration of *Brown*.[14]

Second, the position of this scholarship within the legal discourse might be best defined by what it is not, i.e., it is not at Harvard anymore (and has some strong proponents at Yale, with all its symbolic history of the opposition); it is not Law and Economics and not Critical Legal Studies (but it has a tendency to the left, as mentioned above); it does not aspire to represent collective thought or to 'include' all theories of law under one framework; its existence is actually limited to the narrow imagined arena, where law is supposed to exist in its uniqueness as a separate discipline, capable of providing its own language to generate public norms.

---

12 Id., at 788.
13 Id., at 749: 'Law is politics, politics is the making of decisions that affect the community, and the dynamic of politics ought to be dialogic practical reasoning rather than coercive rule or rights enforcement.'
14 Id., at 744–5.

Third, the naturalistic-positivistic meta-text of the post-war era is switched, as part of the 1960s intellectual climate, into a more interpretive-conversational mode. Instead of speaking about 'institutional settlement' and organic rationality, there is a belief in 'an ongoing conversation about the pursuit of activist values in an incredibly complex world'.[15] Science is no longer a proper paradigm for the handling of legal issues, nor even the social sciences with their judgmatical quality.[16]

There is an imagined social progressive compromise at the core of public law scholarship that cannot find strong supporters at the more iconic place of Harvard. The torn political discourse of the 1980s, which has become the neatly split discourse of today, seems to resist a defined center like the one that exists at Yale. In one of his articles called *The Death of the Law?*[17] Owen Fiss posits the tendency to go to the extreme of the CLS and the L&E as endangering 'the proudest and noblest ambitions of the law',[18] and calls for belief in public values in order to save the law from losing its 'generative force of our public life'.[19] As I will try to demonstrate, his detached position is constructed as a pure negativity of the post-war scholarship without having a definite genre of pragmatism to cling to, and thus, having only a weak American voice.[20]

I would like to engage a few texts of Owen Fiss, thought to be one of the main opponents of the dispute resolution movement. First, I would like to show how, in his forward to the Harvard Law Review in 1978, he excluded a philosophy of dispute resolution, projecting it as archaic and regressive.[21] Then, I will analyze his famous *Against Settlement* article and unpack his arguments in order to show his biased attitude toward this discourse. This

---

15   Id., at 750.
16   See the discussion of the social sciences in the Legal Process Materials in the chapter 'Settled Law and the Law-That-Is-Not-but-Ought-To-Be: Hart and Sacks and the Pragmatic Philosophy of Dispute Resolution (Or: Why Couldn't Henry Hart Speak?)', part 2.2.5.
17   Owen M. Fiss, 'The Death of The Law?', *Cornell L. Rev.* 1 (1986).
18   Id., at 1.
19   Id., at 14–15: 'In order to save the law, we must look beyond the law. We will never be able to respond fully to the negativism of critical legal studies or the crude instrumentalism of law and economics until a regenerative process takes hold, until the broad social processes that fed and nourished those movements are reversed. The analytical arguments wholly internal to the law can take us only so far. There must be something more – a belief in public values and the willingness to act on them.'
20   See also the discussion of Kronman's position in the chapter 'In Search of the Dispute: on Lawyers and Legal Philawsophers at Harvard Law School (Or: Some Private Hope and Public Irony)', part 4.4.
21   Owen M. Fiss, 'The Supreme Court 1978 Term: Forward: The Forms of Justice', 93 *Harv. Law Rev.* 1 (1979).

sequence aims to examine critically the relationship between what I perceive to be two trajectories of the 1950s jurisprudence: the public law scholarship and the Alternative Dispute Resolution movement.[22]

In his 1978 article, 'The Supreme Court 1978 Term: Forward: The Forms of Justice', Fiss describes the qualities and the history of the 'structural reform'. This genre of constitutional litigation emerged during the Warren court era, in which the courts had to 'reconstruct social reality' and to transform the status quo. 'Adjudication is the social process by which judges give meaning to our public values. Structural reform – the subject of this essay – is one type of adjudication,' says Fiss.[23] This basic assumption is developed and transformed during the article, until eventually he concludes that the old perception of adjudication as a dispute resolution mechanism is not only obsolete, but wrong.

> Gone is the triad, the icon of justice holding two balances, and in its place a whole series of metaphors are offered to describe the structural suit. Some, emphasizing the distinctive party structure, speak of town meetings, others, emphasizing the posture of the judge, speak of management or the creation of a new administrative agency.[24]

The paradigmatic notion of adjudication as aiming at achieving private justice between two parties is switched for a public image of a town meeting or an administrative work. What is most striking in Fiss's argument is that, in contrast to a historical evolutionary argument such as the one which appears in Abram Chayes' article, 'The Role of the Judge in Public Law Litigation'[25] – an argument that presents the dispute-resolution model as traditional but still existing, and the structural reform as new and supplementary – Fiss presents a picture of dispute-resolution role of adjudication as false and misleading:[26]

---

22 For the intellectual history argument behind this link see the chapter 'In Search of the Dispute: On Lawyers and Legal Philawsophers at Harvard Law School (Or: Some Private Hope and Public Irony)'.
23 Id., at 2.
24 id., at 28.
25 Abram Chayes, 'The Role of the Judge in Public Law Litigation', 89 *Harv. Law Rev.* 1281 (1976).
26 See also Owen M. Fiss, 'The Social and Political Foundations of Adjudication', 6 *Law and Human Behav.* (1982) 121: 'Adjudication is the process by which the values embodied in an authoritative legal text, such as the Constitution, are given concrete meaning and expression. In my judgment, this has always been the function of adjudication, clearly embraced and legitimated by article III, and continues with the role of courts under the common law, but within recent decades a new *form* of constitutional adjudication has emerged.'

'I doubt whether dispute resolution is an adequate description of the social function of courts. To my mind, courts exist to give meaning to our public values, not to resolve disputes.'[27]

In contrast to the old story of the judge as a stranger deciding between two people 'in the state of nature' who are 'squabbling over a piece of property' and coming to an impasse, Fiss understands the courts to have a different 'social logic'. The old story might be replaced by another one: 'The sovereign sends out his officers throughout the realm to speak the law and to see that it is obeyed.'[28] Disputation becomes 'a mode of judicial operation', and accordingly, 'dispute resolution may be one *consequence* of the judicial decision'.[29]

There is a sharp opposition by this perception to the Legal Process idea of the case and its significance. Instead of the idea of settlement as the horizon of decision making in adjudication, and in opposition to the idea of a slow, reasoned elaboration of a dispute until its problematic can be viewed and resolved, 'the sovereign sends out his officers ... to speak the law and to see that it is obeyed'. The sovereign knows the law, the law embodies public values, and the disputing individuals are only instruments to enhance this scenario. Who is this sovereign and how does he know 'the law', which is presented in Fiss's writing as public values? In another article, he suggests that they are 'the values embodied in an authoritative legal text, such as the Constitution',[30] but he does not provide a definite answer. It appears his assertions ('axioms' might be a better expression here, a concept he uses later to describe Fuller's assumptions) are the flip side of the apologetic response we would have expected from a law professor trying to justify the Warren court's activism. It seems Fiss is interested in creating a new mythology of the adjudication, but the step he takes here away from the dispute, from the concrete, from the settlement seems to ideologically eliminate the pragmatic, anti-foundationalist element within the decision making process, an element which was alive and present within the Legal Process Materials. Adjudication should deal only with public values. If there exist some few insignificant disputes that do not threaten or implicate public values, they should not be handled by courts, but rather by arbitrators; neither should they make 'an extravagant use of public resources'.[31] The Supreme Court justice, the Yale

---

27 Fiss, *supra* note 1, at 29.
28 Id.
29 Id., at 30.
30 Fiss, *The Social and Political Foundations of Adjudication*, *supra* note 26, at 121.
31 Id.

law professor, and the lawyers (elite law school graduates) have become philosopher-kings dealing with public values, and what was considered private before, located at the bottom layer of Hart and Sacks' pyramid, is public altogether, ready for judicial manipulation and handling. If there are other disputes and courts not enjoying these 'structural' characteristics they should not bother the system. Even when assuming that each dispute has a public value dimension, and also acknowledging the fact that each dispute has only contextual dimensions, stories, and social understandings that are interacting together in concrete, singular circumstances, Fiss's position seems to be the mirroring of the Legal Process notion of the bottom layer.

Fiss's idea of the judge and the law professor in relation to the layman's perception of law and its role seems to sharply signify the split that occurred within the law school between the dispute resolution-oriented practitioners and the theoretical, 'high-principled' academics.[32] The public law model is explicitly interested only in appellate courts' high decisions that might influence the social structure, while the interest in the remaining 99 per cent of cases that are settled or solved outside the courts are none of its concern. The image is no longer that of society in endless settlement and resettlement and of a decision process which is itself a settling of the private and public, but of a kind of norms pyramid which is handling everything through grand public principles. These norms are created, in contrast to the Kelsenian picture, by the adjudicative judge. This twist toward the judge follows the idea, fully endorsed by Fiss, that a simple application of a norm is impossible (and that generalities do not decide concrete cases).

---

32 A characterization of a typical 'New Public Law Scholar' as appears in Eskridge and Peller's article 'The New Public Law Movement' might be appropriate here: 'Our typical New Public Law Scholar then attended an elite law school in the late 1960s or 1970s. The law school environment at that time embodied the best of the legal process tradition, emphasizing a vigorously reformist approach to the status quo, whose overall legitimacy was broadly assumed. Often reflecting his or her own graduate school experience and the eclectic pedagogical agenda at the major law schools, the typical budding New Public Law scholar from the beginning of his or her academic career has been interested in intellectual developments outside law, especially developments in political theory and economics. He or she is also an avid reader of CLS scholarship and is impressed with its vision but believes it is "too negative" (referring here to Fiss in the footnote, M.A.) ... His or her audience is not primarily the practitioner, nor is it the radical lawyer or even the public defender; instead, it is other boomer eliteslaw professors, legislative counsels, journalists, and sundry intellectuals of the baby boom generation or later ...': William N. Eskridge, Jr and Gary Peller, 'The New Public Law Movement: Moderation as a Postmodern Cultural Form', 89 *Mich. Law Rev.* 707, 745 (1991).

In his notion of 'disciplining rules' and of adjudication as restrained by 'an interpretive community',[33] Fiss garbs in contemporary interpretive terms the old Holmsian intellectual fantasy of the law as a closed world to inhabit,[34] that which Ronald Dworkin also enacts when he provides the mythology of Hercules.[35] The discourse of law provides formal limits and guidance to the deciding judge. It offers bounded objectivity through its professional and internal qualities. The specialized legal wisdom it produces should handle society from above.[36]

The way in which Fiss depicts Lon Fuller's ideas in his article illustrates his step more vividly.[37] He describes three different approaches that have been taken to establish a priority for dispute resolution as an ideal against which structural reform is to be judged. Fuller is described as taking the axiomatic approach:

> It postulates some formal attribute of a social process as a morally necessary attribute, on the basis of which the structural and dispute resolution modes are to be evaluated ... It places adjudication on a moral plane with two other activities exalted by consent theory, voting, and bargaining, and then tries to construct an ideal form of adjudication that preserves this connection with consensual activity, now in a highly individualized form.[38]

---

33 See for example Fiss, *The Death of Law, supra* note 17, at 11: 'When I read a case like *Brown v. Board of Education,* for example, what I see is not the unconstrained power of the justices to give vent to their desires and interests, but rather public officials situated within a profession, bounded at every turn by the norms and conventions that define and constitute that profession ... In sum, the justices are disciplined in the exercise of their power. They are caught in a network of so-called "disciplining rules" which, like a grammar, define and constitute the practice of judging and are rendered authoritative by the interpretive community of which the justices are part. These disciplining rules provide the standards for determining whether some decision is right (or wrong) and for justifying it (or for contesting it). They constrain, not determine, judgment.'

34 See the chapter 'The Maturing of the Pragmatic Idea in law and Society (Or: The Fall, and the Rise of Philawsophy)', part 1.4, and the reference there to the Fiss-Fish debate.

35 See the chapter 'In Search of the Dispute: On Lawyers and Legal Philawsophers at Harvard Law School (Or: Some Private Hope and Public Irony)', part 4.3.

36 See also McThenia and Shaffer, *For Reconciliation, supra* note 49, at 1660: 'He comes close to arguing that the branch of government that resolves disputes, the courts, is the principal source of justice in fragmented modern American society.'

37 Robert G. Bone claims in his article about dispute resolution and public law models that: 'In large part because of Fiss's work, Fuller has become the paradigm of public law litigation.' Robert G. Bone, 'Lon Fuller's Theory of Adjudication and the False Dichotomy Between Dispute Resolution and Public Law Models of Litigation', 75 *Boston Univ. Law Rev.* 1273, 1279 (1995).

38 Id., at 39.

Fuller's argument in his 'Forms and Limits'[39] article is presented here under the rubric of one optional axiomatic path to support a dispute resolution focus. Fiss then goes on to state: 'The most sustained effort to build a case for dispute resolution on the basis of moral axioms is Lon Fuller's essay *The Forms and Limits of Adjudication*.'[40] Fiss separates the axiomatic elements in Fuller's theory in a way that covers their equivalence to his own 'axiomatic assumption'. It seems he, too, like Fuller, 'postulates some formal attribute of a social process as a morally necessary attribute'. Perhaps only the word 'formal' does not fit here, as Fiss is trying to support the procedure of substance, not of form. But isn't this a new kind of formalism, one in which the judge and the scholar decide the cases directly from the values, and the individual is only an uninteresting stimulator of the process? Is it not formal also in the sense of believing in an internal language of the law, in a possibility for control and objectivity through the adoption of disciplining rules? His acknowledgment here that his conception of adjudication starts from the top down, while Fuller's goes from the bottom up, only reinforces this impression.[41] When Fiss thinks of the neglected individual who has the actual dispute, he does not predict any good from the focus on 'his' perception:

> A conception of adjudication that strictly honors the right of each affected individual to participate in the process seems to proclaim the importance of the individual, but actually leaves the individual without the institutional support necessary to realize his true self. In fact, the individual participation axiom should do little more than throw down an impassable bar polycentrismto the one social process that has emerged with promise for preserving our constitutional values and the ideal of individualism in the face of the modern bureaucratic state – structural reform.[42]

The public law model of Fiss seems here to suggest salvation to the individual through the public value focus of the judge. His right to participate in the process should not be 'axiomatically' supported, and instead of that adjudication will help him 'to realize his true self', in Fiss's terms. This realization is taking place through overcoming the 1950s public-private separation, which depicts polycentrism as a barrier to adjudication. Polycentrism here becomes the paradigm for decision making in adjudication,

---

39   Lon Fuller, 'The Forms and Limits of Adjudication', 92 *Harv. Law Rev.* 353 (1978).
40   Fiss, *supra* note 1, at 39.
41   Id., at 40.
42   Id., at 44.

while the 'managerial discretion', which is needed to determine value judgments, is done by judges. Paternalism and arrogance, as well as the distance from Martinelli – the Legal Process's 'Cantaloupes' hero – are implicit in this description.[43] In both Fiss's and our time, Martinelli should probably be using ADR services. His dispute in its singularities is not the concern of the theoreticians of adjudication.[44] Coming back to Fuller's notion of adjudication, he distinguishes it from negotiation and election by the way the individual participates in it. In negotiation, the participation is bargaining; in election, it is voting. Adjudication, in contrast to these two social processes, includes participation through proof and reasoned argument. The limits of adjudication are determined by the level in which the rights of the individuals to participate in the process are preserved, and this is why polycentric problems are not suitable for adjudication. Multiple repercussions might stem from any decision regarding just one of the issues. 'Each crossing of strands is a distinct center for distributing tensions.'[45] Polycentric elements exist 'in almost all problems submitted to adjudication',[46] and therefore 'it is a question of knowing when the polycentric elements have become so ... predominant that the proper limits of adjudication have been reached'.[47] Fiss perceives this idea of Fuller as being in opposition to the structural reform and, accordingly, to the public law model he suggests. Fuller's mistake, Fiss claims, in developing the polycentric argument is in having at the core of his conception of adjudication's limits the individual's right to participate in a proceeding that might affect him adversely.

A closer look reveals that Fiss's argument is problematic from several perspectives, and will send us back to 'the forms and limits' to learn more about Fuller's polycentrist argument and its implications.

---

[43] See also McThenia and Shaffer, *For Reconciliation, supra* note 49, at 1660: 'Fiss's argument rests on the faith that justice – and he uses the word – is usually something people get from the government. He comes close to arguing that the branch of government that resolves disputes, the courts, is the principal source of justice in fragmented modern American society.'

[44] The political and the 'spectral' motives behind the sorting out of the structural reform (and its *Brown* background) as a model for any adjudication are emphasized when, from a procedural perspective, this mode of litigation is perceived as part of a general phenomenon of the emergence of 'the managerial judges'. Judith Resnik describe the varieties of its manifestations as including post decision judicial work, pretrial phases activity, and during other activities. See Judith Resnik, 'Managerial Judges', 96 *Harv. L. Rev.* 376 (1982).

[45] Fuller, *supra* note 39, at 395.

[46] Id., at 397.

[47] Id., at 398.

First, as I have already mentioned, Fiss brings this 'axiomatic' strategy as a possible way to support the view of dispute resolution as an ideal against which structural reform is to be judged. Actually, Fuller's writing cannot support that view because he does not call for any ideal of adjudication. In contrast to Fiss, who is assuming an interpretive mode, Fuller is committed, according to his time, to a naturalistic-positivistic picture, where the outside pyramid of disputes in the 'world' are handled and settled by the inside navigating force of adjudication. The private and public are still conceptually separated at his time and adjudication is supposed to handle them in harmony. In Fiss' text, there is only the public: the value making of the interpretive judge (who is constrained by disciplining rules). Fuller speaks from the bottom and works up, as Fiss acknowledges, and his effort is neither to depict an ideal nor to support some essential notion of adjudication. According to the definitions he gives, he describes the limits of the process, but the definitions themselves are flexible and ready for revision. It is uncertain what these definitions imply in terms of structural reform. As mentioned above, Fuller acknowledges the polycentric element in each decision: he knows that the question is 'where to draw the line'.

> ... any suggestion of a notion like 'true adjudication' goes heavily against the grain of modern thought. Today it is a mark of intellectual liberation to realize that there is and can be no such thing as 'true science', 'true religion', 'true education', or 'true adjudication'. It is all a matter of definition. The modern professional university philosopher is particularly allergic to anything suggesting the doctrine of essence and takes it as a sure sign of philosophic illiteracy when a writer speaks of 'the essence of art' or 'the essence of democracy'.[48]

When Fuller speaks of 'modern thought' and uses the word 'today', he refers to the 1950s, the decade in which his article was written. His non-essentialist approach reflects pragmatism, at the time a legitimate part of mainstream legal consciousness. Accordingly, the definition of adjudication he suggests is tentative, dependent on the context and only 'a matter of definition'. It does not necessarily imply a position against structural reform because polycentrism is all over, as Fuller mentions. It can always try to examine the lines again. As I try to show, when dealing with the Legal Process scholarship, the notion of adjudication in Hart and Sacks, following Fuller, was of adjudication as a navigating voice of reason between public and private

---

48   Id., at 356.

– between reciprocity and social aims, and not straight within the 'state of nature', as Fiss has tried to depict.[49] It assumes indeed a naturalistic meta-text, but a workable program is offered to the institutions of society to be handled through a mechanism which differentiates the public and private again and again. Actually, the centrality Fuller gives to adjudication as demarcating the public and the private is adopted and accepted by Fiss. It is just that he would like to draw a picture of a judge perpetually articulating the public without assuming a place of 'reciprocity' that should be publicly acknowledged, or a negotiation which happens naturally. The exclusion of the private as a non-interesting place for the judge, a place which does not deserve even for a theory to be acknowledged, is endorsement of the more internal-eternal work of Fuller's *Consideration and Form* or *The Reliance Interest*, where the legal scholar is given the 'conflicting considerations consciousness', in Duncan Kennedy's terms.[50] Fuller might agree, in his conceptual framework, to use adjudication to enhance some public values, but the private reciprocity pole of each decision will keep existing within this move.[51] Thus, it turns out that nothing essential in Fuller's writing goes against structural reform. Fiss cannot see this flexibility. He reads Fuller as axiomatic from a different point in time, through a different generation's eyes. As the 'special editor's note' in Fuller's article indicates, the initial version of the article was circulated in 1957, but was first published only in 1978. Fiss's response is indeed updated to the publication. He says the essay 'was not updated to account, either as a descriptive or normative matter, for the intervening twenty years, the civil rights era. It is as though the period never occurred – an erasure of some portion of the history of procedure.'[52]

Indeed, Fiss's writing represents the 1970s public law ideas, and as such does not take into account the Legal Process era and the pragmatic sensitivities that were common knowledge in Fuller's time. It is, indeed, 'as though the

---

49   For an argument against Fiss's dichotomy between the traditional model and the structural one, see Andrew W. McThenia and Thomas L. Shaffer, 'For Reconciliation', 94 *Yale L. J.* 1660, 1663–65 (1985).

50   See the discussion of these pieces and of Kennedy's reading in the chapter 'Settled Law and the Law That-is-Not-But-Ought-To-Be: Hart and Sacks and The Pragmatic Philosophy of Dispute Resolution (Or: Why Couldn't Henry Hart Speak?)', part 2.2.3.

51   For an effort to construct a contemporary progressive jurisprudence through the notions of Hart and Sacks and partly Fuller, see Anthony J. Sebok, *Legal Positivism in American Jurisprudence* (1998), and the discussion in the chapter 'Settled Law and the Law That-Is-Not-But-Ought-To-Be: Hart and Sacks and the Pragmatic Philosophy of Dispute Resolution (Or: Why Couldn't Henry Hart Speak?)', part 2.4.3.

52   Fiss, *supra* note 1, at 39.

period never occurred'. The theoretical legal discourse is run from the top and works down.

Referring to other characteristics of form in the article, its name, 'Forms of Justice', seems to stand in a metonymic relation to Fuller's article of two decades earlier, 'The Forms and Limits'. Fiss strives to close the gap in this very influential article of this very famous writer, that gap being the erasure of the civil rights era along with its proceduralist lessons.[53] Another interesting phenomenon to notice is that, looking at Fiss's article, it is not that the pragmatic sensitivities have disappeared. 'Displacement' or 'sublimation' might be proper idioms to describe what happened to them. Both here and in his 'Objectivity and Interpretation' article,[54] the pragmatic craft of 'social engineering' and sensitivity to the case are removed to the stage of implementation of the decision, to the time where the right was recognized and now the proper remedy is sought; as Fiss stated, 'The structural remedy must be seen in instrumental terms.'[55] The same demarcation appears in 'Objectivity and Interpretation':

> There is a third dimension that informs the task of the judge and that probably plays an even greater role in giving legal interpretation its distinctive cast: The judge tries to be efficacious. The judge seeks to interpret the legal text and then to transform social reality so that it comports with that interpretation ... The judge must give a remedy ...[56]

At this stage, the judge is indeed acting as a mediator, or at least as the settling judge from Hart and Sacks' time. He or she should acknowledge 'the need to address complex social situations with creative and often complicated remedies and then to manipulate power so as to make them reality'.[57] Judges understand at this instrumental phase that they 'are not all-powerful. They can decree some results but not all ... the success of the actualization process depends on many other forces, less formal, less identifiable, and perhaps even less reachable.'[58] The Legal Process's settling judge has disappeared from the decision making, which is now based on public values and is not therefore in any sense pragmatic. He reappears at the remedy stage and tries to implement in reality his idealistic views. The social-context perception of adjudication as including three intertwining functions, dispute resolution, regulation, and

---

53   Id.
54   Owen M. Fiss, 'Objectivity and Interpretation', 34 *Stan. Law Rev.* 739 (1982).
55   Fiss, *supra* note 1, at 50.
56   Fiss, *supra* note 54.
57   Id.
58   Fiss, *supra* note 1, at 54.

ameliorative,[59] is replaced by one ameliorative function, with the two others moving to a subsidiary position. This separation between the practical and the theoretical, between reality as the private and theory as the public, is to my mind a paradigm of the post-Legal Process generation consciousness, which has its implications also in its relation to the ADR movement:

> There is no likely connection between the core processes of adjudication, those that give the judge the special claim to competence, and the instrumental judgments necessarily entailed in fashioning the remedy ...[60] The judge might be seen as forever straddling two worlds, the world of the ideal and the world of the practical, the world of the public value and the world of subjective preference, the world of the Constitution and the world of politics.[61]

This image of the straddling judge and the two worlds, the ideal and the practical, also seems to capture Fiss's mind in his 1984 article, his famous manifesto 'Against Settlement'.[62] I use the term 'manifesto' first because of the dogmatic, simple structure used in the article to attack this matter, as I will try to demonstrate.[63] Second, it is very famous in the demarcation of the institutional relationship between ADR and the theoretical jurisprudential discourse. A very typical presentation of the 'dialogue' in an ADR textbook is: 'Yale law professor Owen Fiss led the charge with allegations that the justice system would suffer as the result of publicly supported settlement facilitation,'[64] and that no one has defied him since then is another implicit assumption in this context. The above dichotomy between the practical and the ideal implies scorn and opposition to a discourse such as the ADR idea, which focuses only on the practical. This focus will necessarily result in devastating social consequences in terms of the ideals, and Fiss tries to show how this will happen.

The name of the article, 'Against Settlement', refers to settlement as a negative concept: a compromise, a practical unprincipled solution, a

---

59   See Steven D. Smith, 'Three Functions of Adjudication', 91 *Columbia Law Rev.* 68, 90–91.
60   Fiss, *supra* note 1, at 52.
61   Id., at 58.
62   Owen M. Fiss, 'Against Settlement', 93 *Yale L. J.* 310 (1984).
63   See also McThernia and Shaffer, *For Reconciliation, supra* note 49, at 1660: 'Fiss attacks a straw man. In our view, the models he has created for argument in other circumstances have become mechanisms of self-deception not only for him but for most of those who write about alternatives to litigation.'
64   Stephen B. Goldberg et al., *Dispute Resolution* (2nd edn 1992) 9, 244.

withdrawal. It does not use the ADR movements idiom to describe its aim: 'resolution'. Apparently, both sides of this debate have forgotten the suppressed, 'positive' connotation of settlement, the one that was on the horizon of the Legal Process decision maker. Once upon a time, the public law decision maker was interested only in a settlement; but at the time of this article, it seems relegated to a different legal universe. It is interesting to perceive the different moves of Unger and Fiss from this organizing notion of the 1950s: Fiss goes *against* settlement, as if denying its past enchantment through its current different materialization. He uses an interpretive context to defy it. Unger calls for 'institutional imagination' while accepting the institutional, partly economical framework as the basis for this neo-pragmatism.[65] From another perspective, Fiss preserves the Legal Process posture of a neutral center, while constructing a reverse jurisprudence in the image of the *Brown* decision and enhancing a formalism of value, while Unger continues the anti-formalist sequence by working the progressiveness from within, especially through private law.

Fiss's claims against settlement are unconvincing and I will examine them one by one. In contrast to both his 1978 article and the 'objectivity and interpretation' article, where he posits his views of adjudication, in the beginning of the article here we discover the public value idea only at the article's end. This seems an inversion proper to the discussion of a practical (inferior) matter, the matter of settlement.

His first argument is called '*the imbalance of power*':

> By viewing the lawsuit as a quarrel between two neighbors, the dispute resolution story that underlies ADR implicitly ask us to assume a rough equality between the contending parties. It treats settlement as the anticipation of the outcome of trial and assumes the terms of settlement are simply a product of the parties' predictions of that outcome. In truth, however, settlement is also a function of the resources available to each parties to finance the litigation, and those resources are frequently distributed unequally.[66]

First of all, it is not certain that ADR participants necessarily assume equality. The more salient question is how they deal with an imbalance of power. Secondly, the movement's conception of the alternatives is much less

---

65   See the discussion of Unger's theory in part 3.4: 'From Institutional Settlement to Institutional Imagination: Roberto Unger and the Deweyan Democracy Realized (Or: Pragmatism Taken to its End, and the Program of No Program)'.
66   Fiss, *supra* note 62, at 1015.

limited than the Posnerian approach Fiss adopts toward settlement, as 'anticipation of the outcome of trial' phrased in terms which are 'predictions of that outcome'. Except for the problematic of this description in relation to 'settling in the corridor', where Posner's idea might apply, it ignores the variety of alternatives for which the movement calls, each with its unique structure and special way of operation. Arbitration or early neutral evaluations are not aiming at settlement; yet they are still part of the program he challenges. When settlement is at stake, as in mediation, the idea is quite different from 'splitting the difference' according to the predicted outcome in courts. One of the central ideas of mediation is 'enlarging the pie' and producing more creative solutions than court. Fiss should at least address this idea. If there is more cooperation and a problem-solving approach in the ADR settlement, this might neutralize the imbalance of power.[67] Even if this last assumption is problematic, as indeed it is, Fiss has not dealt with it at all.

Thirdly, even if we assume that the parties do 'split the difference', and that there is an imbalance of power, what makes the settlement worse than adjudication when treating the problem? Fiss's argument is as follows:

> The disparities in resources between the parties can influence the settlement in three ways. First, the poorer party may be less able to amass and analyze the information needed to predict the outcome of the litigation and thus be disadvantaged in the bargaining process ... Second, he may need the damages he seeks immediately and thus be induced to settle as a way of accelerating payment, even though he realizes he might if he awaited judgment ... Third, the poorer party might be forced to settle because he does not have the resources to finance the litigation ...[68]

Fiss is referring here to the 'haves' against the 'have-nots' – the party with the resources against the indigent party, or vice-versa. This typology itself is too basic, his whole argument very general. I will try to unpack it by referring to a few considerations.

---

67 See also McThernia and Shaffer, 'For Reconciliation', *supra* note 49, at 1661: 'Many advocates of the ADR make efficiency based claims. And a plea for ending the so-called litigation explosion, and for returning to law and order, runs through the rules-of-procedure branch of the ADR literature. Bur the movement, if it is even appropriate to call it a single movement, is too varied for Fiss's description. Rather than focusing on the substance of claims made for ADR, Fiss has created a view of the function of courts that he can comfortably oppose.'

68 Id.

3.2.1 The Frequency of the Appearance of the Parties in Court

Have they 'only occasional recourse to the court – one shotters (OSs)', or are they 'repeat players (RPs)'? Marc Galanter offers this typology in his article 'Why the Haves Come Out Ahead'[69] in order to show how the basic architecture of the legal system creates and limits the possibilities of using it as a means of redistributive change. He demonstrates, in a bottom-to-top method of analysis, coming from a social sciences perspective, how the formal, neutral legal system reinforces and augments the misbalance between the parties. According to his analysis, OS's tend to lose for different reasons in court: because of their limited strategic possibilities regarding rules, their greater risk aversion, and their less qualified lawyers. This description seems to undermine Fiss's view that the formal system can neutralize imbalances. Moreover, Galanter claims that RP–OS pairs would not tend to use the alternative 'private remedy system'. (The article was written in 1974, when the ADR movement was not yet born.) More likely, disputes will be dealt with in litigation or in appended systems of settlement.[70] This factual possibility should be examined and can affect the whole argument.

3.2.2 The Ability to Manipulate and to Use a Disadvantage in the Bargaining Situation

Negotiation and settlement are not necessarily disempowering for poor parties. Their OS position can help them be more demanding in interactions with RPs, who, in their position, might worry much more about reputation and image as dealing with OSs. Considering the fact that most of the time, RPs are large institutions or even governmental agencies, this possibility should be taken into account as well. Another way to present this argument is to say that weak parties might use their social role to create commitments.[71]

---

69 Marc Galanter, 'Why the "Haves" Come out Ahead: Speculations on the Limits of Legal Change', 9 *Law & Soc. Law Rev.* 95 (1974).
70 Id., at 134.
71 For a discussion of commitments according to Thomas Schelling's book *The Strategy of Conflict*, and of the paradoxical operation of a weakness during a negotiation, see Michal Alberstein-Davidovitch, *The Dense Negotiation: An Interdisciplinary Offer*, LLM manuscript, Harvard University, April 1997.

3.2.3 The Personal Gain to the Poor Party against the Social Value of the Reformative Rule

Fiss's focus is not clear from his analysis. Is it injustice and loss for the individual, or the overall social loss resulting from lack of a principled decision? From his overall writing, it is obvious that the second target is his concern, but when the above paragraph[72] is read, the most bothersome questions come to mind: What if the party *is* interested in accelerating payment and getting his money now, is considering the deviation from the final expected sum and accepting it? What if she *is* interested in reducing litigation costs, which are very high for her? Should Fiss or the legal system be allowed, in the name of some larger principle, to paternalistically prevent such a party from achieving these outcomes? Is he or she the one who should lead social reform through litigation? Is it feasible at all – especially considering Galanter's demonstration that structurally it is not – or are there different and better ways to mobilize social change?

3.2.4 The Imbalance is Reinforced in Court

Fiss does not convince us that the problem he describes is limited to settlement situations, nor that litigation can somehow avoid them. He also does not consider possibilities to neutralize the actual discrepancies he describes. He could consider, for example, better lawyers or public legal services for the indigent parties, a possibility that Galanter, for example, considers and rejects as reproducing the gap. Fiss, however, refers to this possibility and says:

> I also doubt that institutional arrangements such as contingent fee or the provision of legal services to the poor will in fact equalize resources between contending parties ... Governmental subsidies for legal services have a broader potential ... but ... they are in fact extremely limited, especially when it comes to cases that seek systematic reform of government practices.[73]

So how would the disadvantages be accounted for? Who will protect the poor party? Fiss acknowledges the fact that 'imbalances of power can distort judgment as well', but he continues: 'We count, however, on the guiding presence of the judge, who can employ a number of measures to lessen the impact of distributional inequalities.'[74] His hope seems, at best, unrealistic.

---

72 See *supra* text to note 68.
73 Fiss, *supra* note 62, 1076.
74 Id., at 1077.

Fiss's second argument is *'the absence of authoritative consent'*: In summary, this argument says that settlement produces problems of authorization because, in many cases, not only individuals are involved in the dispute. Regarding trustees and corporations, Fiss says:

> Lawyers or insurance companies might, for example, agree to settlements that are in their interests but not in the best interests of their clients, and to which their clients would not agree if the choice was still theirs. But a deeper and more intractable problem arises from the fact that many parties are not individuals but rather organizations or groups. We do not know who is entitled to speak for these entities and to give the consent upon which so much the appeal of settlement depends.

I think this argument does not need much response. Is an organization an integral 'entity' that as a matter of 'truth' cannot agree to settle? Is it not a matter of policy, a matter for other bodies of law such as corporations or insurance companies to decide according to the matter, and have not the Legal Realists said it long ago?[75] Is this the ultimate place where the idea of agency should be abandoned?

A different version of the claim is aimed at 'groups such as ethnic or racial minorities, inmates of prisons, or residents of institutions for mentally retarded people'.[76] The problem with these groups is that they 'may have an identity or existence that transcends the lawsuit, but they do not have any formal organizational structure and therefore lack any procedures for generative authoritative consent'.[77] Again, the same question arises. Is it a matter of an 'inner quality' of the group, to make it incapable of generating consent; and if it is a matter of representation, should we not treat it directly,[78] and in the way the court solves it? Fiss admits that 'going to judgment does not altogether eliminate the risk of unauthorized action', but:

> Judgment does not ask as much from the so-called representatives. There is a conceptual and normative distance between what the representatives do and say and what the court eventually decides, because the judge tests those statements and actions against independent procedural and substantive standards.

---

75   See for example Felix Cohen, 'Transcendental Nonsense and the Functional Approach', 35 *Colum L. Rev. 809 (1935)*.
76   Id., at 1079.
77   Id.
78   Fiss indeed tries to deal with some procedural mechanism to achieve this aim. But, as I will show soon, he finds them unsuitable to guarantee 'real consent'.

> The authority of judgment arises from the law, not from the statements or actions of the putative representatives ...[79]

As in the case of the disparities in resources, Fiss's belief in the ability of the judge to neutralize the imbalance seems at best banal, detached from the reality of disputes, and unsupported. Maybe it is also in contrast to the adversary idea. It is true that what he probably has in mind is the structural reform and cases like *Brown*; but does the new movement aim at settling such cases, or only to act in their shadow, as if there is a private realm that does not necessitate the intervention of the public? Must it hold the model of adjudication which Fiss ascribes to it?[80] In a response to Fiss's article, two of the supporters of ADR, Andrew McThenia and Thomas Shaffer, try to bring their own counter-projection and to emphasize their distance from the place Fiss tries to impose on them.

> The soundest and deepest part of the ADR movement doesn't rest on Fiss's two-neighbors model. It rests on values – of religion, community and work place – that are more vigorous than Fiss thinks. In many, in fact most, of the cultural traditions that argue for ADR, settlement is neither an avoidance mechanism nor a truce. Settlement is a process of reconciliation in which the anger of broken relationships is to be confronted rather than avoided, and in which healing demands not a truce but confrontation. Instead of 'trivializing the remedial process', settlement exalts that process. Instead of 'reducing the social function ... to one of resolving private disputes', settlement calls on substantive community values.[81]

In a response article called 'Out of Eden', Fiss claims the authors 'appear to be moved by a conception of social organization that takes the insular religious community as its model'.[82] He does not perceive them as wrong, just 'beside the point',[83] because the movement is not driven by 'love' but by 'concerns of efficiency and politics'.[84] He might indeed be interested in

---

79 Id.
80 See also Carrie Menkel-Meadow, 'For and Against Settlement: Uses and Abuses of he Mandatory Settlement Conference', 33 UCLA L Rev. 485, 486 (1985): 'Several articulate and sensible critics have asked us to consider what we gain and lose when we divert cases away from the formal adjudication system.'
81 McThenia and Shaffer, *supra* note 49, at 1664.
82 Owen Fiss, 'Out of Eden', 94 *Yale L. J.* (1985) 1669.
83 Id., at 1670.
84 Id.

attacking some ideas of the ADR movement, and to call for the disentangling of the private and public interest in each dispute. But because all he has in mind is the *Brown* model, he fails to see the ways in which the war is much more day-to-day, more focused on the dispute, closer to 'the case'. From the other side, the big public decisions are also not the ultimate cure for the social problems they try to solve. His attack makes it easier for the ADR movement to keep walking, (little) hand in (big) hand, with the 'public-law' movement, as if it does not contest its claims. They are dealing with practical, private cases while their big theoretical brothers from the public-law model (and other subgroups in opposition) will handle the social.[85]

The image Fiss has of settlement is indeed that it is the private place where the power of consent provides the authority of the decision. He explicitly states that this is what stands at the core of the 'no authoritative consent' argument:

> ... the judge's approval theoretically should turn on whether the group consents, but determining whether such consent exists is often impossible, since true consent consists of nothing less than the expressed unanimity of all the members of the group ... The judge's approval instead turns on how close or far the opposed settlement is from what he imagines would be the judgment obtained after suit. *The basis for approving a settlement, contrary to what the dispute resolution story suggests, is therefore not consent but rather the settlement's approximation to judgment*[86] (my emphasis: M.A.).

In response to Fiss here, I would say that what the 'dispute resolution story' suggests, to my mind, is indeed not some presence of the meeting of wills as its theoretical foundation.[87] This classic idea that was long ago abandoned conceptually within the legal realm (in the core discourse of public law theory), might be considered as rejected by the ADR discourse as well. It does not look for autonomy or any other essence as the basis of its call. It is

---

85 More on this division between the peace maker negotiator and the intellectual see the chapter 'In Search of the Dispute: on Lawyers and Legal Philawsophers at Harvard Law School'.
86 Fiss, *supra* note 62, at 1082.
87 See also Fiss, 'The Social and Political Foundation of Adjudication', *supra* note 26, at 127: 'The resurgence of the dispute resolution model is not an isolated phenomenon, but occur within a larger political context characterized by a renewed interest in market economies and theories of laissez-faire and, more generally, by a reaffirmation of the theory of social contract. At the heart of each phenomenon is a renewed belief in the private character of all ends.'

pragmatism at its best (or worst) here; it is the same settlement that the process people sought, based on 'problem-solving', with all its multifarious meanings and uses, incorporated into the practical realm of settling disputes. The dispute resolution call might be indeed, as Fiss suggests, a comeback of ideas 'from relative invisibility in the 1960s to enjoy a renewed popularity in the 1980s',[88] but they are not only the abstract ideas of the social contract and natural harmony, but a distinct cultural genre of American modernity. The appeal of this call is probably not due to the abstract entity it suggests, nor its distance from a 'real consent' of meeting of wills, but because of its promise of a solution, an American resolution without abstractions that suits the case and solves the problem. 'The approximation to judgment' is indeed one criterion of decision making, but not necessarily the ultimate one. Settlement is always done in a social context and involves variant rules regimes, scripts and narratives.

The third argument Fiss suggests is *the lack of a foundation for continuing judicial involvement.* Here he refers to a special kind of case, where 'judgment is not the end of a lawsuit but only the beginning':[89]

> The parties may sometimes be locked in combat with one another and view the lawsuit as only one phase in a long continuing struggle. The entry of the judgment will then not end the struggle, but rather change its terms and balance of power. One of the parties will invariably return to the court and again ask for its assistance, but because the conditions that preceded the lawsuit have unfortunately not changed.[90]

Is this is what courts are for? For parties 'locked in combat with one another', are they not parties having continuing relationship, exactly the type that will do much better in mediation? Is the purpose of running the system merely in order to run it again and again, and to accelerate conflict?

> The drive for settlement knows no bounds and can result in a consent decree even in the kinds of cases I have just mentioned, that is, even when a court finds itself embroiled in a continuing struggle between the parties or must reform a bureaucratic organization.[91]

---

88   Id., at 126.
89   Id.
90   Id., at 1083.
91   Id.

Fiss's last and most substantial argument, called *justice rather than peace*, relates to the above scorn for the 'drive for settlement'. In this argument, Fiss returns to his basic understanding of adjudication as enhancing public values. In contrast to settlement, it is not 'war' that is depicted, but 'justice'. The public decision of the judge is justice; the private settlement of the parties is based on sheer power, on pre-legal assumptions. Settlement has become the degraded concept, not the utopic horizon.

> To be against settlement is only to suggest that when the parties settle, society gets less than what appears and for a price it does not know it is paying. Parties might settle while leaving justice undone ... Although the parties are prepared to live under the terms they bargained for, and although such peaceful coexistence may be a necessary precondition of justice, and itself a state of affairs to be valued, it is not justice itself. To settle for something means to accept less than some ideal ...[92]

Paraphrasing Fiss's claim, I would say that to adjudicate something is always to accept less than some ideal, that there is a trade-off and compromise in each decision. On the other hand, private settling can never be indifferent to public values, but might sometimes reach a level beyond or beneath them.

The concluding part of the manifesto describes the real divide between Fiss's understanding of adjudication and that of the ADR people, represented, according to him, by Derek Bok:

> Someone like Bok sees adjudication in essentially private terms: The purpose of lawsuits and civil courts is to resolve disputes, and the amount of litigation we encounter is evidence of the needlessly combative and quarrelsome character of Americans ... I, on the other hand, see adjudication in more public terms: Civil litigation is an institutional arrangement for using state power to bring a recalcitrant reality closer to our chosen ideals.[93]

Here we find again his working from the top down: adjudication should enhance our public ideals, as most cases have a public dimension. This is why settling must always mean giving up some ideal. On the other hand, ADR people like Bok see adjudication in private terms, and that is why cases should be adjudicated only in extreme cases where public questions are involved. Fiss refuses here to accept what he calls 'a 'two-track' strategy':

---

92   Id., at 1085–6.
93   Id., at 1089.

'sorting cases into two tracks, one for settlement and another for judgment'.[94] He claims this strategy 'would drain the argument for settlement of much of its appeal'.[95] This refusal, which is actually against a very common 'compromise' between the two discourses,[96] indeed invites a rephrasing of the overall claim of the dispute resolution movement in a way that will apply to all adjudicated cases. This approach puts aside the abstract question if a dispute is public or private, and sees it as irrelevant. In Fiss's writing, we have to resist the drive to settle in any small case, and we should use our legal training to each tell the law time and time again because everything is public. We have to be evaluative, to be the intellectual progressives who preserve the aspiration of law to be philawsophical, to be just, to be the liberative power for society.[97]

But Derek Bok has a completely different attitude about what it is to be a lawyer, and he promotes in 1982 a call for conciliation and settlement that seems to have a prophetic power in today's perspective. In an article called 'Law and Its Discontents: A Critical Look at Our Legal System',[98] Bok, then the president of Harvard University, criticizes legal education for 'preparing students for legal combat'.[99]

> Professors spend vast amounts of time examining the decisions of appellate courts, but make little effort to explore new voluntary mechanisms that might enable parties to resolve various types of disputes without going to court in the first place. We have long debated whether lawyers exacerbate controversy or help to prevent it from arising. Doubtless, they do some of each. But no one can dispute that law schools train their students more for conflicts than for the gentler

---

94 Id.
95 Fiss, 'Against Settlement', at 1087-8.
96 See, for example, Lawrence Susskind and Jeffery Cruikshank, *Breaking the Impasse* (1987): 'When fundamental constitutional rights are at stake, we properly turn to our judicial system. It is certainly conceivable that after the courts have defined these rights, some form of consensus building might assist in protecting them, or in reconciling them with other valid interests. We leave it to others to decide whether consensual approaches to dispute resolution can (or should) be used in resolving constitutional questions.'
97 The progressiveness of Fiss as emerging through a 'straightforward' depiction of law as containing the values, which are the liberal right ones, parallels, in that sense, the Legal Process claim, to provide a discourse which is both internal and external, lacking the obscure knots of the Realists. Fiss's picture, nevertheless, as I have already tried to show, is inverse to that of the Legal Process and thus, very explicit in its arrogance of pretending to possess the place of the true prevailing social values.
98 Derek Bok, *Law and Its Discontents: A Critical Look at Our Legal System* (The Record of the Association of the Bar of the City of New York), vol. 38, 12.
99 Id., at 29.

arts of reconciliation and accommodation. This emphasis is likely to serve the profession poorly. Already, lawyers devote more time to negotiating conflicts than they spend in the library or the courtroom, and studies show that their efforts to negotiate are more productive for their clients. *Over the next generation, I predict that society's greatest opportunities will lie in tapping human inclinations toward collaboration and compromise rather than stirring our proclivities for competition and rivalry.* If lawyers are not leaders in marshaling cooperation and designing mechanisms which allow it to flourish, they will not be the center of the most creative social experiments of our time[100] (my emphasis – M.A.).

Instead of investing the intellectual energies in maneuvering within appellate courts' decision and in working the law from within, instead of emphasizing the evaluative dimension of legal decision making and supporting an enlightened imposition of progressive ideas, instead of dreaming of a public discourse which handles society from above, why won't we let a different language, that of collaboration and compromise, guide our legal conduct? Why see an enemy in place where there can be a friend, and where perceiving a friend is much more beneficent to both parties? This 'Bokian' call seems to have its own strength and appeal, and indeed at once has inspired and been influenced by the emergence of the ADR movement at Harvard Law School. The process in which each language has received its own institutional place within the legal academy, and the current abyss that exists between them and the professional ideals which they call for, are examined in the chapter 'In Search of the Dispute: on Lawyers and Legal Philawsophers on Harvard Law School'.

3.3 Overcoming History: Posner and the Economy of Pragmatism's Classics (Or: Staying at the Bottom Layer)[101]

Posner's picture of legal history summarizes the 'classic' historical sequence, which is described in various ways throughout my work. In his book *Overcoming Law*,[102] he gives the narrative of 'the revolt against formalism'.

---

100 Id., at 30.
101 Richard Posner's approach to jurisprudence, economics and law is discussed and elaborated in his many books, articles, and through an enormous secondary literature which deals with it. I have no pretension nor intention to cover all these resources and hence, my aim is here not to capture his jurisprudence, to attack it or to elevate it. Posner functions in my writing as an example and as a genre of pragmatism that I am interested in describing in relation to the Legal Process jurisprudence.
102 Richard A. Posner, *Overcoming Law* (1995).

There is a story about law, told mainly but not only by adherents of the critical legal studies movement, that goes as follows. Legal thinking in the late nineteenth century in England and the United states was formalistic: law, like mathematics, was understood to be about the relations among concepts rather than about the relations between concepts and reality. The student of geometry does not establish the relation between the square of the hypotenuse of a right-angle triangle and the squares of the two sides by measuring triangular objects ... this reifying approach (as distinct from an instrumental one) to legal concepts was, the story continues, overthrown in the 1920s and 1930s by legal realism, the first anti-formalist school of academic legal thought. The formalists fought back, in the 1950s with the jurisprudence of 'legal process' and, in the following decade and continuing right up to the present, with 'law and economics', that is, the application of economics to law. According to the story that I am recounting, law and economics replaces legal conceptualism with economic conceptualism, evaluating legal outcomes by their conformity to economic theory but still keeping away from the facts. The antidote to this conceptualism is pragmatism, the theory (or anti-theory) that debunks all pretenses to having constructed a pipeline to the truth and that, along with its twin, postmodernism, underwrites (thus illustrating the anti-foundational as foundational) the radical critique of law by feminist jurisprudence, critical legal studies, and critical race theory.[103]

In contrast to the above view, which posits pragmatism as the eternal revolt against formalism, while law and economic studies are the next step or transformation of legal formalism, Posner perceives his movement to be that of the real pragmatist. The conceptualism of the Law-and-Economics movement is posited as contrasting the 'anti-theory', which 'debunks all pretense to having constructed a pipeline to the truth', of the others – the postmodernists, the radicals, the feminists and the critical race theorists. The pragmatists refute any formula while the economists still hold one. Posner tries to show how this formula is the original pragmatic one. In his article 'What Has Pragmatism to Offer Law?'[104] he describes the classical history of pragmatism, as questioned and described throughout my book.[105]

---

103 Id., at 2–3.
104 Richard Posner, 'What Has Pragmatism to Offer Law?', in *Pragmatism in Law And Society* (Michael Brint and William Weaver, eds, 1991) 29.
105 I call this history 'classical', because in contrast to the many narratives I examine during the various chapters, where each time pragmatism appears as having discursive relations with another pragmatism, or as a story told from some perspective, the presentation of Posner posits pragmatism as an entity, through positivistic lenses, which appears and reappears in history as the 'real' one or just as a pretension.

> Histories of pragmatism usually begin with Charles Sanders Pierce ... From Pierce the baton is handed to William James, then to John Dewey ... Parallel to and influenced by the pragmatists, legal realism comes on the scene, inspired by the work of Holmes, John Chipman Grey, and Cardozo and realized in the work of the self-described realists, such as Jerome Frank, William Douglas, Karl Llwellyn, Felix Cohen, and Max Radin. Pragmatism and legal realism join in Dewey's essay on law. But by the end of World War II both philosophical pragmatism and legal realism have expired, the first superseded by logical positivism and other 'hard' analytic philosophy, the other absorbed into the legal mainstream and particularly into the 'legal process' school that reaches its apogee in 1958 with Hart and Sacks' *The Legal Process*. Then, beginning in the 1960s with the waning of logical positivism, pragmatism comes charging back in the person of Richard Rorty, followed in the 1970s by critical legal studies – the critical son of legal realism – and in the 1980s by a school of legal pragmatists that includes Martha Minow, Thomas Grey, Daniel Farber, Philip Frickey, and others. The others include myself, and perhaps also, as suggested by Professor Rorty in his essay, Ronald Dworkin – despite Dworkin's overt hostility to pragmatism – and even Roberto Unger.[106]

Posner's narration of the history of pragmatism parallels the various chapters of my book and delineates their 'positivistic' intellectual history march: at first there were Pierce, James and Dewey. Parallel to them was Holmes (here Posner offers Cardozo and Chipman Grey on the same line). His writing was 'realized', in his terms, by the Legal Realists. By the end of World War II, philosophical pragmatism was 'expired' and superseded by logical positivism and analytical philosophy. Legal Realism was absorbed into the mainstream, particularly into the Legal Process school. Then, in the 1960s, there is a comeback of pragmatism from philosophy in the writing of Richard Rorty (a new actor with whom I am not dealing directly in this book). In the 1970s, the parallel legal revival arises under the banner of Critical Legal Studies. A school of legal pragmatism, which I do not discuss directly, begins to thrive in the 1980s,[107] and the major question for this part is where is Posner located within this story.

Searching for the common core of pragmatism throughout history, Posner offers three elements:

---

106 Id., at 30.
107 Thomas Grey's article about Holmes' pragmatism is the focus of part 1.4 in the chapter 'The Maturing of the Pragmatic Idea in Law and Society (Or: The Fall, and the Rise of Philawsophy)'. His genre of pragmatism which has an interpretive background and a general advice to 'not be obsessive with your theories' is a paradigm for the brand of pragmatism which this school promotes.

> The first is a distrust of metaphysical entities ('reality', 'truth', 'nature', etc.) viewed as warrants for certitude whether in epistemology, ethics or politics. The second is an insistence that propositions be tested by their consequences, by the difference they make, and if they make none, set aside. The third is an insistence on judging our projects, whether scientific, ethical, political, or legal, by their conformity to social or other human needs rather to 'objective' 'impersonal' criteria. These elements in turn imply an outlook that is progressive (in the sense of forward-looking), secular, and experimental, and that is commonsensical without making a fetish of common sense – for common sense is a repository of prejudice and wisdom as well as a fount of wisdom.[108]

This definition is very vague, and Posner acknowledges that. He refers to the epigraph to his article, which is a quote by Eliot saying that 'the great weakness of Pragmatism is that it ends by being of no use to anybody'. Posner, nevertheless, finds much use in pragmatism and his version, or genre of pragmatism, seems to allude to a very American common sense which has its 'pragmatic origin', but assumes, as always in these debates, a metaphysic and foundational text of its own. In his book *The Problems of Jurisprudence* he explores his notion of pragmatism.

> I shall argue against 'artificial reason', against Dworkin's 'right answer' thesis, against formalism, against overarching conceptions of justice such as 'corrective justice', 'natural law', and 'wealth maximization' – though not against modest versions of these normative systems – but also against 'strong' legal positivism. I shall argue for an 'activity' theory of law – the theory that underlies Holmes's prediction theory; for behaviorism and therefore against 'rich' conceptions of mentalism, intentionality, and free will; for the critical as distinct from constructive use of logic; for the idea that judge's proper aim in difficult cases is a reasonable result rather than a demonstrably right one; and for a concept of the judge as a responsible agent rather than as a conduit of decisions made elsewhere in the political system. More, I shall argue for objectivity as a cultural and political rather than epistemic attributes of legal decisions, for balancing rule-of-law virtues against equitable and discretionary case-specific considerations, for making law more receptive to science ... and for a consequentialist theory of interpretation. I shall argue in short for a functional, policy-saturated, nonlegalistic, naturalistic and skeptical, but decidedly non cynical, conception of the legal process; in a word (although, I fear, an inadequate word), for a *pragmatic* jurisprudence.[109]

---

108 Id., at 36.
109 Richard A. Posner, *The Problems of Jurisprudence* (1990), at 26.

Posner seems to have no doubts regarding his perception of reality; of the individuals functioning within it with their inner worlds and explanatory psychology; of science and objectivity; of culture and decision making. His epistemology and metaphysical background stay much as those inferred from the Legal Process materials: there is a world of individuals living under interdependent conditions, there is a market, a judicial system that must function in an efficient way.[110] His emphasis on a 'functional, policy saturated' conception of law and on behaviorist psychology and social sciences goes back to the mode of scientification of law between the World Wars. He continues to support the American model of scientification which reaches its peak and end (in a sense) in the post-war era which is perceiving law as a bundle of facts, and devaluing the importance of its formal rules as being metaphysics.[111] His positivistic naturalistic epistemology seems to support an equivalent project to that of the Realists as described by Henry Schlegel. He denies any pretension of law to hold an inner language, a metaphysics of its own, and calls for the empirical consequences of it to be the focus of the legal scholar. The economical framework he imposes on law, brings to the center the instrumental quality of his 'non-metaphysical' notion of law.

> The brand of pragmatism that I like emphasizes the scientific virtues (open-minded, no-nonsense inquiry), elevates the process of inquiry over the results of inquiry, prefers ferment to stasis, dislikes distinctions that make no practical difference – in other words, dislikes 'metaphysics' – is doubtful of finding 'objective truth' in any area of inquiry, is uninterested in creating an adequate philosophical foundation for its thought and action, likes experimentation, likes to kick sacred cows, and – within the bounds of prudence – prefers shaping the future to maintaining continuity with the past. So I am speaking with an attitude

---

110 See also Eskridge and Frickey in the introduction to Hart and Sacks, at cxxii: 'The rediscovery of scarcity by our political and economic culture has coincided with an increased emphasis on efficiency in our legal culture. This theme was prefigured in Hart and Sacks' insistence that legal decision makers consider the consequences of the rules they adopt ... The Law and Economics movement developed these ideas more systematically, and to an increasingly receptive audience, in the 1970s ... Both Law and Economics and the Legal Process start with the desire of human society to maximize the collective satisfaction of its members and acknowledge that legal rules can contribute to this goal. Also like Hart and Sacks, law-and-economics approaches legal issues from an *ex ante* perspective: What legal rule will create the best incentives for efficient behavior in the future?'
111 See the discussion of this American inscription in the chapter 'Settled Law and the Law-that-Is-Not-But-Ought-To-Be: The Pragmatic Philosophy of Dispute Resolution (Or: Why Couldn't Henry Hart Speak?)', part 2.4.3.

rather than a dogma; an attitude whose 'common denominator' is a 'future oriented instrumentalism that tries to deploy thought as a weapon to enable more effective action'. Most of this book is concerned with attacking the dogmas and letting pragmatism emerge as the natural alternative.[112]

The 'common denominator' Unger mentions is defined through a quote taken from Cornell West, and it is interesting to close a circle and go back to a progressive philosopher who writes about the 'the American evasion of philosophy' as his reference to the most proper definition of pragmatism.[113] The political agenda of West aligns much more with Roberto Unger than with Posner, and indeed they co-authored a book called *The Future of American Progressivism: An Initiative for Political and Economic Reform*,[114] where they offer 'the use of politics to reshape governmental and economic arrangements in ways that escape the stereotypes of entrenched ideologies'.[115] Still, West, with his broad popular definition of pragmatism as it is perceived outside law today, is an adequate 'common denominator' for Posner to address, while adopting the opposite political stance. As I try to show later,[116] Unger's stepping outside the theoretical discourse of law and his choice to be political signify giving up on the idea of working the progressiveness from the inside, and in that sense it exposes a straightforward level of politics where he (as well as West) and Posner can compete. On the more intellectual level, their debate might look less commensurable and includes a subversive impulse from Unger's side.[117]

---

112 Id., at 28.
113 See also Posner, *What Has Pragmatism to Offer Law?*, supra note 63, at 36. See the presentation of the origin of pragmatism as presented by West in the chapter *The Maturing of the Pragmatic Idea in Law and Society (Or: The Fall, and the Rise of Philawsophy)*, part 1.2.
114 Roberto Mangabria Unger and Cornell West, *The Future of American Progressivism* (1998).
115 Id., at 40. Unger and West bring forward a specific political agenda, and describe nine planks 'in a progressive platform faithful to these ambitions': Taxes: from liberal pieties to redistributive realities; Pensions, saving, and investment: the resources for growth; Children and education: the future first; Racial discrimination and class in justice: how not to forget about one while dealing with the other; Economic vanguardism outside the vanguard: narrowing the gap between the advanced and backward sectors of the economy; An organized society and an empowered labor force: the tools and the resources of association; Politics, money, and media: quickening the tempo of democracy. Id., at 59–85.
116 Part 3.4.
117 See the discussion of Unger's position and its transformations in part 3.4, as well as the description of Unger's mappings of the Law and Economics movement.

In his 'Pragmatic Adjudication' article, Posner differentiates between pragmatism as 'a philosophical position' and 'applied' pragmatism. His interest is in the latter.[118] The 'philosophical position' is 'the level well illustrated by a recently published book in which Richard Rorty and his critics go at each other hammer and tongs over such questions as whether language reflects reality, whether free will is compatible with a scientific outlook, and whether such questions are even meaningful'.[119] Pragmatic adjudication, in his view, cannot be derived from pragmatism, the philosophical stance.

> A pragmatist judge always tries to do the best he can do for the present and the future, unchecked by any felt *duty* to secure consistency in principle with what other officials have done in the past.[120]

Unlike the Legal Process imperialistic perception of law, Posner does not perceive adjudication as the voice of reason through a navigating force between the public and private. The belief in the craft-like wisdom of 'reasoned elaboration' does not appear in his writing. 'The judge wants to come up with the best decision having in mind present and future needs, and so does not regard the maintenance of consistency with past decisions as an end in itself but only as a means for bringing about the best results in the present case.'[121] In contrast to Holmes' obscure prediction theory and the bad man's cynical acid, Posner for the first time seems, to be taking Dewey's writing literally, applying him as if no epistemological shift has occurred since his time (and indeed, maybe it has not, in Posner's eyes). The suspicion in generalities is applied to legal rules and their status becomes immediately instrumental, as tools to reach social goals.[122] Posner's appeal to Cardozo as his guiding voice of his 'pragmatic jurisprudence' supports this reading.

> I sometimes think we worry ourselves overmuch about the enduring consequences of our errors ... In the endless process of testing and retesting, there is a constant rejection of the dross; the tides rises and falls, but the sands of error crumble. Law is forward-looking. This is implicit in an instrumental concept of law – which is the pragmatic concept of law, law as the servant of human needs. Not the origin, but the goal, is the main thing. There can be no wisdom in a choice

---

118 Richard A. Posner, 'Pragmatic Adjudication', 18 *Cardozo Law Rev.* 1 (1996).
119 Id., at 1.
120 Id., at 4.
121 Id., at 5.
122 See the discussion of the difference between Dewey and Holmes in the chapter 'The Maturing of the Pragmatic Idea in Law and Society (Or: The Fall, and the Rise of Philawsophy)', part 1.4.

of a path unless we know where it will lead ... The rule that functions well produces a title deed to recognition ... The final principle of selection of judges ... is one of fitness to an end.[123]

This mixture of quotes from Posner and Cardozo illustrates the equivalency between a state of mind and of texts which, as Llewellyn has already suggested, share 'generous but unrealistic faith in inevitable incremental progress'.[124] Cardozo is an American classic – 'the most widely read American work on legal thought', as Morton Horwitz suggests,[125] and Posner takes this classic to his own realm to offer its updated economic version.

In other words, while Posner refuses to revolt against formalism again and takes this American event as an important insight that should guide us today in its formal conclusions (i.e., philosophy is dead, metaphysics and rules are minor to their consequences as their evaluative criteria),[126] Unger takes this event in its substance and spirit, and perceives a world different in its texture and institutions than the one Dewey saw. Unger's effort to preserve the Deweyan pathos would be, therefore, to construct a plan which is inherently open to its auto-transformation, to endure the paradox of the invention oneself, and to begin from scratch.[127] To say that one is modern and the other post-modern or radical is to assume a point in time or in discourse when there was full presence to itself, where pragmatism was the ultimate transparent perspective from which to perceive reality as it was. As my writing so far tries to show, pragmatism since its origin brings forward an impossible formula, a myth and a sort of religious pathos that receive their meaning only through a particular historical context, within a particular struggle against other ideas and myths. Even if there was such an imagined moment of transparency in the 1950s, it was only in writing in the format of 'basic problems in the making and application of law', within the discourse of law, and after the theoretical freshness of the

---

123 Posner, *The Problem of Jurisprudence*, supra note 66, at 29.
124 See the discussion of the relation between Cardozo's pragmatism and the Realists' in the chapter 'The Maturing of the Pragmatic Idea in Law and Society (Or: The Fall, and the Rise of Philawsophy)', part 1.4.
125 Morton J. Horwitz, *The Transformation of American Law 1870–1960: The Crisis of Legal Orthodoxy* (1992), 189.
126 The optimism and the activism in Posner's approach thus parallels that of both Roger Fisher and the Legal Process text: 'The pragmatic attitude is *activist* – progressive, "can do" – rejecting both the conservative counsel that whatever is is best and the fatalist counsel that all consequences are unintended. The pragmatist believes in progress without pretending to be able to define it, and believes that it can be effected by deliberate human action'. Posner, *Overcoming Law*, supra note 102, at 4–5.
127 See the discussion of Unger in part 3.4.

ideas had already vanished from other discourses. Along the same lines, it can be argued that Unger and Posner, in their theoretical writing,[128] promote different notions of histories. Posner perceives the moment of the discursive emergence of American modernity as an actual event that revealed a truth, and its theoretical message can be applied again today by economics as it then was. He takes 'the original narrative' as the one right answer. Unger, and maybe other contemporary pragmatists, from the brand defined as 'postmodern', perceive the event as a dynamic structure, almost a religious impulse – 'a religion of possibility'[129] – which should keep transforming the discourse and reinvent history. While on the surface they enhance different brands of pragmatism, promoting opposite political positions, actually they represent two versions of the notion of 'the revolt against formalism'. Posner perceives it as a past event; Unger takes it as an ongoing commandment for any possible regime, as a paradox to endure. A parallel polarity might be read in James Kloppenberg's description of two rival camps struggling over the legacy of pragmatism in contemporary philosophical discourse:

> Early twentieth-century pragmatists envisioned a modernist discourse of democratic deliberation in which communities of inquiry tested hypotheses in order to solve problems; such contemporary pragmatists as Richard J. Bernstein and Hilary Putnam sustain that tradition. Other contemporaries such as Richard Rorty and Stanley Fish present pragmatism as a post-modernist discourse of critical commentary that denies that we can escape the conventions and contingencies of language in order to connect with a world of experience outside texts, let alone solve problems in that world.[130]

Putnam and Bernstein sustain the original tradition, and Rorty and Fish undermine its foundation and point to its fictional manipulative quality, but insist on its pathos. Their non-contemporaneous play is part of the complex

---

128 I describe Unger here in his first-stage theoretical mode of writing as the critical legal studies movement person, and not in his later more political appearance. I describe the transformation from one style to another later in part 3.4.
129 See Unger and West, *supra* note 114, at 10–11: 'To hold the American religion of possibility is to believe that each of the problems that oppress, weaken, and frighten us as individuals can be confronted, problem by problem, through human effort and ingenuity. Americans resist seeing particular problems as the manifestation of hidden, hard constraints ... Social opportunity as a condition and problem solving as an attitude fail to describe the most potent and fundamental strand in the American religion of possibility: *faith in the genius of ordinary men and women.*'
130 James T. Koppenberg, 'Pragmatism: An Old Name for Some New Ways of Thinking?', in *The Revival of Pragmatism* (Morris Dickstein, ed., 1998) 83, 84.

revival of vitality of pragmatism in contemporary discourse.[131] The materialization of this difference in the American legal discourse is stressed when their conception of private and public is examined.[132]

In Posner's writing there is a definite private, visible and concrete, and a compatible public which needs different considerations. 'The defining characteristic of the Chicago approach is the straightforward application of microeconomic (or price-theoretic) analysis to the law.'[133] Within this approach, 'the use of economics to guide decision making in the open areas of law ought to be discussable without immersion in the deep waters of political and moral philosophy'.[134]

> Far from being reductionist, as its detractors believe, economics is the instrumental science par excellence. Its project is not to reduce human behavior to some biological propensity, some faculty of reason, let alone to prove that deep within us, pulling the strings, is a nasty little 'economic man'. It is to construct and test models of human behavior for the purpose of predicting and (where appropriate) controlling that behavior. *Economics imagine the individual not as 'economic man' but as – a pragmatist*[135] (my emphasis – M.A.).

The individual whom Posner imagines is a pragmatist, an American. This subject is a crystallization of a very 'common sense' intuitive perception we have of what it is to live 'ordinary' life. He or she 'behaves' in ways we can predict and control. Their choices are private, and the economist's role is to consider them, and not to change their preferences.[136]

---

[131] Revival and vitality are taken from name of two contemporary books about pragmatism which I discuss in their symbolic significance in the chapter 'The Maturing of The Pragmatic Idea in Law and Society (Or: the Fall, and The Rise of Philawsophy)'.

[132] For Unger's private-public demarcation, see part 3.4.

[133] Nicholas Mercuro and Steven G. Megema, *Economics and The Law: From Posner to Post-modernism* (1997) 57: 'As such, this approach embodies the following premises: (1) individuals are rational maximizers of their satisfactions in their non-market as well as their market behavior; (2) individuals respond to price incentives in non-market as well as market behavior; and (3) legal rules and legal outcomes can be assessed on the basis of their efficiency properties, along with which comes the normative prescription that legal decision making should promote efficiency.'

[134] Posner, *Overcoming Law*, *supra* note 102, at 21.

[135] Id., at 15–16.

[136] Id., at 23: See, for example, his attitude toward homosexuality: 'Many people of conservative bent are distressed by the thought that some people are committing homosexual acts, even adults, even in private. That distress could be thought as an external cost of homosexuality – a cost that homosexuals impose on other people, akin to the cost of pollution – and hence a ground for limiting the freedom of homosexuals.'

It is true that some people insist on treating quite narrow and technical legal questions as microcosms of the vastest social issues. They see antitrust cases as raising issues of political liberty rather than merely of efficient allocation of resources, contract cases as raising issues of human autonomy rather than merely of transaction costs, corporate cases as raising issues of democracy rather than issues concerning optimal investment, criminal cases as raising deep issues of free will and autonomy rather than the issue of how to minimize the social costs of crime ... I think the economist can easily hold his own in these debates by showing that the most fruitful framework for analyzing this range of legal questions is economic one.[137]

What Posner sees when he observes people's behavior is individuals functioning in a 'Chicago law and economic' manner, i.e., under a formal model of economics. In contrast to the Legal Process perception of their interaction, the social pie is not depicted as dynamic.[138]

In economics, formalism was taken to be the abstract *deductive* reasoning of orthodox economic analysis that enthroned universally valid reason, assumed passive, rational utility maximizing behavior, and demonstrated an inordinate concern over the equilibria of comparative statics.[139]

In contrast to this formalism exists another brand of economics named 'institutional', which is considered part of the historical 'revolt against formalism'.[140] Posner rejects this genre, and his choice is to insert the old

---

137 Id., at 23.
138 See Eskridge and Frickey, in the introduction to *Hart and Sacks,* at cxxii: 'Unlike Hart and Sacks, however, law and economics writers in the 1970s reasoned from assumptions of a "static pie" and were greatly more skeptical of state regulation. By way of illustration, a Posnerian approach to the "Case of the Spoiled Cantaloupes" would agree with Hart and Sacks' insistence that the harsh *ex post* penalty suffered by Martinelli might be justified by the *ex ante* goal of assuring sellers that the cantaloupes they ship will be paid for. But a law and economics scholar would be more skeptical (especially if of the Chicago School) of the whole idea of state licensing of fresh fruit transactions and would want to expand the legal process agenda to consider deregulation (as has actually occurred) ... A Posnerian might turn to formal economic models and empirical studies to cast light on issues of contract and regulatory interpretation. The less formal empiricism of Hart and Sacks' "Case of the Spoiled Cantaloupes" might not be sufficient.'
139 Nicholas Mercuro and Steven G. Megema, *Economics and the Law: From Posner to Post-Modernism* (1997) 102.
140 Id. 'Institutional economics has often been described as part of a "revolt against formalism", a revolt that took place in law, in history, and in economics at about the same time. Institutional economics, as part of that revolt, was led by a group of young American

(theoretically dead) general idea of the revolt, while rejecting its economical parallel manifestation.[141] His model of Law and Economics is hence formal economics with the 1950s pragmatic informal style of law.

> The empirical projects of the legal realists, which not only failed but in failing gave empirical research rather a bad name among legal academics, illustrate the futility of empirical investigation severed from a theoretical framework. Modern economics can furnish the indispensable theoretical framework for the empirical research that law so badly needs.[142]

This model of economics is becoming the right answer to the entire history of philosophy that occurred from Plato until Nietzsche.[143]

> The economic approach to law that I defend – the idea that law should strive to support competitive markets and to simulate their results in situations in which market transaction costs are prohibitive – has affinities with both Kantian and

---

scholars who, after World War I, engaged in a critique of the predominate, formalistic economic doctrines of the day.'

141 A few propositions which characterize institutional economy can illustrate its heterodoxical character and its affinity more with the Realists' critique, like that of Hale, and also with Unger's perception: '* Economic behavior is strongly conditioned by the institutional environment within which economic activity takes place, and simultaneously, economic behavior affects the structure of the institutional environment. * The mutual interaction between the institutions and the behavior of economic actors is an evolutionary process, hence the need for an "evolutionary approach" to economics. * In analyzing the evolutionary processes contained therein, emphasis is directed to the role play by the conditions imposed by modern technology and the monetary institutions of modern, mixed-market capitalism. * Emphasis is entered upon conflict within the economic sphere of society as opposed to harmonious order inherent within the cooperative, spontaneous, and unconscious free play of economic actors within the market. * There is a clear and present need to channel the conflict inherent in economic relationships by structuring institutions to establish a system of social control over economic activity ....'

142 Posner, *Overcoming Law, supra* note 102, at 19.

143 See also Posner, *The Problems of Jurisprudence, supra* note 109, at 239: 'Holmes wrote *The Common Law* just a few years before Nietzsche's great work *On the Genealogy of Morals*, and both employ an effective method of skeptical analysis: the genealogical. In the *Genealogy* and other works Nietzsche tried to undermine the ontological status of Christian morality by arguing that moral beliefs reflect the needs and circumstances of the dominant groups in the communities that happen to hold them. Morality, in other words, is relative rather than absolute; in fact, morality is public opinion. *The Common Law* does the same thing with law. By tracing legal doctrines to their origins and thus relating each doctrine to a particular constellation of social circumstances, Holmes showed the absurdity of supposing, as did the nineteenth-century formalists against whom he was writing, that legal doctrines were unchangeables formal concepts like the Pythagorean theorem.'

utilitarian ethics: with the former, because the approach protects the autonomy of people who are productive or at least potentially so (granted, this isn't everyone); with the latter, because of the empirical relation between free markets and human welfare. Although it is easily shown that the economic approach is neither deducible from nor completely consistent with either system of ethics, this is not a decisive objection from a pragmatic standpoint. Pragmatists are unperturbed by a lack of foundations.[144]

It becomes clear from Posner's writing that the notion of economics functions almost like that of pragmatism (and indeed might deserve a distinct separate book to deal with it), but actually Posner insists that what is at stake is not economics for its own sake. In his 1999 book *The Problematics of Moral and Legal Theory*,[145] he refers to psychology, evolutionary biology, and statistics; and his overall project seems to be, in this context, the scientification of law through establishing a close link between it and the social sciences.[146] In a chapter called 'The Suppression Thesis: the Path Away from the Law', he put forward his vision for the legal profession:

> The hope for law to become a genuine profession, in the sense in which the developments in other occupations are teaching us to understand professionalism, lies in what I like to call, with deliberate provocation, 'overcoming law' or, alternatively, the 'suppression thesis'. The thesis is that what we understand as the law is merely a transitional phase in the evolution of social control. Holmes hinted at this at his essay 'The Path of the Law ...'[147]

> We know more about the social world than Holmes could have known. We should be able to avoid his mistakes. No doubt we should make our own. Prudence as well as realism suggest that the entanglement of law with morality, politics, tradition and rhetoric may well be permanent and the path to complete professionalization therefore permanently blocked. But we should be able to go a long way down that path before reaching the obstruction. We should try, at any rate, which will require more emphasis in the legal academy than at present on economics, statistics, game theory, cognitive psychology, political science, sociology, decision theory and related disciplines. In trying we shall be joining a great and, on the whole, a beneficent national movement toward the professionalization of all forms of productive work.[148]

---

144 Posner, *What Has Pragmatism to Offer Law?*, supra note 104, at 42.
145 Richard A. Posner, *The Problematics of Moral and Legal Theory* (1999).
146 Id., at 210–12.
147 Id., at 206–7.
148 Id., at 211.

224 *Pragmatism and Law*

Posner aims at 'complete professionalization', and his offer to resurrect the link between the social sciences and the law is not different from Brian Tamanaha's call, discussed elsewhere, for a 'realistic socio-legal theory'.[149] His effort to criticize and correct the obscure parts in Holmes' 'path of the law' is indeed part of his effort to kill, in a way, or overcome the discourse of law, to deny its internals knots and mysteries, to transform it into a technology. In that way he is very different from Cardozo, who spoke pragmatism like poetry. Interestingly enough, Posner's notion of advanced professionalism is posited in contrast to what he defines, by using a sociological terminology as a 'professional mystique': 'When a belief in a profession's knowledge claims is not justified by the profession's actual knowledge, we have a case of "professional mystique". The more impressive and convincing that mystique, the more secure the profession's claim to the privilege of professional status.'[150] Some of the techniques he lists for preserving the mystique in case of shaky knowledge recall my initial description of the discursive characteristics of the Holmsian discourse.[151]

> One is to cultivate an *obscurantist style of discourse* in order to make the profession's process of inquiry and inference impenetrable to outsiders ... a fourth technique of professional mystification is the cultivation of *charismatic personality* – the selection of membership in the profession of people whose appearance, personality, or personal background creates an impression of deep, perhaps inarticulable, insight and masterful, unique competence ... Seventh, a profession is likely to employ *altruistic pretense*. It will try to conceal the extent to which its members are motivated by financial incentives in order to bolster the claim that they have been drawn to the profession by the opportunity to pursue a calling that yields rich intellectual rewards or gratifies a desire to serve ... Ninth, the profession will resist the systematization of professional knowledge; it will be *anti-algorithmic*. As long as 'the means of production of a profession's knowledge-based service is contained in their heads', the profession's monopoly is secure.[152]

The obscure style, the charismatic figures (like the prophets I describe in my writing), the anti-algorithmic mode, the promise of a non-financial

---

149 See the chapter 'In Search of the Dispute: on Lawyers and Legal Philawsophers at Harvard Law School (Or: Some Private Hope and Public Irony)', part 4.3.
150 Posner, *The Problematics of Moral and Legal Theory*, *supra* note 145, at 187.
151 See the chapter 'The Maturing of the Pragmatic Idea in Law and Society (Or: The Fall, and the Rise of Philawsophy)', part 1.4.
152 Id., at 187–9.

incentive as in the Holmsian call to listen to the echoes of infinity in the study of law – all of these characteristics that provide, for some legal scholars, the reason to be academics, are for Posner the mark of an immature situation we should overcome and from which to move to some Weberian model of rationality. The whole process of the professional discourse becoming the 'philawsophical' one, substituting the role of a past grand philosophy, is denied through this position. The Warren court and the 1950s emblematize, according to this view, the ultimate failure of this mode of unscientific reasoning, and indeed, according to Posner, have a traumatic affect on the legal profession:

> Beginning in the 1960s, the legal profession in all its branches became associated with policies that in time came to be largely discredited. These polices included the judicial activism of the Supreme Court in the heydays of Earl Warren's chief justiceship; a related knee-jerk receptivity to every 'liberal' proposal for enlarging legal rights – and incidentally lawyers' incomes; the plain incapacity of legal reasoning, as demonstrated by modern economics, to make sense of the legal regulation of competition and monopoly; a relaxation of the barriers to litigation that contributed to an enormous, unsettling and unforeseen increase in the amount of litigation; and a host of lawyer-fostered statutory 'reforms' in fields ranging from bankruptcy and consumer protection to employment discrimination, safety regulation, and environmental protection that often had perverse, unintended consequences. The traumatic impact of these failures on the legal profession's self-confidence has been much less than the traumatic impact that the Vietnam War had on the military profession. But there has been some impact, which, along with other factors, has spurred the legal profession to become more professional in the good sense.[153]

The policies of the Warren court and its mode of reasoning signify the failure of the old logic. The 'traumatic impact' that Posner describes through the professional economic position he occupies is very different from the one experienced by the progressive intellectual. In fact, it can be perceived as inverted: 'traumatized' by the operation of the Warren Court itself and not by the failure of legal intellectuals to justify it.[154] Still, there is an agreement regarding the disorienting, and at the same time, constitutive effect of that era. Indeed, we are already on our way to complete rationality and

---

153 Id., at 192.
154 See the chapter 'Settled Law and the Law-That-Is-Not-But-Ought-To-Be: Hart and Sacks and The Pragmatic Philosophy of Dispute Resolution (Or: Why Couldn't Henry Hart Speak?)', and the discussion of the equivalent paths of The Warren Court and The Legal Process writing at the hegemonic moment of the postwar.

professionality; and the time has come to stop believing in the life of the law.

> Developments since the 1960s have seemed to make, and to an extent *have* made, the law more professional in the good sense, the sense in which a profession earns its status and attendant privileges by deploying a body of genuine, specialized, socially valuable, knowledge based skills rather than by cultivating professional mystique. The process by which professional mystique is superseded by fully rational methods is an aspect of what Max Weber called 'rationalization'.[155]

The same phenomenon mourned by Kronman and grieved by Ann Mary Glendon, as I discuss elsewhere,[156] is perceived by Posner as healthy progress. Indeed, the activist mode of the negotiation people and the contemporary call of Mnookin for the lawyer to become a problem solver might go together with this trend.[157] Even Unger's retreat from the internal position might signify the same move, which is the professionalization of law through scientific a-historic social sciences and by an imposition of technocratic manuals and acquisition of skills in a world present to itself. The mystique that might exist in the belief in the social sciences themselves is not examined or dealt with within this context. The anti-formalist mode of pragmatism turns here to an anti-intellectual call, or maybe to a call to become an intellectual of a certain kind – one who believes in programs and in scientific success as his horizon of thought. This might be the same businessperson or peacemaker that the program on negotiation enhances.[158] But it can also be just a law-and-economic scholar.

3.4 From Institutional Settlement to Institutional Imagination: Roberto Unger and the Deweyan Democracy Realized (Or: Pragmatism Taken to its End, and the Program of no Program)

In their introduction to the Legal Process Materials, Eskridge and Frickey describe the response of Roberto Unger to this course as marking, together

---

155 Id., at 190–91.
156 See the chapter 'In Search of The Dispute: On Lawyers and Legal Philawsophers at Harvard Law School (Or: Some Private Hope and Public Irony)', part 4.4.
157 See the chapter 'In Search of The Dispute: On Lawyers and Legal Philawsophers at Harvard Law School (Or: Some Private Hope and Public Irony)'.
158 Id.

with Duncan Kennedy,[159] the 'end of consensus' which the 1960s have brought.[160]

> In an essay submitted to Sacks after taking his legal process course, Roberto Unger questioned the materials' insistence that law is best understood through a method similar to that deployed by the social sciences. Instead, he argued, law is more closely related to the arts and humanities.[161]

In different ways, Unger is commenting on the Legal Process writing, offering his neo-pragmatic approach to transform and displace its ideas. His pragmatism is different from that of either Richard Rorty or Thomas Grey, since it is commenting on the Legal Process picture of the world, and assumes, in a way, its naturalism and positivism. The foundations he assumes, in other words, are not literary or philosophical, and in that sense he shares the same epistemology as the Legal Process Materials.

There are a few aspects which reflect the response to the 1950s jurisprudence. First, his idea of 'institutional imagination' has a direct relationship to the 'institutional settlement' of the Legal Process school.

> The institutional and imaginative frameworks of social life supply the basis on which people define and reconcile interest, identify and solve problems. These frameworks cannot be adequately explained as mere crystallized outcomes of interest-accommodating or problem-solving activities. Until we make the underlying institutional and imaginative structure of a society explicit we are almost certain to mistake the regularities and routines that persist, so long as the structure is left undisturbed, for general laws of social organization.[162]

The underlying institutional and imaginative structure of society in the Legal Process Materials was not explicit enough, under the logic of the above

---

159 See the discussion of Kennedy's response in the chapter 'Settled Law and the Law-That-Is-Not-But-Ought-To-Be: Hart and Sacks and the Pragmatic Philosophy of Dispute Resolution (Or: Why Couldn't Henry Hart Speak?)', part 2.4.4.
160 Hart and Sacks, at cxxi.
161 Id., at cxx. Eskridge and Frickey assume that 'this criticism probably impressed Sacks, who kept Unger's essay and apparently supported Unger's as well as Kennedy's appointment to the Harvard Law School faculty during his deanship'. Actually, at least so far as Kennedy is concerned, his appointment was by Derek Bok, who is another figure this chapter deals with. Sacks' boxes, where Unger's paper was found as an exam notebook, are currently not accessible due to the HLS library's special collection restriction.
162 Roberto Mangabria Unger, *Politics: The Central Texts* (1997), 5–6.

paragraph. It was suffering from 'institutional fetishism'.[163] In a section of his book called *A Radically Anti-Naturalist Social Theory*, Unger explains how any 'problem solving' activity is done in a given institutional and imaginative framework. Challenging this framework, and constructing it in a way that diminishes the distance between 'context-preserving routines and context-transforming conflict',[164] is the best way to overcome constraints and reach freedom.

> The aim is not to show that we are free in any ultimate sense and somehow unrestrained by casual influences upon our conduct. It is to break loose from a style of social understanding that allows us to explain ourselves and our societies only to the extent that we imagine ourselves helpless puppets of the social worlds we build and inhabit or of the lawlike forces that have supposedly brought these worlds into being.

In place of the Legal Process picture of individuals interacting freely at the bottom layer in a natural evolutionary manner, we should assume individuals who play out social scripts that have a ideological and historical dimension. This acknowledgement should not make us abandon the belief in process altogether. Once we acknowledge that full freedom is impossible at the bottom layer, we can also realize the liberating force of reflection and of a perpetual movement of institutional and structural transformation. Revelation of a structure already contains the seeds for its transformation. 'We can always break through all contexts of practical or conceptual activity. At any moment people may think or associate with one another in ways that overstep the boundaries of the conditional worlds in which they had moved till then.'[165] The humanistic pathos in his writing substitutes the rationalist scientific utopia of the Legal Process with a mysterious call to repeatedly question the basic conditions of social life, to challenge the scripts we all play while pretending to act as the free agents of the market. Richard Rorty claims that this humanism

---

163 Id., at ix: 'Institutional fetishism, for Unger, is the imagined identification of highly detailed and largely accidental institutional arrangements with abstract institutional concepts like representative democracy, a market economy, or a free civil society. The institutional fetishist may be the classical liberal who identifies representative democracy and the market economy with a makeshift set of governmental and economic arrangements that happen to have triumphed in the course of modern European history. He may also be the hard-core Marxist who treats these same arrangements as an indispensable stage toward a future, regenerate order whose content he sees as both preestablished and resistant to credible description.'

164 Id., at 9.

165 Roberto Mangabria Unger, *Passion: An Essay on Personality* (1984), 8.

actually represents a Brazilian pathos which suits a new democracy, and that Unger is, in spite of his many years and influence spent in America, 'a man whose mind is elsewhere',[166] but my claim is that his position as a partial outsider helps him to capture the American pragmatic impulse in law and take it to its end.

> To live and move in the conditional world is, then, constantly to be reminded of its conditionality. To gain a higher freedom from the context is to make the context more malleable rather than to bring it to a resting point of universal scope.[167]

Unger wants not to let the context get to a resting point, and proposes a system that enables a perpetual change in the structures of interdependence at the bottom layer. One of his central theses is that 'All the major aspects of human empowerment or self-assertion depend on our success at diminishing the distance between context-preserving routine and context-transforming conflict.'[168] Institutional imagination is a crucial condition for focusing on this constructive distance.[169] The process of its operation parallels an evolutionary mechanism.

> Context-breaking remains both exceptional and transitory. Either it fails and leaves the pre-established context in place, or it generates another context that can sustain it and the belief or relationship allied to it. An insight may enter into conflict with established criteria of validity, verification, and sense, or with a settled conception of fundamental reality. But if it is worth believing at all, then there will be criteria that can be retrospectively constructed with the aim of preserving it.[170]

An insight which presents a challenge to the established context may or may not prevail in transforming it in a way the context will retrospectively

---

166 Richard Rorty, 'Unger, Castoriadis, and the Romance of a National Future', 82 *Northwestern Univ. L. Rev.* 335, 336 (1988). 'To get the right mood to read passages like these, we rich, fat, tired North Americans must hark back to the time where our own democracy was newer and leaner.' See also id., on page 351: 'His theoretical writing is shot through with a romanticism for which we the Alexandrians no longer have the strength.'
167 Unger, *Politics, supra* note 162, at 23.
168 Id., at 9.
169 See also Bernard Yack, 'Toward a Free Marketplace of Social Institutions: Roberto Unger's "super Liberal" Theory of Emancipation', 101 *Harv. L. Rev.* 1961 (1988).
170 Unger, *Passion, supra* note 165, at 9.

acknowledge it. No simple interaction happens in the bottom layer of the ordinary, nor a simple event occurs in history, without the possibility of a retrospective re-reading of it if the context has been transformed due to its operation.

> We ordinarily admit into our thoughts only that measure of seemingly disordered reality to which we can give an active response. To limit the perception of reality is the natural strategy of intellectual survival: the mind fears being overwhelmed by more than it can imaginatively order. But unless we occasionally move at the edge of our imaginative capabilities we cannot hope to extend our vision of reality and to refine our conception of how things may be ordered.[171]

Before the Second World War, some of the Realists adopted a behaviorist psychology, and a notion of law that assumes individuals have a private inaccessible 'black box', which we only try to examine and manipulate through behavior and external events. In Unger's writing, the inner life is based on formative contexts which are social. There is no natural context.

> There is no past, existent, or statable catalogue of social worlds that can incorporate all the practical or passionate relationships that people might reasonably, realistically, and rightly want to strike up. So the power to make society always goes beyond all the societies that exist or that have existed, just as the power to discover the truth about the world cannot keep within the forms of discourse that are its vehicles.[172]

We want to transcend our context and this is the only valid objectivity to assert. If we will only acknowledge that the creativity of inventing ourselves anew is a condition of life, a genuine freedom will emerge.[173]

---

171 Unger, *Politics, supra* note 162, at 32.
172 Unger, *Passion, supra* note 165, at 9.
173 See also Ernest Weinrib, 'Enduring Passion', 94 *Yale L.J.* 1825 (1985): 'Unger seeks a conception of the self which supports the radical program of "superliberalism" ... Within this conception, the self is located at the intersection of two large issues. One, termed by Unger the problem of solidarity, concerns the contradictory demands of repulsion and attraction occasioned by the presence of others who can be neither wholly trusted nor wholly avoided. Sensing danger but longing for confirmation, the self struggles to find the truth of its own identity in the life of the passions, where virtue and vice are variations on the themes of love and hate. The other issue Unger calls contextuality. Here Unger points both to the particularity of the context in which one finds oneself and to one's capacity to rise above and thus be liberated from the constrictions which this particular context would otherwise impose.'

Everything is contextual, and all contexts can be broken, in Unger's writing, but the assertion itself has a context, and within it, institutions and a legal system that structure them are the ultimate guarantee for freedom and for human happiness. In contrast to the Realists' progressive fathers of the Critical Legal Studies movement, and in contrast to the legacy of Holmes, which provides the jurist-intellectual a safe place to inhabit, Unger chooses to present a new ideal of a Dewyan democracy and to provide, this time from within law, after the maturing stage of the 1950s, the external hysterical picture (of the world and the American society). Instead of a natural evolutionary image of society, we have a contextual evolutionary one, which assumes concrete historical arbitrary stories, and aspires to transform them. The context which this discourse assumes and in which Unger's program should operate is that of institutions, and in that sense he responds to the Legal Process materialization of the world. Behind this idea of institutions and its specific style of naturalism lies a whole set of epistemological and philosophical questions that Unger seems to take for granted, just as the Legal Process authors did before him. In that sense, Unger suggests one naturalism to substitute for another and his image of law and adjudication, unlike Dworkin's, is not interpretive and hermeneutic.

Unger goes against the private-public dichotomy of the Legal Process, and since, as has been shown above, he does not believe that pure private ordering is possible, the legal system that he imagines questions again and again the structures of social order and makes sure they are in perpetual transformation. From the notion of adjudication as the navigating force between private and public, through the use of reason, he moves to a plural logic of reason, navigating between the institutions, redefining the public and private again and again in each decision making.

Second, following the focus on the grand social picture, Unger's emphasis is no longer on adjudication as the voice of reason to handle the public and the private, and through the years his call becomes mainly for a political change. His 'revolt against formalism' is in that sense 'the next step' after the 'success' or the incorporation of the revolt manifested by the second stage of the pragmatism of law, as described by Morton White and elsewhere.[174] When he refers to the 'critique of formalism' as one of the two 'overriding concerns of the Critical Legal Studies movement',[175] he gives a description of the Legal Process jurisprudence as his target formalism.

---

174 See the chapter 'The Maturing of the Pragmatic Idea in Law and Society (Or: The Fall, and the Rise of Philawsophy)'.
175 Roberto Mangabria Unger, *The Critical Legal Studies Movement* (1986).

> By formalism I do not mean what the term is usually taken to describe: belief in the availability of a deductive or quasi-deductive method capable of giving determinate solutions to particular problems of legal choice. Formalism in this context is a commitment to, therefore also a belief in the possibility of, a method of legal justification that contrasts with open-ended disputes about the basic terms of social life, disputes that people call ideological, philosophical, or visionary. Such conflicts fall far short of the closely guarded canon of inference and argument that the formalist claims for legal analysis. This formalism holds impersonal purposes, policies and principles to be indispensable components of legal reasoning. Formalism in the conventional sense – the search for a method of deduction from a gapless system of rules – is merely the anomalous, limiting case of this jurisprudence.[176]

The legal universe Unger has in mind is made of policies, principles, and legal rules. This picture of law handling a society that is honeycombed with disputes is that of the Legal Process Materials. The 'materialization' of the functional, and the central role of adjudication as providing the voice of reason to navigate between the institutions, are part of this image. The process formalism, in terms of the pragmatic idea and in light of Fuller's perception, is the belief in the ability to use reason to differentiate between two types of disputes: those that are 'open-ended', about the basic terms of social life, and those that are given to reasoned elaboration.

> Legal doctrine or legal analysis is a conceptual practice that combines two characteristics: the willingness to work from the institutionally defined materials of a given collective tradition and the claim to speak authoritatively within this tradition, to elaborate from within in a way that is meant, at least ultimately, to affect the application of state power. Doctrine can exist, according to the formalist view, because of a contrast between the more determinate rationality of legal analysis and the less determinate rationality of ideological contests.[177]

The more determinate rationality of legal analysis was assumed when rules, principles and purposes were perceived as the organic medium of decision-making. The 'reasoned elaboration' idea assumed a relationship to other institutions which have a different logic of operation. The private-public demarcation at the core of this picture is challenged by Unger. His attack on 'legal doctrine' or on 'legal analysis' is a comment on the 1950s picture of a

---

176 Id., at 1.
177 Id., at 2.

harmonic mediation of the external view of the world and the internal view of the legal decision maker. He actually accepts the discourse of the 1950s with its pragmatic knot as the boundary he would like to transgress, as the fetishism he strives to overcome. His writing targets the pretension to provide the Hart and Sacks-like harmonic picture of a manageable coordination between institutions through the rigorous working of the small things. 'Successive failures to find the universal legal language of democracy and the market suggest that no such language exists.'[178] Instead of the idea of 'settlement' and a reasoning that searches for the 'maturing of collective thought', Unger posits imagination and the endless transformations of the structure and the institutions we inhabit. Reason is not an intellectual movement based on the status quo, but it is a constant challenge to the status quo by acknowledging its momentary character.

Unger does not give up the effort to find a universal language; neither does he reject the basic picture of the legal universe of rules, principles, and polices. His offer is to enlarge the picture by pointing to the social visions that lie behind them, and to construct a system that enables them perpetually to challenge and enhance a society with endless transformations. Following this broadening of the legal universe and the shift to the meta-level behind the principles and policies – the social visions – Unger's imagined empowered democracy is assumed, as in the utopic vision of the 1950s, to settle and resettle imagination and constraints, through institutional transformations.

Adjudication, which at first in his *Critical Legal Studies* book captures Unger's major interest, ceases to be the hegemonic discourse as his writing proceeds. Eventually, in his last book named *Democracy Realized: the Progressive Alternative*, he offers a political manifesto for the new progressive state. It is interesting to follow the 'evolution' of the grand program of Unger, from his initial involvement in *The Critical Legal Studies Movement*[179] and his call for a deviationist doctrine until his latest manifesto. He begins with the work from within.

> Deviationist doctrine moves across the empirical boundary in two different ways. One way is familiar and straightforward: to explore the relations of cause and effect that lawyers dogmatically assume rather than explicitly investigate when they claim to interpret rules and precedents in the light of imputed purpose ... The other way the empirical element counts is more subtle and systematic: it opens up the petrified relations between abstract ideas or categories, such as

---

178 Id., at 6.
179 Id.

freedom of contract or political equality, and the legally regulated social practices that are supposed to exemplify them.[180]

Deviationist doctrine works from inside the body of the law, and at the beginning, Unger offers a subversive methodology in the name of a movement which claims to stand in the place of the Legal Realists and produce 'the next step' of the pragmatism of law. Their work is done from the inside, but in a subversive manner it affects and questions the outside in each particular decision.

> The starting point of our argument is the idea that every branch of doctrine must rely tacitly if not explicitly upon some picture of the forms of human association that are right and realistic in the areas of social life with which it deals ... Without such a guiding vision, legal reasoning seems condemned to a game of easy analogies. It will always be possible to find, retrospectively, more or less convincing ways to make a set of distinctions, or failures to distinguish, look credible. A common experience testifies to this possibility; every thoughtful law student or lawyer has had the disquieting sense of being able to argue too well or too easily for too many conflicting solutions. Because everything can be defended, nothing can; the analogy-mongering must be brought to a halt.[181]

In contrast to Kennedy, who describes from his insider's prophetic position this indeterminacy of legal reasoning as the semiotic of legal argument,[182] and in contrast to the Process scholars who believe this indeterminacy can be achieved through reasoned elaboration by exercising the maturing of collective thought, Unger avoids the detached (position of Kennedy) or the simplistic positions (that of the Legal Process). In stepping outside the legal world and its life, he points to diverse views and to the need to have a specific social vision, to operate some choice. Still, it is impossible to locate an ideology or a social vision of any doctrine in a simple way, since the body of law in any field never coincides with one metascheme.[183] 'It is always possible to find

---

180 Id., at 17.
181 Id., at 8.
182 See part 1.5 in the chapter 'The Maturing of the Pragmatic Idea in Law and Society (Or: The Fall, and the Rise of Philawsophy)'.
183 See also John J. A. Burke, *The Political Foundation of The Law and The Need for Theory with Practical Value: The Theories of Ronald Dworkin and Roberto Unger* (1992), 44–5: 'According to Unger, American law contains diverse, and immaturely formed, normative concepts capable of supporting counter interpretations of legal doctrine and of providing radically different content to law. Deviationist doctrine identifies latent normative concepts of law and takes them to their logical conclusion.'

in actual legal materials radically inconsistent clues about the range of application of each of the models, and indeed, about the identity of the models themselves.'[184]

> There emerges the characteristic figure of the modern jurist who wants – and needs – to combine the cachet of theoretical refinement, the modernist posture of seeing through everything, with the reliability of the technician whose results remain close to the mainstream of professional and social consensus. Determined not to miss out on anything, he has chosen to be an outsider and an insider at the same time. To the achievement of this objective he has determined to sacrifice the momentum of his ideas. We have denounced him wherever we have found him and we have found him everywhere.[185]

Law, in this paragraph, is the inescapable context from which we would like to perceive everything. The modern jurist who aims to 'catch an echo of the infinite',[186] just as Holmes suggested, and who pursues his social views through the legal work, will soon find him or herself frustrated by not being able to simply move to the external terrain. The fear of taking the critique of formalism to its end will soon result in another kind of formalism. The law-and-economics and the rights-and-principles schools represent in that sense a symptomatic response from the right and center, which supplies 'a watered-down version of the enterprise of nineteenth-century legal science'.[187] Each school is offering a foundation; the economists offer the market: 'the identification of the abstract market idea or the abstract circumstances of maximizing choice with a particular social and institutional complex'.[188] The rights-and-principles school offers either moral consensus or 'a transcendental moral order whose content can be identified quite apart from the history and substance of a particular body of law'. Alternately, it offers a mediating position (this seems like Dworkin's position) of 'a moral order resting mysteriously upon more than consensus'.[189] Unger sees the Process school as part of these

---

184 Unger, *The Critical Legal Studies Movement, supra* note 175, at 10.
185 Id., at 10–11.
186 Oliver Wendell Holmes, *The Path of the Law* in *American Legal Realism* (William W. Fisher III, Morton J. Horwitz, Thomas A. Reed, eds, 1993), 15, 24.
187 Unger, *The Critical Legal Studies Movement, supra* note 175, at 14.
188 Id., at 12.
189 Id. at 13. 'The intended result of all this hocus-pocus is far clearer than the means used to achieve it. The result is to generate a system of principles and rights that overlaps to just the appropriate extent with the positive content of the laws. Such a system has the suitable degree of revisionary power, the degree necessary to prove that you are neither an all-out and therefore ineffective apologist nor an irresponsible revolutionary.'

covering experiences, and does not perceive the constitutional moment in this era for his writing as well.

> The single most striking example in twentieth-century American legal thought has been the development of a theory of legal process, institutional roles, and purposive legal reasoning as a response to legal realism. The most credible pretext for these endless moves of confession and avoidance has been the fear that, carried to the extreme, the critique of objectivism and formalism would leave nothing standing.[190]

Unger perceives the process effort as part of other 'endless moves of confession and avoidance' to carry the critique against formalism to its end. Only the Critical Legal Studies people have overcome their fear 'to pursue the critical attack *a outrance*. When we took the negative ideas relentlessly to their final conclusions, we were rewarded by seeing these ideas turn into the starting points of a constructive program.'[191]

The location of Unger's 'deviationist doctrine' is on the boundary between holding a 'formal' theory while trying to enhance it politically, or under the cover of some legal school of thought (Law and Economics or the public law scholars,[192] as discussed above), and accepting the ruling style. He refuses to choose between accepting the ruling style or 'being political'. 'Either resign yourself to some established version of social order, or face the war of all against all.'[193]

> The implication of our critique of formalism is to turn the dilemma of doctrine upside down. It is to say that, if any conceptual practice similar to what lawyers now call doctrine can be justified, the class of legitimate doctrinal activities must be sharply enlarged ... We agree neither on whether we can in fact develop this expanded or devationist doctrine nor on what exactly its methods or boundaries should be. But we know that only such an expansion could generate a conceptual practice that maintains the minimal characteristics of doctrine – the willingness to take the extant authoritative materials as starting points and the claim to normative authority – while avoiding the arbitrary juxtaposition of

---

190 Id.
191 Id., at 14.
192 Id., at 12: 'Each of these theories is advanced by a group that stands at the margin of high power, despairs of seeing its aims triumph through governmental politics, and appeals to some conceptual mechanism designed to show that the advancement of its program is a practical or moral necessity.'
193 Id., at 15.

easy analogy and truncated theorizing that characterizes the most ambitious and coherent examples of legal analysis today.[194]

Deviationist doctrine works from the inside and refutes generalization as to its specific operation. It moves across the empirical and normative boundary; it is willing 'to recognize and develop the conflicts between principles and counter principles that can be found in any body of law'.[195] 'To incorporate the final level of legal analysis in this new setting would be to transform legal doctrine into one more arena for continuing the fight over the right and possible forms of social life.'[196] The arena Unger chooses is of private law theory, where Fuller has founded his 'conflicting considerations consciousness',[197] the core of the theoretical thinking in law.

That is how, in Unger's *What Should Legal Analysis Become?*,[198] decision making in law wears the counter-image of the settling one of the Legal Process. It is 'a marriage between social realism and social prophecy'.[199]

> The heart of most legal analysis in an adjudicative setting should and must be context-oriented practice of analogical reasoning in the interpretation of statutes and past judicial decisions ...
>
> The practice of purposive analogical reasoning should, however, differ in two crucial respects from the method recommended by rationalizing legal analysis and its supporting cast of theories. First, it should acknowledge no drive toward systematic closure and abstraction: the conceptual ascent of purposive judgments toward prescriptive theory-like conceptions of whole fields of law and social life. Second, it should attempt to avoid any rigid contrast between the prospective and the retrospective genealogies of law: between law as it looks to those who struggle, in politics and political opinion, over its making and law as it looks after the fact to its professional and judicial interpreters. The purposes guiding the analogist must be just as eclectic in character as those motivating the contestants in original law making.[200]

---

194 Id.
195 Id., at 17.
196 Id., at 18.
197 See the discussion of Duncan Kennedy's treatment of Fuller and his 'Consideration and Form' article in the chapter 'Settled Law and the Law-That-Is-Not-But-Ought-To-Be: Hart and Sacks and the Pragmatic Philosophy of Dispute Resolution (Or: Why Couldn't Henry Hart Speak?)'.
198 Roberto Mangabria Unger, *What Should Legal Analysis Become?* (1996).
199 Id., at 23.
200 Id., at 114.

The exposure of the political choice and the indeterminate character of law derive a style of anti-formalism that questions any formal institutional constraints on a judge at each decision making. Since there is a possibility to re-imagine again and again all the conditions of social life, the oscillation between the prospective and the retrospective, the conceptual and the prescriptive, the theoretical and the practical are part of each small decision making that tries to take the critique to its end.[201] This is how Unger describes the decision making in private law cases when reaching the end of his *Critical Legal Studies* Book.

> Toward the center of this spectrum, deliberate agreement and state-made or state recognized duties become less important, though they never disappear entirely. The closer a situation is to the center, the more clearly do rights require a two stage definition: the initial tentative definition of any entitlement must now be completed. Here the boundaries are drawn and redrawn in context according to judgments of both expectations generated by interdependence and the impact that a particular exercise of a right might have upon other parties to the relation or upon the relation itself.[202]

The pragmatic tension between the grand program and the sensitivity to the singular case is preserved here, and at this stage inhabiting the body of the

---

[201] See also Unger, *The Critical Legal Studies*, *supra* note 175, at 88: 'The first model of deviationist doctrine begins by analyzing the major thematic commitments of a particular branch of law and legal doctrine as well as the specific doctrine categories that serve these commitments. It then makes explicit the assumptions about social fact and the social ideal on which those categories rest and subjects them to criticism by the light of more or less widely accepted ideals and understandings ... At this point the first model of deviationist doctrine switches to a different and independently justified view of how the area of social life with which it deals should be ordered. This view implies the institutional reconstruction of major aspects of major society. Finally, the model shows how this programmatic conception can serve as a regulative ideal for the development of current doctrine. The second model of critical doctrine starts by conceiving a broad field of law as the expression of a system of principles and counter-principles whose actual or proper relation to each other can be represented in clashing ways. It then shows how these rival approaches appear in a series of instances of exemplary difficulty. The counter-vision worked out through the analysis of these foci of controversy brings a changed understanding of the proper relation between counter-principles and principles. This understanding can be clarified through generalization into a more comprehensive legal theory. Once generalized it may be applied, and revised through its application, to other related branches of law. Finally, the larger justifications and implications of the suggested developments can be made explicit.'

[202] Id., at 81.

law requires a journey which seems to take, as in Holmes' writing, the form of an organic occurrence. The analysis moves between one level of discourse to another, spreading and transforming like a virus, oscillating between the social visions and the concepts, between the vertical and the horizontal.[203] Each singular decision making is an opportunity to draw the boundaries again and to raise the basic questions 'according to judgments of both expectations generated by interdependence and the impact that a particular exercise of a right might have upon other parties to the relation or upon the relation itself'. The interdependence is happening in a concrete social context, and this context can be transformed, or at least influenced, through operation in each singular dispute. One of the possibilities is to affect 'the relation itself'.

As time goes by, Unger is increasing interested in the social level, in providing a scheme for his 'empowered democracy', and the dispute and adjudication in general are of less concern to him. His 1998 book *Democracy Realized: the Progressive Alternative* is focused on a general political program that can re-organize the Western countries and is concluded by a manifesto composed of thirteen theses. The book contains a political plan for developing a real democratic experimentalism, and the only reference to legal analysis and to his old developed notion of it as a subversive mechanism is through his short conclusive announcement of its failure to mature.

> The institutional arrangements for production and exchange should be as open to experimental variation as all other parts of social life. The assumptions about property underlying this turn contrast with the view, still characteristic of much economics, that the market economy has a single natural and necessary basic form, expressed in the classical, nineteenth-century legal system of unified, sharply demarcated property rights. The formative episode in the development of twentieth-century legal thought was the redefinition of property as a bundle of legal relations and the simultaneous development of the awareness that property rights inevitably conflict. No single logic of the property regime can settle such conflicts; decisions of policy are required to resolve them. This legal thesis, however, has failed to develop into the conception, central to this argument for reconstruction, that market economies like representative democracies and free civil societies can take radically different institutional forms. *Legal thought has yet to complete its rebellion against institutional fetishism. The partisans of democratic experimentalism should not wait for it to do so*[204] (my emphasis, M.A.).

---

203 See *supra* note 201.
204 Roberto Mangabria Unger, *Democracy Realized: The Progressive Alternative* (1998), 203–4.

Twentieth-century legal thought has failed to develop into Unger's conception, and that is why the partisans of democratic experimentalism should not wait for its full rebellion. His 1998 call for democracy realized offers a grand global picture of a universal progressive scheme, and leaves the little work of doctrine and details to those left behind, the internals to the legal discourse.

Third, what seems to begin with the prevalence of form and process in the Legal Process tradition seems to turn in Unger's writing into a kind of obsession with form, a project of creating 'a form of no form', a 'structure of no structure'. His notion of a system of rights based on an incommensurable mixture of solidarity, market, immunity, and destabilization rights[205] is a materialization of the pragmatic sentiment of self-destruction, of a perpetual movement loyal only to its continuance.

> The institutional program of empowered democracy has its counterpart in a program for the transformation of personal relations. Call this program cultural revolution. There are both causal and justificatory links between the institutional proposals and their personalist extension. Like any institutional order, the institutions of empowered democracy encourage certain changes in the character of the direct practical or passionate relations among individuals, and they depend for their vitality upon the perpetuation of these qualities. At the same time the ideas inspiring the cause of empowered democracy also support a criticism of the fine texture of social life.[206]

The 'empowered democracy' of Unger tries perpetually to question 'the fine texture of social life'. It combines an interest 'to deny authority to any entrenched scheme of authoritative models of human association'[207] with the need to adapt the proper institutional structure to deal with the existing modes of interaction. The private is acknowledged to be conditioned by the public,

---

205 The system of rights which Unger offers illustrates the substantive elements which already exist in his early writing. It shows his external vision of his empowered democracy, his grand theory that tries to balance the different aspects of a human life. His rights are not perceived in a regular way; they are usually treated in legal context: 'We have come to think of the vocabulary of rights as ordinarily limited to the legal definitions of institutions and practices and therefore to state-described and state-enforced law. The following discussion presupposes this narrower conception of right while effacing the clarity of its boundaries. For the system of rights described here is meant to transcribe an institutional structure that weakens the contrast between devotion to the common good and the pursuit of private interests.' See Unger, *Politics, supra* note 162 at 367. Id., at 385.
206 Id., at 399.
207 Id., at 400.

while still being handled by the latter. Hence, in Unger's system of rights there is a heterogeneous structure standing in the basis of the social organization. Within his system exist side by side the following components: *Immunity rights*, the traditional liberal rights (which secure against governmental or private oppression), extended by welfare entitlements which guarantee 'access to the material and cultural resources needed to make a life'.[208] These include education; *Market rights*, which are 'the rights employed for economic exchange in the trading sector of society';[209] and are equivalent to the familiar economical legal regime which deals with the market; *Destabilization rights*, which 'protect the citizen's interest in breaking open the large-scale organizations of the extended areas of social practice that remain closed to the destabilizing effects of ordinary conflicts and thereby sustain insulated hierarchies of power and advantage'.[210] These rights enable to challenge again and again all the conditions of social life; and *solidarity rights*, which 'give legal form to social relations of reliance and trust'.[211]

The mixture suggests that at the very core of the organization of society, there is an asymmetry and a gap that should be acknowledged in its heterogeneity. There are formal familiar rights of market operation and individual liberties and welfare, but besides them there is a type of rights that threatens to undermine their neatness and compatibility. The public-private demarcation is said to be questioned and transformed again and again through this framework. This is the anti-formalist germ of Unger's contemporary pragmatic call. His response to a possible complaint that his solidarity rights are too fluid in their relational emphasis illustrates this point:

> It may be objected that an unenforceable right is no right at all and that merely to speak of such entitlements is to disinter the illogical language of natural rights with its implicit but halfhearted allusion to a natural, absolute context of social life. But it is a mistake to identify the positivism of governmental enforcement and the idea of innate and internal entitlements as the only two senses that rights language may bear. A system of rights, in the sense employed by this discussion of all rights, is fundamentally the institutionalized part of social life, backed up by a vision of possible and desirable human association. The limits to rights are the limits to institutionalization itself.[212]

---

208 Id., at 385.
209 Id., at 377.
210 Id., at 387.
211 Id., at 391.
212 Id., at 395.

Institutionalization is the key for the construction of the public and private, and in Unger's early writing, there is a possible institutional framework that will enable its self-transformation. The system it creates can also be worked from within the legal realm. Its work, maybe through Marxist subversion, is done through the hard work of working on the legal doctrine and exposing its ideological roots. This hope seems to disappear from his current writing. His last call for democracy realized is an effort to reframe a new style of liberalism that has an open-ended economy. Two hopes characterize Unger's democratic experimentalism.

> The first hope of the democrat, according to democratic experimentalism, is to find the area of overlap between the conditions of practical progress and the requirements of individual emancipation. Prominent among such conditions and requirements are the institutional arrangements of society. Practical or material progress includes economic growth and technological or medical innovation, supported by scientific discovery. It is the development of our power to push back the constraints of scarcity, disease, weakness, and ignorance. It is the empowerment of humanity to act upon the world. Individual emancipation refers to the freeing of individuals from inherited advantage, shaping the life chances of individuals.[213]

> If the first hope of the democrat is the hope of building in the zone of overlap between the conditions of practical progress and of individual emancipation, the second hope is that this work respond to the felt needs and aspiration of ordinary men and women. Democracy cannot go forward as the recognized gift of a cunning history to a reluctant nation.[214]

In a manner that can be described as 'straightforward', and in a structure comprised basically of two parts – an argument, and a manifesto – Unger weaves his ideal democracy as built upon institutional innovation and alternative pluralisms. His anti-formalist heterogeneous mediation of the incommensurable transforms here to a more coherent detailed scheme of a progressive regime. His program does not promote anymore an obscure complex operation through an internal mechanism from within law, but prefers to ignore this discourse altogether. In that sense, he seems to take the equivalent and opposite trajectory of the negotiation people in providing a 'practical' political straightforward approach to the highest public questions. In the negotiation writing at Harvard, the same genre of writing is provided for all

---

213 Unger, *Democracy Realized*, *supra* note 204, at 5.
214 Id., at 10.

private affairs.[215] The singular dispute and the basic universal question of liberal democracy receive a treatment, which has a relation to the 1950s jurisprudence, in Roger Fisher's writing as well as Unger's. The fact that they are both prominent figures at Harvard Law School is not a coincidence, according to my writing. Neither of them is satisfied (at least currently, for Unger) with the 'spectator position' of the academic legal scholar.[216]

The pragmatic sentiments of engineering and grand programs are brought in Unger to their peak and maybe, in a way, to their manifest impossibility.[217] The main ideas in his writing are of a plan of no plan, an economy of no economy, an open-ended experimentalism of hyper-transformations, until finally he reaches a full transparent hysteric political discourse, with no ironic distance, fully present to itself, not having an academic posture at all. Unger becomes, in his genre of writing, Roger Fisher. It seems as if a return of Dewey, in a new costume, occurs in Unger's texts. Nevertheless, this time it is not the progressiveness of founding, as in Dewey, but the progressiveness of the children, or grandchildren, who can no longer hold to the original text, the children who have brothers and sisters, legal and illegal, but still try to offer a revised pragmatic script as their ultimate text. They still try to revolt against formalism.

From another place and continent, a very different but equivalent political humanistic program can be read, by way of an example again, in the writing of Jacques Derrida.

> Even beyond the regulating idea in its classic form, the idea, if that is still what it is, of democracy to come, its 'idea' as event of a pledged injunctions that orders one to summon the very thing that will never present itself in the form of

---

215 See the discussion of the problematic aspects of defining this project as private and the elaboration on this link in the chapter 'In Search of the Dispute: On Lawyers and Legal Philawsophers at Harvard Law School (Or: Some Private Hope and Public Irony)'.
216 See the discussion of Fisher's activism in the chapter 'In Search of the Dispute: On Lawyers and Legal Philawsophers at Harvard Law School (Or: Some Private Hope and Public Irony)'.
217 There is also a kind of arrogance, not so different from that of Fiss, in constructing a regime of endless transformations for human beings that in most cases 'find satisfaction within settled contexts and experience the disruption of those contexts not as empowerment, but rather as deprivation'. William A. Galston, 'False Universality: Infinite Personality and Finite Existence in Unger's Politics', in Robin W. Lovin and Michael J. Perry, eds, *Critique and Construction: A symposium on Roberto Unger's Politics* (1990) 14, 2. 'To the extent that modernism craves transformative efficacy, it is driven toward revolution from above – that is, toward coercion. It is no accident that in its rage against the stolid persistence of bourgeois society, modernism has repeatedly flirted with fascism.'

full presence, is the opening of this gap between an infinite promise ... and the determined, necessary, but also necessarily inadequate forms of what has to be measured against this promise. To this extent, the effectivity or actuality of the democratic promise, like that of the communist promise, will always keep within it, and it must do so, this absolutely undetermined messianic hope at its heart, this eschatological relation to the to-come of an event *and* of a singularity, of an alterity that cannot be anticipated.[218]

'Democracy to come'[219] of Derrida and 'empowered democracy' of Unger are two ideals built on the mourning[220] or the overcoming (respectively) of the Marxist critique. One of them is built from literary materials and is surrounded by a messianic aura, while the other is built on a solid picture of a world composed of institutions and sophisticated economies.[221] One is suggesting to endure the paradox and to understand how the 'condition of possibility of the event is also its condition of impossibility'[222] while the other simply offers to build 'institutional and cultural worlds that become more supportive of our context-transcending powers'.[223] Although they manifest distinct intellectual cultures and carry different histories, despite their territorial and contextual distance, in spite of their extremely different styles and disciplinary locations, in my thesis narrative they represent two different

---

218 Jacques Derrida, *Specters of Marx: The State of the Debt, The Work of Mourning and The New International* (Peggy Kamuf, trans., 1994), 1993, 65.
219 Id., at 64: 'At stake here is the very concept of democracy as concept of a promise that can always arise in such a *diastema* (failure, inadequation, disjunction, disadjustment, being "out of joint"). That is why we always propose to speak of a democracy *to come*, not of a *future* democracy in the future present, not even of a regulating idea, in the Kantian sense, or of utopia – at least to the extent that their inaccessibility would still retain the temporal form of a *future present*, of a future modality of the *living present*.'
220 Id., at 88: 'To continue to take inspiration from a certain spirit of Marxism would be to keep faith with what has always made of Marxism in principle and first of all a *radical* critique, namely a procedure ready to undertake its self-critique. This critique *wants itself* to be in principle and explicitly open to its own transformation, re-evaluation, self-interpretation.'
221 Unger, *Democracy Realized, supra* note 204, at 3: 'The focus of ideological conflict throughout the world is changing. The old contest between statism and privatism, command and market, is dying. It is in the process of being replaced by a more promising rivalry among the alternative institutional forms of economics, social, and political pluralism. The basic premise of this new conflict is that market economies, free civil societies, and representative democracies can assume many different institutional forms, with radically different consequences for society.'
222 Derrida, *Specters of Marx, supra* note 218, at 65.
223 Unger, *Democracy Realized, supra* note 204, at 9.

languages: American and perhaps European (which, as in any case of languages, have translation problems), which do not necessarily say different things. Exposing here the metaphysical against the ordinary, the philosophical against the legal, the aesthetic and literal against the economic, goes back to the 'origins' of the difference between these two discourses.[224] Eventually, perhaps, these two prophets might give the same formula of progressiveness and justice,[225] that is, to transcend: to throw an insight without foundation and to wait and hope for its retrospective settling.[226] It seems that behind the familiar anti-formalist mode of Unger's writing lies also the singularity of the *Brown* decision and its effect on American society. The transformation of his theory and his 'loss of hope' in the legal discourse can be perceived also as the disenchantment of *Brown*, and together with it the belief in the ability of

---

224 See the chapter 'The Maturing of the Pragmatic Idea in Law and Society (Or: The Fall, and the Rise and Philawsophy)'.
225 See, for example, Derrida, *Specters of Marx*, *supra* note 218, at 27: 'Beyond right, and still more beyond juridicism, beyond morality, and still more beyond moralism, does not justice as relation to the other suppose on the contrary the irreducible excess of a disjointure or an anachrony ... some "out of joint" dislocation in being and in time itself, a disjointure that, in always risking the evil, expropriation and injustice against which there is no calculable insurance, would alone be able to *do justice* or to *render* justice to the other as other? ... Otherwise, justice risks being reduced once again to juridical-moral rules, norms, or representations, within an inevitable totalizing horizon.'
226 In Unger's writing there is a possible democratic hospitality towards a style like Derrida's: 'No one genre of thinking, talking, and writing enjoys the privilege best to represent today a progressive, programmatic imagination. We can think discursively, prophetically, or poetically; systematically or by fragment and parable; with a particular context in mind or on a workable scale; linked to particular parties or movements or disconnected from them; extending actual experience or anticipating possible experience; for the here and now of immediate feasible changes or for the remote and speculative future of unborn humanity; with a wealth of empirical detail and justificatory argument or with nothing but the suggestive and dogmatic invocation of a manifesto. These forms have different uses. They complement one another'. As to Derrida's response to Unger, he might claim that the poetic and the non economical genre are a precondition for producing an event that can count as progress: '... it would be just as easy to show that without this experience of the impossible, one might as well give up on both justice and the event. That would be still more just or more honest. One might as well give up also on whatever good conscience one still claims to preserve. One might as well confess the economic calculation and declare all the checkpoints that ethics, hospitality, or the various messianisms would still install at the borders of the event in order to screen the *arrivant*'. The American 'hospitality' here is, undoubtedly, also a certain kind of imperialism which accepts the other genre so long as it shares the same 'pragmatic', i.e., the American language; but since this dissertation is written from an American place, it allows itself the violence of inclusion, but again, as written in the introduction, just for the sake of the dispute, of some singularity that has still not occurred.

adjudication to produce major social transformations. The problem of segregation and discrimination and racism was not resolved by *Brown*, but the promise it enhanced as to the ability to transform society through a grand institutional design, conducted by a legal facilitator, seemed to capture the mind and imagination of Unger's generation of students. The example of Brown hence became a model for possible further transformations in the society in the future, and drove Unger's empowered democracy. The fact that it had its own singularities, obviousness and particular history, combined with an overall substantial failure,[227] did not prevent Unger at first from adopting it as a proof for the feasibility of his project.

> Formative contexts must be reproduced in the banal activities of daily life such as the forms of economic exchange, the habits of party-political competition, and the discourse of moral and legal controversy. These activities generate an endless series of petty conflicts – a Brownian motion of social life. These disputes are the small wars fought to save a social world from the wars that can pull this world apart. [228]

The physical notion of a 'Brownian motion' can symbolize also the Brownian hope to use the adjudicative branch to transform society through a bottom-to-top process. It also emphasizes again the naturalistic aspect of Unger's theory. Instead of the dynamic pie and the harmonic evolution in society in a settlement and re-settlement, we have a Brownian motion, of disputes as little wars that can always 'escalate into context transforming struggles'.[229] This view mediates the 'deep-structure social theorist position', who is the Marxist, the 'wrong' position in the Legal Process Materials, and the 'positivist social scientist',[230] who is assuming possession (like Posner) of 'the true stuff of social life'.[231] The first gives too little credit to the low-level disturbances as capable of influencing the big order. The second gives them too much credit as the only social happening ('the exercise of problem solving and interest accommodation that plays so large a role in his understanding of society'[232]).

---

227 See the chapter 'Settled Law and the Law-That-Is-Not-But-Ought-To-Be: The Pragmatic Philosophy of Dispute Resolution (Or: Why Couldn't Henry Hart Speak?)'.
228 See Unger, *Politics, supra* note 162, at 73.
229 Id., at 74.
230 Id., at 169.
231 Id.
232 Id.

> The Brownian notion of social life – the emerging of destabilizing opportunity out of stabilizing methods – provides the occasion for influences that may shape long-term context change. These influences, working in concert or in opposition, account for a remarkable possibility. Contexts may change in quality as well as content.[233]

This economical picture of culture as a notion of problem solving activities that transform the context in which they operate is reenacting a belief in process, and the impossibility of its workability is materialized again into a whole system of rights, which Unger tries to delineate.[234] His destabilization rights, market, immunity, and solidarity rights construct a universe where incremental changes are combined with transformative ones to create a new framework of society and of law functioning within it.

The incremental change, which carries the seeds of a new structure and of a transformation, is a new horizon for the pragmatic spirit, and in that sense Unger's matured antiformalism brings pragmatism and the intellectual history pathos of this whole thesis to their modern inherent formula of impossibility.

> The conception of intellectual history underlying this critical diagnosis is not the image of intellectual systems eventually collapsing under the weight of contrary evidence until a theoretical revolution replaces them with alternative theories. It is rather the picture of a twofold process of dissolution and construction: as the intellectual traditions dissolve they also provide the materials and the methods for their own substitution. In this view of the situation of social thought, we need to explicate and to extend the fragments of an alternative social theory already implicit in the self-subverting activities of contemporary social thought.[235]

To explicate and to extend fragments of alternative social theory by using the self-subverting elements in the existing system is to believe in academic theoretical progress inhabiting a discourse and to bounce against its boundaries. This is the first layer of Unger's writing, which speaks as an internal to the discourse of law while trying to affect the world. This seems still to be the weapon of Duncan Kennedy, actually the first leader of the Critical Legal Studies movement, who speaks in his *Critique of Adjudication* about the internal critique as a 'viral strain'. The 'next step' of Unger's program, as it seems to emerge from *Democracy Realized*, discussed above, is to overflow

---

233 Id., at 171.
234 See *supra* note 205.
235 Id., at 9.

this discourse altogether. He becomes 'pragmatic' in the 'brutal' straightforward manner of adopting a political theory, offering a plan, providing a manifesto.

3.5 The End of the Day (and of the Century)

Several conclusions can be inferred from the debate in this chapter.

First, the idea of settlement which was central to the discourse of the 1950s, and part of its style of pragmatism, has become degraded in progressive eyes in the following generations. In Owen Fiss, this response is manifested in a complete denial of the dispute resolution function of adjudication, and in his call 'against settlement'. In Roberto Unger's writing, the core of his progressive vision lies in his offering a structure that is inherently unsettled, and in substituting imagination for settlement

Second, the imagined center that the public law scholarship offers, as manifested in Fiss's writing, is constructed as a pure negativity of the postwar Legal Process scholarship at Harvard: The *Brown* decision is the constitutive moment of the opposition; the pathos is progressive and not conservative, but it is imagined to be located between the 'real' political poles of CLS and L&E; the mode is interpretive and not natural; the bottom-to-top pragmatic sensitivity of working the dispute from its emergence is switched by a top-to-bottom idea of handling it from above; there is almost no private ordering, and what is there, if any, is insignificant; there is a conversation and a dialogue instead of an organic rationality and reasoned elaboration, but the optimism here is still that of the 1950s, that of finding a language to control through adjudication, by adopting formalism which is based on higher values.

Third, Posner and Unger represent two equivalent contemporary moves to eliminate the intellectual obscure mode of the legal discourse. Posner does so by offering a social science emphasis and by hoping for a path away from the law. Unger begins by occupying the internal space of working the progressiveness from the inside, but eventually gives up on the subversive intellectual work and prefers the straightforward political genre.

Fourth, Unger and Posner represent two non-contemporaneous readings of the revolt against formalism. While Posner takes it as a fixed truth to be followed and applied, Unger begins by taking it as a living commandment that can be followed from within the discourse of law. Eventually he moves to a political genre of a concrete program and a religious style of argument.

Fifth, the notion of pragmatism has multifarious meanings in contemporary discourse. My reading of Posner illustrates how an effort to capture this 'theory' as having a fixed meaning already has a specific location in time and place, and carries a political agenda. The difference between Posner and Unger, who does not define himself as a pragmatist but still carries this idea to its end, is that in Unger's texts, the pragmatic impulse is materialized in its paradoxical quality, in its open-ended messianic horizon. The Marxist specters in Unger and Derrida are thus posited in their possible equivalency.

In some sense, it can be said, finally, that we are all pragmatists, a certain particular kind, since we have experienced some of this power of the American discourse as part of being modern, as part of being contemporary. At the end of the day (and of the century), perhaps the question to be asked is not that of finding another language, another local complexity to dwell in, but rather, the question of the possible mediation between languages, between genres of discourse that are heterogeneous, like the dispute resolution discourse and the jurisprudential, or even the French and the American and perhaps the quest for the anti-imperialist mode of negotiation, which always aims to work on the difference and not to escalate it. It is Morton Horwitz whom I choose to conclude this 'taking sides' chapter sequence. The following quotes are taken from his conclusion to his book *The Transformation of American Law*. He warns that:

> One of the most discouraging spectacles for the historian of legal thought is the unselfconscious process by which one generation's legal theories, developed out of the exigencies of particular political and moral struggles, quickly come to be portrayed as universal truths good for all time. This process of reification draws deep sustenance from a religious and unhistorical American culture.[236]

Then he continues to say:

> Only pragmatism, with its dynamic understanding of the unfolding of principle over time and its experimental appreciation of the complex interrelationship between law and politics and theory and practice, has stood against the static fundamentalism of traditional American conceptions of principled jurisprudence.[237]

Pragmatism is the answer to the extremist's tendency to portray a contingent and context-dependent claim as a universal truth, which is part of the American religious and historical American culture. Pragmatism is the

---

236 Morton J. Horwitz, *The Transformation of American Law 1870–1960* (1992), 271.
237 Id.

coming back to history, to reality, the standing-again, static fundamentalism. Pragmatism, as posited here, is a multi-meaning notion which sometimes functions as religion itself. If you do not believe in it, it is empty and shallow. If you do, you had better construct your very own genre of it within the American family. In the same spirit, this chapter ends claiming to be only contemporaneous and not to represent universal truth here at Harvard Law School, 29 March 2000.

Chapter 4

In Search of the Dispute: On Lawyers and Legal Philawsophers at Harvard Law School (Or: Some Private Hope and Public Irony)[1]

4.1 Introduction

In terms of the previous chapters, this one continues with a contemporary manifestation of two versions of pragmatism, which I have already dealt with before, as organizing the educational message of Harvard Law School in its 'iconomical' position. One is the pragmatism of the 1950s, optimistic and harmonious, as found today in the texts of the negotiation scholars of Harvard. The second is contemporary pragmatism in law, based on the Holmsian legacy, which constitutes the canon of a diverse and torn theoretical discourse. I present the first through the writing of Roger Fisher, Robert Mnookin, and other negotiation scholars at the Law School. I examine the second through depicting Ronald Dworkin as the writer of the mythological script of the contemporary jurist-intellectual. Dworkin posits himself in his 'law as integrity' notion preserving the place of the Holmsian believers in the life of the law, reconstituting the pragmatism of law in its next step. Fisher, on the other hand, infiltrates the optimistic self-righteous pragmatism of the 1950s into contemporary studies in social science by producing a new activist mode of negotiation. In contrast to a difficult conversation in negotiation, where there is no bottom line and no need of such a line, according to Dworkin in hard cases, there is one right answer. This chapter tries to show how and why this is true.

My argument can be divided into a few sub-arguments:

First, my approach is selective. I describe a bounded area of negotiation studies, focusing mainly on the Harvard Negotiation Project, a sub-organization under the umbrella of the Program On Negotiation (PON) at Harvard Law

---

[1] The subtitle is a paraphrase of Rorty's 'public hope and private irony' idea. Richard Rorty, *Contingency, Irony, and Solidarity* (1989).

School. From the theoretical discourse, on the other hand, I pick up Dworkin as the prominent figure, without discussing many other theories or positions that surround or contradict him. I claim that the Negotiation Project, with its 'Harvard stamp', is marketing a practical interest in dispute resolution, which was a major interest of theoretical thinking until the post-war era. The transformation of this interest within the institution of Harvard can provide a case study – an example – for the theoretical shifts in the broader cultural level. I furthermore claim that Dworkin, as the mediator of the English tradition of law and analytic philosophy with the American experience, and as the provider of the unrefuted script of the jurist-intellectual, is appropriate to serve as the prophet of the jurisprudential realm.

Second, my approach does not accept the hierarchy of high and low culture, and I read the 'do it yourself' books of the negotiation writers as embedding theories and cultural texts as much as they Dworkinian writing does by using the abstract reflective thought from the theoretical genre. I refute any notion of common sense, 'practical', personal, straightforward or 'pragmatic' to account for the textual difference between the two discourses I examine.

Third, the intellectual history of the interest in dispute resolution in law reveals that the focus on dispute resolution and negotiation in the practical discourse of today is an 'illegal' offspring of the theoretical interest in this notion until the post-war era. The Legal Process era is said to be the transitional moment where this interest in the dispute was brought to its end, and I present the theoretical discourse of the next generation as suppressing this focus by shifting to a 'public law' mode. The discourse of Dworkin, accordingly, is progressive, due to the retelling the American mythology of a distinct philosophical kingdom in law. This story organizes a theoretical discourse, which is no longer interested in the lawyering lesson or the actualities of the court life, but is occupied with the broad value disagreements that occupy society.

Fourth, based on the inferred claim of the theoretical discourse to provide progressive and political lessons, and the counter-pretension of the negotiation approach to provide none, while still focusing on the dispute to be solved, I describe their inverse operation. While the paradigmatic contemporary intellectual develops an ironic posture of 'nowhere to go', in terms of Pierre Schlag's description,[2] the peacemaker-businessperson wears the activist mode of taking positions and intervening to enforce them, in politics as well as in business life. Side by side in the Law School, these two figures promote a

---

2 Pierre Schlag, 'Normative and Nowhere to Go', *Stan. Law Rev.* 167 (1990).

compact split self-identity, that can account for the current stage of critique in law in general.

Fifth, the split I discern between the a-historic scientific epistemology characterizing the social sciences which surround negotiation studies today and the interpretive mode characterizing the intellectual realm is posited as organizing the institutional abyss between these two realms. The use value of the 'no dialogue' idea between the negotiation activist and the ironic, paralyzed intellectual will be questioned while emphasizing the different genres of discourse they inhabit.

4.2 Negotiation and the Process School

Harvard Law School's curriculum includes courses in diverse legal fields, as well as courses on negotiation and alternative dispute resolution. Although the diverse courses other than negotiation do not have a unified 'approach' or theoretical view, I claim they generally represent a modern theoretical understanding of an indeterminacy of values, of a complex public discourse in which the quest for objectivity and 'right' solutions is doubted or at least contested. In contrast, the negotiation discourse, as part of the Law School's elective educational experience,[3] offers a unified approach in which the process of a well-conducted negotiation can potentially overcome each value disagreement. 'Put most simply, the Program on Negotiation is working to change the way people, organizations and nations resolve their disputes – shifting the process from 'win-lose' outcomes to 'mutual gains' solutions.[4]

One way to reconcile the theoretical dead-end consciousness with the Program on Negotiation's utopian-sounding framework is to say that the negotiation approach is aimed at the private, where its constructive assumptions can work. But the quote above speaks about 'people, organizations, and nations', indicating concern for and focus upon public matters as well. Another way to reconcile the skeptical approach toward the use of criteria in theoretical legal discourse with constructiveness in the negotiation sphere is to refer to the difference between the general and the particular. The Law School registration bulletin implies this point of mediation together with the public-private distinction:

---

3   See, for example, Harvard Law School Catalogue 1998–1999, 164.
4   Brochure, 'The Program of Negotiation at Harvard Law School', 2.

In very general terms, a balanced program is one that includes courses primarily devoted to public regulation as well as courses concentrating on relations between private parties ... courses that offer a broad perspective on the law and legal institutions as well as courses that afford students supervised experience where they learn to apply legal knowledge and skills in contexts like those faced by practicing professionals.[5]

Be theoretical, study jurisprudence and regulation, but also be practical, sensitive to a case, trained as a lawyer who controls the actuality of business life. One should take the Negotiation Workshop, for example. Take a lawyering course. In a Negotiation Workshop offered by the Program,[6] one of the concluding plenary sessions suggests this mediation by dividing the 'reasonable' against the 'personal',[7] respectively, on a chart presented to Workshop participants: 'Some possibly reasonable assumptions' are that 'the prospects for the world are pretty gloomy ...', that 'the most important intercepts in any negotiation are conflicting ...' that 'there are no objective standards of fairness ...'. These stand opposed to the 'personal': 'Some personal assumptions' are that 'it is more fun being an optimist than a pessimist', that 'in every negotiation the parties have shared interests', that 'some standards of legitimacy are objectively more legitimate than others'.

Another idea might be to present the negotiation studies as a 'common-sense' approach:

HNP (Harvard Negotiation Project, M.A.) is perhaps best known for the development of the theory of 'principled negotiation', as presented in *Getting to Yes: Negotiating Agreement Without Giving In*. First published in 1981, *Getting to Yes* is an international best seller that outlines a common-sense approach to negotiation to literally millions of people in 25 different languages. In clear, straightforward writing, *Getting to Yes* shows negotiators how to: focus on interests, not positions; invent options for mutual gains; and use independent standards of fairness to avoid a bitter contest of wills.[8]

Twenty-two years have passed since Herbert Wechsler's *Neutral Principles*[9] article was published, defending a process position in the public law realm,

---

5   Preliminary Registration Bulletin, 1998–1999, Harvard Law School, 73.
6   The Winter 1999 Negotiation Workshop, Harvard Law School, Harvard University.
7   'Some Contrasting Assumptions', handout distributed in the Negotiations Workshop, Winter 1999 (unpublished, on file with *The Program on Negotiation*).
8   Id., at 18.
9   Herbert Wechsler, Toward Neutral Principles of Constitutional Law, 73 *Harv. L. Rev.* 1 (1959).

and situating neutral principles back into law, but this time within the negotiation realm. It is not a theoretical school of process anymore, but a practical project.[10] According to the above quote, millions of people in 25 languages have accepted this common-sense approach to resolving their conflicts and to avoiding a battle of wills.[11] It is a straightforward writing and through it we find a practice, a process that could use 'independent standards of fairness' to reach an acceptable solution. This process is presented as common sense, but what is 'common sense'? Is it not assuming a theory without questioning it? Rorty might have agreed with this idea:

> The opposite of irony is common sense. For that is the watchword of those who unselfconsciously describe everything important in terms of the final vocabulary to which they and those around them are habituated. To be commonsensical is to take for granted that statements formulated in that final vocabulary suffice to describe and judge the beliefs, actions and lives of those who employ alternative final vocabularies.[12]

Against these dichotomies of the private-public, general-particular, reasonable-personal, reflexive-commonsensical, I would suggest an intellectual history argument in favor of two versions of pragmatism: the pragmatism of the 1950s promoted by the process school in jurisprudence, and contemporary pragmatism, which is labeled literary, interpretive or postmodern.[13]

Nowadays, from an intellectual perspective, belief in a process that can determine any substantial choice might seem impossible, and even a mere pretension, to return to some intuitive non-origin, to a place beyond criteria. However, this belief, as I show elsewhere,[14] was actually central to jurisprudential thinking during the 1950s:

---

10 See the discussion of this article and its depiction as 'neutorious' by today's intellectuals in the chapter 'Settled Law and the Law-That-Is-Not-But-Ought-To-Be: The Pragmatic Philosophy of Dispute Resolution (Or: Why Couldn't Henry Hart Speak?)', part 2.4.3.
11 Roger Fisher and William Ury, *Getting to Yes: How to Negotiate Agreements Without Giving in* (1981). As Roger Fisher answers one of his reviewers, 'in times when the book was even less popular: *Getting to Yes*, however, is beyond recall. With twelve ... editions and a third of a million copies in print, the book will have to take care of itself'. Roger Fisher, 'Reply to The Pros and Cons of *Getting to Yes*', 34 *Jour. Legal. Educ.* 115, 120 (1984).
12 Rorty, *Contingency, Irony, and Solidarity, supra* note 1, at 74.
13 I discuss the epistemological rift between the interpretive and the naturalistic-positivistic mode in chapters two and three. Dworkin's pragmatism, which is examined in this chapter, is defined through his writing as interpretive.
14 See the chapter 'Settled Law and the Law-That-Is-Not-But-Ought-To-Be: The Pragmatic Philosophy of Dispute Resolution (Or: Why Couldn't Henry Hart Speak?)'.

In particular, many people have rejected the whole notion of purpose in social organization. At bottom, they have argued, the social problem is a problem simply of deciding who gets what. This view starts with the obvious fact that there is not enough in the world of all the things that people want to go around among the people who want them. The gist of the social situation is then seen baldly, as no more than a continuing struggle among conflicting claimants to get what they can. In this view, the whole apparatus of social order, law included, becomes little more than a substitute or a mask for force, providing a cover of legitimacy for the decisions that have to be made among the various contestants.

These materials proceed upon the conviction that this is a fallacy – 'the fallacy of the static pie'. The fact – the entirely objective fact – seems to be that the pie – that is, the total of actually and potentially available satisfactions of human wants – is not static but dynamic. How to make the pie larger, not how to divide the existing pie, is the crux of the long-range and primarily significant problem.[15]

The Legal Process people believed (probably collectively,[16] as do the negotiation people nowadays[17]) in 'the entirely objective fact' of a dynamic 'pie'.[18] They spoke about the lawyer's primary role being 'problem solving',[19] and believed that the indeterminacy of criteria could be resolved by a formal process. Nevertheless, a salient difference from that approach is that the

---

15 Henry M. Hart, Jr and Albert M. Sacks, *The Legal Process: Basic Problems in the Making and Application of Law* (William N. Eskridge, Jr and Philip P. Frickey, eds) 1994, at 102. (Hereinafter 'Hart and Sacks').
16 The Legal Process Materials are said to be 'the maturing of a collective thought', and in the citation itself we find reference to Lon Fuller as the originator of the expression 'the fallacy of the static pie'. Id., note 2.
17 Teamwork is characteristic of writing in negotiation literature. Most of the 'best sellers' typical of the Harvard Negotiation Center are written by more than one person, and no reference is made to the authorship of one part or another. The book speaks as a product of collective thought.
18 Within the same epistemological framework, Richard Posner's Law and Economics approach 'overcomes' the optimism of this dynamic pie by speaking of scarce resources and the Chicago model of economics. See the chapter 'Taking Sides: Margins and Phases of Pragmatics of Legal Process Disciples (Or: The Pragmatists that We Are)', part 3.3.
19 See Henry Hart, speech to first-year class, 1948, How to Go About the Job of Studying Law: 'My notion of a lawyer can be summed up in one word. To my mind, he is essentially a problem-solver. A good lawyer, it follows, is one who is good at solving problems. A poorer lawyer is one who is not so good.' Box 22–9, Special Collection, Langdell Library, Harvard Law School, Harvard University, Cambridge. See also the equivalent negotiation perspective in Robert H. Mnookin, et al., 'Beyond Winning: How Lawyers and Clients can Create Value in Legal Negotiations' (draft, December 1998), 1–5.

negotiation people do not speak of 'the social problem', but rather of the private problem of the bargaining situation.

> At the Harvard Negotiation Project we have been developing an alternative to positional bargaining: a method of negotiation explicitly designed to produce wise outcomes efficiently and amicably ...[20]

> The third major block to creative problem-solving lies in the assumption of a fixed pie: the less for you, the more for me. Rarely if ever is this assumption true ... Even apart from a shared interest in averting joint loss, there almost always exists the possibility of joint gain. This may take the form of developing a mutually advantageous relationship, or of satisfying the interests of each side with a creative solution.[21]

The focus here is on negotiation, not on the social level as a whole. In other words, while the process people are interested in producing the proper norm by reflecting *ex ante* through diverse institutional perspectives, the negotiation people believe that after all the norms have been created, an *ex post* process reconciles between them by moving to another level, the level of the parties' interests. In terms of the Legal Process Materials, we are here at the 'private ordering' realm.

> The overwhelming proportion of the things that happen and do not happen in American society pass without any later question. Many of these acts and omissions are the result of decisions which people make in the exercise of a private discretion, accorded to them by official recognition of a private liberty ... the billions and billions of events and non-events which in one or another of these fashions stir no later question may be thought of as forming the bottom layer, or base, of the pyramid about to be described.[22]

The above description of Hart and Sacks' 'Great Pyramid of Legal Order' is of the 'bottom layer' – the private ordering institution.[23] This position does not exclude enlarging the pie at the private level, as the negotiation people claim today. Conversely, it assumes this possibility for the public and the private realm as well. There is an interdependence at both levels, and in each

---

20 Fisher and Ury, *Getting to Yes*, *supra* note 11, at 10.
21 Id., at 70.
22 'The Great Pyramid of Legal Order', Hart and Sacks, *supra* note 15, at 286.
23 See the discussion of this pyramid in the chapter Settled Law and the Law-That-Is-Not-but-Ought-To-Be: The Pragmatic Philosophy of Dispute Resolution (Or: Why Couldn't Henry Hart Speak?).

of them the effort is to maximize efficiency for the benefit of all. This is part of the post-war optimistic mediation of the external and internal in law, as discussed in another chapter.[24]

At this bottom layer, there are individuals pursuing self-interest and asking to fulfill their goal in a purposive activity.

> Here enters the most fundamental of the conditions of human society. In the satisfaction of all their wants, people are continuously and inescapably dependent upon one another ...[25] People who are living together under conditions of interdependence must obviously have a set of understandings or arrangements of some kind about the terms upon which they are doing so. This necessarily follows from the fact that interdependent living is collaborative, cooperative living. People need understanding about the kinds of conduct that must be avoided if cooperation is to be maintained. Even more importantly, they need understandings about the kinds of affirmative conduct that is required if each member of the community is to take his due contribution to the common interest.[26]

The Legal Process Materials are indeed 'the last great attempt to a grand synthesis of law in all its institutional manifestations'[27] and, as an analytical endeavor to approach problems from a bottom-to-top perspective, they describe the emergence of the law as a natural, cooperative phenomenon in the development of society. Most of the disputes in society are resolved through a private ordering mechanism, and a horizon of growth and progress is the natural consequence of preserving the institutional settlement between this private realm and other social institutions.

This 1950s idea of people having interests and purposes that can be answered and fulfilled only in a social interaction recurs in the negotiation literature. This notion of the private is at times posited as 'common sense' and as an inevitable conclusion drawn from observing the social world. In other places, it arrives from the interdisciplinary surrounds of negotiation, whether social-psychological or economic, and wears an academic appearance:[28]

---

24 See the chapter 'Settled Law and the Law-That-Is-Not-but-Ought-To-Be: The Pragmatic Philosophy of Dispute Resolution (Or: Why Couldn't Henry Hart Speak?)'.
25 Id., at 1.
26 Id., at 3.
27 Garry Peller, 'Neutral Principles in the Fifties', *U. Mich. J. L. Reform* 561, 568 (1988).
28 See, for example, Jeffery Z. Rubin and George Levinger, *Levels of Analysis: In Search of Generalizable Knowledge*, in *Conflict Cooperation and Justice* (Banker, et al., eds, 1995) 13.

One of the more important distinguishing features of bargaining is the fact that it is a voluntary relationship. Bargainers come together in an attempt to resolve their conflict(s) of interest not because they have to but because they choose to. Each can make a variety of offers and demands, and each is free to leave the relationship – or threaten to do so – at any time. And it is precisely because bargaining is a voluntary relationship that it is also of mutual dependence, that is, interdependence.[29]

There is a voluntary relationship, based on choice, in the core of a bargaining situation, and this choice implies an interdependence of the participants in the deal. In his 1979 famous article 'Bargaining in The Shadow of The Law: The Case of Divorce',[30] which is frequently quoted in legal writing on negotiation, Professor Robert Mnookin, another negotiation prophet at Harvard today, indeed draws the link between The Legal Process 'private ordering' notion and his own writing:

> We see the primary function of contemporary divorce law not as imposing order from above, but rather as providing a framework within which divorcing couples can themselves determine their post-dissolution rights and responsibilities. This process, by which parties to a marriage are empowered to create their own legal enforceable commitments, is a form of 'private ordering'.[31]

The private is 'redeemed' again in law, in Mnookin's 1979 writing, and in Roger Fisher's 1981 *Getting to Yes*, and the influence of the 1950s jurisprudence is apparent in the 'biased' optimism, which their discussion promotes.

In social psychology terms, the interdependence which exists in any bargaining situation can exhibit three kinds of dynamics.

> *Motivational orientation* (MO) refers most generally to one's bargainer's attitudinal disposition toward another and may be usefully described in terms of three extreme cases ... A bargainer has a *cooperative* MO to the extent that he has a positive interest in the other's welfare as well as in his own. A *competitive* MO denotes an interest in doing better than the other, while at the same time doing as well for oneself as possible. A bargainer with an *individualistic* MO is

---

29 Jeffery Z. Rubin and Bert R. Brown, *The Social Psychology of Bargaining and Negotiation* (1975), 197.
30 Robert H. Mnookin and Lewis Koornhauser, 'Bargaining in The Shadow of The Law: The Case of Divorce', 88 *Yale L. J.* 950 (1979).
31 Id., at 950.

simply interested in maximizing his own outcomes, regardless of how the other fares.[32]

The negotiation can take a cooperative, competitive, or individualistic mode. Descriptively, these three possibilities capture the variety of choices for the parties involved. The actual dynamic in each case is a matter of the bargainer's 'attitudinal disposition'. In more business-oriented studies, the same balanced picture of an indeterminate interdependence recurs in different terms. David Lax and James Sebenius in their book *The Manager as Negotiator*[33] present a prisoner's dilemma inherent in any negotiation, based on the tension between creating and claiming value.[34]

> A deeper analysis shows that the competitive and cooperative elements are inextricably entwined. In practice, they cannot be separated. This bonding is fundamentally important to the analysis, structuring, and conduct of negotiation. There is a central, inescapable tension between cooperative moves to create value jointly and competitive moves to gain individual advantages. This tension affects virtually all tactical and strategic choice. Analysis must come to grips with it: negotiators must manage it. Neither denial nor discomfort will make it disappear.[35]

The idea that negotiators should 'balance the tension between creating and claiming value' seems to be a balanced mediating approach between the extremities of the competitive and the integrative styles. We can find it later in Robert Mnookin's book dealing with the lawyer overcoming three basic tensions in each bargaining.[36] Nevertheless, borrowing from other disciplines

---

32 Rubin and Levinger, id., 13. See also Rubin and Brown, *supra* note 29, 198.
33 David A. Lax and James K. Sebenius, *The Manager as Negotiator: Bargaining for Cooperation and Competitive Gain* (1986), 29–45. See also Mnookin, *supra* note 14, 1.
34 See Lax and Sebenius, id., 30: 'Value creators tend to believe that, above all, successful negotiators must be intentive and cooperative enough to devise an agreement that yields considerable gain to each party, relative to no-agreement possibilities. Some speak about the need for replacing the "win-lose" image of negotiation with "win-win" negotiation, from which all parties presumably derive great value ...'. And on page 32: 'Value claimers, on the other hand, tend to see this drive for joint gain as naïve and weak-minded. For them, negotiation is hard, tough bargaining ... To "win" at negotiating – and thus make the other fellow "lose" – one must start high, concede slowly, exaggerate the value of concessions, conceal information, argue forcefully on behalf of principles that imply favorable settlements, make commitments to accept only highly favorable agreements, and be willing to outwait the other fellow.'
35 Id., at 30.
36 See infra text accompanying notes 77–8.

is accompanied in the negotiation studies at Harvard by the 'legal' footprint of the 1950s scholarship. The balanced neutral presentation of the possible dynamics in each bargaining situation is put aside in favor of a more constructive, optimistic description of this interdependent moment. This biased construction is done through the old pragmatic notion of 'problem solving'. Roger Fisher's choice to ignore the competitive (or also individualistic) aspect of the negotiation is presented in some places as overcoming a bias named 'the mythical fixed pie of negotiation'.[37] This idea recalls 'the fallacy of the static pie', described above in the Legal Process Materials.[38]

> Negotiators often fail to reach integrative solutions partially resulting from a systematic intuitive bias to assume that their interests necessarily and directly conflict with the other party's interests ... The fundamental assumption of a fixed-pie may be rooted in social norms that lead us to interpret most competitive situations as win-lose. The win-lose orientation is manifested in our society in athletic competition, admission to academic programs, corporate promotion systems, and so on. Individuals tend to generalize from these objective win-lose situations and create similar expectations for other situations that are not necessarily win-lose.[39]

In the more 'legal' version of negotiation (i.e., in the Harvard Negotiation Project, which Fisher has established), the 'interests' focus is presented as common-sense understanding. The other possibilities of a more competitive interdependence among disputants are not dealt with directly, as if the approach itself, when accepted, will solve the inherent tensions and competition which exist in any interaction, or resolve the above described bias in favor of the static pie. The descriptive approach in law might actually be perceived as a prescription for negotiators, but it is not a pure moral pathos which drives it, as Gerald Wetlaufer suggests.[40] Roger Fisher himself concedes this prescriptive

---

37 Margaret A. Neal and Max H. Bazerman, *Cognition and Rationality in Negotiation* (1991), 61.
38 See *supra* text accompanying note 15.
39 Neale and Bazerman, *supra* note 37, at 61-62.
40 See Gerald B. Wetlaufer, 'The Limits of Integrative Bargaining', *Geo. L. J.* 369 (1996). The author claims that 'the full argument in favor of cooperation and truth telling rests only in part on the possibility of integrative bargaining, but partly also on the negotiator's long-term pecuniary self-interest, on his non-pecuniary self-interest, and on considerations of ethics'. I agree with the description he gives for the limits of the idea of integrative bargaining. Still, I find that his appeal to 'ethics' (the utilitarian version or the notion of 'harm') in order to fill the missing foundation ignores the ideological contextual dimension of the 'win-win' idea. It is not necessary to say that 'Plato's Socrates may have gotten it

view when he admits that he is more concerned with 'what intelligent people ought to do' than with 'the way the world is'.[41] When he states that *Getting to Yes* 'blurs a desirable distinction between descriptive analysis and prescriptive advice',[42] he fails to realize how this blurring is done in name of an old dominant idea, at the core of the process pragmatism in law. This is 'the pragmatic leap' of *Getting To Yes*.

> The basic problem in a negotiation lies not in conflicting positions, but in the conflict between each side's needs, desires, concerns and fears.[43] They are the silent movers behind the hubbub of positions.[44] Behind opposed positions lie shared and compatible interests as well as conflicting ones ... a close examination of the underlying interests will reveal the existence of many more interests that are shared or compatible than ones that are opposed.[45]

The fact that this idea appears without a footnote (and in a book whose first page declares that '... the authors alone are responsible for statements of fact, opinions, recommendations, and conclusions expressed. Publication in no way implies approval or endorsement by Harvard University ...') does not

---

right' in order to promote the integrative idea. Pragmatism is enough for that mission and its cultural flavor is much more appealing.

41 See Roger Fisher, *supra* note 11, at 120, who, while responding to White, claims that his book excludes the competitive inevitable aspect of bargaining,

42 Id., 120–21: '*Getting to Yes* as a whole, I believe, blurs a desirable distinction between descriptive analysis and prescriptive advice. Descriptively, it sorts facts into useful categories: positions vs. interests; people issues vs. substantive ones; inventing vs. deciding; discussing what negotiators will or won't do vs. discussing what they ought to do. Those distinctions, like distinctions between reptiles and mammals, or between short snakes and long snakes, are objectively true, and despite possible difficulties in drawing lines, exist as facts in the real world. Whether or not they are useful is another question. We go beyond suggesting these descriptive categories by advancing some prescriptive rules of thumb, indicated by the chapter heading in the book.'

Using this natural-science image of biology, and making the fact-clue distinction while the facts are considered 'objective truth', locates Fisher even earlier than the 1950s and the Legal Process Materials. Hart and Sacks believed, according to their Zeitgeist, that the social sciences were different from the natural ones in being more judgmatical. See *Pragmatism: From Progressivism to Postmodernism* (Robert Hollinger and David Depew, eds,1995), 227. Also see Hart and Sacks, 107: 'These materials proceed upon the conviction that the science of society is essentially a judgmatical, or prudential, science demanding modes of inquiry and reflection which are sharply at variance with the procedures conventionally thought to be appropriate to the natural sciences.'

43 Fisher and Ury, *Getting to Yes*, *supra* note 11, at 40.
44 Id., at 41.
45 Id., at 42.

imply a non-theoretical medium to its content. The theoretical posture throughout negotiation materials is legal, and is common-sense pragmatism of the 1950s combined with some updated complementary theoretical approaches in the social sciences. What 'collective consciousness' does the Harvard Negotiation Center present? This expression itself, as the post-war chapter suggests, has a pragmatic flavor (and a problematic of its own).[46] Collective consciousness is assumed when an evolutionary epistemology is conditioning the theoretical debate.[47] On its surface, *Getting to Yes* differs from the pragmatism of the 1950s because it does not aim at the public discourse, and does not offer new ways or rules with which to address issues of rights, interpretation of rules or allocation of decision making between social institutions. It does not have any jurisprudential agenda; legal rules occupy a very limited place within its structure as only one kind of possible criteria to use as principles of decision making. In fact, a prominent characteristic of today's studies of negotiation is the loss of interest 'to live within law' and to learn its body. Dispute resolution people approach the dispute from a completely external position of its occurrence in reality as a problem to solve. There is no 'grand synthesis', no 'great effort'. Still, it exudes a genuine belief in the process of negotiation as having the potential to overcome *any* problem. When moving to the Alternative Dispute Resolution (ADR) movement, which might be considered the 'mother' of legal interest in negotiation,[48] we find the same insistence on a vision as in the negotiation writing, and not a mere practical orientation or an efficiency goal.

---

46 See the discussion of the post-war era as chracterized by collective conciousness, and the counter-accounts in the chapter 'Settled Law and the Law-That-Is-Not-But-Ought-To-Be: The Pragmatic Philosophy of Dispute Resolution (Or: Why Couldn't Henry Hart Speak?)'.
47 'The organism manifests itself as what it truly is, an ideal or spiritual life, a unity of *will*. If, then, society and the individual are really organic to each other, then the individual is society concentrated. He is not merely its image or mirror. He is the localized manifestation of its life.' Dewey, *supra* note, 192. See also the discussion of the way evolution is built in Dewey's pragmatism in the chapter 'The Maturing of the Pragmatic Idea in Law and Society (Or: The Fall, and the Rise of Philawsophy)'.
48 Frank E. Sander, *Dispute Resolution Within and Outside the Courts – An Overview of the US Experience* (unpublished manuscript, 1994), 1. 2: 'An important by-product of the recent interest in alternative dispute resolution has been to refocus our attention on negotiation as a vital and pervasive process that can be taught and is not, as was so often assumed until recently, a skill one is either born with or not. We have found in our teaching at Harvard Law School that there are important theoretical questions that have been recently addressed by scholars.'

In my view, the basic thrust behind the multi-door approach is to provide more effective and responsive solutions to the disputes, not, as it sometimes claimed, to relieve our court dockets or to save time and money. The latter consequences may often come about, but they should not be the raison d'être.[49]

To give 'more effective and responsive' solution to the dispute is to believe in the ability of the ADR approach to enlarge the pie, to achieve something better than splitting the difference. It is the idea that there is something inherently good in approaching the singular dispute through a variety of processes instead of one, imposed solution by a judge. 'Fitting the forum to the fuss',[50] as Professor Sander suggests in one of his articles, is to acknowledge the inherent hybridity, heterogeneity and multiplicity that can overcome each difficult legal or social question. In Lon Fuller's terms, it is acknowledging the pervasiveness of polycentrism.

Coming back to the Negotiation Project, its theoretical posture organizes the educational experience of law students pursuing this specialty. Harvard Law School offers this course as an elective course for first-year law,[51] as well as the now famous and very popular Negotiation Workshop for participants in and outside the law school. The experience this Workshop offers is extremely different from that of other courses in the Law School:

> We're going to be working together intensively and collaboratively ... Assignments for each night have been consolidated in the workbook. Each night you will be asked to reflect on your experiences that day, and to review your thoughts and learning in your journal ... To stimulate and give texture on important topics in the course, we have included several sets of discussion problems ... Each afternoon after class you should turn to the relevant page of the workbook and follow the instructions.[52]

In contrast to other contexts, where grades are given and are considered a crucial part of the learning experience, students are advised not to take the course for a letter grade and to instead choose the pass/fail option.[53] During

---

49 Id., at 1.
50 F. Sander and S. Goldberg, 'Fitting the Forum to the Fuss: A User-Friendly Guide to Selecting an ADR Procedure', in *Dispute Resolution : Negotiation, Mediation, and Other Dispute Resolution Techniques*, 1995 Supplement, 81.
51 Harvard Law School Catalog 1998–1999, 81.
52 *The Workbook*, Negotiation Workshop, Harvard Law School, 1.
53 'We encourage you to elect the pass/fail option. Our desire is to be able to give participants candid and helpful feedback on their performance as negotiators, and encourage them to experiment with different negotiation styles and approaches.' Negotiation Workshop

the 'summer camp'-like experience of the Workshop, the whole team of professors, teachers, and teaching assistants arrive each morning together, whether or not they are scheduled to lecture.[54] Students are encouraged 'to learn a great deal from one another',[55] and a very communal cooperative atmosphere (in contrast to the alienated environment in other courses) is intended to emerge. The Workshop is filled with simulations, role-plays and video taping, where the students are supposed to practice and improve their negotiation skills. The operation of these simulations can be described also in terms of the 'common-sense' discussion above:[56] There is a theory to prove, and some appeal to the ordinary – to the experience that is 'out there' (beyond theory) – is made. This 'experience', which can be also defined as the old pragmatic idea of the 'ordinary', is constructed in scientific laboratory tools in the Negotiation Workshop. The 'actual' experience is built through the simulation in the image of the theory, reinforcing it and educating subjects that will prove it again. In contrast to Jerome Frank's intellectual interest in experience that I describe later when referring to a possible jurisprudential version of negotiation,[57] in negotiation studies nowadays experience is constructed artificially through laboratory methods of simulations, in the image of the 1950s reality principle.

Above all, there is the idea of growth and learning during the Workshop. Students are asked to reflect each day on their experiences, and then to reflect again on each journal entry when the course ends.

> We ask that each of you approach the Workshop with a mind that is open to

---

General Memorandum, Winter 1999, 9 (unpublished, on file with the Program on Negotiation).

[54] In an article written in 1984, Sander describes the pioneers' spirit that still prevails among the ADR people. I think the description can suit the current state of mind of the program as well. 'Those scholars who found themselves working in this newly emerging field ... felt like a lonely band on a pioneering mission. Thanks to some developments ... there is now a wealth of materials, information, and company for those who wish to take this exciting journey. Yet the pioneering spirit prevails. The entire legal system, as well as the law schools, have tended to place a predominant emphasis on adversary court adjudication. The result has been to undervalue the role of accommodative problem solving.' Frank E. Sander, 'Alternative Dispute Resolution in the Law School Curriculum: Opportunities and Obstacles', 34 *J. Legal Educ.* 229, 236 (1984).

[55] Id., at 7.

[56] See also later, regarding Dworkin's idea of 'bare convictions'. The logic of experimental economy seems to also be of the same sort. See Michal Alberstein, 'Negotiating Through Paradoxes: Rationality, Practicality, and Naïve Realism (Or: Enjoy your Biases)', forthcoming in *Studies in Law, Culture and Society* (2000).

[57] See *supra* notes 136–63 and accompanying text.

learning about yourself and about others. We hope that you will welcome surprises.[58] You should view it as an opportunity to engage in ongoing self-examination and personal growth ... You should treat journal writing as something you do for yourself. It will allow you to follow your progress and serve as a useful reference for the future. We urge you not to hold back on thoughts and feelings that you would like to express in your journal ... You are encouraged to 'dig deep' in terms of your reflections about your experiences ...[59]

By asking students to 'dig deep' and by assuming their personal growth and change through the Workshop, the negotiation people refer to what I perceive as their departure from the 1950s pragmatists. They do have a 'private' dimension in this sense, manifested by referring to a psychological background behind the positions. Interests, as described above, are not only needs; they are also 'desires and fears'.[60] The idea is that, behind the competing rules, there are compatible and answerable feelings, some diverse but subjective partisan perceptions, and some manageable identity stories. This insight is strengthened and developed in the recent, advanced product of the Negotiation Workshop, the 'Difficult Conversations' book, recently published.

> Surprisingly, despite what appear to be infinite variations, all difficult conversations share a common structure ...[61] We need to understand what the people involved are thinking and feeling but not saying to each other. In a difficult conversation the real action is below the surface ...[62] In studying hundreds of conversations of every kind we have discovered that there is a structure to the mess ... It turns out that no matter what the subject, our thoughts and feelings fall into the same three categories or 'conversations ...'
>
> 1. The 'What Happened?' conversation. Most difficult conversations involve disagreement about what has happened or what should happen ...
> 2. The Feeling Conversation. Every difficult conversation also asks and questions about feelings. Are my feelings valid? Appropriate? Should I acknowledge or deny them, put them on the table or check them at the door? What do I do about the other person's feelings? What if they are angry or hurt?
> 3. The Identity Conversation. This is the conversation we each have with ourselves about what this situation means to us. We conduct an internal

---

58 Negotiation Workshop General Memorandum, 2.
59 Id., at 4.
60 See at 7, notes 27–9.
61 Id., at 4.
62 Id., at 5. Douglas Stone, Bruce Patton and Sheila Heen, *Difficult Conversations: How to Discuss What Matters Most* (1999).

debate over this means we are competent or incompetent, a good person or bad, worthy of love or unlovable ...[63]

In a difficult conversation, according to the above, 'the real action is below the surface', at the level of the three conversations the authors wish to teach us to handle. The personal growth assumed during the Workshop, as described above, is probably based on the psychological effects of dealing with these conversations. 'Difficult conversations do not just involve feelings; they are at their very core *about* feelings.'[64] But what are the psychological assumptions that are at stake? What is the underlying text of a project which offers a manageable procedure with which to overcome each communication problem? I will try to start answering these questions by briefly referring to each of the conversations.

Regarding the 'What Happened?' Conversation, the assumption is that '... we each have different stories about what is going on in the world'.[65]

> Our stories are built in often unconscious but systematic ways. First, we take information. We experience the world – sights, sounds and feelings. Second, we interpret what we see, hear and feel; we give it all meaning. Then we draw conclusions about what's happening. And at each step, there is an opportunity for different people's stories to diverge.[66]

There is a 'ladder of inference' design near this description and on it are the three steps: our observations, our interpretations, and our conclusions. As participants in difficult conversations, we might each have different information. Even if we all have the same information, we might interpret it differently due to past experience or implicit rules. Our conclusions might also be partisan, reflecting our self-interest. In this text, there is a notion of 'reality', which can be perceived correctly or through a bias in this text, but a closer examination might reveal a circular argument which leaves us only with the constructed idea of reality (which is already contaminated with perceptions).[67] It is long since that reality 'for itself' is hard to be located.

Regarding the 'Feeling' Conversation, the idea is: 'Have your feelings (or they will have you).' The psychological or psychoanalytical perspective,

---

63 Id., at 7.
64 Id., at 13.
65 Id., at 28.
66 Id., at 30.
67 For an elaborate discussion of the inherent problematic in the 'partisan perception' idea and its 'reality' assumption see Alberstein, *Negotiating through Paradoxes, supra* note 56.

which mobilizes the 'new approach' to negotiation studies, assumes that awareness and reflections on feelings and 'inner processes' can enhance our negotiating function.

> There are ways to manage the problem of feeling. Working to get feelings into the conversation is almost always helpful as long as you do so in a purposeful way ... By following a few key guidelines you can greatly increase your chances of getting your feelings into your conversations and into your relationships in ways that are healthy, meaningful and satisfying: first, you need to sort out just what your feelings are; second, you need to negotiate with your feelings; and third, you need to share your actual feelings, not attributions or judgments about the other person.[68]

Feelings are depicted here as 'a problem' we can manage 'in a purposeful way'. We should negotiate with them and not treat them as gospel.[69] An equivalent account of feelings is given from the psychoanalytic perspective in Melissa Nelken's article 'Negotiation and Psychoanalysis: If I'd Wanted to Learn About Feelings, I Wouldn't Have Gone to Law School':[70] 'Most people find that their increased understanding of what goes on in *them* during a negotiation has tangible benefits in terms of the results they achieve.'[71]

The feelings are 'the inside':

> Psychoanalysis focuses on mental processes that are unconscious: the wishes, fears, beliefs, and defenses that motivate our actions without our being aware of them. It asserts that our conscious stance in the world results from a complex internal process, going back to earlier childhood that involves compromises among conflicting feelings. The value of the analytic process for the individual lies in a growing capacity for self-observation and the concomitant ability to make choices about behaviors that had previously seemed immutable.[72]

In this view of psychoanalysis, by digging into past events and into internal processes, an orthopedic[73] growth of the ego and the negotiator are supposed

---

68 Id., at 90.
69 Id., at 99.
70 Melissa L. Nelken, 'Negotiation and Psychoanalysis: If I'd Wanted to Learn about Feelings, I Wouldn't Have Gone to Law School', 46 *J. Legal. Educ.* 420 (1996).
71 Id., at 428.
72 Id., at 421.
73 I use the expression 'orthopedic of the ego' following Jacque Lacan, who uses it in different places to differentiate his Lacanian post-structural psychoanalysis perspective from the psychological and psychoanalytic discourses he opposes.

to result. The value of the process is a 'growing capacity for self-observation', and it is clear how, in this text, this view of success is the opposite of the legal masculine 'rules talk': 'Law, by contrast, is aggressively rational, linear and goal oriented. Law, many lawyers say, is based on facts, not feelings; it is logical; and success is measured by whether you win or lose in court or by the dollar amount of the settlement.'[74] The lawyer is ironic toward the idea of growth in the feeling conversation, because restraining and taming the feelings in a conceptual structure are what his/her legal-subject position is all about. The professional lawyer operates in a world of logic and rationality, within an assumed body.

Assuming that negotiation studies are today becoming very popular, and remaining in my paradigmatic research object of Harvard Law School, what is the educational message for a student who learns both about the masculinity of law (law as a hermetically closed world where the internal mastering of an assumed body of law is the main target) in regular classes, and about the femininity of negotiation life or 'common sense' in a Workshop? Even if different students explore both sides of the curriculum, what is the pragmatic of this contradicting message; what makes it win? It seems like some years have passed from Duncan Kennedy's 1983 polemics *Legal Education and the Reproduction of Hierarchy*,[75] and the current disciplining tools insert the feminine sensitive approach as part of the official picture. Through manuals, flip-charts and skill exercises, the student receives a counter discourse to the legal one he/she inhabits. This discourse offers a picture quite equivalent to that of the 1950s: of a purposive interaction between individuals pursuing their self-interest in the private ordering realm. The acknowledgement of the feelings dimension for these individuals is the updated term to 'settle in theory', in order to complete the external view of the world outside the law school.[76] The future lawyer absorbs the two genres in their compatibility.

Regarding the 'Identity' Conversation: 'The conversation has the potential to disrupt our sense of who we are in the world, or to highlight what we want

---

74   Id., at 421.
75   Duncan Kennedy, *Legal Education and the Reproduction of Hierarchy: A Polemic against the System* (1983).
76   For another approach to legal education, balancing the emotional with the rational through a feminist perspective, see Carrie Menkel-Meadow, 'Feminist Legal Theory, Critical Legal Studies, and Legal Education, or "The Fem-Crits Go to Law School"', 38 *J. Legal Educ.* 61 (1988). The author compares the CLS critique of legal education with the feminist one, and emphasizes the strong voices of women using their real-world experience in their teaching, undermining the demarcation of the private and public, emotional and rational, objective and subjective.

to be but fear we are not.'[77] We are concerned about the question of whether we are competent, we are good persons, and we are worthy of love.[78] The advice is, in general: 'First, you need to become familiar with those identity issues that are important to you so you can spot them during a conversation. Second, you need to learn to integrate new information into your information in ways that are healthy.'[79]

There is an interesting description here that I think captures the whole 'three conversations' approach of the book in dealing with identities. There is an attitude, which can be generally labeled as anti-foundational or pragmatic, that assumes no need of closure and in general accepts indeterminacy. Still, this framework does not disturb the authors in their collective effort to speak in the name of the constructive agenda of the program (the Negotiation Project in its advanced approach, offered each practitioner coming to Harvard Law School the opportunity to study negotiation). In contrast to views that will depict this genre as 'post-modern', depicting the unifoundational mode as a sign of a contemporary 'post' phenomenon, I posit its organizing text as that of American modernity, the pragmatic philosophical text: hysterical, external, practical, and general.[80] Claiming within a practical discourse seems to enable the negotiation people to preserve this discourse and to make it appealing and popular again. What might have been considered radical and skeptical at the adjudication discourse is used here as a source of learning and growth.

> Once you've identified which aspects of your identity are most important to you or seem most vulnerable, you can begin to complexify your self-image. This means moving away from the false choice between 'I am perfect' and 'I am worthless', and trying to get as clear a picture as you can about what is actually true about you.[81]

What is 'actually true' is beyond yes-and-no questions. This is a more complex perception; it has an open thematic. 'We each exhibit a constellation of qualities, positive and negative, and constantly grapple with how to respond to the complex situation life presents.'[82]

---

77 Id., at 112.
78 Id.
79 Id., at 116.
80 See the discussion in the chapter 'The Maturing of the Pragmatic Idea in Law and Society (Or: The Fall, and the Rise of Philawsophy)'.
81 Id., at 118.
82 Id.

> What, then, is the bottom line …? … the bottom line is that there is no bottom line … Indeed, a self-image that allows for complexity is healthy and robust; it provides a sturdy foundation on which to stand.[83]

In contrast to an image of a self-controlled judge deciding a case by using external criteria, in the negotiation realm we have the image of an individual who has drifted into a difficult conversation, acknowledges his split identities and their indeterminacy, and is surprised by this learning process.

> So it is with difficult conversations. Working through your identity issues is extremely helpful. And still, the conversation will bring its share of surprises, testing your self-image in ways you hadn't counted on. The question is not whether you will get knocked over. You will. The real question is whether you are able to get back on your feet and keep the conversation moving in a productive direction.

The possibility of being 'knocked over' is assumed in this text as a natural moment. The ability to keep the conversation going while being surprised from time to time stands in contrast to the later rigorous journey of the Dworkinian jurist-intellectual. This attitude might have been considered skeptical in the jurisprudential realm, but here we find it as the mainstream constructive approach, which each law student and each lawyer attending the Workshop learns and absorbs.

> The truth is, there is no 'right choice'. There is no way to know in advance how things will really turn out. So don't spend your time looking for the one right answer about what to do. It's not only a useless standard, it's crippling. Instead, hold as your goal to *think clearly* as you take on the task of making a considered choice. That is as good as many of us can do.

The truth of 'no 'right choice'' here stands in contrast to 'there is one right answer' later in Dworkin. In a negotiation, we have to stop looking for an answer, and instead allow ourselves to learn and grow through the interaction. The command to 'think clearly' recalls the old, pragmatic idea of experience overcoming the decision making moment, transcending the choice of criteria and the subject-object distinction.[84] In another current negotiation book written

---

83 Id.
84 '… reason is experimental intelligence, conceived after the pattern of science and used in the creation of social arts; it has something to do. It liberates man from the bondage of the past, due to ignorance and accident hardened into custom. It projects a better future and

by Mnookin, Peppet, and Tulumello, the same 'progressive' spirit takes an equivalent mode:

> The rewards for becoming a collaborative, problem-solving negotiator are manifold. Professionals who have developed the skill and desire to engage in problem-solving negotiations can help make the world a better place as well as lead more satisfying professional lives. That is our belief, and that is why we have written this book.[85]

Mnookin, Peppet, and Tulumello's book continually returns to three basic tensions involved in any negotiation, and the lawyer is supposed to manage them through acquiring the skill of a problem-solving negotiator. These are the tensions between creating and distributing value; the tension between empathy and assertiveness; and the tension between principals and agents. The lawyer negotiator is located, in the fantastic invisible line, somewhere between or outside the distributive and the integrative, the empathic and the assertive, between principal and agent. He or she is 'beyond winning', as the book's title suggests.

The hysteric, progressive, practical mode of this discourse is a combination of classical,[86] common-sense-like and legal pragmatism of the 1950s, inserted also into psychological, economic, and psychoanalytical approaches of today. The hopeful mediating way in which a difficult conversation is handled through such an approach stands in contrast to the restricted way in which a hard case is decided in the ostensibly more intellectual part of the school. The internal wisdom of dealing with law in non-practical terms brings forward a contradicting message regarding how to resolve a problem or a dispute.

4.3 The Integrity Voyage: Dworkin and the Process School

I would like to contrast the 'difficult conversations' approach with Dworkin's

---

assists man in its realization, and its operation is always subject to test in experience. The plans that are formed, the principles that man projects as guides of reconstructive actions are not dogmas. They are hypotheses to be worked out in practice, and to be rejected, corrected and expanded as they fail or succeed in giving our present experience the guidance it requires.' John Dewey, *Reconstruction in Philosophy* (1920), 96.

85 See Mnookin, *supra* note 19, at 2.
86 See the discussion of the discursive chracteristics of general pragmatism in the chapter 'The Maturing of the Pragmatic Idea in Law and Society (Or: the Fall, and the Rise of Philawsophy)', part 1.2.

'Hard Cases' treatment in jurisprudential thought.[87] Dworkin, in my view, takes themes and ideas prevalent in the jurisprudential pragmatic thought of the 1950s, turning them into an 'advanced theoretical approach' by giving them an analytical philosophy and hermeneutic revisions. This sequence has equivalency with the 'advanced negotiation approach' of the 'difficult conversations' people and with the *Getting to Yes* or going *Beyond Winning* approaches described above. These approaches were described as updating the pragmatic style of the 1950s to account for contemporary business studies, and social and cognitive psychology insights. Dworkin does so through more humanistic discourses.

Is the practical, sensitive mediator of the *Difficult Conversations* material the other side of Hercules, the mythological judge decision-maker in *Hard Cases?* Are these two images contradictory? Are they complementary? What allows both these figures to be optimistic and constructive in their realms? My answer will be given again through the intellectual history argument which will reveal their distinct genres of discourse. I describe Dworkin as enacting the mythological script of the living within law, established by the old Holmsian legacy of Oliver Wendell Holmes.

Coming back to the 1950s jurisprudence again, Dworkin himself has an affiliation with the Legal Process school that I would like to explore.

> I shall argue that even when no settled law disposes of the case, one party may nevertheless have a right to win. It remains the judge's duty, even in hard cases, to discover what the rights of the parties are, not to invent new rights retrospectively. I should say at once, however, that it is no part of this theory that any mechanical procedure exists for demonstrating what the rights of the parties are in hard cases. On the contrary, the argument supposes that reasonable lawyers and judges will often disagree about legal rights ...[88]

The point Dworkin tries to make here on the positivist-analytical tradition, manifested mainly by H.L.A. Hart, is that, in contrast to the 'hard cases' image of a place beyond rules, where the judge operates like a legislator and 'invents' law, hard cases are the core example of practicing law and the paradigm for

---

87 Duncan Kennedy takes Ronald Dworkin in his book 'as the paradigm of contemporary responses to the liberal dilemma ... Its virtue lies in that it is canonical, admirably complete, and ... by far the most sensitive of the lot to the internal tensions the project has to overcome – the most legal realist'. Duncan Kennedy, *A Critique of Adjudication* (1977), 119.
88 Ronald Dworkin, *Taking Rights Seriously* (1977) 81.

understanding judicial decision making in general.[89] The non-mechanical way of decision making in hard cases, where no 'settled law' disposes of the case, is characteristic of the whole judicial endeavor, according to Dworkin, and should not be treated as the exception (the penumbra, against the core, in Hart's description). The notion of 'settled law', which Dworkin mentions, rings with the Legal Process dichotomy between 'settled law' and 'the law that is not but ought to be'.[90] This distinction helps the authors overcome the question of the relationship between law and morals, or at least to bring it to some settlement.

> Law and morals come into a different relation when the question is one of altering a previous settlement, or settling a matter previously unsettled. Is it not plain that here an ethic of a different order has an indispensable role to play in assisting the decision-maker in the evaluation of purposes and of the possible means of advancing them? Is it not plain also that in this context a hard and fast line between law and morals cannot be drawn? Questions of the kind which have been suggested pervade these materials ...[91]

Hart and Sacks leave question marks, and an inquiry (I use here the pragmatic notion) that still has not been made.[92] Dworkin's 'solution' seems to proceed from this same point of the 'plain' impression that 'an ethics of a different order has an indispensable role to play in assisting the decision maker'. His theory of adjudication uses the 'impressions' of the participants in the practice of law, and the institutional characteristic of the activity as the validating background for the use of discretion in law. Although he claims a failure of

---

89 See, for example, Marshall Cohen, *Preface* to *Ronald Dworkin and Contemporary Jurisprudemce* (Marshal Cohen, ed., 1984), ix: 'Dworkin has cast much of his legal writing in the form of an attack on legal positivism, in particular on the form of legal positivism expounded in H.L.A. Hart's classic work, The Concept of Law.'
90 Hart and Sacks, *supra* note 15, at 109: 'Insistence on the distinction between law and morals can at times be understood as an expression, in substance, of the principle of institutional settlement. That principle requires that a decision which is the due result of a duly established procedure be accepted whether it is right or wrong – at least for the time being. Thus it seems to call for a distinction between settled law and the law-that-is-not-but-ought-to-be.' See also the chapter 'Settled Law, and the Law-That-Is-Not-But-Ought-To-Be: The Pragmatic Philosophy of Dispute Resolution (Or: Why Couldn't Henry Hart Speak?)', part 2.2.
91 Hart and Sacks, at 110.
92 See also the chapter 'Settled Law, and the Law-That-Is-Not-But-Ought-To-Be: The Pragmatic Philosophy of Dispute Resolution (Or: Why Couldn't Henry Hart Speak?)'.

Hart and Sacks' 'emphasis on tactics'[93] and stresses only their instrumental claim,[94] he actually returns to their idea of process in a different version.

Dworkin projects Hart and Sacks as instrumental, as he projects pragmatism in general, and claims that they avoided the hard question, i.e., what is it to follow a rule? But throughout his critique, he ignores the intellectual climate that surrounded the Legal Process Materials. Writing in the fifties, within an intellectual collective consciousness (very different from Dworkin's time, where the legal academy wore diverse structures of mainstream thought and political margins), Hart and Sacks have addressed the question of following a rule by the pragmatism of their time. As I show elsewhere,[95] Dewey's idea of experience was incorporated into the idea of reasoned elaboration in the Materials, and the whole notion of 'institutional settlement' was part of a process/form trend which took place in many other academic fields. Through the fifties, and by the time Dworkin writes his jurisprudence theory, the classical Deweyan, evolution-based pragmatism disappears from the philosophical and cultural forefront, and a new kind of logical positivism-pragmatism and a general analytical-philosophical perspective emerge instead.[96] Right after it, a new phase of post-modern,

---

93   Dworkin, *supra* note 87, at 4: 'The emphasis on tactics had a more lasting effect within the law schools. Scholars like Myers, McDougal, and Harold Lasswel at Yale, and Lon L. Fuller, Henry Hart, and Albert Sacks at Harvard, though different from one another, all insisted on the importance of regarding the law as an instrument for moving society toward certain legal goals, and they tried to settle questions about the legal process instrumentally, by asking which solutions best advanced these goals.'

94   Dworkin, *supra* note 87, at 6: 'The instrumental branch of post-realism also reframed the question, though in a different way. Hart and Sacks, in their brilliant materials on the legal process, suggested that conceptual questions about rules could be bypassed by putting the issue this way: How should judges reach their decisions in order best to advance the goals of the legal process? But their hope that this would avoid the puzzles about rules was vain, because it proved impossible to state the goal of the legal process without those problems appearing at a later stage.'

95   See the chapter 'Settled Law and the Law-That-Is-Not-But-Ought-To-Be: The Pragmatic Philosophy of Dispute Resolution (Or: Why couldn't Henry Hart Speak?)'.

96   See Robert Hollinger and David Depew, *Pragmatism: From Progressivism to Postmodernism* (1995). The authors differentiate between three phases of pragmatism: classical, positivist and postmodernism.

See at xv: 'In the first period, classical pragmatism became linked to the diffuse social and political movements known as progressivism. This link was formed, on the epistemological side, by what John Dewey called "the influence of Darwinism on philosophy ...". A second phase of American pragmatism began when sophisticated advocates of logical positivism or logical empiricist views about philosophy, scientific method, and social engineering began arriving in American in flight of Nazi tyranny in the late 1930s and early 1940s ... Beginning in the 1960s, a cultural reaction against

more hermeneutic literary pragmatism emerges. Dworkin writes within this new intellectual climate,[97] which is why he fails to see how some ideas that were a 'common-sense' understanding during the 1950s, such as the idea of experience transcending the subject-object split, can no longer cover the problematic in 'following a rule'. His attack on positivism anchors at the institutional perspective of the Legal Process time and, following it, perceives the legal realm as consisting of rules, principles, and policies.

> I want to make a general attack on positivism ... My strategy will be organized around the fact that when lawyers reason or dispute about legal rights and obligations, particularly in those hard cases when our problems with these concepts seem most acute, they make use of standards that do not function as rules, but operate differently as principles, policies, and other sorts of standards. Positivism, I shall argue, is a model of and for a system of rules, and its central notion of a single fundamental test for law forces us to miss the important roles of these standards that are not rules.[98]

Dworkin attacks H.L.A. Hart here in his own terms. If the understanding of what law *is* should proceed from the assumption that it is a language game, a social activity, and should trace the ways it is operated and understood by the participants in the practice, my claim is that the participants' real understanding is that they are not driven only by rules, and that there are principles, policies, and other kind of standards in the picture. This picture, which Dworkin presents throughout his writing as universal, is actually the

---

fetishized scientific and technocratic worldviews, and new attraction to aestheticizing, expressive, and participatory conceptions of the lifeworld, began to take shape ... This cultural shift stimulated and was in turn intensified by a widespread revolt against positivist philosophy of science by students of many disciplines ... Pragmatism began to disentangle itself from positivism, scienticism, and technologism, and to link itself with the humanities.'

[97] For a detailed account of the similarities between Dworkin's jurisprudence and the process approach, see Vincent A. Wellman, 'Dworkin and the Legal Process Tradition: The Legacy of Hart and Sacks', 29 *Ariz. L. Rev.* 413 (1987). I find Wellman's approach too analytic and thus avoiding the intellectual abyss that exists between the Legal Process and Dworkin, turning the former to neglected and 'theoretically undeveloped' and the latter to the current canon of jurisprudence. See, for example page 414, n8: 'This article, however, does not make any claims about a possible causal connection between Hart and Sacks' manuscript and the genesis of Dworkin's views. While the historical link between them is an interesting topic, the purpose of this essay is to articulate the conceptual similarities between their respective views'. See also a discussion of this article in the chapter 'Settled Law and the Law-That-Is-Not-But-Ought-To-Be: The Pragmatic Philosophy of Dispute Resolution (Or: Why Couldn't Henry Hart Speak?)'.

[98] Dworkin, *supra* note 87, at 22.

American Legal Process understanding of law and not a result of any empirical study; inversely, it is *a priori* truth. His 'general theory' of law is based on some 'common-sense' understanding of the local (large) community he occupies, an understanding that is a result of a contingent, specific way in which American legal thought has questioned itself from the end of the nineteenth century until his time. Dworkin adopts a Legal Process framework.[99]

Dworkin's process emphasis is sharpened when he develops the idea of 'law as integrity' in his 'Law's Empire':

> Law as integrity denies that statements of law are either the background-looking factual reports of conventionalism or the forward-looking instrumental programs of legal pragmatism. It insists that legal claims are interpretive judgments and therefore combine backward-and forward-looking elements; they interpret contemporary legal practice seen as an unfolding political narrative. So law as integrity rejects as unhelpful the ancient question whether judges find or invent law; we understand legal reasoning, it suggests, only by seeing the sense in which they do both and neither.[100]

The fantasy of finding this Archimedean point, this balanced position which does 'both and neither', the invisible line between past and future, the backward-looking and forward-looking at once, are part of Dworkin's building his writing as a mainstream position. A strong emphasis in this endeavor is his exclusion of each opposition that does not share his interpretive conviction. The external skeptic is unable to defy, according to Dworkin, the interpretive quest of Hercules, because he speaks in the name of metaphysics, which Hercules does not assume. 'Hercules might agree never to use the nearly redundant words "objective" or "really" to decorate his judgments', says Dworkin, 'which have the same meaning for him without these words'.[101]

---

99 See William N. Eskridge, Jr and Gary Peller, 'The New Public Law Movement: Moderation as a Postmodern Cultural Form', 89 *Mich L. Rev.* 707, 731 (1990): 'There are some striking similarities between the legal process synthesis of the 1950s and Ronald Dworkin's theory of "law as integrity", which posits a judge interpreting a statute, the constitution, or a common law decision has a duty to render an interpretation that best fits the text and overall principles of law. Dworkin's theory relies on the legal process distinction between "policies" and "principles" and on the importance of coherence arguments in law'. See also Eskridge and Frickey's introduction to Hart and Sacks, *supra* note, xvii: 'Ronald Dworkin's *Taking Rights Seriously* followed Hart and Sacks' distinction between principles and policies, and accepted Whechsler and Bickel's position that constitutional activism must be justified by principles that are something more than policy judgments.'
100 Ronald Dworkin, *Law's Empire* (1986), 225.
101 Id., at 267.

For me, it recalls 'the bottom line is that there is no bottom line' of the 'difficult conversations' people above. The literary image, which the decision making in law now wears, allows the interpretive judge to develop a new kind of pragmatics, no longer classical and inherently progressive, but more complex and analytical. In contrast to a position that depicts Dworkin as exploring 'the classic legal process themes through a more systematic analytical philosophy',[102] I would claim that the interpretive turn Dworkin adopts is a collaboration with disciplines that were not accessible as a theoretical foundation to the legal scholar. The literary and the political-scientific are entering law through his writing and inserted into a familiar pragmatic structure. From there on, and through other intellectual developments,[103] the theoretical legal discourse wears different colors.[104] It is no more ahistorical and it does not adopt the scientific paradigm as its foundation. Some may call this shift 'the linguistic turn', and posit it as the idea that 'meaning is constituted in and through language',[105] but without essentializing this transition as carrying a concrete 'meta theory', I would like to stress that it is here where the rupture can be located. Still, within this perception (and perhaps due to it), within this 'soft', interpretive framework, there is one right answer.

> Judges who accept the interpretive ideal of integrity decide hard cases by trying to find, in some coherent set of principles about people's rights and duties, the best constructive interpretation of the political structure and legal doctrine of their community. They try to make that complex structure and record the best

---

[102] Eskridge and Peller, *supra* note at 731.

[103] I discuss the proliferation of schools and the politicization of legal theory in the chapter 'Taking Sides: Margins and Phases of Pragmatics of 'Legal Process' Disciples (Or: The Pragmatists That We Are)'.

[104] See, for example, James T. Koppenberg, 'Pragmatism: An Old Name for Some New Ways of Thinking?', in *The Revival of Pragmatism* (Morris Dickstein, ed., 1998), 83: 'When David A. Hollinger recounted the career of pragmatism in the *Journal of American History* in 1980, he noted that pragmatism had all but vanished from American historiography during the previous three decades. In 1950, Hollinger recalled, Henry Still Commager had proclaimed pragmatism "almost the official philosophy of America"; by 1980, in Hollinger's judgment, commentators on American culture had learned to get along just fine without it.'

[105] For an example of a discussion of this phenomenon, see William W. Fisher III, 'Text and Contexts: The Application of American Legal History of the Methodologies of Intellectual History', 49 *Stan L. Rev.* 1065, 1066–7 (1997). Fisher discusses 'modern American intellectual history', but his discussion applies to the general discursive phenomenon which I try to articulate here.

these can be. It is analytically useful to distinguish different dimensions or aspects of any working theory. It will include convictions about both fit and justification. Convictions about fit will provide a rough threshold requirement that an interpretation of some part of the law must meet if it is to be eligible at all ... Hard cases arise, for any judge, when his threshold test does not discriminate between two or more interpretations of some statute or line of cases. Then he must choose between eligible interpretations by asking which shows the community's structure of institutions and decisions – its public standards as a whole – in a better light from the standpoint of political morality.[106]

While basically accepting the idea of 'no bottom line' when answering the external skeptic, Hercules judges can pursue 'the best constructive interpretation of the political structure and legal doctrine of their community'. Their 'working theory' has the dimension of 'fit' and 'justification', and in hard cases they use their convictions 'by asking which shows the community's structure of institutions and decisions – its public standards as a whole – in a better light from the standpoint of political morality'. Operating in this bounded context of the law, their choices are made in name of literary motives of interpretation and of showing 'how law is like literature'. Their 'working theory', nevertheless, is the pragmatism of law.

There is a deep belief that this process overcoming value judgments, and the non-instrumental pathos here goes together with pragmatism's original emphasis on indulging in the generalities, of experiencing without a fixed aim.[107] I find it as re-enacting, in contemporary terms, the Holmsian idea of the life of the law.[108]

I find that Dworkin's reflections on his own epistemological background serve my conclusion above. In some places, he describes his approach as a 'common-sense' understanding: 'It would be silly ever to announce if it had not been denied by so many legal philosophers.'[109] 'Ordinary lawyers practicing their profession think that some judicial opinions really get the law

---

106 Id., at 255-6.
107 See Dewey, *supra* note 50, at 180–81: 'Upon the whole, utilitarianism has marked the best in the transition from the classic theory of ends and goods to that which is now possible ... But ...it never questioned the idea of a fixed, final and supreme end. It only questioned the current notions as to the nature of this end; and the inserted pleasures in the position of the fixed end ... Like every theory that sets up fixed and final aims, in making the end passive and possessive, it made all active operations *mere* tools.'
108 See also the chapter 'The Maturing of the Pragmatic Idea in Law and Society (Or: The Fall, and the Rise of Philawsophy)'.
109 Ronald Dworkin, *Pragmatism, Right Answers, and True Banality* in: *Pragmatism in Law and Society* (1991), 359.

right or straight and that others do not.'[110] But 'common sense', 'ordinary', and what 'really is' are no more than a cover to some concrete cultural perception, as in the negotiation case. Where he is pressed to trace his political philosophy foundations, within a framework called the 'Dewey lectures', he reaches his bottom line:

> How should we search for truth once we have finally abandoned the unintelligible idea of reasons beyond bare conviction? We should think as hard as we can about what we find important, we should puzzle and ponder, doubt and rethink. But in the end, when we have managed not only conviction but reflective conviction, we should believe what we believe, and act up to and out of it, free from the constraints or apologies of bad philosophy. Is that a quest for a certainty? Yes ... What should we do? Act and think with tact, imagination, purpose and then confidence. Is that what John Dewey really said, after all? Maybe.[111]

Yes, I think this is what Dewey said. I find it similar to the instruction of the negotiation people to 'think clearly', not so different from their 'it is more fun being an optimist then a pessimist'.[112] One of the differences between this 'bottom line' and negotiation's 'bottom line that there is no bottom line' is that, while the negotiation people stop here and make it their motto, for Dworkin it is only the starting point. Conceptually, he proceeds with the description of the substance of his convictions in the name of an imaginary community of 'we'.

> We have a variety of convictions about value, some of which we hold particularly firmly: we think ... that there is simply nothing else to think but what we do think. Of course, having a conviction, even one we cannot resist, does not insure that the conviction is right ... Still, our present convictions are what we presently believe. Some of these convictions claim, as a matter of their content, objective truth. I mean nothing more than they claim to be true independently of anyones' belief or desire that they be true. The cardinal principles of humanism I described, and the conceptions of democracy, equality and liberty that we constructed to enforce these principles, claim objective truth ...[113]

The bottom line is: stick to your common-sense, reflective convictions. There, in your ordinary intuitions, you find the cardinal principles of humanism as Dworkin describes them and the conceptions constructed to enforce them

---

110 Id., at 361.
111 Ronald Dworkin, *Justice for Hedgehogs* (Harvard colloquium draft 2/23/99, unpublished, on file with the author), 36.
112 See *supra* text to note 7.
113 Dworkin, *Justice for Hedgehogs, supra* note 111, at 34.

(democracy, equality, liberty). These convictions 'claim their truth' upon you, and create a variant of the internal motive of the pragmatic search:

> Some goals have an appropriate role to play, a role that assists, rather than corrupts, inquiry, and the goals I mentioned – the goal of finding the best way of living successful life together, or, more generally, of understanding the universe in terms that allow us to live lives appropriate to our understanding of it – are among these. On this view, appropriate *goals supply external motives that do not replace but guide the internal goal of the search for truth*. The two goals function as pairs of equations that must be solved simultaneously: we want to find a truth we can live with and out of, a truth that satisfies both the mind and the narrow bone (my emphasis – M.A.).

In contrast to the 'empiricist creed's' idea, '[t]he inquiring mind must not itself shape what it discovers',[114] which is actually the pragmatic comment on utilitarianism, as described elsewhere,[115] and in answer to the 'larger skeptical attack' that followed it, i.e., 'The American pragmatists',[116] Dworkin returns to his mediating central point of Hercules above,[117] to that fantastic position of looking backward and forward, between past and future. This time, he is between 'mind' and 'narrow bone' in Yeats, between appropriate goals and truth, between the internal and external motives of inquiry. This is part of Dworkin's building himself a literary canon[118] in the judicial realm. But to our debate, what is important is that in a very circular way, the 'common sense' receives content, the content that Dworkin's convictions should guide the pragmatic search from now on.

The pragmatism of Dworkin is different from that of the Legal Process era, more current, sometimes post-modern, though detesting this movement.[119]

---

114 Id., at 32.
115 See the discussion of Dewey's comment on utilitarianism in the chapter 'The Maturing of the Pragmatic Idea in Law and Society (Or: The Fall, and the Rise of Philawsophy)'.
116 Id., at 33.
117 See *supra* text to notes 93–4.
118 Referring to the same literary techniques and to the textual creation of a canon, regarding the writing of chief Justice Ahron Barak in Israel, see Roei Amit (in Hebrew*)* '(Re)construction of a Canon', 21 *Eyunei Mishpat* (1997) 81.
119 'I believe that what Professor Rorty calls the "new" pragmatism has nothing to contribute to legal theory, except to provide yet another way for legal scholars to be busy while actually doing nothing.' 'Pragmatism self-destructs wherever it appears.' Dworkin, *supra* note 108 at 359, 361.
   And in another place: 'That is now the staple core of all the relativism, neo-pragmatism, post-modernism and other examples of the intellectual e-coli bacteria that now plagues

Its mode is more interpretive, less positivistic and naturalistic in its assumption.[120]

> [W]e can understand the metaphors and mysteries, and also account for their appeal, if we take them to express an *interpretive model* of adjudication ... The model distinguishes between the positive law – the law in the books, the law declared in the clear sentences of statutes and past courts decisions – and the full law, which it takes to be the set of principles of political morality that taken together provide the best interpretation of the positive law. It insists on a certain understanding of the idea of interpretation: a set of principles provides the best interpretation of the positive law if it provide the best justification available for the political decisions the positive law announces. It provides the best interpretation, in other words; it shows the positive law in the best possible light.[121]

The 'metaphors and mysteries' of law's quest of itself are given a literary narration in Dworkin, built on a positive framework. Like the Holmsian legacy of law as experience, his theory anchors at the particular elements of the legal body as perceived by the English philosophical tradition of his time. The referral to 'the legal elephant'[122] as the object of contemplation and as a bounded present entity is establishing in contemporary, non-organic terms the place of the internal jurist. This basic script is a repetition and an abstract articulation of the Holmsian idea of the life of the law. In progressive eyes, this is *the first* abstract articulation of this core idea. In other words, the interpretive idea and the image of law as a chain-novel[123] are built into an

---

us'. Dworkin, *supra* note 110 at 33. The scientific *E coli* bacteria image, and the counter image of 'true philosophy' that 'acts up' with no 'constraints' or 'apologies', give a different perspective on the humanism Dworkin promotes. It also fits with the externals' exclusion, described later.

120 Regarding the difference between classical and contemporary pragmatism see also Kloppenberg, 'Pragmatism: An Old Name for Some New Ways of Thinking?', *supra* note 104, at 84. 'First, the early pragmatists emphasized "experience", whereas some contemporary philosophers and critics who have taken "the linguistic turn" are uneasy with that concept. Second, the early pragmatists believed their philosophical ideas had particular ethical and political consequences, whereas some contemporary thinkers who call themselves pragmatists consider it merely a method of analysis.'

121 Ronald Dworkin, 'Law's Ambition for Itself', 71 *VA. L. Rev.* 173 (1985).

122 See the discussion of Thomas Grey's reading of Holmes' pragmatism in the chapter 'The Maturing of the Pragmatic Idea in Law and Society (Or: The Fall, and the Rise of Philawsophy)'.

123 See Ronald Dworkin, 'How Law is Like Literature', in *Taking Rights Seriously*, *supra* note 88.

old, self-perpetuating structure, that of the pragmatism of law.[124]

Dworkin's exclusion of the external skeptic as having 'a metaphysical theory, not an interpretive or moral position',[125] emphasizes his built-in constructiveness, which leaves his theory undefeated internally and a prominent candidate for being considered the current mainstream approach.

> The only skepticism worth anything is skepticism of the internal kind, and this must be earned by arguments of the same contested character as the arguments it opposes ... I shall offer arguments about what makes one interpretation of a social practice better than another, and about what account of law provides the most satisfactory interpretation of that complex and crucial practice.[126]

The internal kind are skeptical of the one who accepts the idea of the life of the law, and is ready to engage in the particular process Dworkin offers him in his 'law as integrity' notion. The idea implies a closed world, where principles and a structured interpretive voyage, as described above, are the given and undisputed context. In such a sequence, whenever a certain choice is disputed as not being the 'one right answer', the challenge can be accepted, and the answer to it will be found through more work, more interpretive elaboration, and more reflection. It does not matter if you object to the method, because, first of all, and before having any external claim, 'you have to do the work'. Any debate will be among the believers in the life of the law and in the Dworkinian method. Whenever an external skeptic tries to challenge Hercules, her/his arguments are irrelevant, are immediately excluded. Hercules does not claim for a metaphysic, and that is how he cannot be defeated. He believes in the life of the context.

---

[124] Richard Rorty supports the same argument by saying that 'It is true that Ronald Dworkin still badmouths pragmatism and insists that there is "one right answer" to hard legal questions. On the other hand, Dworkin says that he does not want to talk about "objectivity" any more. Further, Dworkin's description of "law as integrity" in *Law's Empire* seems to differ only in degree of elaboration from Cardozo's account of "the judge as legislator" in *The Nature Of Judicial Process*. So I find it hard to see what the force of the phrase "one right answer" is supposed to be. Dworkin polemics against legal realism appear no more than an attempt to sound a note of Kantian moral rigorism as he continues to do exactly the sort of thing the legal realist wanted done.'
Richard Rorty, *The Banality of Pragmatism and the Poetry of Justice*, in Pragmatism in Law and Society (Michael Brint and William Weaver, eds, 1991), 89. Dworkin, of course, opposes this view in the same book. See Ronald Dworkin, *Pragmatism, Right Answers, and True Banality*, *supra* note 109, at 359–88.

[125] Dworkin, *supra* note 100, at 79.

[126] Id., at 86.

Dworkin tries to incorporate the social and cultural changes within the intellectual climate of his time and to account for the Warren court activism through creating a constructive theory of adjudication.[127] As part of a generation that resists the 1950s jurisprudence, with its assumed conservativism towards social change, he can no more accept the openness of texts which mediated the external with the internal, the masculine with the feminine.[128] His appeal to external resources is only while preserving the strict commitment of the obsessed Hercules who lives within law. Within this context, through the notion of 'rights' he promotes the progressive political agenda emerging from the interpretive journey.

The political climate of Hercules is another prominent characteristic that differentiates him from the process scholarship and from negotiation studies as well. Dworkin operates within a diverse and political theoretical discourse that has only an imagined, narrow center.[129] Today there is no longer a 'matured collective thought' among theorists of law, and there are actually many competing versions of what is law, and many histories of it. The current, jurisprudential theoretical discourse is characterized by a split, and on Dworkin's side, there are different kinds of pragmatists (left and right),[130]

---

[127] See also Dworkin, *Law's Ambition of Itself, supra* note 121: 'The famous decisions of the "Warren Court" built a jurisprudence of individual constitutional rights against the state; the justices who wrote the famous opinions said these rights were created not by the bare text of the Constitution, nor by the specific, concrete intentions of its "framers", nor by their own fiat, but itself by the constitutional structure itself working itself pure. They relied, that is, on the mysteries latent in the antique metaphors. They have been attacked with the same arguments, and all the fervor and ridicule, that the earlier positivists and Realists used against what they called natural law; but now the attack comes from the right, not the left, of the political spectrum. Today's skeptics are conservatives, not progressive or even liberal.'

[128] The characteristics of general and legal pragmatism, including the opposition of the masculine internal to the feminine external, are dealt with in the chapter 'The Maturing of the Pragmatic Idea in Law and Society (Or: The Fall, and the Rise of Philawsophy)'. The mediation which occurred in the 1950s is dealt in the chapter 'Settled Law and the Law-That-Is-Not-But-Ought-To-Be: The Pragmatic Philosophy of Dispute Resolution (Or: Why Couldn't Henry Hart Speak?)'.

[129] See the discussion of the public law scholarship in part 3.2 in the chapter 'Settlement Aversion: Owen Fiss and the Public Law Scholarship (Or: What Happened to Old Martinelli?)'.

[130] See the chapter 'Taking Sides: Margins and Phases of Pragmatics of 'Legal Process' Disciples (Or: The Pragmatists That We Are)'. See also Brian Z. Tamanaha, *Realistic Socio-Legal Theory: Pragmatism and a Social Theory of Law* (1997), 7. 'The short-term transition in US legal theory is the seemingly overnight convergence upon pragmatic philosophy of many of these competing jurisprudential schools ... Prominent

and other legal theories that do not accept his view. Dworkin is a prominent participant in a very diverse discourse of opinions about the role and the nature of law.[131] Pierre Schlag, in his article 'Normative and Nowhere to Go',[132] calls this discourse 'normative legal thought'. In different ways (which I find convincing though overly 'commercial'), he describes the blooming of 'self-referential instrumentalist rhetorical structures',[133] which do not have any relation to the real 'field of pain and death' (using Cover's terms[134]) of the law.

> 'What should we do? What's the point?' asks normative legal thought. 'If normative legal thought isn't going anywhere, what should we do instead?' 'What do you propose?' 'What's the solution? ...'[135] In fact, normative legal thought is so much in a hurry that it will tell you what to do even though there is not the slightest chance that you might actually be in a position to do it. For instance, when was the last time *you* were in a position to put the difference principle into effect (referring to Rawls' theory), or to restructure the doctrinal corpus of the first amendment? 'In the future, we should ...' When was the last time you were in a position to rule whether judges should become pragmatists, efficiency purveyors, civic republicans, or Hercules surrogates?[136]

Schlag claims that, as legal thinkers become increasingly aware of the fantastic character of normative legal thought, 'the enchantment of normative legal thought weakens and withers'.[137] Schlag takes a postmodern position

---

representatives of the left, centre, and right in US legal theory – of critical legal studies, critical feminism, critical race theory, law and economics, and of the mainstream – scholars who otherwise hold sharply divergent opinions about law, have begun to assert that pragmatism points the way.'

131 See also *Kennedy, Critique Of Adjudication, supra* note 87, at 113–18. Referring to the proliferation of schools and political positions within jurisprudence, Kennedy describes them as responding to 'the liberal dilemma', which is the need to bring together the liberal project of the judiciary since World War II, and the legitimation of the rule of law. I find that Kennedy's linear description of Realist and Legal Process, as sharing the same project as the schools that followed them, misses the 1950s rupture, which makes the ideology debates of the post Legal Process generation distinctly different from the ones before. I discuss this subject in the chapter 'Taking Sides: Margins and Phases of Pragmatics of 'Legal Process' Disciples (Or: The Pragmatists That We Are)'.
132 See Schlag, *supra* note 2.
133 Id., at 186.
134 Id., at 187, and see Robert M. Cover, 'Violence and the Word', 95 *Yale L. J.* 1601 (1986).
135 Id., at 177.
136 Id., at 178–9.
137 Id., at 182.

of acknowledging 'the crash'. From another, more agonizing angle, Brian Tamanaha says that 'the current state of US legal theory consists of what some have called post-modern jurisprudence: a plethora of competing approaches, each representing a particular normative or interest group perspective, each arguing that law should serve the interest they tout. Legal theory has become thoroughly openly politicized.'[138] For me, Schlag's 'nowhere to go' metaphor seems emblematic to the academic discourse, with its proliferation of schools and economy of diversity. It stands in contrast to *Getting to Yes* and to the idea that we can 'negotiate an agreement without giving in'. While Schlag declares the inherent 'postmodern' external inability to be normative and to decide between values (because there is no bottom line), Dworkin agrees and extended an offer for him to be internal and to adopt his interpretive script. Fisher agrees while offering to allow him to give up the pretension of being normative *ex ante*, and concentrate on the dispute to solve, where everything can be mediated and the pie enlarged. The Legal Process people are probably the only real opposition to this skeptic position, because their text offers the mediation of the external and the internal while keeping an optimistic spirit, 1950s style. The Materials, as part of post-war thought, were much more inviting to external views.

> Are the positions that have been taken thus far in these materials conventional and generally accepted? Might a representative chairman of the Republic National Committee, for example, be expected to agree with them? A chairman of the Democratic National Committee? A representative union leader? A representative president of the United States Chamber of Commerce? Of the American Bar Association? A representative member of the Soviet Russian Politburo? A younger professor of anthropology in an American university representative of the most recent trend of thought in this field? Of economics? History? Philosophy? Political Science? Psychology? Sociology? Does it make any difference to a hardheaded practicing lawyer whether the positions are accepted or rejected – or simply ignored?[139]

This 'query' is brought within 'introductory text notes on the nature and function of law', after a 'note on the nature of institutional decisions'. Except for the institutional hypothetical respondents mentioned here, there is the young professor of anthropology, representative of the most recent trend of thought in the field, the psychology professor, and the philosophy professor. There is the obvious question of whether their opinion is important to a 'hard-headed'

---

138 Tamanaha, *supra* note 130, at 7.
139 Hart and Sacks, *supra* note 15, at 113.

practicing lawyer, but there is also the implicit question of whether this hard-headed lawyer is the graduate we are trying to produce. The most important element is that reflections through different perspectives, cultural and not only institutional, are presented as part of dealing with law. There are not 'externals' by definition to the legal discourse. We can find the same pragmatic openness in the writing of Roger Fisher in 1969, when he deals with effective influence in international relationship. At the time, Fisher was still a law professor, teaching international law at Harvard.

> The sociologist, the anthropologist, the cultural historian, the military strategist, and the diplomat each have a contribution to make toward our understanding of international conflict. Each can tell us something, but how can we best put these pieces together?[140]

Fisher's genuine pragmatic belief is that it is possible to bring all the diverse perspectives to bear on one question, through the mediation of law. The solution he gives to the multiplicity of opinions is to find 'a common question, where each has something to contribute to the answer'.[141] Fisher brings the underlying idea as a statement of a natural fact, a common wisdom, although it has a specific history and controversiality.[142] Facts and theories have no objective importance. If they are important, it is because they are important to somebody for some purpose. His 'practical' orientation is taking an already theoretically dead text of general pragmatism, while Dworkin's 'political theory' follows a more updated version of this text. Fisher's next step will be to step out of the legal discourse, into the world of negotiation and business, where mediation and settlement are again the natural answer.

4.4   Legal Histories of Negotiation, and Alternatives

What is the story/history of the emergence of interest in dispute resolution and negotiation during the 1980s? How is the story related to the decline of interest in dispute resolution in the theoretical realm? Where should the

---

140 Roger Fisher, *Effective Influence of Decision in an International Setting* (1969), Harvard Special Collection (with permission of the author).
141 Id.
142 'The most obvious conclusion would seem to be the impotency and the harmfulness of any and every ideal that is proclaimed wholesale, and in the abstract, that is, as something in itself apart from the detailed concrete existences whose, moving possibilities it embodies.' Dewey, *Reconstruction in Philosophy, supra* note 84, at 129.

Dworkin response to the post-war intellectual climate be located against the response of Roger Fisher, an actual pilot during the war, to its perceived reality? As in many places throughout my writing, there is no one right answer, and there are only different stories told from different perspectives. Nevertheless, as part of the epistemological split I discern between the jurisprudential and practical discourse nowadays, the 'official' story is presented by me as suppression. The familial status of the dispute resolution interest in relation to the post-war era jurisprudence, can be probably best described as an 'illegal' offspring. Understanding this status requires more inquiry into some aspects of the difference between the intellectual climate in the 1950s and that of today.

What might a 'legal' offspring of the jurisprudence prior to the 1950s have looked like? Was there a stage before the 1950s collective consciousness mediation between all external and internal voices during which the question of the dispute was asked seriously and believed to be a matter of progressive interest? It seems that there were a few such moments, and one of them was part of the Realists' progressive attack on classical legal thought. Jerome Frank, one of the prophets of that era, was considered an 'enfant terrible',[143] later becoming a judge and a government administrator himself, promoted an educational curriculum that put much more emphasis on clinical experience and the study of the dispute. In his article 'A Plea for Lawyer-Schools',[144] published in *Yale Law Journal* at 1947, he promotes this view through scorning the Harvard emphasis on books and on the study of doctrine.

> When I was at law school I sat next to a Chinese student who had learned his English in Spain. As a consequence, when he took his notes on what the American professors said, he took them in Spanish. On inquiry, I ascertained that he actually thought them in Chinese. University law teaching today is involved in a process not unlike that. It is supposed to teach men what they are to do in court-rooms and law offices. What the student sees is a reflection in a badly made mirror of a reflection in a badly made mirror of what is going on in the work-a-day life of lawyers. Why not smash the mirrors? Why not have the teachers acting as enlightened interpreters of what is thus observed?

The call to 'smash the mirrors' is accompanied in Frank by the description of the 'brilliant neurotic Christopher Columbus Langdell'[145] whose spirit

---

[143] See the discussion of Frank in the chapter 'The Maturing Of the Pragmatic Idea In Law and Society (Or: The Fall, and the Rise of Philawsophy)', part 1.4.
[144] Jerome Frank, 'A Plea for Lawyer Schools', 56 *Yale L. J.* 1303 (1947).
[145] Jerome Frank, *Courts on Trial* (1950) 225.

'choked American legal education'.[146] It is repeated in his book *Courts on Trial*,[147] rendering also a constructive 1949 answer (characterized by 'the basic *Zeitgeist* of a post-fascist democracy'[148]) to his skeptical 1930 *Law and the Modern Mind*.[149] The need to study 'what is going on in the work-a-day life of lawyers' is part of a broader progressive call to brings back law to 'reality'.[150] Still, as I try to show elsewhere,[151] this emphasis in Frank on the dispute is marginalized through today's reading of this movement, due to its deviation from the stronger myth of 'the life of law' (or of the pragmatism of law). At the time Frank writes his article, there is still the theoretical possibility of assimilating law with medicine, thereby to require a clinical education as a major part of the law student experience:

> Is that not a shocking state of affairs? Think of a medical school which would turn out graduates ignorant of how medicine 'should be applied and is applied in daily life'. In this connection it is important to note that, according to Flexner,

---

146 Id., at 227.
147 Id.
148 Neil Daxbury, 'Jerome Frank and the Legacy of Legal Realism', 18 *Jour. Law and Soc.* 175, 185 (1991).
149 Jerome Frank, *Law and the modern Mind* (1930). See also the discussion of this book in the chapter 'The Maturing of the Pragmatic Idea in Law and Society (Or: The Fall, and the Rise of Philawsophy)', Part 1.4.
150 See, for example, an equivalent call already extant in 1907: 'It is the business of the Law School to prepare its students to be good attorneys. The training of the School is directed into this one profession – the practice in law. Its teaching draws mainly from the one great domain of jurisprudence. The principles of law may be illustrated, reinforced, made rich and impressive, by historical allusion, by the treasures of literature, as the teacher illuminates his instruction by subsidies from these outlying fields; but the one thing to be done is to equip the law student so thoroughly that he may act well his part as a lawyer ... In order to accomplish the fine result of turning out good lawyers the teachers of law must have a clear view of the characteristics of their own age – its conditions in business, in politics, in social and civil movements, in legislation, in governmental administration. Adaptation is what makes learning of any kind effective at given time or place. Dogma, whether in the realm of theology, medicine, or law, that is not vitalized from age to age that it is made adaptable to the immediate interests and life of men, becomes effete and useless. Theoretic or speculative learning may be ever so elaborately set forth, but unless the erudition is taken out of the domain of theory and applied to the actual conditions in which men are acting and where "things are as they are", it counts little for the man who takes his place in the arena of active life.' W.E. Huntington, 'Laboratory Work in the School of Law', *Bostonia*, vol. 7 (4) 15, 16 (1907).
151 See the chapter 'The Maturing of the Pragmatic Idea in Law and Society; Or: The Fall, and the Rise of Philawsophy'.

in the best equipped medical schools, the student 'makes and sees made through physical examinations, painstaking records, varied and thoroughgoing laboratory tests, at every stage in the study of the patient'.[152]

The 'physical examination' of the law student, as well as his 'laboratory tests' and records taking, are done at the law office. The term 'clinical education' is itself 'in origin an analogy to medical education',[153] and the Flexner report is a 1910 'survey of the conditions in American and Canadian medical schools',[154] signifying the transformation of medical schools into 'factories for the production of well-trained doctors and the pursuit of medical research'.[155] Still, although the progressive pathos in the Flexner report,[156] might be equivalent to the progressive sentiment of Frank, there is something different about law, which the 1921 *Reed Report*,[157] the legal equivalent of the Flexner project, tries to capture:

> [T]he main end of legal education is to qualify students to engage in the professional practice of the law. This is a public function, in a sense that the practice of other professions, such as medicine, is not. Practicing lawyers do not merely render to the community a social service, which the community is interested in having them render well. They are part of the governing mechanism of the state. *Their functions are in a broad sense political*[158] (my emphasis – M.A.).

---

152 Frank, 'A Plea for a Lawyers' School', *supra* note 144, at 1319.
153 H. Packer and T. Ehrlich, *New Directions in Legal Education* 39 (1972).
154 Kenneth M. Lundmerer, *Learning to Heal: The Development of American Medical Education* 4 (1985).
155 Id., at 167: 'To Flexner, only one type of medical school was acceptable: university schools, with large full-time faculties and a vigorous commitment to research. Although the report was not original – everything in it had been said by academically inclined medical educators since the 1870s – it has a galvanizing effect on public sentiment, making the achievement of the ideal much more attainable. In addition, it made a choice among the commenting models of medical education, supporting the most uncompromisingly academic model.'
156 Id., at 5: 'These were the same educational ideas as those associated with the progressive education movement.' And also at 167: 'Modern medical teaching ... involved the same educational concepts as those developed by John Dewey and associated with the progressive education movement. Spokesmen for both the medical and elementary school emphasized the importance of carefully constructing the educational environment so students could learn from their sensory experiences in an individualized fashion.'
157 Alfred Z. Reed, *Training for The Public Profession of The Law* (1921).
158 Id., at 3.

Whatever the function of the word 'political' within this report,[159] and in the text above, it is crucial for the understanding of the disparate unfolding of the progressive impulse in medicine and law. In contrast to the scientific posture in medicine as a social service, which needs skills and direct experimentation,[160] the progressive pragmatic idea of learning from 'sensory experiences in an individualized fashion'[161] conveys an ambiguous message within law. Because if, as the *Reed Report* suggests, practicing lawyers are part of the governing mechanism, their mode of intervention is characterized by constructing the actual field they try to influence. In other words, instead of 'smashing the mirrors' as Jerome Frank suggests, in law there is an endless mirroring production, and within it even the 'laboratory' character of the 'legal hospital' is a matter of perspective. Frank, as legal progressive, offers a humanistic dimension to law, and tries to intellectualize legal practice. Contemporary interveners like Fisher will construct it in a more scientific manner. Frank and Fisher might be considered to be offering two activist versions of dispute resolution. While the first one arises from within the body of law as having a life and political tendencies, the other arrives from the outside, perceiving the legal rules as one source of data within the multi-dimensional external existence

---

159 There is a particular professional struggle around the status of night law schools which stands behind the initiation of the Reed Report and has significance for the consequences of the 'political' quality of law. Keeping the privilege of practicing law from becoming a class monopoly necessitated accessibility of legal studies for people who cannot attend full-time schools. See Jerold S. Auerbach, *Unequal Justice: Lawyers and Social Change in Modern America* 109–13 (1976): 'For nearly a decade lawyers had looked enviously at the medical profession, which succeeded in eliminating schools and restricting professional access at the very moment when the number of law schools and new lawyers was increased ... The Reed report hit the profession with an explosive impact which spread shock waves through the American Bar Association and the Association of American Law Schools. When the storm had subsided, the associations stood arm-in-arm against their common enemy: night law schools and the immigrants who crowded into them.'

160 This construction seems problematic today even in regard to medicine. Even if it is assumed that the scientific paradigm itself has a founded meaning, and not just a performative force to reflect a contemporaneous episteme, as in Foucault's descriptions of *The Birth of The Clinic*, its hegemonic status seems to be not obvious anymore. Though traditional medical education and the clinical operation of doctors are controlled by scientific paradigm, it seems there is much more awareness of the indeterminacy of the professional wisdom it provides. The entering of alternatives and of more flexible modes of treatment and self-determination in medicine prove that the context construction is always a question of time, place, and social background. The 'scientific per se' does not exist, only its functioning within a text: the relation to what is considered the non-scientific, the supplementary, etc.

161 Id.

of the dispute. The clinical programs in today's law schools are the residue of Frank's grand reform offer,[162] but their limited scope and marginal location indicate a prevailing 'theory-practice' line that favors the scientific, business-oriented embrace of the practice – practice as peacemaking.

From another perspective, the opposition between Fisher and Frank, in its non-contemporaneous characteristic, illustrates a sequence which is repeated throughout my work. There is a crisis after the 1950s, which begins earlier in philosophical realms, a response to the horrors of World War II, reflected in a loss of access to reality in humanist theoretical accounts of today. The Frank-style belief in a laboratory that will intellectualize actual problems in a satisfying way is unappealing for a discourse which distrusts science, and which points to the constructive-textual element in each situation.

Coming back to Frank, the educational reform he suggests, equivalent to that recommended by the Flexner report in medicine, carries the following ideas:

1. A considerable proportion of the teachers in any law school should be men with less than five to ten years of varied experience in actual legal practice.
2. The case system, so far as it is retained, should be revised so that it will in truth and fact become a case system and not a mere sham case system. 'The study of cases which will lead to some small measure of real understanding of how suits are won, lost, and decided should be based to a very marked extent on reading and analysis of complete records of cases – beginning with the filing of the first papers, through the trial in the trial court and to and through the upper courts. A few months properly spent on one or two elaborate court records, including the briefs ... will teach a student more than two years spent on going through twenty of the case-books now in use.'[163]
3. Law students should be given the opportunity to see legal operations. Their study of cases, at the very minimum, should be supplemented by

---

162 See Robert L. Doyel, 'The Clinical Lawyer School: Has Jerome Frank Prevailed?', 18 New Eng. L. Rev. 577, 587 (1983). In this article, the author examines the development of clinical programs in the fifty years that have passed since 'A Plea for a Lawyers' School'. He perceives Frank as going 'too far' in his call, but indicates some ways to improve the practical skills of lawyers by using more of his ideas. His 'pragmatic' solution of acknowledging various educational goals of legal education ignores the historical context of Frank's writing with the possible radical disciplining mechanism it could offer at his time.
163 Id., at 1315.

frequent visits, accompanied by law teachers, to both trial and appellate courts.
4. As in medical schools, law schools should develop legal clinics where students can acquire practical skills. The teacher-clinicians would disclose to their student assistants, both in and out of 'office hours', the general aspects of the specific cases with which they dealt. Theory and practice would thus constantly interlace.[164]

Law schools, in Frank's vision, should function as a sort of 'sublimated law office'. The study of cases should leave the library in favor of a close look at the records, the actuality of the arising dispute and its transformations and flips through time. There should be an effort to reflect theoretically on the basic human ordinary manifestations of the dispute in court, and much less interest in theoretical questions that have no bearing on the concrete problem. The singular dimension of the dispute as understood only through a close inspection is accompanied by the theoretical call to include any possible general perspective within this mode of inquiry:

> It would consider 'strictly legal problems' in the light supplied by the other social studies (miscalled 'social sciences') – history, ethics, economics, politics, psychology and anthropology. Mere pre-legal courses in those fields, unconnected with the live materials of human action with which lawyers must cope, have proved a failure. The integration ought to be achieved inside the law schools.[165]

The call seems similar for the previous 'query' within the Legal Process Materials above,[166] where different academic figures, administrators, or ordinary people are supposed to respond to the positions taken before. Still, in contrast to the glorious text of the Materials, which assumes the mediation of the external with the internal and the harmonious debate among these people, Frank assumes that the 'outside' position is never heard 'for itself'. The interdisciplinary settlement has to be done always by the lawyer through the internal incorporation of the theories he or she has absorbed, through the singular dispute. Following this idea, Frank is suspicious of the social sciences in a tone that we can barely find today in dispute resolution studies, at least in law.

---

[164] Id., at 1317. And also: 'The student, with the aid of his teachers, would learn legal rules and doctrines in the exciting context of live cases ... it is like the difference between kissing a girl and reading a treatise on osculation.'
[165] Id., at 1320.
[166] See *supra* text to note 139.

> The so-called 'social sciences approach ...' tends to foster, among law teachers and their students, an indifference, and therefore, an insensitivity to the unique particular features of particular lawsuits. And sensitivity to those uniqueness is imperative, if the trial courts are to do real justice, to avoid cruel callous injustices.[167]

Walter E. Wolkomer in his book *The Passionate Liberal: the Political and Legal Ideas of Jerome Frank*[168] claims that Frank's remedy for this danger of the social sciences was the genesis of the introduction of the humanities into the law schools. 'The humanities produce the capacity in man to obtain what Frank called poetic, moral insights.'[169] Neil Daxbury introduces this move as being aimed to develop 'in the lawyer of the future the ability to identify with the particular feelings of the individuals'.[170]

Frank believed that theory has to be connected with life, and the life that the lawyer should learn is that of the dispute. He thought that educating a professional enlightened student should be the prominent goal. His rejection of the practice-theory distinction as a valid justification for avoiding this mediation of the general and the singular seems relevant today:

> *An interest in the practical should not preclude, on the contrary it should invite, a lively interest in theory. For practices unavoidably blossom into theories, and most theories include practices, good or bad.* Like Mr. Jourdin who was surprised to learn that all his life he'd been talking prose, so those 'practical lawyers' who decry legal theory as frivolous are, despite themselves, legal theorists, legal philosophers. But their philosophies, their theories, are usually inarticulate, so that they delude themselves and surrender in practice to their own unexamined, uncriticized principles[171] (my emphasis – M.A.).

Practical lawyers who 'decry legal theory as frivolous, are, despite themselves, legal theorists'. Frank offers law schools, which function as a human laboratory of experience and of the same pragmatic 'ordinary' at the origin of pragmatism. It is not only the humanist call to acknowledge people's feelings, as in negotiation studies today. It is also, possibly, the effort to intellectualize these feelings (as in *Courts on Trial*), together with 'libidanizing' the theories (as in *Law and the Modern Mind*). It is the inner tension in Frank's

---

167 From Walter E. Volkomer, *The Passionate Liberal: The Political and Legal Ideas of Jerome Frank* (1970), 74.
168 Id.
169 Id., at 74.
170 Daxbury, *supra* note, 148, at 187.
171 Frank, 'A Plea for a Lawyers' School', *supra* note 144, at 1321.

writing between the jurisprudence of therapy and that of despair,[172] and it is the coming back to the Holmsian commandment to endure the obscurities, but not those of the generalities, but of their actual crystallization, in fact, in the state of 'becoming'. In negotiation terms, it is a commitment to describe the game, while acknowledging the fact that it already transforms and transfigures while we describe it.[173] In a generation that no longer believes collectively in the prevalence of science and in the power of the laboratory to generate new social insights, and in an academic institutionalization which tends to 'philawsophy' and political diversity, Frank's call cannot be heard. Although there have been a few efforts to revive his ideas, and although in clinical programs nowadays we can still find a more humanistic emphasis, the intellectual call to deal with the singular as the proper place to mediate the grand theories is not popular today. There are many laws today: the one of the economist, of the critical, the public law scholar, and of many other groups and schools. The law of the dispute within this new mode does not exist, and the interdisciplinarity allowed for today's practitioner is of a limited kind – that of economics and other scientific disciplines. To be a lawyer in a law office today, in contrast to Frank's vision, is to be practical through scientific and not humanistic disciplines.

There is a sociological story behind this disappearance of 'the law of the disputes'. The 1960s saw a huge increase in US law schools enrollments, which had effects in terms of both quality and scope of interest of the students, and in the theoretical content of the academic interest. Mary Ann Glendon describes this shift by pointing to 'the best and brightest' character of the new students, their progressive enthusiastic spirit, and to 'the new faculty' at American elite law schools, a character built on a more interdisciplinary interest and less of a doctrinal focus.[174] The transformation which has emerged,

---

172 See Daxbury, *supra* note 148, at 193: 'When, in 1957, Thurnman Arnold characterized Frank's jurisprudence as the jurisprudence of therapy, he was implicitly responding to an article by Philip Mechem, published in 1936, in which Frank, Llewellyn, and another Yale realist, Edward S. Robinson, were condemned collectively as the "chief contemporary prophets of a hopeless nihilism", namely, "the jurisprudence of despair".' I disagree with Daxbury's suggestion that the pragmatic embrace of the clinical idea demonstrates 'a genuine intolerance for the scholar'. Frank operates in a time where it is still possible to see the practice and theory as going together, in an era where Kronman's lost lawyer is functioning as an intellectual whose professional work as a lawyer goes together with his love of theory.
173 See Michal Alberstein-Davidovitch, *The Dense Negotiation: An Interdisciplinary Offer*, (LLM manuscript, Harvard University).
174 Mary Ann Glendon, *A Nation Under Lawyers: How The Crisis in The Legal Profession is Transforming American Society* (1994), 199–229.

following these changes, has resulted in her view in 'the law school without law', and in a disrespect for the private practice of law as a career choice.

> Professorial disdain or indifference toward the sorts of careers most of their students will follow manifests itself in myriad ways. Few would openly declare, as has Yale's Owen Fiss, that 'law professors are not paid to train lawyers, but to study the law and to teach their students what they happen to discover'.[175]

Within this process, the dispute is forgotten, and I describe this theoretical shift elsewhere while dealing with Owen Fiss in his Yale and public law position.[176] When trying to account for the history of the ADR movement, this process illustrates the sociological background for the theoretical discourse's loss of interest in theorizing the dispute, and for the emergence of a meta-discourse addressing itself to other professors of law and not to future lawyers.[177] The practice of this professional discourse is marked by political diversity, indeterminacy of values, and an overall ironic position of 'normative and nowhere to go' as described above.[178]

Beside the sociological background, there is an epistemological abyss between the pre- and the post-post war interest in dispute resolution. Today's camps of negotiation and jurisprudence are institutionally divided through their incommensurable modes of perceiving and understanding a legal problem. While a negotiation person assumes a scientific instrumental picture, sometimes accompanied by 'organic' or 'natural' components such as emotions, the jusrisprudential paradigmatic professor takes an interpretive

---

175 Id., at 217.
176 See part 3.2 in the chapter 'Taking Sides: Margins and Phases of Pragmatics of Legal Process Disciples (Or: The Pragmatists That We Are)'.
177 Criticism of this phenomenon, and efforts to return to Frank's notion of a law school, are still done today, and they have equivalencies, in my view, to Kronman's nostalgic longing for 'the lost lawyer'. See, for example, Stephen Wizner, 'After the War: Poverty Law in the 1980s: What is a Law School?', 38 *Emory L. J.* 70, 1. (1989): 'Why, then, is there such widespread dissatisfaction with the state of legal education? Law students believe that today's law schools do not prepare them to be lawyers, and program them to aspire, or resign themselves, to narrow and materialistic career opportunities ... Faculty appointments and promotions are based upon the production of legal scholarship that often has only a tengenerial relationship to the work of lawyers and the problems of clients. The public views lawyers – law school graduates – as a necessary evil, at best, and more often as greedy, sleazy technicians who prosper from the problems and misfortunes of others.' It is not that a clinical education is not possible nowadays in my view. It is rather the need to combine the practice emphasis with an updated humanist sophisticated theory that I find so necessary.
178 See *supra* text to notes 124–31.

mode regarding any phenomenon, including science. While the negotiation person perceives the dispute as a singular and private interaction between the parties involved, the intellectual character denies any claim for the existence of a private dimension, per se, of the dispute.[179] It is always the manifestation of some deeper social forces.

The above split explains why a linear, smooth evolutionary historiography of the ADR movement, emerging from the constitutive text of the Legal Process, is not convincing.[180] The fact that *Getting To Yes* repeats the 1950s genre implies more about a subconscious or subtextual influence than about a reflexive link (from Fisher's side). The 'public law' element of the Materials has vanished from this genre. This is also why a description of it as being concerned with progressive ideas cannot be accepted. Such progressive narration is offered by Albert Sacks, one of the 'fathers' of the Legal Process Materials. (Sacks is the secondary partner, compared to the older Henry Hart, and the more famous of the two for their 'failure'.)[181] Sacks, staying loyal to his 'historical figure', cannot step out of his own shoes and acknowledge the abyss between 1950s jurisprudential thought and the generation that followed. Sacks does not acknowledge the inferior academic position of 'the practical' today, nor the particular institutionalization of dispute resolution studies at Harvard Law School, as resulting from the intellectual rupture that occurred in the 1960s. He correctly draws a link between his Materials and the current interest in dispute resolution, but he refers only to the attention in the Materials to a 'mechanism of private ordering, including negotiation, mediation, arbitration, and settlement'.[182] He mentions this course as one of the exceptions to the lack of concern for dispute resolution in the post-war era.[183]

---

179 See also the discussion of the relation between the position of Roberto Unger and that of Richard Posner in the chapter 'Taking Sides: Margins and Phases of Pragmatics of Legal Process Disciples (Or: the Pragmatists That We Are)'.
180 For an equivalent mode of positivist history writing, which remains unconvincing, see Valerie A. Sanchez, 'Towards a History of ADR: The Dispute Processing Continuum in Anglo-Saxon England and Today', 11 *Ohio St. J. disp. Res.* 1 (1996). The author examines documents 'from the period spanning the seventh through eleventh centuries, A.D.' and tries to draw analogies to modern dispute resolution and ADR activity. Her dismissal of the cultural background and the extremely different social environment of the two eras, renders her claims of a new role for law within a multidoor courthouse framework very unconvincing.
181 See the chapter, 'Settled Law and the Law-That-Is-Not-But-Ought-To-Be: The Pragmatic Philosophy of Dispute Resolution (Or: Why Couldn't Henry Hart Speak?)'.
182 Albert Sacks, 'Legal Education and the Changing Role of Lawyers in Dispute Resolution', 34 *Jour. Legal Educ.* (1984) 237, 239.
183 Id., at 238.

He portrays, in my view, an 'alternative' image of the current ADR movement as being mainly concerned with 'the role of lawyers' in society. When he describes academic developments since the 1950s, he perceives them as conditioning the emergence of the ADR movement: 'If these developments had not occurred, the subject of Alternative Dispute Resolution would be nonexistent or unrecognizable.'[184] One of these developments centers around 'the problems created by the explicit recognition during the 1960s and the 1970s that the traditional operation of the legal system would often have a differential impact on groups identified by various characteristics – e.g., race, sex, or poverty'.[185] Touching here upon the most painful problem of the relationship between the 1950s process-collective perception and the Warren court activism, considered the 'public law' problem of the Legal Process school, Sacks sees no reason to revise his linear description.

> One must be careful to avoid the easy assumption that traditional dispute resolution must be wrong and should give way to new approaches. We need, rather, to define the nature of the claim, if any, which flows from differential impact and then consider which legal processes and institutions are most appropriate. The same is true of those claims that, in an earlier period, would have been perceived to be individual and therefore 'private', and are now asserted on behalf of some class or group, in the nature of a 'public action'.[186]

I claim that this is more or less the answer Lon Fuller would have given to Fiss's accusations of his 'dispute resolution' orientation. This is a typical 'pragmatic' dealing with the 'public law problem',[187] but the generation that followed Hart and Sacks could not adopt it. The theoretical progressive interest in dispute resolution was suppressed, and the ADR movement arrived through the back door and from the ground, under the banner of an orientation to the practice. This new focus on the dispute is not concerned with the social dimension of law. When Sacks speaks about the 'increased use of interdisciplinary approaches'[188] contributing to the emergence of the movement, he again fails to see the unity of ADR's interdisciplinary surroundings as emblematizing its intellectual isolation, or at least its distinctiveness. The social sciences that have generally entered negotiation studies are economics, social

---

184 Id., at 240.
185 Id.
186 Id.
187 See part 3.2 in the chapter 'Settlement Aversion: Owen Fiss and the Public Law Discourse (Or: What Happened To Old Martinelli?)'.
188 Sacks, *supra* note 182, at 241.

and cognitive psychology, game theory, and other perspectives that do not include the studies that, in jurisprudence, have contributed to the heat of the debates and to the diversity of schools. The interpretive turn, the literary perspective, the hermeneutic, and the political have not entered ADR.[189] The pragmatism that exists in this realm is from the kind which supports 'communities of inquiry and tested hypotheses in order to solve problems'.[190] Thus, its voice manages to be unified, utterly collective. This does not imply that there are not economical powerful parts and margins in law, nor that there are no humanist and interpretive ideas in some sub-area of negotiation. But, remaining at the paradigm of Harvard Law School, the core and periphery seem to be organized around these distinct interdisciplinarities.

When Sacks describes one of the developments that have brought the dispute resolution interest to a 'critical examination of the legal profession', he seems again to suffer from the 'blind spot' of reporting from the intellectual prism of a different generation. When recounting the new interest of ADR in the role of lawyers, he portrays the movement as being interested in the same public emphasis he described before.[191]

> It was inevitable that some law teachers would turn their attention to a number of critical questions of public concern. To what extent does the indigent – or for that matter the ordinary middle class person – have effective accesses to required legal services? To what extent is an average person who has somewhat gotten into the justice system treated fairly ... More generally, are we able to give a systematic account of what we mean by 'satisfactory' or 'adequate' legal services? Can such an account be given without addressing the role of the lawyer-representative in reforming the law as well as enforcing or invoking it?[192]

---

[189] For a discussion of the lack of interest in contemporary pragmatism in the social sciences, see Alan Wolfe, 'The Missing Pragmatic Revival in American Social Sciences' in *The Revival of Pragmatism, supra* note 104, at 199. The author claims that 'social science, dealing with human beings, has a humanistic dimension and thus ought to be influenced by pragmatism. But social science, because it is obligated to take cognizance of the real world, finds itself with a pragmatism problem. Of the many strengths of pragmatism, realism is not one.'

[190] James T. Koppenberg, 'Pragmatism: An Old Name for Some New Ways of Thinking?', in *The Revival of Pragmatism, supra* note 104, at 83, 84. See the discussion of this brand of pragmatism in relation to the one which is defined 'postmodern' in the chapter 'Taking Sides: Margins and Phases of Pragmatics of Legal Process Disciples (Or: The Pragmatists That We Are)', part 3.3.

[191] See *supra* text to notes 176–8.

[192] Sacks, *supra* note 182, at 242.

Sacks invokes an ideal lawyer, who aims at 'reforming the law', who cares about the indigents, who operates in 'complex interactions of public and private interests'.[193] In principle, perhaps he is right in saying that these issues 'grow directly out of the courses and seminars on alternative dispute resolution'. In a hypothetical, linear intellectual sequence since the 1950s, this might have occurred.[194] Actually, this ideal lawyer might have been the goal of the new critical professors. In the book *How Harvard Rules*,[195] Jamin Raskin claims that 'liberal professors, CLS, and the clinical movement should take the lead in showing law students how desperately their skills and imagination are needed in so many parts of the country to revitalize public institutions and the democratic project'.[196] In various ways, he shows their failure to do so. It is the same failure as the one to revitalize Jerome Frank's clinical law school (the progressive–Realist–CLS man going together with the clinical), as was described above.

In fact, however, the negotiation orientation has a counter image of the lawyer. Using Anthony Kronman's terminology, Sacks has in mind the ideal of the 'lawyer-statesman',[197] combined with the ideal of 'scientific law reform'. The 'lawyer-statesman' is a devoted citizen who cares about the public good, and is prepared to sacrifice his own well-being for that good. He is a paragon of judgment, and has the wisdom and traits of prudence and practical wisdom.[198] Replacing him nowadays, according to Kronman, is the 'scientific law reformer'. He or she is instead concerned with 'the structural arrangement of the legal order as a whole and not the resolution of particular disputes of the sort that lawsuits and other concrete controversies typically involved'.[199] The scientific law reformers proclaim that 'law could be most effectively

---

193 Id.
194 In another way, such a combination occurs in a few places where dispute resolution is taught, but I view these phenomena as marginal when perceived through the theoretical-jurisprudential discourse.
195 B. Raskin, *Laying Down the Law: The Empire Strikes Back* in *How Harvard Rules: Reason in the Service of Empire* (1989).
196 Id., at 358. See also 357: 'What is missing from the CLS is a powerful sense that the rule of law can be a force for good, and therefore that people teaching in and studying at the Law School can participate in a movement for social reconstruction.'
197 Anthony T. Kronman, *The Lost Lawyer: Failing Ideals of the Legal Profession* (1993).
198 Id., at 14–17. I find that Kronman's description of the lawyer-statesman's philosophical foundations imposes an analytical scheme of Kantian and Aristotelian ideas of judgment upon a discourse that does not have these sensitivities. In my view, his two ideals both find expression in the classic pragmatic thought within law. I elaborate this claim in the chapter, 'The Maturing of the Pragmatic Idea in Law and Society (Or: the Fall, and the Rise of Philawsophy)'.
199 Id., at 19.

reformed through the application of certain methodical and rigorous techniques' – that its problem could be solved in a 'scientific' fashion, using mainly social sciences.

I find Henry Hart to be the last representative of these two ideals, combined together in the Legal Process pragmatic writing. The effort to deal with law through all its institutional manifestations, and at the same time to keep sensitivity to the dispute and its singularity through the idea of reasoned elaboration, demonstrates an old pragmatic tension between the grand theory and the embrace of the ordinary. This mediating approach has consequences in terms of Hart's silence and other gestures of his perceived 'failure' to articulate a theory.[200] He was one of the last 'statesman-lawyers', and Kronman nostalgically mourns the disappearance of his kind of people. He tries to preserve the inheritance he believes, which arrives from the generation of Hart and Sacks, and to educate future lawyers in their spirit, but do both Sacks the grandfather and Kronman the father manage to address the new generation's ideals? An overview of the negotiation literature at Harvard indicates that no public or institutional concerns should bother the new lawyer. The emphasis on the 'dispute' changes the focus of lawyers from being interested in the 'public good', as engineers of the social structure, to the role of mere negotiator, no different from business people, civil service scholars, or social psychologists in their functioning. They are not interested in producing norms, nor in the metaphysical question of what is right or wrong. Their assumption is that after a dispute has emerged and the positions are put on the table, a solution will come from reaching another level. Going below or beyond the level of positions is going beyond the law, the legal rules. In that sense, the negotiation people could be considered radical, anti-foundational, leading a revolution in the legal discourse.[201] Turning the legal endeavor into a less

---

200 For the discussion of the discursive mediation within the Legal Process Materials, and of the perceived theoretical failure of Hart and Sacks, see the chapter 'Settled Law and the Law-that-Is-Not-But-Ought-To-Be: The Pragmatic Philosophy of Dispute Resolution (Or: Why Couldn't Henry Hart Speak?)'.

201 For such an interpretation, see Sara Cobb, 'Neutrality as a Discursive Practice', 11 *Studies in Law, Politics and Society*, 69, 71: 'In fact, the stated goal of mediation is to move beyond the "story" and "positions" (to use Fisher and Ury's 1981 perspective), rupturing the relationship between the disputant and their story in the move toward settlement.' Also see Sara Cobb, 'A Narrative Perspective on Mediation', in *New Directions in Mediation* (Joseph P. Folger and Tricia S. Jones, eds, 1994), 48, 51. The author suggests that post-structural approaches to narrative would be useful for 'filling in' the storytelling metaphor in mediation. One reason she gives for this offer is that the ideology of mediation is 'antithetical to the structural approaches to narrative – the distinction between *story*

megalomaniac one that is more sensitive to 'a case', with all its delicately interwoven social stories, could be fascinating. Yet, the negotiation people tell a different, more grounded story. Like the 'scientific law reformer', their context is the social sciences, but instead of behaving like engineers or producing grand social projects, they deal with perceptions, with feelings, and with an inter-subjective framework that assumes war games.[202] They describe reality from the angle of the singular dispute to be solved *ex post* and not through any *ex ante* position. A prominent idea in this literature is that there is an inherent 'prisoner's dilemma' or 'negotiator's dilemma' in any negotiation. Lawyers should be cooperative because this is efficient and enhances their self-interest. They do not have to care about the social good in order to fulfill their new role as 'problem-solvers'.

This mathematical, purely rational though controversial[203] assertion goes

and *discourse*, between events and their representation, if adopted, would lead mediators to look for the "real" story, the one that purports to have the best fit between the telling and the events themselves. However, the focus in mediation is not on accurate representations of real events, for indeed, mediation presumes that there is no *one* true story; rather, the focus in mediation is on the differences/similarities in the representational forms themselves ....'

I find her idea that mediation has not 'one true story' to be compelling and right. Descriptively, however, the negotiation and mediation people do have one true story, as I discuss later; and her views, at least in the meantime, are still marginal.

202 I do not discuss in this paper the paranoiac structure at the core of game theory, or its possible reading through Lacanian psychoanalytical post-structural understandings of the relation of inter-subjectivity. See Jacques Lacan, *The Seminar of Jacques Lacan, Book I: Freud's Papers on Technique* (Jacques Alain Miller, ed., John Forrester trans., 1988) 1975, 224: 'We are at war. I am moving forward over a plain, and I assume myself to be under a gaze lying in wait for me. If I am assuming that, it is not so much that I am afraid of some sign of my enemy, some attack, because as soon as that happens the situation becomes more relaxed and I know who I am dealing with. What matters the most to me is knowing what the other imagines, what the other detects of these intentions of mine, I who am moving forward, because I must screen my movement from him. It is a matter of ruse ... The theory of games, as it is called, is a fundamental method for the study of this relation. Simply because it is a mathematical theory, we are already on the symbolic plane. However you define the field of an intersubjectivity, its analysis always requires certain numbers of numerical givens, which, as such, are symbolic.'

See also Jean-Luc Nancy and Philippe Lacoue-Labarthe, *The Title of the Letter* (Francois Raffoul and David Pettigrew, eds, 1992) 1973, 70: 'Game theory, better said strategy, is an example of this, where one profits from the entirely calculable character of a subject which is strictly reduced to the formula of a matrix of signifying combinations.'

203 'We have, in certain respects, allowed ourselves to be dazzled and seduced by the possibilities of integrative or "win-win" bargaining. That, in turn, has led to a certain amount of overclaiming. The reason, I think, is that if we hold these possibilities in a certain light and squint our eyes just hard enough, they look for all the world like the holy

together with a strong yet soft emphasis on feelings, and with the intense experience of negotiation workshops, which expose students to an atmosphere counter to the usual competitive environment of the Law School.[204] In this respect, Sacks evolutionary description mentions correctly that one of the major academic developments since the 1950s is that today, there is 'greater awareness of psychological and emotional factors'.[205] In a tone no less passionate than that of the public law scholar, the lawyer-statesman, or the social engineer, the negotiation people promote, probably successfully, their vision of the legal profession:[206]

> In our vision of legal problem-solving, lawyers and businesspeople recognize the systems nature of legal negotiations, and can 'think systematically' about how they, as individuals, contribute to the difficult negotiations they are embroiled in. Rather than blame each other or the other side, lawyers and clients focus on what they can do to improve their negotiations without exposing themselves to unacceptable risk of exploitation. And rather than merely complain about the legal process, legal culture, or problems with fees and incentives, they see the ways that the various relationships and inputs in the system of a legal negotiation as a whole can be used as leverage points for change ... It is not a simple story, and there are no magic formulas. *But the results – working to*

---

grail of negotiations. They seem to offer that which we have wanted most to find. *What they seem to offer – though in the end it is only an illusion – is the long sought proof that cooperation, honesty, and good behavior will carry the day not because they will benefit society as a whole, but because they are in everyone's individual and pecuniary self-interest.* But however much we may want "honesty" to be "the best policy" in this strong sense, the discovery of integrative bargaining has not, at least so far, provided that long sought proof' (my emphasis – M.A.). See Gerald B. Wetlaufer, *supra* note 40, at 369.

204 See *supra* text to notes 63–9. Also in the General Memorandum of the Workshop: 'To help facilitate this learning we ask you to offer feedback to your co-negotiators and yourself after each negotiation simulation in the Workshop ... We urge you to be open, honest, and frank, both with other participants and with yourself ... Because we ask you to use the Workshop as an opportunity to experiment with your negotiating style, no weight will be assigned to the specific results you achieve in any of the negotiation exercises ... The Workshop includes participants from outside the Law School and people from many different countries and cultures. We believe this diversity of experience provides many opportunities to learn from and coach each other and we urge you to take full advantage of this.'

205 Sacks, *supra* note 182, at 241.

206 See, for example, HLS Adviser February 25, 1999, Volume 30, Number 24: 'The Harvard Negotiation Law Review and the Harvard Negotiation Research Project are co-sponsoring a major symposium on the role of lawyers as problem solvers, to be held in spring of 2000.'

change the legal profession and the way we do business – are clearly worth the effort[207] (my emphasis – M.A.).

'Legal culture' as mentioned in this paragraph is not some social aspect of the dispute or of its normative content. It is 'the expectations, scripts and roles – often implicit and embedded – by which both lawyers and clients attach meaning and interpret behavior in the legal context'.[208] Taking 'the challenge of legal culture', in the authors' view, is to consider its two central assumptions regarding problem-solving: '... that negotiations are zero-sum and that lawyers must be highly assertive to best meet their clients' interests',[209] and that there are 'ambivalent assumptions that lawyers often have about clients and clients about lawyers'.[210] An equivalent account of culture is given by Rubin and Sander[211] when trying to describe the contribution of culture to negotiating styles. When the description is more general and not specific to lawyers, culture is a 'hook' that makes it easy for one negotiator what he or she sees emanating from that 'different person' seated at the other side of the table.[212] Culture, like labels and stereotypes, enables us 'to reduce cognitive complexity to simple terms'.[213] In order to handle a dispute, we must acknowledge how much it is built on perceptions, to acknowledge our biases and predisposition at the level of the individual. This is a science of the 'real world'.

4.5 Progressive Miscommunication: Two Disciplines of Interdisciplinarity

The incommensurable quality of the interaction between the dispute resolution discourse and that of law is reflected in their repetitive miscommunication and their self-addressing arguments, which encourage reciprocal autism. The progressive critical scholars who attacked the dispute resolution focus and the informalism shift failed to see that it is not that the ADR movement has an implicit regressive ideological motive, nor that it has an anti-formalist agenda. The progressive vision of this practical discourse is to focus on the dispute as

---

207 Mnookin, Peppet, and Tulumello, *supra* note 19, Introduction, 7–8.
208 Id., at 7, 1.
209 Id., at 2.
210 Id.
211 Jeffery Z. Rubin and Frank E.A. Sander, 'Culture, Negotiation and the Eye of the Beholder', *Neg. Jour.* (1991) 249.
212 Id., at 251.
213 Id., at 250.

a 'problem solved' by turning the 'rights' discourse into only one small part of the picture. Professor Sander responds in this spirit to Able's critical description of *The Politics of Informal Justice*,[214] by offering that this writing might be examined against empirical data and provide a basis for an elaborate academic research:

> Similarly some of the recent works critical of the alternatives movement could be used for a searching examination of the impact of non-court processes on the disadvantaged – whether, in the parlance of the critics, these processes constitutes a form of 'second-class justice' and serve to co-opt the poor.[215]

The 'parlance' of the critics is indeed different from that of Sander, and an inquiry into the diverse discourses they inhabit can account for what I define as the 'progressive miscommunication' between the masters of the practice and the artists of the theoretical. When Christine Harrington says that 'the reforms associated with informalism and the ideology itself are found to be closer to an order maintenance style exercising state authority than to matters of social justice',[216] or when Jerold Auerbach claims that 'alternatives prevent the use of courts for redistributive purposes in the interest of equality by consigning the rights of disadvantaged citizens to institutions with minimal power to enforce or protect them',[217] they have in mind a different view than that of Sander of both the rule and the role of law in society. They have in mind a reformist law and an activist legal intervention, which promotes social justice and transforms society. A dispute resolution emphasis is perceived through their eyes as suppressing this progressive mode. But must Sander accept their consciousness or style in order to pursue his constructive, pioneering mission? It seems like he has enough contextual background, enough theoretical support, to put aside their comments, or just to transform them into a more concrete pragmatic inquiry. He might even convincingly

---

214 See Richard Able, *The Politics of Informal Justice* (1982), vol. 1: The American Experience, 4: 'The present legal retrenchment is seen as a reaction to the progressive theories' victories of the 1960s and early 1970s. The state, at the behest of the capital, is seeking to dampen "inflated" expectations, to defuse protest. Law, which had been heavy politicized, must now be "depoliticized" – which actually means that its conservative political content must be hidden.'
215 Frank E.A. Sander, *Alternative Dispute Resolution in the Law School Curriculum*, supra note 54, at 232.
216 Christine B. Harrington, *Shadow Justice: The Ideology and Institutionalization of Alternatives to Court* (1985), 2.
217 Jerold S. Auerbach, *Justice Without Law* (1983), 144.

say that they have diverse partisan perceptions of reality. It is all 'in the eye of the beholder', as one of his articles suggests.[218] In this same spirit, he elegantly avoids confronting Fiss's ideological war 'against settlement' and dispute resolution focus in general,[219] by offering that 'such a thesis might form the core of a seminar devoted to the proper role of courts and their alternatives in our society'.[220]

In an interesting way, a 'Sander' perception of the dispute can go together with a complex Ungerian or Fissian understanding of the social, although in terms of epistemology and meta-text, the Sander approach alludes much more to Posner (or to Putnam)[221] with their 'metaphysics' or epistemology of the world. The 'original text' pragmatism can work here together with the more updated modern one.

Within the dispute, there is some unexplainable element influencing what we 'see', which a negotiation person might call 'construal' or 'bias', while a jurisprudence scholar will name a 'cultural script'. What we 'see' has an inseparable relationship with what we expect to see, taught to see, posit in opposite relation to what we 'do not see', what we 'fantasize'. Sander has no fantasy of a progressive enemy in his discourse, and that is why he can invite a cooperative work with Fiss, who projects Sander's work as dangerous. The undermining of the critique, and the irrelevance of it to the actual work of the practical people, are achieved through the heterogeneity of perceptions, and through the dispute resolution persistence to see a friend even when an enemy can be imagined. This persistence might become nowadays a more subversive mechanism than the old internal theoretical working from within a text.

According to the above discussion, the operation of the 'efficiency', or the 'court crisis solution' stories behind the ADR movement emergence, can be perceived in a complex way. The idea of 'litigation explosion' or 'legal pollution' is usually considered to be the 'cover story' to the ideological, regressive tendencies of the movement. Auerbach says that beneath the description of 'legal explosion' lurks 'a conservative effort to restore courts to the abstemious purity of judicial restraint – and to deter them from further encouraging legal change in the interest of disadvantaged groups'.[222] Abel

---

218 See Sander, *supra* note 211, at 127.
219 See also part 3.2 'Settlement Aversion: Owen Fiss and the Public Law Discourse (Or: What Happened to Old Martinelli?)'.
220 Sander, *supra* note 54, at 232.
221 See the discussion of Unger, Fiss, and Posner in the chapter 'Taking Sides: Margins and Phases of Pragmatics of Legal Process Disciples (Or: The Pragmatists That We Are)'.
222 Auerbach, *supra* note 217, at 121.

asks if the savings that informal alternatives are supposed to create will not benefit only 'those who use the formal courts regularly'[223] and create a system 'worth less' to its users.[224] He goes on to claim that 'reducing court caseloads by creating alternative institutions tends to render courts more attractive to potential litigants, thereby restoring caseloads to their former levels, with the result that the total cost to the state of subsidizing litigation *and* informal alternatives increases significantly'.[225] Galanter, in relation to this concern, proves convincingly that 'respect for the available evidence suggests a more benign reading of our current situation than is found in the discourse that depicts us in a lawsuit crisis'[226] or litigation explosion. Actually, the ADR people do not see themselves as practical and efficiency-oriented, as their critics suggest. They do mention the Pound Conference, which dealt with 'popular dissatisfaction with public overuse of the legal system',[227] as an important moment in their history,[228] but they insist on a more broad and theoretical vision than simply the relief of court dockets.[229] Using sociological and empirical methods when Galanter interprets, the 'litigation explosion' view as resulting from 'the weakness of contemporary legal scholarship and

---

223 Richard L. Abel, 'Conservative Conflict and the Reproduction of Capitalism', 9 *UCLA L. Rev.* (1981) 9, 246.
224 'Not only are they less well endowed with both coercive power and due process guarantees than formal courts, but participants may also invest less of themselves in the process, so little, in fact, they got nothing significant in return.' Id., 246.
225 Id.
226 Marc Galanter, 'The Day After the Litigation Explosion', 46 *Maryland Law Rev.* (1986) 1, 37. See also Marc Galanter, 'Reading the Landscape of Disputes: What We Know and Don't Know (and Think We Know) About Our Allegedly Contentious and Litigious Society', 31 *UCLA Law Rev.* (1983) 4. In this article, Galanter shows how the 1980s' and late 1970s' concern about the legal health of American society is unfounded in reality, where 'contemporary patterns of disputing should be seen as a relatively conservative adaptation to changing conditions, including ... changes in the production of injuries, knowledge about them, education, and so forth'.
227 Galanter, id., at 63. Also see *The Pound Conference: Perspectives on Justice in the Future* (Leo Levin and Russel R. Wheeler, eds, 1976).
228 Stephen B. Goldberg and Frank E.A. Sander, *Dispute Resolution* (2nd edN, 1992) 7: 'At the 1976 Pound Conference, leading jurists and lawyers expressed concern about increased expense and delay for parties in a crowded justice system. A task force resulting from the conference was intrigued with Professor Frank Sander's vision ... The task force recommended public funding for pilot programs using mediation and arbitration ....'
229 Id.: 'While courts and litigators focused on a variety of dispute resolution processes to reduce the courts' and parties' costs, other ADR advocates saw mediation as a means to serve different interests.' See also Sander, *supra* note 48. (Not only efficiency, but raison d'être.)

policy analysis',[230] he fails to see that the elite are attuned to the 'top of the system',[231] accompanied by neglect of the complex structure of the development of disputes, as a result of a practical-theoretical distinction which has its own ideological and historical background. The 'practical' lawyers (Supreme Court Justices, other judges and lawyers who practice in large firms) and not 'the elite' as a whole[232] are concerned with the court crisis, and the ADR movement answers their concern. By wearing the 'practical' costume, they 'do not need' a theory to solve their practical concern. They will probably not read Galanter's article. The theoretical-elite lawyers, on the other hand, indeed are not concerned with disputes and have an undeveloped sociological scholarship. But they have a compelling excuse for this neglect. They are too busy now with public law questions for a discourse that focuses on the legitimacy of the judiciary in general in a modern society. That is why they analyze mainly appellate courts' rhetoric and their colleague-scholars' articles. The split between the discursive genres that the dispute resolution scholars and the theoretical people inhabit is well demonstrated through the three points in time that were the focus of the Pound Conference, where the ADR movement is said to have been established.

> What has come to be known as the 'Pound Revisited Conference' might, from its title, be thought of as commemorative event, a retrospective look at the administration of justice in the United States over the preceding three-quarters of a century. Its themes and substance, however, mark it as clearly prospective in focus. The keynote address, emphasizing 'the need for systematic anticipation' of the demands of the Twenty-First Century, struck a note that carried through the entire conference.[233]

The 'retrospective look' was going back to Roscoe Pound's famous address to the bar in 1906.[234] Pound discussed then 'the causes of popular

---

230 Galanter, *supra* note 226., at 71.
231 Id., at 61.
232 Id.: 'The scholarly foundation of the "litigation explosion" view is the product of a narrow elite of judges (mostly federal), professors and deans at eminent law schools, and practitioners who practice in large firms and deal with big clients about new cases. Because they are attuned to the "top" of the system – to appellate courts, to federal courts, to that small segment of law practice that deals in large cases, and thus to the concern of the large clients – such elites tend to have a limited and spotty grasp of what the bulk of the legal system is really like.'
233 A. Leo Levin, 'Epilogue', in *The Pound Conference, supra* note 214, at 289.
234 See Warren E. Burger, 'Agenda for 2000 A.D – A Need for Systematic Anticipation', in *The Pound Conference*, id., at 23: 'We open this meeting of judges, lawyers and scholars

dissatisfaction with the administration of justice',[235] and under the heading of 'causes lying in the peculiarities of our Anglo-American legal system',[236] he mentions 'the lack of general ideas or legal philosophy, so characteristic of Anglo-American law, which gives us petty tinkering where comprehensive reform is needed'.[237]

> For one thing, it keeps us in the thrall of a fiction. There is a strong aversion to straightforward change in any important legal doctrine. The cry is *interpret it*. But such interpretation is spurious. It is legislation. And to interpret an obnoxious rule out of existence rather than to meet it fairly and squarely by legislation is a fruitful source of confusion. Yet the bar are trained to it as an ancient common law doctrine, and it has a great hold upon the public.[238]

The need to stop tinkering and provide general ideas or legal philosophy is presented in Pound as resisting the common law emphasis on interpretation instead of legislation. But Pound's framework, the need to legislate itself is in the need of giving a theory of law, a comprehensive philosophical narrative, which incorporates general pragmatism. In the Holmsian-Realists-Dworkinian discourse of law that follows him, there is no need of such a theory. The open texture of law, and the need to endlessly interpret it from diverse perspectives, is becoming the philawsophical pathos of contemporary theories of law. Seventy years after Pound's speech, in 1976 and in the same chamber,[239] this need for a comprehensive system of thought is repeated in the Pound Conference. The call is given in the context of solving a practical problem of 'the litigation explosion'. Justice Warren E. Burger, who opens the conference describes Pound's address as a 'map of the territory',[240] and in his speech he

---

> here at the scene of Roscoe Pound's 1906 speech to the American Bar Association in order to remind ourselves of what he said and to underscore the sobering reality that progress is slow and that much remains to be done. On that occasion Pound gave to our profession, and to the country, the first truly comprehensive, critical analysis of American justice and of problems that had accumulated in the first 130 years of our independence.'

235 Roscoe Pound, 'The Causes of Popular Dissatisfaction with the Administration of Justice', in *The Pound Conference, supra* note 214, at 337.
236 Id., at 338.
237 Id., at 343.
238 Id., at 346.
239 See Charles S. House, 'Introduction to the Conference', in *The Pound Conference, supra* note 214, at 17: 'We are here on an historic occasion, not only as part of our participating in our country's bicentennial, but, of course, as you all know, to celebrate the speech of Roscoe Pound in this very chamber 70 years ago. We are here once again to consider the causes of popular dissatisfaction with the administration of justice.'
240 Id., at 25.

considers the administration of justice since its occurrence, as well as the need to answer the demands of the twenty-first century.

> Because the world has experienced more changes in these 70 years than in the preceding 700, we must be prepared to lift our sights even higher than Pound had in mind, for the year 2000 will be on us swiftly ...[241]

> Perhaps what we need now are some imaginative Wright Brothers of the law to invent, and Henry Ford of the law to perfect, new machinery for resolving disputes.[242]

The Wright Brother and Henry Ford of the law indeed came in that conference in the figure of Frank Sander, a professor from Harvard who offered 'to explore alternative ways of resolving disputes outside the courts'.[243] In the time between 1907 until 1970, what was considered the academic interest of a legal scholar with a theoretical pathos (Pound) transformed into the academic interest of a legal scholar who is interested only in the practice of resolving disputes (Sander). The social engineering function is left to the interpretive judge and not to the 'philosophical' legislature as Pound wanted, but this Hercules judge is inherently bounded in a context of indeterminate principles and rules. This American judge of the theoretical jurisprudential discourse is not interested in resolving the dispute or in the problem of 'the litigation explosion'. She/he is committed to the internal voyage of playing with the generalities from within. The judge of the ADR scholar, on the contrary, is interested only in resolving and engineering the dispute, but he/she ignores the philosophical-interpretive quality of law all together. The soon-arriving twenty first century, which was the horizon of the 1976 conference, inherits a developed and institutionalized system of alternatives, that has become, to some extent, the system itself (a field of 'dispute resolution' and not just 'alternatives'). In many places, there is today, a multiplicity of procedures offered through the model of a 'multi-door courthouse',[244] and the idea of a

---

241 Id., at 24.
242 Id., at 25.
243 Id., at 89.
244 See *Dispute Resolution*, *supra* note 228, at 432: 'Perhaps the most encompassing mechanism for institutionalizing systematic ADR referral in the public sector is the multi-door courthouse (MDC). The MDC is a multifaceted dispute resolution center that is premised on the notion that there are advantages and disadvantages in any specific case to using one or another dispute resolution process. Hence instead of just one "door" leading to the courtroom, such a comprehensive justice center has many doors through which

peripheral alternative can be switched by the notion of a core of diversified options. Adjudication does not function as the central focus of this discourse[245] in its institutionalized manifestations, and being a practitioner might demand mastering its nuances and not only performing the old role of the lawyer. Within this coming to terms with the 'practical' 1976 problem, a distinct discipline[246] of interdisciplinarity in law has emerged. The social sciences and the scientific pathos are back again through the back door in the discourse of law, and a mode of inquiry that has ceased to appeal in the jurisprudential theoretical realm since the 1950s is re-emerging in this practical sphere.

Putting aside social questions in some important parts of the ADR discourse is, hence, part of a scientific mode and a private-public distinction, both prevalent within law during the 1950s. After these scientific a-historical modes of inquiry were developed in other social sciences,[247] they re-emerged within law through the interest in negotiation and the ADR movement.

---

individuals can get to an appropriate process. Among the doors may be ones labeled "arbitration", "mediation', "mini-trial", "summary jury trial", and "case evaluation" ... The key feature of the multi-door courthouse is the initial procedure: intake screening and referral. Here disputes are analyzed according to various criteria to determine what mechanism or sequence of mechanisms would be appropriate for the resolution of the problem.'

245 As Sander, Goldberg, and Rogers mention in their book *Dispute Resolution*, id. at 243, referring to the academic theoretical impulse: 'There are undoubtedly some judges who still cling to the traditional notion that the sole function of judges is to adjudicate. From time to time their view has found powerful support among academics, as is evident from the article of Professor Owen Fiss ... But the burgeoning caseloads in many courts, particularly urban ones, have created increasing pressure for judges to process more expeditiously their swelling dockets ... Thus for many judges the question is no longer whether to encourage settlement but how best to do so.'

246 I use here the notion of discipline in its Foucauldian sense, i.e., except from being a bounded field of study, it is a disciplining mechanism of a distinct kind of subjects, operating according to the particular grid of incentives and hierarchies, which is different from that of the jurisprudential discourse.

247 This gap between the 'politicized' jurisprudential realm and the scientific, a-historic social science perspective is emphasized in Brian Tamanaha's effort to bring 'realistic socio-legal' theory into law, in order to make it more scientific, against the post-modern threat. 'It will be the only predominantly descriptive, non-normative alternative available among current schools in legal theory, with a critical capacity which plays no favourites among the competing schools of normative legal theory, be they on the left, center, or right.' Tamanaha, *supra* note 130, at 8. I find Tamanaha's projection of the 'post-modern' to be one-sided, and misleading, and accordingly, the 'remarriage' he offers between these two discourses is fantastic. I discuss an equivalent offer of Richard Posner in part 3.3 in the chapter 'Taking Sides: Margins and Phases of Pragmatics of Legal Process Disciples (Or: The Pragmatists That We Are)'.

Coming back to my example of Harvard and its practice-theory demarcation, the Negotiation Project at Harvard Law School represents an image counter to the indeterminacy and relativism in the jurisprudential realm. In the spirit of the 1950s, updated by the surrounding social sciences of the 1990s, new lawyers are taught to negotiate while cooperating, without giving in. The establishment of the mediating position in each discourse is determined by the distinct genre of pragmatism that conditioned it. While the negotiation realm speaks in a collective optimistic voice, in the spirit of the 1950s and in contemporary vocabulary, the jurisprudential realm unifies its diverse voices through a script of the committed legal worker, in his integrity voyage. In the negotiation discourse, we do not find the 'political' margins, but more of a collective consciousness. The a-historical dimension of American social sciences surrounds the writing, and explains this 'scientific' posture.[248] Unlike Dworkin, Mnookin[249] tries neither to prove liberalism nor to ignore capitalism. His texts assume capitalism as a state of nature: the rational and the individualistic lawyer is making deals and negotiating agreements, and he or she is the subject of Mnookin's programs. The problems this lawyer encounters reflect the deviations from what is considered the normal, i.e., scientific, rational decision-making. The social sciences have a distinct apparatus of knowledge to deal with such deviations. The idea of partisan perceptions, of emotions as natural and given, and of cognitive biases supplies the complementary 'irrational' that the lawyer needs to handle.

> We all face a complex world. To make sense of it, we develop perceptions that work as a kind of shorthand, a template that we impose on what would otherwise be a welter of chaotic data.[250]

---

[248] 'History can be used to achieve a critical understanding of historical experience and allow us to change the social structures that shape it. In contrast, the models of the social world that have dominated American social sciences in the twentieth century invite us to look through history to a presumably natural process beneath. Here the social world is composed of individual behaviors responding to natural stimuli, and the capitalist market and modern urban society are understood, in effect, as part of nature. We are led toward quantitative and technocratic manipulation of nature and an idealized liberal vision of American society. As twentieth-century American culture becomes increasingly eroded, it behooves us to look closely at this a-historical strategy.' Dorothy Ross, *The Origins of American Social Science* (1991), xiii-xiv.

[249] I refer from here on to Mnookin as representative of the book's approach, without mentioning the other two authors.

[250] Roger Fisher, Elizabeth Koppelman, and Andrea Kupfer Schneider, *Beyond Machiavelli* (1994), 21.

This is the problem of *partisan perceptions*: the biased selection, storage and recall of information and experience. Sometimes this is called the confirmation bias[251] (my emphasis – M.A.).

Irrationality and emotion often make decision making very difficult. What's more, uncertainty, irrationality, and emotion are inherent facets of legal negotiation, and they often erect barriers to problem-solving.[252]

What would have been considered radical and subversive in the legal realm – the claim that perception of facts is always subjective, that our judgments are full of biases, and that it is all a matter of settling and the way we present a matter – is assumed here nonchalantly as a state of nature, as a problem we can try and then master. The same inversion was described before when dealing with *Difficult Conversations*.

Despite the reactionary flavor that can be ascribed to such a scientific ahistorical position, besides the danger inherent in sending the woman to reflect on her contribution to a harassment situation,[253] beside the reduction in turning interesting discussions into manuals,[254] and good and bad news,[255] there is something attractive about the way the negotiation people invite us to 'negotiate' a difference. Without probing into their intentions, inner motives, or social and cultural characteristics, their idea – that there is always a

---

251 Mnookin, Ch. 8, 14.
252 Id., Chs 8, 9.
253 See *Difficult Conversations, supra* note 62, at 78–9. The authors present a story about Sydney, a woman who was leading a team of engineers on a consulting assignment. They were all men, older than she by fifteen years. One of the team members who was first hostile started telling her how beautiful she was, stood close to her, stroked her hair. 'Initially, like many of us, Sydney fell into a blame frame. She judged Miguel's behavior as inappropriate and felt victimized by it. But along with blame came several doubts. Just as she would get up to tell Miguel his behavior was wrong, Sydney worried that she was overreacting or misinterpreting his actions. Perhaps it was just a cultural difference.' When Sydney learns the lesson of the chapter 'Abandon Blame: Map the Contribution System', she stops blaming Miguel and instead tells him that she might have sent a confusing signal, that he should tell her if there are other things she has done that were ambiguous or that suggested she might be interested in something else. 'Sydney would learn important information about her own impact, and also set the stage for discussion of Miguel's contribution.'
254 See *Difficult Conversations*, 234: 'Road Map to Difficult Conversations'. See also the 'Seven Elements' card distributed to each Workshop participant: 'Negotiation: Define your Goal ... reach an agreement that: Satisfies *interests*; is an elegant, no waste solution among the best of many *options*; is *legitimate* for all – no one feels taken; is better than our *BATNA*; includes *commitments* that are operational and durable; there is effective *communication*; the process helps build the kind of *relationship* we want.'
255 See Mnookin regarding culture, and many other issues in his book.

manageable meta-level behind our positions – captures attention from all over the world (and from all the schools of Harvard), and produces outcomes in the 'real world'.

The activist, impatient tone in which the negotiator is advised above, in Mnookin's text, not to 'complain' about legal process or legal culture and instead to try to be pragmatic and to use what exists as a leverage of action, is emblematic of the legal negotiators at Harvard. 'In this book we have adopted the style of a handbook or how-to manual, to encourage an activist and problem-solving approach among people who like to – or must – think about tough problems.'[256]

> Most university courses and scholarly texts approach international relations from the standpoint of a spectator. They seek to produce an explanatory structure ... If we want knowledge in order to improve the world, than predictability is the wrong standard. We need to turn from what is inevitable to those things we can change.[257]

The standpoint of the spectator is that of academic contemplation, in Roger Fisher's text. The indeterminate quality of thoughtful speculation is an impediment for producing knowledge in order 'to improve the world'. The 'Harvard approach' is supposed to overcome the bar to reality by revitalizing the pragmatic idea in the context of dispute resolution. The authors fully acknowledge their relationship of the legal training of the authors to their prescriptive approach to international conflicts.

> One can study international relations much as one studies law, taking the facts as given but the decision as open. Students of law do not try to guess how a particular judge, with his or her personal idiosyncrasies, would decide the case. Rather they consider how a judge – any judge – in that position and faced with that choice *ought* to decide that case. What would be a sound way for a judge to analyze such a dispute? How would we, as experts, advise a judge faced with that choice to decide? Through such a process we develop our own ability to reach wise decisions.[258]

---

256 Roger Fisher, *Beyond Machiavelli, supra* note 250, at 4. The reference to Machiavelli as a model is made by Fisher already in 1969, *supra* note: 'In trying to understand international affairs it is useful to ask: what is the advice which a wise and up-to-date Machiavelli would give to a modern prince?'
257 Id., at 8–9.
258 Id., at 11–12.

When you study law, the authors tell us, you learn to develop normative arguments. You do not predict the idiosyncratic decision of the judge (and neither do you care about it on the theoretical level, according to them) as a social scientist would do. Instead, you operate your faculty of judgment; evaluate; give expert advice. You have to be purposeful and not reactive. The whole idea of facilitation and cooperative brainstorming is transformed here into a very activist intervention by the peacemaker-lawyer. In contrast to a softer – mediating image of the 'problem-solving' approach as hostile to legal rules and focused on cooperation and mutual understanding,[259] there is much more choice and more positioning[260] in the way the actual third party (or the imaginary one each negotiator tries to play) is supposed to act. His action is aimed at a state of 'becoming', in philosophical terms, where no previous theory can determine the outcome.

This is one of the nuances that the legal perspective gives to negotiation studies. The law student who learned the indeterminacy of legal argument is called upon by the Negotiation Project to be determinate and to 'ask a different question'.[261] Unlike Unger who gives up on the idea to work from within, Roger Fisher perceives the possibility of working from within and without at once, being just as valid and appealing as it was in the 1950s. Under the banner of 'dispute resolution' or 'brainstorming', we can advance, just as judges once did, with the notion of 'reasoned elaboration', a solution that will bring harmony and settlement. We can find 'neutral principles' again through the singular dispute. The pragmatic progressive spirit of the 1950s has been

---

[259] Carry Menkel-Meadow, 'Toward Another View of Legal Negotiation: The Structure of Problem Solving', 31 *UCLA L. Rev.* (1984), 794: 'Problem solving is an orientation to negotiation which focuses on finding solutions to the parties' sets of underlying needs and objectives'. 797: 'As Carol Gilligan noted in her study of gender differences in moral reasoning, there may be more solutions when one takes account of both parties' needs than when one tries to evaluate the moral hierarchy of whose needs are more deserving ... Whether a focus on the needs of both parties is a particularly female mode of problem-solving is still unknown.'

[260] See also Robert A. Baruch Bush and Joseph P. Folger, *The Promise of Mediation* (1994), 39, criticizing the way the problem-solving approach in mediation has become formalistic and limited: 'Mediators are willing to take strong measures to influence the outcome of a case, based on their own sense of what would be a good solution, and they are willing to do so even if it means challenging and redirecting the parties' own views.'

[261] 'Better questions are not about who is right and who is wrong, or about one-shot solutions, but about the process for dealing with conflicting views about right and wrong, and for dealing with the inevitable changes that lie ahead ... If we are right, the quest for better and better questions is going to be endless.' Id., at 144.

transformed and displaced, but has not disappeared at all; the utopic horizon for the new lawyer is to be a good negotiator.

The same pathos existed in Fisher's writing in 1965. In a preliminary draft of a book he never published, *Enforcing International Law*, Fisher writes:

> Like a lawyer arguing a case, I may sometimes get carried away with the merits of the position being urged. This does not trouble me much. As a firm believer in the adversary system I am convinced that wise decisions are more likely to result from having competing views advanced forcefully than from having everyone play the role of judge.[262]

Fisher does not envision any problematic in the indeterminacy of rules or in taking decisions in case of conflicting principles. His 'common-sense' pragmatism is all over his texts, stated as a condition of nature, and he does not need any justification or quote in order to assume Dewey's scientific inquiry.

> To the extent that the ideas and hypotheses are implausible or inadequate they may stimulate the development of more accurate theories of governmental control. Every political theory is necessarily an approximation.[263]

This common-wisdom pragmatism also enables Fisher to depict the intellectual occupation with questions like following a rule as useless, or sometimes even dangerous. Relating to the Realists' critique, he says: 'The realists went overboard in considering applications to domestic law. They tended to underestimate the extent to which most men and particularly, most judges, are influenced by principle and by rule.'[264] The Realists went to the extreme,[265]

---

[262] Roger Fisher, *Improving Compliance with International Law* (2nd draft, 1969) (unpublished, with permission of the author, on file in Harvard Law School Special Collection) 1–4.

[263] Id.

[264] 'Law and Policy in International Decisions: Urging decision-makers to cut international law to fit their policy undermines the basic policy of having law' (*Science*, 23 February 1962, vol. 135).

[265] Fisher opposes the Realist view of McDougal and the Realist school for overemphasizing the role of policies. He goes against the claim: 'Instead of training lawyers in legal techniques and technicalities', legal education 'must be conscious, efficient and systematic training for policy making'. He also opposes McDougal's views that 'both relevant policies and technical rules are commonly and necessarily formulated in pairs of opposites and ... the appropriate function of such formulations is not to dictate decisions but to guide decision makers to all the factors in a context which could be taken into account in making

and Fisher takes the middle way. He claims that the Realists 'tended to underestimate the extent to which most men and particularly, most judges, are influenced by principle and by rule'. They underestimated 'the value of professing to be bound by rules and of behaving as though bound'.[266] His ideas of 'following a rule' (the same 'hard question' that Hart and Sacks failed to answer, according to Dworkin's argument),[267] seem to recall the organic rationality notion in the Legal Process era – the idea that 'any legal rule reflects a balance, drawing a line between two opposing general principles and saying that each shall be valid only up to the line, and that beyond it, the other shall prevail'.[268]

> In almost every dispute, there are conflicting principles involved. In a lawsuit each side urges that a different principle should be the controlling one. A resolution of the dispute does not necessarily mean that either principle need to be abandoned; it often means that, at this point, a particular accommodation between them has to be worked out, leaving both principles intact.[269]

As in the Legal Process time,[270] but continuing until today in the negotiation intellectual posture, there is a declared openness to viewers from all over the interdisciplinary range.

> One of the major difficulties facing work on conflict resolution lies in relating one bit of wisdom to another. We know that men are affected by their emotions, their fears, their perception of their role, economic considerations, law, politics, religion, idealism, and even by reason. The sociologist, the anthropologist, the cultural historian, the military strategist, and the diplomat each has a contribution to make toward our understanding of international conflict. Each can tell us something, but how can we best put these pieces together?[271]

---

rational decisions'. Fisher says his claim is that 'the deciders are not actually bound by rules and prescriptions, but rather have them at their disposal'. In response to this attitude, which he considers nihilist (p. 3: 'he abandons the premise that rights and duties are governed by rules. To do so is to undercut the very foundations of fairness and order upon which the attainment of his policies depends. To accept his policy-science is all but to ignore the policy of having law').

266 Id. at 2.
267 See *supra* text to notes 124–31.
268 See Hart and Sacks, *supra* note 19, at lxv. For more discussion of the organic rationality notion see the chapter 'Settled Law and the Law-That-Is-Not-But-Ought-To-Be: The Pragmatic Philosophy of Dispute Resolution (Or: Why Couldn't Henry Hart Speak?)'.
269 Roger Fisher, 'Fractionating Conflict', *Daedalus* 920 (1964).
270 See *supra* text to notes 132–3.
271 Roger Fisher, *Effective Influence of Decision in an International Setting* (1969).

The assumption is that we can find 'a common question, where each has something to contribute to the answer'.[272] There is no fear of external critics, and this openness continues in the current attitude of the program on negotiation. Law has a limited role within this framework, important but still limited, and one among many other perspectives.

> Law thus operates as a restraint by making certain courses of action, if illegal, either ineffective or counterproductive. That illegality operates as a restraint is the obverse of the fact that legality may save as a tool.[273]

Legal rules can help in offering one set of criteria to solve a problem, to resolve a dispute, which is always a unique situation calling for reflections from diverse perspectives.

> The danger inherent in big disputes and the difficulty of settling them suggests that, rather then spend our time looking for peaceful ways for resolving big issues, we might better explore the possibility of turning big issues – even issues like Hitler and Communism – into little ones ... Viewed from this perspective, adjudication appears not as a process for settling big conflicts, but rather as one that is valuable because it tends to fragment conflict situations by cutting off and serving up for decision one small issue at a time.[274]

This idea of fractionating, which derives from a dispute-oriented pragmatism, gives prevalence to 'no meta-discourse' and assumes the singularity of each dispute.

> Instead of identifying every issue as a part of a cold war to be dealt with as a single major conflict, it would seem wiser to insist that each issue, whether or not it reflects basic and fundamental differences, be dealt with independently on its merits.[275]

In 1965, Fisher complains that his students do not understand his activist approach.[276]

---

272 Id.
273 Roger Fisher, *International Conflict for Beginners* (1969).
274 Fisher, *supra* note 269, at 921.
275 Id., at 940.
276 See also Roger Fisher, *Improving Compliance with International Law*, *supra* note 262, at 1-1: '*An inquiry for a purpose*: The problem is being examined for a purpose. It is designed to attain a better understanding of what ought to be done. It is possible to examine international affairs from a more detached point of view. Some of the best political scientists

Some Private Hope and Public Irony 319

I find that when I discuss the process by which law affects governments, a typical reaction of a student or friend is, 'I don't think it will work'. Then I reply that I am trying to be practical and that therefore it is irrelevant whether the particular idea 'will work', our misunderstanding becomes almost complete.[277]

The student could not understand this pragmatic mode in the academic context. Fisher gave up the idea of 'enforcing international law' or 'bringing law to bear on governments' through purely academic writing. In 1969, this same idea recurs in Fisher's book *International Conflict for Beginners*,[278] a guide for statesmen, illustrated with cartoons, and having almost no footnotes:

> This approach sharpens facts by confronting them with the cutting edge of choice. I am often told that I spend my time prescribing what decision makers ought to do while true social science is concerned with what decision makers actually do. I flatly reject this view that it is more scientific to adopt the vantage point of a pure spectator rather than a potential actor. For a pure spectator there are no criteria of relevance ... The handbook form excludes nothing, I believe, but rather tries to marshal the facts in a more useful fashion.[279]

The previous idea of an activist mode of decision making while putting aside scientific questions appears here in a how-to-do-it guide. Later it is sold to the student or to the layperson as a best-seller manual for *Getting it Done* or *Getting to Yes*. Fisher's second chapter in the 1969 book *Give them a Yesable Proposition*,[280] in relation to the enforcement of the United States' international demands,[281] has transformed into a cooperate approach of solving disputes.

---

believe that a scholar should be a detached observer, that accuracy of perception comes from not being too closely involved. It is sometimes deemed bad form to corrupt one's analysis with personal notions of what ought to be done. For such a person international affairs are a spectator sport. The commentator produces program notes explaining to the less skilled what is going on and predicting what is likely to happen. He can comment on the difficulties and dilemmas of the day without feeling any duty to explain what any particular official or government ought to do. Like a historian, he can point out significant trends and forces. He can thus impart some meaning to the chaos of facts.'

277 Roger Fisher, Enforcing International Law (preliminary draft, 1965) (unpublished, on file with Harvard Law School Special Collection, with permission of the author) at 1–1.
278 Roger Fisher, *supra* note 273.
279 Id., at xvi.
280 Id., at 15.
281 'Putting our objective in the form of a yes-able proposition makes us think through our position and the ways in which we will want to go about exerting influence. Too often our demand – the decision we desire – is vague simply because our own thinking is vague ... Trying to write out some sample decisions which we would like Cuba or China

The activist prescriptive pathos is still there, questioning from within the neutrality and 'softness' of the approach. In contrast to the academic frustration described above, today's student understands perfectly well this mode of argument, and buys one of millions of copies. In some sense, Fisher has fulfilled his American dream.

In an interesting way, the academic character, which represents the private irony of the post-modern intellectual,[282] is posited at Harvard as walking hand in hand with the self-satisfied, business approach of the negotiation student and future lawyer who aims to 'change the world' with his 'problem-solving' approach.[283] Rorty's idea of public liberal hope suddenly returns through this modest and private window. Wherever this pragmatic couple is going, it's certainly not nowhere.

---

or Algeria or East Germany to make in the next six months or next year is a highly educational exercise. It should make us think about our conduct toward those countries. It tends to make us be realistic, to understand what is in the realm of the possible, and to bring the limitations of their political reality into the calculations of what we would like to have them do.' Id., at 15–16.

[282] See *Rorty, supra* note 2, at 87: 'In the ideal liberal society, the intellectuals would still be ironists, although the non-intellectuals would not. The latter would, however, be commonsensically nominalist and historicist. So they would see themselves through and through, without feeling any particular doubts about the contingencies they happen to be.'

The intellectuals in the Law School seem to represent the 'public' aspect of the school as academic, the law as a normative concept. The commonsensical negotiation people represent the private aspect of law teaching, the business making, and the 'hope to negotiate without giving in'.

[283] See Mnookin, *supra* note 19, at 2.

Chapter 5

From Philawsophy to Dispute-Resolution (Or: Layers of Mediation, and Models of Engagements in Reality)

5.1 Introduction

This short concluding chapter aims to shift the focus of inquiry from the relation between legal theory and negotiation studies within the legal academy, to an internal look at the evolving discipline of dispute-resolution and its intellectual layers. My aim is to provide a narrative in which models of mediation are described as evolving in parallel to the intellectual climate of their time. By presenting mediation studies as being conditioned by time and place, I try to demarcate the lines between developments within the field and other social phenomena. I also try to point to 'the next step', or the next model that might answer current 'burning' disputes, those which involve mainly identity struggles.

In relation to the previous chapters, this one concludes a sequence which traces the evolution of the pragmatic idea within the legal discourse, by aspiring to escape or transcend the internal or autopoetic[1] mode of law towards the 'external' appearance of the field of dispute-resolution. Briefly, and through a very preliminary overview of the field of dispute-resolution I intend to mark what I perceive as a terrain of hope. An elaborate intellectual discourse on dispute-resolution, which might be nurtured and encouraged through academic activities in years to come can strive to transform the internal-external detachment explored in this book. Instead of focusing on the complex relation between philosophy and law, while trying to draw a map of major intellectual transformations within the legal discourse of the twentieth century, the

---

1   By using the notion 'autopoiesis' I refer to the rich European jurisprudence which describes the relation between law and society as conditioned upon a systematic detachment, logical circularity and self-reference within law. See Gunther, Teubner, eds, *Autopoietic Law: A New Approach to Law and Society* (1988). I do not discuss here this approach and its relation to the American legal discourse analysis which is performed throughout this book, and this theoretical synthesis is left for further projects.

following narrative assumes 'from philosophy to dispute-resolution' as its organizing scheme.

The field of dispute-resolution developed in the second half of the twentieth century in response to the major atrocities and horrific wars that occurred during that time, and its development has transformed diplomacy and negotiation from practical studies into a reflexive theoretical field. The gradual development of a meta-discourse which questions the idea of 'resolving a dispute' parallels in a way the sequence in law of questioning the idea of 'following a rule', which is described in various ways in the previous chapters. The emergence of a modern profession dedicated to the question of 'the dispute', and the gathering of lawyers, psychologists, psychoanalysts, social workers and diplomats around the singular spectacle of a dispute, whether it is a major global catastrophe or a local family affair is the subject of this chapter. My aim is to show how the effort to implement basic universal philosophical truths always requires the delicate art of dispute-resolution, and within that effort the legal realm with its internal struggles provides only one perspective which should be imposed on the conflict situation at stake. The legal scholar, the feminist and the law and economic person must listen to the social worker and the therapist, while listening to the parties involved, and the 'truth' of the resolution of a dispute can emerge only through the diversity of their judgments and offers of interpretation.

The shift to dispute-resolution studies and the effort to step away from legal discourse, cannot avoid using again the prism of the insider, that of the dispute-resolution professional, and its own mystique. This new professional identity of the mediator is depicted within my text as the emerging profession of our time, and should be fostered and developed, according to this logic, on both practical and theoretical levels. The mediator is the professional who combines legal with psychological, psychoanalytical, and philosophical knowledge, and who endlessly aspires to work with the difference and not against it. The challenge of this both theoretical and practical endeavor will be described as evolving throughout the intellectual layers accumulated through the following narrative.

My argument can be divided into the following claims:

First, the evolution of the field of dispute-resolution since the Cold War is generally characterized by a discursive transformation from interpretive paranoid schemes of war and of prisoners' dilemma into models of intervention in reality through interpretive schemes of peace and an emphasis on process.

Second, there is a parallel between the appearance of new ideas of dispute-resolution and the development of the feminist movement. Feminism functions within this argument as a form of ongoing cultural criticism and as a mode of discursive intervention which aims to transform and replace the existing social order.

Third, the emergence of the new modern professional identity of the mediator of our time is a product of tension between the lawyer and the therapist, and thus the contemporary model the interpretive one, which is posited as working on this tension, combines theoretical insights of both disciplines.

Fourth, the sequence of intellectual development which is described throughout this chapter includes the incorporation of ideas which are considered 'post-modern', such as 'the death of the subject' or 'language games', in a constructive frame of a mediation model. This incorporation occurs within the model named as 'interpretive'.

Fifth, there is a correspondence between the decline of a 'discourse of rights' within the legal domain and the emergence of an 'identity discourse' as supplementing and substituting it. The development of jurisprudence of dispute-resolution which can be based on interpretive models of mediation will be presented in relation to that phenomenon.

Sixth, in the context of the internal-external dichotomy which recurs in this book, the mediator role calls for a new mystique to guide those internal to the discourse. The new formula can depict the identity conversation and the idea of 'working on the gaps' as the pragmatism of the time (the pragmatism of dispute-resolution) and thus emphasizes the contemporary sequence 'from philosophy to dispute-resolution'.

5.2 The Scientific Model: Mediators as Detached Observers

At a very fundamental level, still constituting the 'mainstream' epistemology of the dispute-resolution field of studies, stands a rational scientific perception of conflict management, which assumes the ability to bridge gaps, eliminate biases and organize contradictory views into a coherent resolution through the spectator position of the dispute-resolution scientists. Disputants, according to this perception, suffer from cognitive and strategic biases and are entrenched within their subjective worldviews. Assuming this extreme incommensurability of the positions involved in a conflict, the mediator's role is to provide a non-biased focal point at which the contradictory perspectives of the parties can converge.

The 'scientific' paradigm is the prevailing mode of interpretation within the academic studies of negotiation and conflict resolution.[2] Here I use the expression 'scheme of interpretation' while already employing the interpretive mode that characterizes my entire reading of the field, and the jurisprudential-legal discourse in the other chapters of this book. This mode is translated into the most contemporary updated model of mediation, one that contains the other layers offered here.[3]

When The Program On Negotiation at Harvard Law School published a canonic book in the field of conflict management in the year 1999, it was entitled 'Barriers to Dispute-Resolution' and it was characterized by the collaboration of scholars from cognitive psychology, social psychology and game theoreticians.[4] The mode of inquiry characterizing their writing can be described in relation to three categories:

First, the *reality* of the dispute is perceived as external to the scientific viewer of it. The scholar in this context is capable of watching, inspecting and intervening in this actual reality. The ideal situation is the undisturbed laboratory environment, and each deviation is interpreted though this measure.

Second, the standpoint of the scholar or the mediator in this context is *external* to the occurrence of the dispute. S/he is a viewer and thus is able to neutralize cultural, cognitive and social gaps without imposing any of her/his own. There is no moral or value judgment which s/he should apply. A failure of a mediation effort within this context is the materialization of the inherent contradictory and extremely subjective character of the conflicting reality, composed of its complementary biases.[5]

Third, considering the fact that the academic discipline of conflict resolution is still evolving, there is extreme *heterogeneity* and diversity among the genres of discourse which constitute this field. In fact, a common language has not yet emerged within this context. The development of this discourse as having bearing on the practical world frequently transformed its leading imported texts into superficial simplifications of wisdom which, in the 'spheres of origin' of it (whether it is psychology, sociology, game theory or law),

---

2   For a textual critical analysis of some of the ideas in the discourse see: Michal Alberstein, 'Negotiating through Paradoxes: Rationality, Practicality and Naïve Realism (Or: Enjoy your Biases)', 22 *Studies in Law, POlitics and Society* 197 (2001).
3   See Part 5.5 later.
4   See Kenneth Arrow et al., *Barriers to Conflict Resolution* (1999).
5   See also the discussion of the negotiation discourse and its contrast to the jurisprudential one in the chapter 'In Search of The Dispute: On Lawyers and Legal Philawsophers at Harvard Law School (Or: Some Private Hope and Public Irony)', parts 4.4 and 4.5.

might have depth and complexity. Becoming part of a discourse which is assumed to lead practitioners and which develops an orientation toward manuals and straightforward bottom lines might affect the whole 'original' quality of the knowledge involved.

5.3 The Pragmatic-legal Model: Mediators as Biased Interveners

In 1981, when Fisher and Ury publish their famous best seller *Getting To Yes*, the occupation with conflicts became 'biased' toward peace for the first time and a practical interest in dispute-resolution could be identified. This can be defined as the formal birth of the field of dispute-resolution as such, after the academic interest was focused mainly on the study of war games and diplomacy. As discussed in the previous chapter, Fisher was interested in moving away from the spectator position and in avoiding the relativistic descriptive mode of the average social scientist of his time. His call has an anti-intellectual mode in the American spirit, but through a discursive perspective. What he calls for is reflection on the antagonistic actual game in order to convert it into a cooperative, efficient business. In other words, the pragmatic legal model provides a meta-discourse on what is required to resolve a dispute and incorporates the state of mind of the biased intervener in favor of mediation as the new 'science of the disputes'. The message of *Getting To Yes* is to take one step back from the biased interaction which the scientific model describes, and impose a biased constructive scheme of interpretation on the dispute in a way that will enable it to produce more gains to both parties, enlarge the pie and channel emotional expressions into constructive tracks, or at least contain them to avoid disturbances. Acknowledging the futility of the competitive game enables the drafting of new rules from a higher level of perception. This is the 'descriptive-prescriptive' attitude which Roger Fisher portrays in the previous chapter, while answering his critics.[6] It assumes the pragmatic lawyer as its operator and preacher. Its relation to the legal discourse is described in the fourth chapter.

In relation to the *reality* of the dispute, the pragmatic model offers the option of not taking it for granted. The possibility of intervening in reality and helping to reshape it into some conciliatory framework makes its existence relevant 'for itself' only in a limited sense. In 'theory', the pragmatic mediator

---

6   See the chapter 'In Search of The Dispute: On Lawyers and Legal Philawsophers at Harvard Law School (Or: some Private Hope and Public Irony)', part 4.5.

might be as 'realistic' as her/his friend operating according to the scientific model. His/her idea of the actual measurability, visibility and the naturalist character of reality may still go together with an effort to transform it while aiming at the future and handling the dispute.

The position of the mediator within this model is *internal* to its happening, trying to intervene in it. This discourse offers a mode of dealing with disputes in an effort to transform it and change reality. It suggests speaking about the game of negotiation and agreeing on changing its rules to the benefit of all; switching from a position game to an interests one is the key art of dispute handling according to this perception.

The pragmatic model is part of a *homogenous* discourse that offers a common sense guide which can work and be taught in any place and time, in any language and attract people of all ages, with no relation to their intelligence or any previous knowledge. As the previous chapter aims to show, the 'collective consciousness' mode characterizes the writing of the originators of this model and their followers at The Program On Negotiation at Harvard Law School.[7] The cultural location of this project is manifest, emerging from Harvard and reflecting American values. Its belief in the possibility of finding neutral objective principles of negotiation goes back to ideas that prevailed in the theoretical public discourse only for a short time during the 1950s.[8]

5.4 The Transformative-psychological Model: Mediators as Process Experts and Therapists

The two previous models belong to a liberal modernist tradition, which can also be defined from a contemporary perspective as 'masculine'. The disputing subjects can be defined according to these models as individuals who are maximizers operating under market conditions to promote their interests and achieve their goals. The scientific model describes their interdependence from an external position, focusing on the inherent complementary biases which constitute their dispute. The pragmatic model tries to intervene and exploit their interdependence by pointing to the benefits and mutual gains which arise from adopting a cooperative attitude. The transformative model assumes, according to my reading, a different style of individuality and goes beyond

---

7 See the chapter 'In Search of The Dispute: On Lawyers and Legal Philawsophers at Harvard Law School (Or: Some Private Hope and Public Irony)', part 4.2.

8 See Herbert Wechsler, 'Toward Neutral Principles of Constitutional Law', 73 *Harv. L. Rev.* 1 (1959).

the liberal market assumptions. It emerged during the 1990s, where a significant landmark was the publication of the book *The Promise of Mediation* by Robert Bush and Joseph Folger.[9] The intellectual and cultural circumstances that gave birth to this model and helped it flourish also relate to contemporaneous feminist ideas, which seem relevant for the understanding of this model's quality and significance. During the same period when *Getting To Yes* was published, the social psychologist Carol Gilligan wrote her book *In a Different Voice*, published in 1982,[10] which became a leading text for a wave of feminism called 'relational' or 'cultural'.[11] In terms of cultural criticism this mode of feminism defied the hegemonic, liberal, masculine logic of individualism and Kantian moral thinking and called for acknowledging the feminine voice as different, by virtue of its carrying another form of logic: Women think in a more pragmatic, non-foundational way; they put relationships and responsibility before rights; they use care and emotion as their primary guide and they prefer flexible, conceptual grids to formal abstract logic. Gilligan's nine year old heroine Amy, who, in the book, tries together with Jack to answer a moral dilemma, originally devised by Kohlberg.[12] The Question is whether or not a man should steal some medication in order to save his dying wife, and when Amy responds to it, she avoids the either-or choice and the analytic metaphysical analysis of Jack. She actually behaves as a natural negotiator. She tries to find mutual interests with the drug seller, to bargain and to brainstorm with him to find a solution. She turns the problem into a cooperative project. In some way Gilligam shows that women are natural negotiators or maybe natural pragmatists or problem-solvers. Her moral lesson is to acknowledge this ethics of care as a valid moral voice, even the highest one. Indeed, in the 1990s relational ideas became the updated promise of moral thought and Bush and Folger adopted this morality in order to revise the old pragmatic model by offering a new one to handle disputes. Gilligan's idea of 'self in relationship' and her primary emphasis on empathy and responsibility became the moral social call behind 'The Promise of

---

9   Robert A. Baruch Bush, *The Promise of Mediation: Responding to Conflict through Empowerment and Recognition* (1994).
10 Carol Gilligan, *In A Different Voice: Psychological Theory and Women's Development* (1982).
11 For the relation between 'The Promise of Mediation' and relational ideals of that time see also Patricia L. Franz, 'Notes & Comment: Habits of a Highly Effective Transformative Mediation Program', 13 *Ohio St. J on Disp. Resol.* 1039 (1998). Franz describes an equivalent relational trend in the realm of management consulting as manifested in Stephen R. Covey, *The 7 Habits of Highly Effective People* (1990).
12 Gilligan, *supra* note 10, at 24–63.

Mediation'.[13] Bush and Folger present this call as universal and true, regardless of gender. It is the 'essence of human moral maturity'[14] and the idea that 'full moral development involves an *integration* of individual autonomy and concern for others, of strength and compassion'.[15]

The basic idea advanced by Bush and Folger is that conflicts are opportunities to learn and grow, and that empowerment and recognition are the most important values to support within a mediation process.

> In this transformative orientation, a conflict is first and foremost a potential occasion for growth in two critical and interrelated dimensions of human morality. The first dimension involves strengthening the self. This occurs through realizing and strengthening one's inherent human capacity for dealing with difficulties of all kinds by engaging in conscious and deliberate reflection, choice and action. The second dimension involves reaching beyond the self to relate to others. This occurs through realizing and strengthening one's inherent human capacity for experiencing and expressing concern and consideration for others, especially others whose situation is 'different' from one's own.[16]

In some sense, this return to the process and to a different notion of transformation is the manifestation of the evolution of the discourse of dispute-resolution, through the more complex thinking about what is involved in resolving a dispute. What was considered new and promising during the eighties, providing the cutting edge of ideology for practitioners and for agents of social change, became old fashioned in some people's eyes during the 1990s, and there were calls to replace its formalism and stagnation by a fresh approach.

> Rethinking the problem-solving orientation starts by questioning the premise that conflicts need to be viewed as problems in the first place. A different premise would suggest that disputes can be viewed *not* as problems at all but as opportunities for moral growth and transformation. This different view is the *transformative orientation* to conflict.[17]

The pragmatic model described above can be explained as responding to the scientific, external position which focuses on the antagonistic and

---

13 See Bush and Folger, *supra* note 9, at 81, 253–9.
14 Id., at 82.
15 Id., at 81.
16 Id., at 81.
17 Id.

subjectivist interaction within a negotiation by emphasizing the mediating mode of a third position, that of the mediator or that of language and the reflective capacity of the negotiator her/himself. The transformative model performs the same gesture upon its brother predecessor and conveys the claim that the emphasis on interests and problem-solving remains embedded in an efficient external state of mind which can help in handling negotiations but does not show the extra value in the reflective capacity and the mediating mode of a third party. This second-order reflection suggests that the efficient interest-based negotiation is only a superficial interpretive scheme to perceive disputes and that in order to reach this problem-solving phase parties need to go through internal transformations which will help them to address one another after facing their inner constructions. According to Bush, mediation can compete with adjudication and offer extra value in order to challenge the traditional 'Owen-Fiss position'[18] towards settlements, only through adopting the transformative ideal.[19]

In relation to the *reality* of the dispute, the transformative approach offers a mediator who is indifferent to it and external. The tacit assumption of the model is that a dispute is a symptom of a conflict between the individuals' perceptions and thus its core existence lies is in the encounter between their inner lives.

The mediator, who is typically a psychologist according to this model, is responsible for handling this inner-perceptions-reconstruction, and thus s/he is *external* to the actual phenomenon of the dispute *and internal* to its analytic psychological organization. The hope is that once the inner antagonism and animosity are solved and empowerment and recognition occur, the negotiation on the actual outcome can be efficient and quick. Nevertheless, the success of the mediation or its actual resolution is meaningless in terms of the evaluation of the mediating process according to the transformative approach, since the main point is the artful handling of the internal worlds of the perceptions involved in it.

The transformative discourse, like the previous pragmatic one, is *homogenous* and straightforward at the level of knowledge which is required to provide actual training for mediation practitioners. It has moral theoretical

---

18   See the chapter 'Taking Sides: Margins and Phases of Pragmatism of Legal Process Disciples (Or: The Ptagmatists that We Are)', part 3.2.
19   See Robert A. Baruch Bush, 'Mediation and Adjudication, Dispute Resolution and Ideology: An Imaginary Conversation' 3 *J. Contemp. Legal Issues* 1 (1989–90). Robert A. Baruch Bush, 'Efficiency and Protection, or Empowerment and Recognition?: The Mediator's Role and Ethical Standards in Mediation' *41 FA L. Rev* 253 (1989).

claims which can compete with the theoretical world of adjudication and it attempts to offer this discourse the most convincing moral challenge, but in fact it focuses on simple ideas which people can adopt or reject while considering their existing practice of mediation.

5.5 The Interpretive Model: Combining Storytelling with Linguistics

In terms of the previous models, this one returns to an academic mode of analysis which has not materialized in an actual social trend or inspired a school of practitioners, at least not yet. The model is named interpretive since it is based on the notion of textual analysis and it challenges the prevailing *academic* model, the scientific one (as described before). In some sense, this model brings into the realm of dispute-resolution the interpretive mode which prevails today in law, as my third and fourth chapters have tried to show. The interdisciplinary, confined quality of the current discipline, which speaks in social science terms and embraces an epistemology of the 1950s, can be switched and updated in my view to incorporate the intellectual shifts of the last decades. These shifts include the actual practical models which developed during that time, but also different waves of feminism; the flourishing of philosophical and political ideas like multiculturalism; the spread and challenge of post-modern thought and other cultural developments.

The following sections aim to construct this model, first through exposing its foundation in linguistics and in the idea of language game and discourse analysis. After introducing this 'substance' the exposition continues by presenting the model's 'form' in relation to the previous models described, and in accordance with post-modern thought. Finally, the relation to legal discourse and the aspiration to achieve a multicultural notion of justice is explored through discussion of the idea of identity conversations.

5.5.1 Language Games and CMM

A basic assumption of the interpretive model is that the material from which conflicts are made is discourse. Conflicts occur in language and in texts, and although they have effects and appearance in 'reality', the only way to understand them and engage in the effort to resolve them is through the texts and genres of discourse which are involved in each case. A prominent existing model which adopts this notion of conflict is based on the communication theory CMM: Coordinated Management of Meaning.

CMM theory posits four key characteristics of the communication process. These postulates are: (1) that the acts performed by persons are reflexively linked to various forms of life; (2) that persons organize the meanings that constitute their forms of life in patterned ways; (3) that persons attribute to their actions certain kinds, degrees, and directions of force; and (4) that the patterns of interaction that persons produce have a non-summative but necessary relationship to the intentions of individual actors.[20]

This method is based on theories of communication and linguistics and incorporates Ludwig Wittgenstein's notions of 'language games' and 'forms of life' to describe the process of mediation.

Mediation is a language game, or recurrent episode, that is reflexively linked to the speech acts that constitute its moment-by-moment realization and to larger patterns, or forms of life, such as relationship, autobiographies, and cultural patterns.[21]

When mediation is assumed as a language game which interacts with the language games that constitute the dispute, the terms neutrality and empowerment acquire a specific significance, which reflects this discursive shift.

I define empowerment as the appropriate elaboration or transformation of disputants forms of life.[22]

Forms of life are the autobiographies, relationships, and cultural patterns that are continuously developed, maintained, elaborated, or transformed in conversation.[23]

Instead of transformation of the self as in the transformative model, here the change is in the language games that establish the forms of life. These forms of life 'carry' the parties within the dispute, and their self-perception is dependant upon them. In other words, the parties are subject to the cultural scripts and narratives which surround them, and at the same time they become subjects in terms of rules of their discourse through the reflexive capacity

---

20 Jonathan G. Shailor, *Empowerment in Dispute Mediation: A Critical Analysis of Communication* (1984) 19.
21 Id., at 20.
22 Id., at 15.
23 Id., at 19.

regarding its boundaries. Their level of control and their ability of learning depends on the extent of reflection they are able to operate on their limited location within discourse. Acknowledging the boundaries of the discourse might help the relevant forms of life to transform.

5.5.2 Post-modern Thought and Incorporation into Mediation

Since mediation is a matter of time and place, and the language of dispute-resolution should reflect ideas and insights which have developed until the moment in time in which the mediation takes place, the interpretive model is said to contain and assume post-modern intellectual ideas as some of its foundational texts. The post-modern mode of inquiry and critique has affected our perception of reality and self, of science and history, and I believe it can be incorporated into a constructive model of mediation. There are, in my view, four intellectual assumptions that lie behind the model:

First, the narrative named 'the death of the subject'. The self or the ego is no longer an epistemologically valid foundation for thinking about mediation in a complex way nowadays. It is not the self and its interests, as in the pragmatic model, which are the focus of the mediation work, and neither is it the self in relationship, as in the transformative model. Instead, there are grids of significations and of interpretations which function within a cultural context, and the individual is a reflection of their operation, which never has a fixed substance.

Second, a mediation effort is always a discursive intervention and not a technocratic operative skill. Mediation itself is a narrative, which has different appearances and assumptions in different cultural contexts and through different perspectives in time. The discourse of mediation is biased towards mediation and presents itself as such, with no pretensions to be 'objective' or 'scientific'. It has an aim, nevertheless, to weave its mediation bias into the conflicting narratives of the parties. In relation to the pragmatic model, which places an emphasis on outcomes and efficiency, this model perceives these goals as part of an economic-individualistic discourse, which does not necessarily characterize the parties' narratives. In relation to the transformative model, which opposes efficiency and problem-solving orientation while focusing only on the process, the interpretive model depicts the reality of the 'outside world' of the dispute as enjoying the title of 'residue' or materialization. A reality of conflict is always a materialization of some deep-level ideological and positional struggles. In that sense, treating only the surface appearances of the parties' battle of wills within a dispute context, according to the pragmatic model assumption, is addressing only the tip of the iceberg. The parties' wills and desires reflect cultural scripts and narratives which should be addressed in their full complexity since their interplay might transform the dispute into a different clash of evident positions or, conversely, turn it into a peaceful resolution. Switching to the transformative model does not suffice either, according to this discursive analysis, since the inner worlds and ideologies cannot always be exposed and be transformed through the encouragement of 'empowerment and recognition'. The constraints of the actual residual reality demarcate the limit for the level of exposure and challenge which cultural narratives and scripts can handle. Pushing the parties too far towards a transformation might provoke inner forces and desires which might prove as impossible to settle. The interpretive model, in that sense, keeps an eye on the external reality and the actual expected outcome, considering them relevant to the context-shaping of resolving the dispute. The feelings and the inner worlds are not the 'true' reality of the dispute and transforming them for itself does not have any inherent value. Parties who are interested in staying at the supposed superficial level of their economic style interaction are encouraged to do so and to use the pragmatic model, which suits their discourse and the way they perceive themselves within it.

Third, the interpretive model emphasizes the incommensurable heterogeneous interaction of genres of discourse within a negotiation. In contrast to the pragmatic model, which assumes a progressive story of enlightened problem-solving and rational brain-storming process toward the mediating outcome, the interpretive model assumes individuals who communicate and respond from separate, unbridgeable worlds of meaning. Each party is entrenched in his/her own narratives and textshis personal and national memories and trauma, her mechanism of perceptions, their cultural and social identities. Imposing a language of 'interests' on this detached interaction of diverse worlds of meaning is a violent act which pretends to establish a common ground where only an epistemological abyss exists. The relation between the narratives and positions of the parties to the mediation can be described by the term 'differend', offered by the French philosopher Jean-François Lyotard:

> As distinguished from a litigation, a differend [*differend*] would be a case of conflict, between (at least) two parties, that cannot be equitably resolved for lack of a rule of judgement applicable to both arguments. One side's legitimacy does not imply the other's lack of legitimacy. However, applying a single rule of judgement to both in order to settle their differend as though it were merely

a litigation would wrong (at least) one of them (and both of them if neither side admits this rule). Damages result from an injury which is inflicted upon the rules of a genre of discourse but which is reparable according to those rules. A wrong results from the fact that the rules of the genre of discourse by which one judges are not those of the judged genre or genres of discourse.[24]

The notion of 'differend' which Lyotard suggests describes the inherent inability of a system of rules to address a wrong, when this wrong is measured through another incommensurable system of rules and from another perspective. According to this notion, the interaction during a conflict is between at least two genres of discourse and thus there are a few incommensurable systems of rules and no agreeable meta-systems to decide between them. In a legal system the adjudication process is supposed to provide this meta-discourse (and has difficulties in finding balanced standards and principles), but when a mediation is at stake there is no way to impose on the parties any external scheme without their consent. Their structural relation is like in an international war between countries or superpowers which represent different cultures. The crucial point about the interpretive model is that the mediation option arises in a paradoxical way through the extremity of the pessimistic, antagonistic picture which it depicts. Acknowledging the cultural textual quality of each world of meaning may enable the parties to use their reflective power to realize the indeterminacy and contingency of their expressed wills and perceptions within the conflict. Acknowledging the fact that they speak from a place cultural, ethnic or anotherhelps to initiate communication between the supposed separate 'galaxies' which constitute the differend. This communication might encourage transformation of the contradictory stories and opposing texts until the differend disappears or is replaced by another, while bringing the current conflict to a settlement. It is not the parties which are transformed directly through the explicit manipulation of the mediator, thus the ego 'empowerment' of the transformative approach does not necessarily occur. Instead it is the diverse contexts in which the parties perceive themselves and their ongoing history which determine the style of intervention needed in each stage and the style of narrative selected by the mediator to handle their interaction

Fourth, according to this model, the perception of the self is always a function of an identity experience. Whether it is a professional or gender-based identity, ethnic, national or religious, the 'hard cases' of mediation, to

---

24 Jean-François Lyotard, *The Differend: Phrases in Dispute* (1988) 1983, xi.

borrow Dworkin's expression regarding controversial adjudication cases which set an example for the whole theory of the discourse, involve identity struggle. A mediation is thus performing a reading which tries to expose and heal the contingency of any identity narrative. Through the reconciliation of interpretations it tries to rebuild a public space in which the private element of the self perception and the public element of the cultural and social identity texts (the universal and the particular, in Hegelian terms) can reach a discrete setting which reflects the new perception of justice of that time and place. Each mediation is a singular event which can reenact its unique notion of justice, according to this perception.

In terms of the feminist idea, and the ways in which this identity, gender-based discourse offers evaluation and critique of the cultural narratives of the time, the interpretive model offers a synthesis of the previous models in favor of an approach which can be named post-feminist or feminism of standpoints: The scientific and the pragmatic models are based on a liberal masculine self perception which assumes the individual is a rational maximizer who aspires to the efficient organization of her/his interests and desires. The transformative model is based on a feminine self-perception which assumes a caring individual who develops in relationships and greatly values her belonging to a community and the mutual understandings that can be reached within it. The perception of the self according to the interpretive model is, instead, a consequence of the waves of feminism which followed Gilligan's movement, and it tries to incorporate the critique of the idea of care and 'a different voice' emanating from the radical branch. If care and a unique style of logic characterize women's thinking only as a function of their historically inferior cultural position, as the radical feminist Catharine Mackinnon would argue,[25] and if no feminine essence exists to articulate a view which is authentic and uninfluenced by cultural and contextual norms, then the feminine and masculine are themselves narratives to be examined within the mediation situation. The separation-connection dichotomy does not necessarily offer an either-or choice for the mediation style. The interpretive model assumes that the interplay between them organizes the mediation process. Furthermore, the exposure of the cultural narratives which provide the background for the differentiation mechanism that construct our identities might help them to transform into better stories or constructions which can co-exist.

---

25 Catharine A. Mackinnon, *Toward a Feminist Theory of the State* (1989).

5.5.3 An Identity Discourse and its Relation to Legal Thought

If the interpretive model is thought to offer the most updated version of a mediation handling, its basic outlines can be also applied to and imported into the legal discourse and examined vis-à-vis the burning question of legitimacy which has dominated the theoretical debate at least since the 1960s. In contrast to the internal debate between legal scholars, who are either divided in their opinions of a meta-discourse for the legal realm, or occupied with finding internal formulas for the actors within the discourse,[26] the interpretive model suggests an opening of the debate to other professional entities and their worlds of meaning. The professional identity of the mediator should be constructed, according to the interpretive model, through the amalgamation of the therapist, the lawyer, the social worker, the diplomat and other dispute-resolution professionals and scholars. I believe that the dichotomy which holds the greatest potential for advancing this engagement is the one between the lawyer and the therapist. In contrast to the therapist, who is the preferred professional of the transformative model, the interpretive mediator does not strive to dig deep while searching for feelings and emotions which might produce empowerment for the self when revealed. Instead s/he tries to contain and handle emotional expression in a way that will promote the settlement process. Venting and 'feelings conversations' are not important in themselves, according to this model, and they have their own contextual and discursive significance, which suggests they are not the 'truth' or the core of any dispute. Since feelings and emotions are always products of cultural scripts and narratives, the readiness to relate to them and to invoke them should be dependant on the overall context of the relevant dispute. An ethnic and religious conflict involving gender questions, traumatic historical memories and a hyper-sensitive outside reality should not be handled solely through the use of therapeutic ideas of exposing emotions, since those could be sheltering the very basic core values of the diverse cultures involved. In contrast to the lawyer, who is the preferred character of the pragmatic model, the interpretive

---

26 See especially the chapter 'Taking Sides: Margins and phases of Disciples of Legal Process Disciples (Or: The Pragmatists that We Are)'. The map in the chapter is drawn in terms of the pragmatic lines and the response of legal scholars to the 1950s jurisprudence, but in general terms what is presented there is the heterogeneity of languages and perceptions which surround the basic questions in law nowadays. The maturing of the legal profession and the reaching of the highest reflexive engagement within this discourse is thus depicted also as the beginning of its decline and the move to a different notion of professional identity. Richard Posner (see part 3.3 of that chapter) promotes this 'social-sciences' oriented identity.

mediator does not aspire to negotiate in the shadow of one single legal system. S/he does not settle only for problem-solving and the limited standards of efficiency, satisfaction and enlarging the pie. Instead she aims to negotiate in the shadow of many laws: the psychological, the legal, the philosophical, and the sociological. This expansion of the discourse enables the mediator to see a multiplicity of narratives and possibilities of readings. Within this new space the mediation solution can respond to the complex context of the dispute and not only to its economic or legal reading.

According to the above description the construction of the new professional identity, that of the mediator, has at least three levels of discursive interaction.

One is the actual complex dispute (i.e. the hard case, as in Dworkin's theory; the one which calls the most sophisticated professional and theoretical ammunition) between the real parties and their diverse detached worlds, where the notion of 'differend' is the most suitable to describe the gap between them. A real complex dispute always involves questions of emotions, identity, diverse historical narratives, and cultural differences. These clashes are weaved into the parties' stories and responses during the process and the mediator tries to reveal as well as to contain some of them in order to move the actual reality of the conflict to a more advantageous place. The main encounter of the parties at this level is with their own worlds of meaning, and trying to reach out to the understanding of the other side is always limited to the perspective and context which limits the perceived landscape which each one can see

The second level of interaction is that of the dispute-resolution professionals who deal with the dispute and try to resolve it. One is the lawyer, who is trained at pragmatic deal-making and aims to arrange the many manifestations of the dispute efficiently. Another is the therapist, who is interested in the internal logic and opportunities for growth which the conflict suggests. Others may be social workers, business people, diplomats or trained negotiators. Their main challenge is to create a dialogic environment which offers the parties a multiplicity of interpretations reflecting the diverse professional discourses of these viewers.

The third and the most reflexive layer of the interaction which occurs in every singular mediation is the academic interdisciplinary comments of scholars from psychology, law, sociology, philosophy, linguistics, political sciences, business studies and some other fields of study. These disciplines have not addressed one another for a very long time and the possibility of making them examine their views vis-à-vis one another with regard to a concrete dispute might produce fascinating new insights. These insights might also help to resolve a concrete dispute through the second-order reflection they offer.

At all three levels of interaction and during the complex discursive performances which take place within the mediation process, the mode of interaction should, in my view, answer the code of a 'discourse of identity'. I take this notion from an article published by an Israeli professor of philosophy named Avi Sagi.[27] He pits two familiar genres of discourse in moral thought against each other – that of rights, and that of identity. In a nutshell and in a very schematic way these two discourses can be described as capturing the difference between a classical liberal mode of thinking and a multicultural global ideology. A discourse of rights assumes an alienated encounter between individuals who have different interests and beliefs and are guided by legal rules which determine the contours of their activities. It is an interaction based on safe contact, where claims and challenges regarding the other's possessions and acts are determined by a third party, which is represented by the law. The parties do not address one another directly, and in that sense they remain subject to a monologic style of communication. The law functions here, in Isaiah Berlin's terms, as protecting the 'negative liberty' of people defending their borders, preventing intervention. This discourse is concerned with restraining the formal limits of human interaction.

At the core of the identity discourse, on the other hand, stands a Levinassic face-to-face encounter with the other. It is a dialogic engagement and a much more dangerous experience, since at the core of this meeting stands the idea that we know how we enter the dialogue, but never know how we will conclude it. The borders of the identity itself are blurred within these meetings, and hence the danger and fear which the parties experience can be sustained. The interactions can, in other words, turn into a Hegelian struggle, since an identity-based conversation inherently entails questioning one's own identity and thus taking the risk of losing it. The game which best characterizes the orientation of the participants to this engagement is that of active listening, of the search for a voice and for a direct touch that cannot be achieved through a monitoring scheme. There is no law which tells the two parties how to interact, and moving halfway toward the other does not guarantee the merging of horizons, since a similar gesture should be done from his/her side too, and with no expectation of reward. It is a game where the distinct identity of the speaker is assumed but the whole interaction is aimed at challenging the prejudices and stereotypes which are associated with the different identities at stake. In other words, handling an identity conversation and participating in a dialogical engagement

---

27 Avi Sagi (In Hebrew), 'Law and Society: Rights Discourse and Identity Discourse in Israel', 16 *Bar-Ilan Law Studies* 37 (2000).

which this discourse calls for, is working on the difference while assuming that new frames of reason and law will emerge through this effort.

It is easy to see from the above dichotomy that the two styles of discourses operate in a dialectic with one another: in order to enter an identity discourse the rights and boundaries of the parties should be acknowledged, and once dialogic progress has been established and developed, a new articulation of it in terms of their rights might emerge. The history of the West, of the feminist movement, of post-colonial ideas and of the queers studies can be represented as following these lines and oscillating between the different poles of identity and rights: the West's construction of its own identity regarding the East and the colonies, the 'original' West and the 'New World'; the different waves of feminism trying at first to promote rights and later entering into dialogic and identity conversation (like relational feminism) with their supposedly alienated enemy; the post-colonial struggle against an identity definition imposed by the Western hegemony; post-structural ideas of logocentrism of Western philosophy. All these phenomena represent a challenge to a right discourse that emerges from a certain identity which provides a genuine 'Other' perspective. This 'other' perspective calls for acknowledgment of and legitimacy for its own logic, which reflects the significance of speaking from a place. The contemporary ideal of multiculturalism, globalization and pluralism can be presented in this context as shifting the center to the peripheries, or in other words: providing an ideology of no center, of multifarious genres of discourse which emerge from the diverse identity positions of the parties. The identity conversation which mediation should encourage through its three levels is thus a reflection of this current contemporary ideology.

Both the most promising and most challenging point about this effort to merge the horizons between political philosophy, law and dispute-resolution is that the identities and narratives contain contradictory images and a logic which do not always transmit an antagonistic life or death Hegelian struggle. Often the stories also parallel one another, share some common history, develop through the influence of another identity, and have a non-contemporaneous character, which might encourage unexpected collaboration. The intellectual and the practical task of the one who is interested in a healing process and not in the escalation is to endure the contradictions and to challenge what is perceived as substantial and as located at the 'core' of her/his identity. Parties can do that by keep listening to one other. They need to trace the places which make their differences echo in a productive way, and to offer interpretations and reframings which avoid crisis and encourage evolving of new self perception and identity constructions. In relation to the legal realm, this conversation can also occur within a Supreme Court through the diverse identities of its Justices.[28]

5.6 From Philosophy to Philawsophy to Dispute-resolution ...

The schematic description of layers of mediation in the above sequence is the effort to present models of mediation as evolving in relation to intellectual movements and to suggest a theoretical-practical model which will contain the previous ones and incorporate ideas of the twenty-first century to cope with its new challenges. An identity conversation which stands at the core of my utopian interpretive model is supposed to go beyond post-modern thought and to enhance a strategy which aims first of all at its own self-criticism and transformation. Within this model, the pragmatic and the psychoanalytic ideas of the twentieth century are beginning to collaborate, since in a Dewyan world of experience and commodities and in a Freudian world of melancholy and an ongoing analysis which always seeks the unknown, disputes can both be still transformed and maintained. Acknowledging the element of need in a dispute in order to survive and grow, and the fact that all our self-definitions contain some constitutive dispute, and that each identity emerges as contradicting the others, may enable this either-or dichotomy to be surpassed. Thus in a complex dispute, a progress can be made through challenging our identity as a daily matter. In that sense, mediating according to the interpretive model is a self-journey and not only a process to be handled for others.

Finally, there is not a wrong model or an outdated one in *a priori* terms. Some conflicts may be handled by scientific 'biases neutralizers', some may be resolved through pragmatic 'problem solving', and others may be handled through the search for empowerment and recognition. The personal style of any mediator dictates her/his own genre for the practical work and each new case calls for a complex singular model to treat it. My main purpose in offering the interpretive model is to portray my own perception of the meta-discourse of mediation, and I hope that presenting it does not mean the beginning of the decline of this business of mediation, since I really hope it flourishes and spreads at least for the next hundred years.

---

28 For an elaboration of this discussion regarding the Isreali Supreme Court see Michal Alberstein (in Hebrew), 'From Ringer to Barda and the Thin Skull of Legal Interpretation', forthcoming in *Bar-Ilan Law Studies* (In file with the author).

Concluding Notes

History

Each chapter has a message regarding history.

Chapter 1 traces the 'royal' narratives of the emergence of American philosophy and of American legal thought, and exposes their discursive dimension. By pointing to the mythical as well as the contingent and religious aspects in each discourse, I have tried to demonstrate their fictional-textual dimension, which is reflected in the multiplicity of lenses that try to depict them. The 'truth' my analysis insists on is the complementary relation between the two discourses of the general and the legal, a relation that has two distinct manifestations in time, through the two stages of pragmatism in law that I have described. The 'matured', explicit self-reflecting version of this genre is posited through the writing of Duncan Kennedy.

Chapter 2 stresses the difference between internal and external-history tellers of the law. The claim is that progressive intellectuals perceive the post-war era through the mechanism of denial and dismissal, in an effort to conceal what they perceive as the conservative failure of the Legal Process school. Outsiders to the discourse of law cannot grasp the riddle, which occupies their friends, and portray this period through formal characteristics of one sort or another. Another message of this chapter is that the post-war era is a crucial moment for the understanding of the contemporary American legal discourse, and for the understanding of the theoretical developments before and after that time.

Chapter 3 explores the way in which interaction between contemporary discourses on law is achieved through their non-contemporaneous character – through their adoption of various meta-texts or genres of pragmatism. I characterize the post-post-war era as having many histories, and this situation is reflected in the impossibility of telling *any* history without already occupying a strategic place within the discourse.

Chapter 4 claims that the genre of discourse that the post-war era produced is still alive in the contemporary studies of negotiation and dispute resolution, combined with current updates from psychology and game theory. Within this discourse, adjudication is not the prominent procedure anymore, but optimism, activism, and writing style prevail in it, as they did in the Legal Process Materials.

Chapter 5 moves to the discourse of dispute resolution to show the evolution of a discourse through time, where each phase and layer claims to contain the previous ones and to provide a more detached reflexive standpoint toward the dispute. The models and perspectives provide a few valid modes of engagement in reality, which can still interact with one another in spite of their non-contemporaneous character.

Progressivism

There is a suspicion toward the progressive sentiment in my writing, not 'for itself', but toward the way it is constructed through discourse and time to conceal current wrongs, or to celebrate some righteous position. In the first chapter this suspicion is applied to Morton Horwitz's portrayal of the Realists as progressives, with this being their main characteristic. It also applies to Holmes' controversial progressivism and the multifarious perceptions of him along time, as progressive and conservative at once. In the second chapter, I show how the hegemonic text of the post-war period is characterized by its written harmony between the outside and the inside. Its politics is that of effacing obscurities, riddles, and knots in favor of a grand picture of law in all its institutional manifestations, built into the instrumental script. This official moment of mediation entails an interdisciplinary progressive openness which could not exist before that time, nor would it last later. Chapter 3 follows the progressive internal subversive pathos of Roberto Unger as it transforms into a straightforward (Roger Fisher-esque) style of discourse, delivered through a political manifesto. The internal subversive progressive act is presented, thus, as a failure. The closer inspection of Unger's counterparts, Fiss and Posner, shows that each one perceives himself as progressive, and develops his progressivism in some reaction to the post-war scholarship. Chapter 4 shows that the intellectual passion at Harvard is promoted and blossoming in the 'private' pole of negotiation and dispute resolution practice. The academic theoretical discourse is too ironic and detached to promote any political message, and Dworkin's Hercules, with his obsessive, internal undefeated quest is its mythological character. This combination might be perceived as the 1950s knot again in its heroic mediation.

Finally, the last chapter bypasses the progressive struggles within law by moving to the sphere of dispute resolution, where the ideals of multiculturalism and pluralism can, in my view, find new channels through the development of a complex discourse of mediation. There I posit the notion of an 'identity conversation' to provide some fresh hope for the new century by obliging us to work on the differences and not to intensify them to a level of escalation.

Discourse

In general terms, I draw the line of an American pragmatic discourse that built itself until the post-war era through the opposition between two genres of discourse. After the post-war era, I describe the lines of discursive responses to the Legal Process crystallization. One is manifested by Unger, Fiss, and Posner (from left to right) and is characterized by resistance to the materials in a reflexive account of what is law. The second line is manifested by Kennedy, Dworkin, and Fisher, and is characterized by a repetition of a distinct previous style of discourse. The writing is perceived to work through engaging written texts: texts about history, about progressiveness, about law, about theory and practice, about adjudication and dispute resolution. The access to the origin, i.e., real history, real politics, real people whom I discuss (even those I actually saw) is inherently denied in my view, and I have no pretense of providing the grand, true history of American legal thought. Nevertheless, to everyone who does purport to do so, I offer my text, that of the bystander and the observer, who says she sees so many differences, but she sees also one big family to which she does not belong, an American Family. The discursive family ties are those of masculinity and femininity, couples relations in general, illegitimacy (of the dispute resolution discursive trajectory); they all come back to the singularity of pragmatism as an organizing text. My perception of the American legal reality I have experienced is exactly between these genres, in the abyss and in the interaction among them: between the dispute resolution pathos and the jurisprudential; between philawsophy and philosophy (or politics); between practice and theory; between fiction and reality. The last chapter aims to escape these American contradictions and reflects my transition to another environment and context, the Israeli one. The narratives and layers of mediation described in this finale were drawn from a different location and the belief they transmit is related to the conditions and characteristics of places and institutions I have not attempted to describe in this book.

Throughout my writing, during the first four chapters, I try to stay locked in my paradoxes, in the same ideas I try to critique, those of pragmatism. I am haunted by the pragmatic spirit, as I have already said, and am fascinated by the multifarious ways it works itself through time and place. A basic lesson of my writing is that there are many of these spirits, and even since the 'origin' of pragmatism, there have been at least two of them, one near another, not necessarily contradictory and actually complementary. The idea of genres of discourses, which signify in their intercourse a political climate, is part of this claim.

Another discursive conclusion, accumulated from implicit claims in each chapter, is that the intellectual passion to transform the law into a closed world to inhabit, a world from which there is a way to open a window to control the whole of the external surroundings, begins with the oracle of law, Holmes, but is developed through the writing of two progressive sequences: the Realists and the CLS. The style of writing and analysis I find in Duncan Kennedy carries the legacy of Holmes, and thus, in an interesting way and from an internal perspective, Kennedy articulates what Dworkin draws in mythological terms, and his academic legal position is as close to the highest as possible. The theoretically obscure genre, which endures the body and is committed to the hard work and to mapping and playing with 'rationality', is the paradigm framework for the jurist intellectual. Progressive history, in that sense, is the one written by the intellectual who has mastered the internal wisdom and can perceive the law in its sophistication and complexity. As in a Hegellian master-and-slave play, the fact that the master of legal consciousness is a leftist intellectual does not prevent the slave from promoting economics as the ground rule for mediating the 'external-political' manifestations of their differences. At the turn of the century, it seems Kennedy portrays the internal mode as a dangerous disease – the 'viral strain' – and Unger chooses to give up on the possibility of an internal critique from within law altogether, preferring the straightforward political. The mainstream construction of 'the world' is probably equivalent to that of the Legal Process time: an economical, complex net of institutions operating through assuming positivism, naturalism, and many other hidden old theories. The Marxist spirit as in the 1970s that might have haunted some of the CLS members has yielded, as in 'real history', to an old specter, that of American pragmatism. But even within pragmatism itself, the obscure genre might be declining in favor of a new (American?) century and millennium that might not need the irony any longer. A possible counter-account of the pathos which drives the discourse of this book is the exhaustion of the psychoanalytic and pragmatic drives, which are primary theoretical and methodological tools of the previous century, in favor of a private passion, or of a reading which tries to 'experience' both the psychoanalytic and the pragmatic as a threshold to overcome.

Finally, in the same way as I opened my writing, there are many possible readings and even more possible conclusions. I had no ambition to produce a text that would be present to itself and convey the conclusions as if there were a way to do so without being already trapped in the position of only one reader, myself. Hence, the space is here left for my readers to perform their own interpretive acts and violence, to draw their lines and conclusions, to 'use' the theories and claims as if such use is ever possible, or to dismiss the whole project as having no pragmatic cash value.

Bibliography

Books

Able, R. (1982), *The Politics of Informal Justice*, Vol. 1.2, New York, Academic Press.
Arrow, K.J. et al. (1999), *Barriers to Conflict Resolution*, New York, W.W. Norton.
Auerbach, J.S. (1976), *Unequal Justice: Lawyers and Social Change in Modern America*, New York, Oxford University Press.
Auerbach, J.S. (1983), *Justice Without Law*, New York, Oxford University Press.
Bush, R.A.B. and Folger, J.P. (1994), *The Promise of Mediation*, San Francisco, CA, Jossey-Bass.
Brint, M. and Weaver, W. (eds) (1991), *Pragmatism in Law and Society*, Boulder, Westview Press.
Bunker, B.B. and Rubin, J.Z. (1995), *Conflict Cooperation and Justice: Essays Inspired by the Work of Morton Deutsch*, San Francisco, Jossey-Bass Publishers.
Cardozo, B.N. (1921), *The Nature of the Judicial Process*, New Haven, Yale University Press.
Cavell, S. (1969), *Must We Mean What We Say?*, New York, Scribner.
Cavell, S. (1981), *Pursuits of Happiness*, Cambridge, Mass., Harvard University Press.
Cavell, S. (2nd edn, 1981), *The Senses of Walden*, San Francisco, North Point Press.
Cavell, S. (1987), *Disowning Knowledge*, Cambridge and New York, Cambridge University Press.
Cavell, S. (1988), *Conditions Handsome and Unhandsome: The Constitution of Emersonian Perfectionism*, Chicago, University of Chicago Press.
Cavell, S. (1994), *A Pitch of Philosophy: Autobiographical Exercises*, Cambridge, MA, Harvard University Press.
Cavell, S. (1996), *Contesting Tears: The Hollywood Melodrama of the Unknown Woman*, Chicago, University of Chicago Press.
Clement, C. (Betsy Wing trans., 1988), *Opera: On the Undoing of Women*, Minneapolis, University of Minnesota Press.
Cohen, M. (ed.) (1984), *Ronald Dworkin and Contemporary Jurisprudence*, Totowa, N.J., Rowman & Allanheld.
Derrida, J. (1967), *Of Grammatology* (Gayatri Chakravotry Spivak trans., 1976) Baltimore, Johns Hopkins University Press.
Derrida, J. (1993), *Specters of Marx* (Peggy Kamuf trans., 1994) New York, Routledge.
Derrida, J. (1996), *Resistances of Psychoanalysis* (Peggy Kammuf and Pascal-Ann Brault and Michael Naaf trans., 1998) Stanford, CA, Stanford University Press.
Dewey, J. (1920), *Reconstruction in Philosophy*, New York, H. Holt and Company.
Dewey, J. (1925), *Experience and Nature*, Chicago, London, Open Court Publishing Company.

Dickstein, M. (ed) (1998), *The Revival of Pragmatism*, Durham, Duke University Press.
Dworkin, R. (1977), *Taking Rights Seriously*, Cambridge, Harvard University Press.
Dworkin, R. (1986), *Law's Empire*, Cambridge, MA, Belknap Press of Harvard University Press.
Emerson, R.W. (Larzer Ziff, ed., 1982), *Selected Essays*, Harmondsworth, Middlesex; New York, NY, Penguin Books.
Festenstein, M. (1997), *Pragmatism and Political Theory: From Dewey to Rorty*, Chicago, IL, University of Chicago Press.
Fisher, R. (1969), *International Conflict for Beginners*, New York, Harper & Row.
Fisher, R. and Ury, W. (1981), *Getting to Yes: How to Negotiate Agreements Without Giving in*, Boston, Houghton Mifflin.
Fisher, R., Koppelman, E. and Schneider, A.K. (1994), *Beyond Machiavelli*, Cambridge, MA, Harvard University Press.
Fisher, W.W., Horwitz, M.J. and Reed, T. (eds) (1993), *American Legal Realism*, New York, Oxford University Press.
Frank, J. (1930), *Law and The Modern Mind*, New York, Brentano's.
Frank, J. (1950), *Courts on Trial: Myth and Reality in American Justice*, Princeton, NJ, Princeton University Press.
Frankfurter, F. (1965), *Of Law and Life and Other Things that Matter*, Cambridge, MA, Belknap Press of Harvard University Press.
Goldberg, S.B., Sander, F.E.A. and Rogers, N.H. (2nd edn 1992), *Dispute Resolution*, Boston, Little, Brown.
Gilligan, C. (1982), *In a Different Voice: Psychological Theory and Women Development*, Cambridge, MA, Harvard University Press.
Glendon, M.A. (1994), *A Nation Under Lawyers: How the Crisis in the Legal Profession is Transforming American Society*, New York, Farrar, Straus and Giroux.
Gordon, R.W. (1992), *The Legacy of Oliver Wendell Holmes, Jr.*, Stanford, CA, Stanford University Press.
Harrington, C.B. (1985), *Shadow Justice: The Ideology and Institutionalization of Alternatives to Court*, Westport, CT, Greenwood Press.
Hart, H.L.A (1961), *The Concept of Law*, Oxford, Clarendon Press.
Hart, H.M. Jr and Sacks, A.M. (Eskridge, W.N. Jr and Frickey, P.P., eds) (1994), *The Legal Process: Basic Problems in the Making and Application of Law*, Westbury, NY, Foundation Press.
Hollinger, R. and Depew, D. (eds) (1995), *Pragmatism: From Progressivism to Postmodernism*, Westport, CT, Praeger.
Horwitz, M.J. (1992), *The Transformation of American Law 1870-1960: The Crisis of Legal Orthodoxy*, New York, Oxford University Press.
Horwitz, M.J. (1998), *The Warren Court and the Pursuit of Justice*, New York, Hill and Wang.
Hull, N.E.H. (1997), *Roscoe Pound and Carl Llewellyn: Searching for an American Jurisprudence*, Chicago, IL, University of Chicago Press.

Kalman, L. (1986), *Legal Realism at Yale 1927–1960*, Chapel Hill, University of North Carolina Press.

Kelsen, H. (Max Knight trans., 1960, 1978 edn) (1934), *Pure Theory of Law*, Berkeley, CA, University of California Press.

Kennedy, D. (1997), *A Critique of Adjudication (fin de siecle)*, Cambridge, MA, Harvard University Press.

Kennedy, D. (1983), *Legal Education and the Reproduction of Hierarchy: A polemic against the system*, Cambridge, Mass.: Afar.

Kronman, A.T. (1993), *The Lost Lawyer: Failing Ideals of the Legal Profession*, Cambridge, MA, Belknap Press of Harvard University Press.

Kuklick, B. (1977), *The Rise of American Philosophy: Cambridge Massachusetts 1860–1930*, New Haven, Yale University Press.

Kuklick, B. (1985), *Churchmen and Philosophers: From Jonathan Edwards to John Dewey*, New Haven, Yale University Press.

Lacan, J. (Miller, J.A. ed., Porter, D. trans.) (1986), *The Seminar Of Jacques Lacan, Book VII: The Ethics Of Psychoanalysis*, Cambridge and New York, Cambridge University Press.

Lacan, J. (Miller, J.A. ed., Forrester, J. trans.) (1988), *The Seminar of Jacques Lacan, Book I: Freud's Papers on Technique*, Cambridge and New York, Cambridge University Press.

Laclau, E. and Mouffe, C. (1985), *Hegemony and Socialist Strategy*, London; New York, Verso.

Lax, D.A. and Sebenius, J.K. (1986), *The Manager as Negotiator: Bargaining for Cooperation and Competitive Gain*, New York, Free Press; London, Collier Macmillan.

Levin, L. and Wheeler, R.R. (eds) (1976), *The Pound Conference: Perspectives on Justice in the Future*, St Paul, MA, West Pub. Co.

Llewellyn, K.N. (1960), *The Common Law Tradition: Deciding Appeals*, Boston, Little, Brown.

Lovin, R.W. and Perry, M.J. (eds) (1990), *Critique and Construction: A Symposium on Roberto Unger's Politics*, Cambridge and New York, Cambridge University Press.

Lundmerer, K.M. (1985), *Learning to Heal: The Development of American Medical Education*, New York, Basic Books.

Mackinnon, C.A. (1989), *Toward a Feminist Theory of the State*, Cambridge, MA, Harvard University Press.

Marke, J.J. (1955), *The Holmes Reader*, New York, Oceana Publications.

Menand, L. (ed) (1997), *Pragmatism: A Reader*, New York, Vintage Books.

Mercuro, N. and Megema, S.G. (1997), *Economics and the Law: From Posner to Post-modernism*, Princeton, NJ, Princeton University Press.

Mnookin, R. (2000), *Beyond Winning: Negotiating to Create Value in Deals and Disputes*, Cambridge, MA, Belknap Press of Harvard University Press.

Nancy, J.L. and Lacoue-Labarthe, P. (Raffoul, F. and Pettigrew, D., eds, 1992) (1973), *The Title of the Letter*, Albany, State University of New York Press.

Neal, M.A. and Bazerman, M.H. (1991), *Cognition and Rationality in Negotiation*, New York, Free Press; Toronto, Collier Macmillan Canada; New York, Maxwell Macmillan International.

Packer, H. and Ehrlich, T. (1972), *New Directions in Legal Education*, New York, McGraw-Hill.

Posner, R.A. (1990), *The Problems of Jurisprudence*, Cambridge, MA, Harvard University Press.

Posner, R.A. (1995), *Overcoming Law*, Cambridge, MA, Harvard University Press.

Posner, R.A. (1999), *The Problematics of Moral and Legal Theory*, Cambridge, MA, Belknap Press of Harvard University Press.

Reed, A.Z. (1921), *Training for The Public Profession of The Law*, The Carnegie Foundation for the Advancement of Teaching, Bulletin no. 15 New York.

Rorty, R. (1989), *Contingency, Irony, and Solidarity*, Cambridge and New York, Cambridge University Press.

Ross, D. (1991), *The Origins of American Social Science*, Cambridge and New York, Cambridge University Press.

Rubin, J.Z. and Brown, B.R. (1975), *The Social Psychology of Bargaining and Negotiation*, San Diego, CA, Academic Press.

Schlegel, J.H. (1995), *American Legal Realism and Empirical Social Sciences*, New York, Academic Press.

Sebok, A.J. (1998), *Legal Positivism in American Jurisprudence*, Cambridge and New York, Cambridge University Press.

Shailor, J.G. (1984), *Empowerment in Dispute Mediation: A Critical Analysis of Communication*, Westport, CT, Praeger.

Smith, J.E. (ed.) (1999), *Classical American Pragmatism: Its Contemporary Vitality*, Urbana, University of Illinois Press.

Stone, D., Patton, B. and Heen, S. (1999), *Difficult Conversations: How to Discuss What Matters Most*, New York, Viking.

Levi-Strauss, C. (Weidenfeld, G. trans., 1966) (1962) *The Savage Mind*, Chicago, University of Chicago Press.

Tamanaha, B.Z. (1997), *Realistic Socio-Legal Theory: Pragmatism and a Social Theory of Law*, Oxford, Clarendon Press; Oxford and New York, Oxford University Press.

Teubner, G. (ed.) (1988), *Autopoietic Law: A New Approach to Law and Society*, Berlin and New York, W. de Gruyter.

Townsend, K. (1996), *Manhood at Harvard: William James and Others*, New York, W.W. Norton.

Twining, W. (1973), *Karl Llewellyn and the Realist Movement*, London, Weidenfeld and Nicolson.

Unger, R.M. (1984), *Passion: An Essay on Personality*, New York, Free Press; London, Collier Macmillan.

Unger, R.M. (1986), *The Critical Legal Studies Movement*, Cambridge, MA, Harvard University Press.
Unger, R M. (1996), *What Should Legal Analysis Become?*, London and New York, Verso.
Unger, R.M. (1997), *Politics: The Central Texts*, London; New York, Verso.
Unger, R.M. (1998), *Democracy Realized: The Progressive Alternative*, London; New York, Verso.
Unger, R.M. and West, C. (1998), *The Future of American Progressivism*, Boston, Beacon Press.
Volkomer, W.E. (1970), *The Passionate Liberal: The Political and Legal Ideas of Jerome Frank*, The Hague, Nijhoff.
Weber, M. (Parson, T. trans., 2nd edn, 1998), *The Protestant Ethic and the Spirit of Capitalism*, Los Angeles, Roxbury Pub.
West, C. (1989), *The American Evasion of Philosophy*, Madison, WN, University of Wisconsin Press.
White, G.E. (1993), *Justice Oliver Wendell Holmes: Law and The Inner Self*, New York and Oxford, Oxford University Press.
White, M. (1949), *Social Thought in America: The Revolt Against Formalism*, New York, Viking Press.
Wittgenstein, L. (3rd edn, 1958), *Philosophical Investigations*, Oxford, Blackwell.

Articles

Abel, R.L. (1981), 'Conservative Conflict and the Reproduction of Capitalism', *UCLA Law Review*, Vol. 9, p. 9.
Alberstein, M. (2001), 'Negotiating through Paradoxes: Rationality, Practicality and Naïve Realism (Or: Enjoy your Biases)', *Studies in Law, Politics and Society*, Vol. 22, p. 197.
Amit, R. (1997) (in Hebrew), '(Re)construction of a Canon', *Eyunei Mishpat*, Vol. 21, p. 81.
Arnold, T. (1960), 'Professor Hart's Theology', *Harvard Law Review*, Vol. 73, p. 1298.
Black, C.L. Jr (1960), 'The Lawfulness of the Segregation Decision', *Yale Law Journal*, Vol. 69, p. 421.
Bok, D. (1983) 'Law and Its Discontents: A Critical Look at Our Legal System', 38 *Rec. A.B. City N.Y.* 12.
Bone, R.G. (1995), 'Lon Fuller's Theory of Adjudication and The False Dichotomy Between Dispute Resolution and Public Law Models of Litigation', 75 *Boston University Law Review*, Vol. 75, p. 1273.
Boyle, J. (1993), 'Legal Realism and the Social Contract: Fuller's Public Jurisprudence of Form, Private Jurisprudence of Substance', *Cornell Law Review*, Vol. 78, p. 371.

Bush, R.A.B. (1989), 'Efficiency and Protection, or Empowerment and Recognition?: The Mediator's Role and Ethical Standards in Mediation', 41 *Florida Law Review* Vol. 41, p. 253.

Bush, R.A.B. (1989–90), 'Mediation and Adjudication, Dispute Resolution and Ideology: An Imaginary Conversation', *Journal of Contemporary Legal Issues*, Vol. 3, p. 1.

Chayes, A. (1976), 'The Role of the Judge in Public Law Litigation', *Harvard Law Review*, Vol. 89, p. 1281.

Cobb, S. (1994), 'A Narrative Perspective on Mediation', in Folger, J.P. and Jones, T. (eds), *New Directions in Mediation*, p. 48.

Cobb, S. (1990), 'Neutrality as a Discursive Practice', *Studies in Law, Politics and Society*, Vol. 11, p. 69.

Cohen, F. (1935), 'Transcendental Nonsense and the Functional Approach', *Columbia Law Review*, Vol. 35, p. 809.

Cohen, M. (1984), in Cohen, M. (ed.), *Preface to Ronald Dworkin and Contemporary Jurisprudemce*.

Cover, R.M. (1986), 'Violence and the Word', 95 *Yale Law Journal*, Vol. 95, p. 1601.

Dawson, J. (1983), 'Legal Realism and Legal Scholarship', *Journal of Legal Education*, Vol. 33, p. 406.

Daxbury, N. (1991), 'Jerome Frank and the Legacy of Legal Realism', *Journal of Law and Society*, Vol. 18, p. 175.

Derrida, J. (1992) 'Force of Law: The "Mystical Foundation of Authority"', in Cornell, D. et al. (eds), *Deconstruction and the Possibility of Justice*, New York: Routledge, p. 2.

Dewey, J. (1925), 'Logical Method and the Law', *Cornell Law Quarterly*, Vol. 10, p. 17.

Dorsen, N. (1991), 'In Memoriam: Albert M. Sacks',105 *Harvard Law Review*, Vol. 105, p. 1.

Doyel, R.L. (1983), 'The Clinical Lawyer School: Has Jerome Frank Prevailed?', *New England Law Review*, Vol. 18, p. 577.

Dworkin, R. (1985), 'Law's Ambition for Itself', *Virginia Law Review*, Vol. 71, p.173.

Eskridge, W.N., Jr and Peller, G. (1990), 'The New Public Law Movement: Moderation as a Post-Modern Cultural Form', *Michigan Law Review*, Vol. 89, p. 707.

Ewald, W. (1988), 'Unger's Philosophy: A Critical Legal Study', *Yale Law Journal*, Vol. 97, p. 671.

Fish, S. (1989), 'Fish v. Fiss', in Stanley Fish, *Doing What comes Naturally: Change, Rhetoric, and The Practice of Theory in Literary and Legal Studies*, Durham, Duke University Press.

Fisher, R. (1964) 'Fractionating Conflict', *Daedalus*, p. 920.

Fisher, R. (1984), 'Reply to The Pros and Cons of Getting to Yes', *Journal of Legal Education*, Vol. 34, p. 115.

Fisher, W.W. Jr III (1997), 'Text and Contexts: The Application of American Legal History of the Methodologies of Intellectual History', *Stanford Law Review*, Vol. 49, p. 1065.
Fiss, O.M. (1979), 'The Supreme Court 1978 Term: Forward: The Forms of Justice', *Harvard Law Review*, Vol. 93, p. 1.
Fiss, O.M. (1982), 'Objectivity and Interpretation', *Stanford Law Review*, Vol. 34, p. 739.
Fiss, O.M. (1982), 'The Social and Political Foundations of Adjudication', *Law and Human Behavior*, Vol. 6, p. 121.
Fiss, O.M. (1985) 'Out of Eden', *Yale Law Journal*, Vol. 94, p. 1669.
Fiss, O.M. (1986), 'The Death of The Law?', *Cornell Law Review*, Vol. 72, p. 1.
Frank, J. (1947), 'A Plea for Lawyer-Schools', *Yale Law Journal*, Vol. 56, p. 1303.
Fuller, L. (1941), 'Consideration and Form', *Columbia Law Review*, p. 799.
Fuller, L. (1978), 'The Forms and Limits of Adjudication', *Harvard Law Review*, Vol. 92, p. 353.
Fuller, L. and Perdue (1936–37), 'The Reliance Interest in Contract Damages' (pts 1 and 2), *Yale Law Journal*, Vol. 46, pp. 52, 373.
Galanter, M. (1974), 'Why the "Haves" Come Out Ahead: Speculations on the Limits of Legal Change', *Law and Society Law Review*, Vol. 9, p. 95.
Galanter, M. (1983), 'Reading the Landscape of Disputes: What We Know and Don't Know (and Think We Know) About Our Allegedly Contentious and Litigious Society', *UCLA Law Review*, Vol. 31, p. 4.
Galanter, M. (1986), 'The Day After the Litigation Explosion', *Maryland Law Review*, Vol. 46, 1. 37.
Gilmore, G. (1961), 'Legal Realism: Its Cause and Cure', *Yale Law Journal*, Vol. 70, p. 1037.
Golding, M.P. (1986) 'Jurisprudence and Legal Philosophy in Twentieth-Century America – Major Themes and Developments', *Journal of Legal Education*, Vol. 36, p. 441.
Grey, T.C. (1989), 'Holmes and Legal Pragmatism', *Stanford Law Review*, Vol. 41, p. 787.
Grey, T.C. (1996) 'Freestanding Legal Pragmatism', *Cardozo Law Review*, Vol. 18, p. 21.
Hantzis, C.W. (1988) 'Legal Innovation Within the Wider Intellectual Tradition: The Pragmatism of Oliver Wendell Holmes, Jr.', *Northwestern University School of Law*, Vol. 82, p. 541.
Hohfeld, W.N. (1913), 'Some Fundamental Legal Conceptions as Applied in Judicial Reasoning', *Yale Law Journal*, Vol. 23, p. 16.
Hart, H. (1959), 'Foreword: The Time Chart of the Justices: The Supreme Court 1958 Term', *Harvard Law Review*, Vol. 73, p. 84.
Holmes, O.W. (1894), 'Privilege, Malice and Intent', *Harvard Law Review*, Vol. 8, p. 281.

Hull, N.E.H (1987), 'Some Realism about The Llewellyn-Pound Exchange over Realism: The Newly Uncovered Privet Correspondence 1927–1931', *Wisconsin Law Review*, p. 921.
Huntington, W.E. (1907), 'Laboratory Work in the School of Law', *Bostonia*, Vol. 7(4), p. 15.
Hyman, J.D. (1976) 'Constitutional Jurisprudence and the Teaching of Constitutional Law', *Stanford Law Review*, Vol. 28, p. 1271.
Karier, C.J. (1992), 'The Rebel and The Revolutionary: Sigmund Freud and John Dewey', in *John Dewey: Critical Assessments* (J.E. Tiles, ed.), p. 42.
Kennedy, D. (1976) 'Form and Substance in Private Law Adjudication', *Harvard Law Review*, Vol. 86, p. 1685.
Kennedy, D. (1991) 'A Semiotics of Legal Argument', in 3 Collected Courses of The Academy of European Law (Kluwer, Netherlands), Book 2, p. 309.
Kennedy, D. (1992), 'Freedom and Constraint in Adjudication: A Critical Phenomenology', *Journal of Legal Education*, Vol. 36, p. 45.
Kennedy, D. (2000), 'From the Will Theory to the Principle of Private Autonomy: Lon Fuller's "Consideration and Form"', *Columbia Law Review*, Vol. 100, p. 94.
Leiter, B. (1999), 'Positivism, Formalism, Realism', *Columbia Law Review*, Vol. 99, p. 1138.
Luban, D. (1996), 'What's Pragmatic about Legal Pragmatism', *Cardozo Law Review*, Vol. 18, p. 51.
McThenia, W. and Thomas, L.S. (1985) 'For Reconciliation', *Yale Law Journal*, Vol. 94, p. 1660.
Menkel-Meadow, C. (1984), 'Toward Another view of Legal Negotiation: The Structure of Problem Solving', *UCLA Law Review*, Vol. 31, p. 794.
Menkel-Meadow, C. (1985), 'For and Against Settlement: Uses and Abuses of the Mandatory Settlement Conference', *UCLA Law Review*, Vol. 33, p. 485.
Menkel-Meadow, C. (1988), 'Feminist Legal Theory, aritical Legal Studies, and Legal Education or "The Fem-Crits Go to Law School"', *Journal of Legal Education*, Vol. 38, p. 61.
Moore, M.S. (1989), 'The Interpretive Turn in Modern Theory: A Turn for the Worse?', *Stanford Law Review*, Vol. 41, p. 871.
Nelken, M.L. (1996), 'Negotiation and Psychoanalysis: If I'd Wanted to Learn about Feelings, I Wouldn't Have Gone to Law School', *Journal of Legal Education*, Vol. 46, p. 420.
Peller, G. (1988), 'Neutral Principles in the Fifties', *University of Michigan Journal of Law Reform*, p. 561.
Posner, R.A. (1996), 'Pragmatic Adjudication', *Cardozo Law Review*, Vol. 18, p.1.
Raskin, B. (1989), 'Laying Down the Law: The Empire Strikes Back', in *How Harvard Rules: Reason in the Service of Empire*, Boston, MA, South End Press.
Resnik, J. (1982), 'Managerial Judges', *Harvard Law Review*, Vol. 96, p. 376.
Roach, K. (1995), 'What's New and Old about Legal Process?', *University of Toronto Law Journal*, Vol. 47, p. 363.

Rorty, R. (1988), 'Unger, Castoriadis, and The Romance of a National Future', *Northwestern University Law Review*, Vol. 82, p. 335.

Rubin, E.L. (1995), 'Institutional Analysis and The New Legal Process', *Wisconsin Law Review*, p. 463.

Rubin, J.Z. and Sander, F.E.A. (1991), 'Culture, Negotiation and the Eye of the Beholder', *The Negotiation Journal*, p. 249.

Sacks, A. (1984), 'Legal Education and the Changing Role of Lawyers in Dispute Resolution', *Journal of Legal Education*, Vol. 34, p. 237.

Sanchez, V.A. (1996), 'Towards a History of ADR: The Dispute Processing Continuum in Anglo-Saxon England and Today', *Ohio State Journal of Dispute Resolution*, Vol. 1, p. 1.

Sander, F.E. (1984), 'Alternative Dispute Resolution in The Law School Curriculum: Opportunities and Obstacles', *Journal of Legal Education*, Vol. 34, p. 229.

Sander, F.E. (1984), 'Dispute Resolution Within and outside the Courts – An Overview of The US Experience' (unpublished, 1994, Harvard Special Collection).

Sander, F.E. and Goldberg, S. (1994), 'Fitting the Forum to the Fuss: A User-friendly Guide to Selecting an ADR procedure, in Dispute Resolution: Negotiation, Mediation, and Other Dispute Resolution Techniques', *The Negotiation Journal*, Vol. 10, p. 49.

Schlag, P. (1990), 'Normative and Nowhere to Go', *Stanford Law Review*, Vol. 42, p. 167.

Smith, S.D. (1990), 'The Pursuit of Pragmatism', *Yale Law Journal*, Vol. 100, p. 409.

Smith, S.D. (1990), 'Reductionism in Legal Thought', *Columbia Law Review*, Vol. 91, p. 68.

Singer, J.W. (1988), 'Legal Realism Now', *California Law Review*, Vol. 76, p. 467.

Wechsler, H. (1959), 'Toward Neutral Principles of Constitutional Law', *Harvard Law Review*, Vol. 73, p. 1.

Weinrib, E. (1985), 'Enduring Passion', *Yale Law Journal*, Vol. 94, p. 1825.

Wellman, V.A. (1987), 'Dworkin and the Legal Process Tradition: The Legacy of Hart and Sacks', *Arizona Law Review*, Vol. 29, p. 413.

Wetlaufer, G.B. (1996), 'The Limits of Integrative Bargaining', *Georgetown Law Journal*, Vol. p. 369.

White, G.E. (1972), 'From Sociological Jurisprudence to Realism: Jurisprudence and Social Change in Early Twentieth-century America', *Virginia Law Review*, Vol. 58, p. 999.

White, G. E. (1973), 'The Evolution of Reasoned Elaboration: Jurisprudential Criticism and Social Change', *Virginia Law Review*, Vol. 59, p. 279.

Wizner, S. (1989), 'After the War: Poverty Law in the 1980s: What is a Law School?', *Emory Law Journal*, Vol. 38, p. 70.

Yack, B. (1988), 'Toward a Free Marketplace of Social Institutions: Roberto Unger's "Super Liberal" Theory of Emancipation', *Harvard Law Review*, Vol. 101, p. 1961.

Index

Abel, Richard 305–7
Ackerman, Bruce 169–70
adjudication 141, 143, 152, 178, 191–200, 209–10, 217, 233, 284, 318, 334, 341
 political 148
ADR movement 137, 187, 196, 200–203, 206–11, 263–4, 296–9, 304–11
aporia 63–4
Aristotelian thought 23
Arnold, Thurman 153–5
Auerbach, Jerold 305–6
Augustine, St 6
autonomy 223

Bentham, Jeremy 45–6, 182
Berlin, Isaiah 338
Bernstein, Richard J. 219
Bickel, Alexander 149
Black, Charles L. Jr 163–4
Blackstone, Sir William 61, 182
Bok, Derek 209–11
Boyle, James 120–22
bricolage 29–30, 75, 83
Brown, Ernest 148
Brown v. Board of Education 156–9, 163–7, 189, 201, 206–7, 245–8
Brownian motion 246–7
Burger, Warren E. 309–10
Bush, Robert 327–9

capitalism 129–30
Cardozo, B.N. 43, 50, 78–80, 83, 213, 217–18, 224

Cavell, Stanley 5–11, 25–8, 68, 86, 132
certiorari 148
Chayes, Abram 191
civil rights 156, 188
Cohen, Felix 90, 213
Cold War 97
concepts, nature of 59
conflict management 323–4
Coordinated Management of Meaning, theory of 330–31
Critical Legal Studies (CLS) 61, 91, 188–90, 212–13, 231, 236, 247–8, 300, 344

Darwinian theory 13–18, 21, 23, 30, 48, 51, 69
Daxbury, Neil 175–7, 181, 294
Demogue, Rene 143
Depew, David 29
Derrida, Jacques 51, 63–4, 67–9, 91–2, 243–4, 249
Descartes, René 24–6
destabilization rights 241, 247
Dewey, John 3, 8, 12, 16, 20–34 *passim*, 38, 43–66 *passim*, 69, 75, 100–101, 112, 160–62, 213, 217–18, 231, 243, 275, 280, 316
'differend' concept 333–4, 337
'difficult conversations' 266–7, 271–3, 278, 313
discourse theory 330–44
discretion, judicial 141
dispute resolution 134–7, 191–7, 252, 287–8, 291, 298–9, 321–8, 330–37, 340, 342;
 see also ADR movement

divorce law 259
Douglas, William 213
Dworkin, Ronald 20, 98, 107, 127, 138, 168, 186–7, 194, 213–14, 231, 235, 251–2, 271–88, 309, 317, 334–7, 340–44

Edwards, Jonathan 3
Emerson, Ralph Waldo 2–18 *passim*, 23, 28, 30
empowerment 233, 240, 246, 328–34, 340
Eskridge, W.N. Jr 40, 103, 150, 163–5, 178, 187–9, 226–7

Farber, Daniel 213
fascism 160–61
feelings, dealing with 267–9, 302–3
feminine approach
  to law 269
  to mediation 335
feminism 322–3, 327, 330, 335, 339
Festenstein, Matthew 31, 67
Fish, Stanley 64, 219
Fisher, Roger 12, 22–3, 115, 243, 251, 259–62, 286–8, 291–2, 297, 314–20, 325, 342–3
Fiss, Owen 64, 98, 111, 185–7, 190–210, 248, 296, 298, 306, 329, 342–3
Folger, Joseph 327–8
formalism, meanings of 231–2
fractionating 318
Frank, Jerome 40, 74, 79, 85–9, 128, 135, 144–5, 213, 265, 288–95, 300
Frankfurter, Felix 40, 182
Freud, Sigmund 67, 340
Frickey, Philip 40, 103, 150, 163–5, 178, 213, 226–7

Fuller, Lon 40, 116–22, 125, 135, 140, 142–3, 166, 168, 176, 192–9, 232, 237, 264, 298

Galanter, Marc 203–4, 307–8
Getting to Yes 254, 259, 262–3, 273, 286, 297, 319, 325, 327
Gilligan, Carol 20, 327, 335
Glendon, Mary Ann 226, 295–6
Gordon, Robert 40, 70
Grey, Thomas 43–54, 61–6, 69–73, 80, 88, 94, 115, 213, 227
Griswold, Erwin 154

'hard cases' 272–9 *passsim*, 317, 334–7
Harrington, Christine 305
Hart, Henry 22, 101–3, 110, 115–17, 122–34, 140–41, 146–55, 161–70, 178–84, 193, 197, 213, 257, 273–6, 297–8, 301, 317
Harvard Law Review 148, 190
Harvard Law School 80–81, 103, 146, 154, 159, 170–1, 183, 211, 242–3, 248, 251–4, 263–5, 270, 297, 299, 312, 314, 324, 326, 342
Hegelian thinking 15, 22, 335, 338–9, 344
hegemony, concept of 109
historical school of jurisprudence 46
Hohfeld, Wesley Newcomb 80–81, 124–5
Hollinger, David 16, 28, 42, 66
Holmes, Oliver Wendell 4–5, 18–19, 31–5, 40–78, 82–4, 88–91, 96–100, 115, 117, 125, 167, 172–3, 186, 194, 213–14, 217, 223–5, 231, 235, 239, 273, 279, 282, 295, 309, 342, 344
Horwitz, Morton 32–4, 39, 43, 73, 79, 82, 88, 90, 103, 114, 119–22,

149, 155–60, 173, 182, 184, 218, 249, 342
Hull, N.E.H. 74–6, 80–82
Hume, David 47, 81

immunity rights 241, 247
individualism 4
institutional settlement, principle of 111–12, 118–19, 125, 275
institutionalization 241–2
intangible satisfactions 108
interpretation of statutes, judicial 152
interpretive model of dispute resolution 330–37, 340

James, William 3, 9, 13, 16–20, 43–4, 55–8, 64, 69, 75, 79, 82, 100–101, 213

Kalman, Laura 169–73, 177
Kant, Immanuel 7–9, 14–15, 19, 46, 81, 222–3, 327
Kelsen, Hans 128–32, 193
Kennedy, Duncan 78, 91–9 *passim*, 119–22, 138, 143, 156, 177–87, 198, 226–7, 234, 247, 269, 341–4
Kloppenberg, James 219
Kronman, Anthony 133, 226, 300–301
Kuklick, Bruce 17, 19, 21

Lacan, Jacques 14, 89
Laclau, Ernesto 108–9
Langdell, Christopher Columbus 63, 70, 170–71, 177, 181, 288–9
language 122–4
 legal 124
language games 331
langue 94
Laski, Harold 40

law schools 210–11, 290–96
Law-and-Economics (L&E) movement 212, 220–23, 235, 248
Lax, David 260
legal culture 303–4
Legal Process school 32–3, 36, 40, 82, 89, 101–40, 143–7, 155–6, 162–8, 175–84, 187–92, 199, 213–15, 227–40, 246–8, 252, 256–8, 261, 273–7, 286, 293, 301, 317, 341–4
Legal Realism 32–40 *passim*, 43, 49, 66, 70–85, 90–92, 96, 98, 100, 103, 114–15, 119–20, 125, 128, 132, 139, 152, 161–2, 167–77, 182, 205, 212–13, 215, 222, 230, 309, 316–17, 342–4
Leiter, Brian 167–8, 173
Lerner, Max 40
Levi-Strauss, Claude 29–30, 94
Lincoln Mills case 149
'litigation explosion' 306–10
Llewellyn, Karl 40, 74–85, 91, 99–100, 113–14, 117, 129, 173, 213, 218
Lochner case 42, 63–6
Locke, John 31
Luban, David 70–73
Lyotard, Jean-François 333–4

Macintyre, Alasdair 121
Mackinnon, Catharine 335
McThenia, Andrew 206
market rights 241, 247
Martinelli, Joseph 112–13, 196
Marx, Karl 51
Marxism 105–6, 344
'maturing of collective thought' 149–54, 183, 284
mediation 136, 321–42
Menand, Louis 13, 19

Metaphysical Club 18–19, 41, 62
Minow, Martha 213
Mnookin, Robert 23, 226, 251, 259–60, 272, 303–4, 312–14
Moore, Michael S. 71, 174
motivational orientation 259–60
Mouffe, Chantal 108–9

negotiation studies 134, 136, 196, 251–72, 280, 301–3, 312–15, 327–9
Nelken, Melissa 268
New Deal 171
Newtonian science 14–15
Nietzsche, Friedrich 222
norms, legal 128–33, 140

'one shotters' in court 203
Othello 26–8

parole 94
Paul, St 21
Peller, Garry 36–8, 103, 149–52, 158–63, 166–9, 184, 187–9
per curiam opinions 148
philawsophy 61, 91, 162, 225, 309
Pierce, Charles 3, 16–20, 23, 43–4, 48, 55–8, 213
Plato 222
Plessy case 156–7
policies, legal 139
policy analysis 92, 97
positivism 166–8, 172–7 *passim*, 213, 275–6, 344
Posner, Richard A. 41, 98, 185–6, 202, 211–26, 246–9, 306, 342–3
post-modern jurisprudence 286
Pound, Roscoe 49, 74–8, 81, 172, 182, 308–10
Pound Conference 307–9
'principled negotiation' 254
principles, legal 138–9
prisoner's dilemma 260, 302, 322

problem-solving orientation 22–3, 108, 208, 226, 228, 256–7, 261, 272, 303, 305, 315, 328–40 *passim*
process theory 38, 166, 176–7, 212
process/substance distinction 161
professional mystique 224, 226
psychoanalysis 268–9
public law theory 188–201 *passim*, 207, 252, 297–8
Putnam, Hilary 9, 219, 306
Pyramid of Legal Order 128–35, 140, 164, 193, 257

race relations 156–9, 164, 246
Radin, Max 213
Raskin, Jamin 300
Rawls, John 285
'realism' in philosophy 70–71
reasoned elaboration 137–40, 148–55, 167, 178–80, 183, 217, 232, 234, 275, 315
reciprocity 135–6, 140–41, 198
Reed Report (1921) 290–91
'repeat players' in court 203
rights 241, 247
rights-and-principles school 235
Rogat, Yosal 40
Rorty, Richard 9, 45, 48, 72, 213, 217, 219, 227–9, 255, 320
Rubin, Jeffery Z. 304
rules, legal 138–9

Sacks, Albert 101, 103, 115, 117, 122–34, 140–41, 147–52, 155, 161–70, 178–81, 193, 197, 213, 257, 274–5, 297–303, 317
Sagi, Avi 338
Sander, Frank E.A. 264, 304–6, 310
Saussure, F. 94–5
Schlag, Pierre 252, 254, 285–6
Schlegel, Henry 78, 173–5, 182, 215

scientification 215, 223
Sebenius, James 260
Sebok, Anthony 148, 156, 166–9, 172, 177
Second World War 157
semiotic of legal argument 138, 234
Shaffer, Thomas 206
Shaw, Lemuel 54
signs, abstract or indexical 122–3
Singer, Joseph 83–4
social order 141–2
social science, law in relation to 127–8, 170–75, 224, 226, 248, 293–4, 302, 311–12
solidarity rights 241, 247
standards, legal 138–9
'statesman-lawyers' 300–301

Tamanaha, Brian 171–2, 175, 177, 224, 286
training of lawyers 210–11, 290–96
Twinning, W. 173

Unger, Roberto 98, 185–7, 201, 213, 216–19, 226–49, 306, 315, 342–4
Unitarian philosophy 17–18

United States Supreme Court 146, 148, 151, 154–6, 284
under chief justice Earl Warren 39, 102, 109, 149, 153, 155, 157, 159, 225
Urry, W. 325

Vienna Circle 130
Volkomer, Walter E. 294

Warner, Joseph Bangs 18
Warren, Earl 39, 102, 109, 149, 153, 155, 157, 159, 225
Weber, Max 50–51, 225–6
Wechsler, Herbert 155–9, 163–7, 184, 254
West, Cornell 2–3, 19, 28–9, 68, 216
Wetlaufer, Gerald 261
White, Edward 151
White, Morton 33–8, 43, 90, 109, 181, 231
win-lose situations 261
Wittgenstein, Ludwig 27, 92, 123, 331
Wright, Chauncey 18–19, 57

Yale Law School 80–81, 86, 169–71